Contemporary
English
CHANGE AND VARIATION

Contemporary English

English

CHANGE AND VARIATION

Edited by

David L. Shores

OLD DOMINION UNIVERSITY

J. B. Lippincott Company

PHILADELPHIA   NEW YORK   TORONTO

ISBN-0-397-47207-2
Library of Congress Catalogue Card Number 79-165977
Printed in the United States of America

Cover design by Jeanette Renich
Interior design by Anne W. Churchman

92107

For David and Keith, my sons

🏵 Preface

Everyone knows that language is variable:

Ye knowe ek that in forme of speche is chaunge
Withinne a thousand year, and wordes tho
That hadden pris, now wonder nyce and straunge.

      ○   ○   ○

I knowed you wasn't Oklahomy folks. You talk queer kinds—That ain't no blame, you understan.' Ever' body says words different, said Ivy. Arkansas folks says 'em different, and Oklahomy folks says 'em different. And we seen a lady from Massachusetts, an' she said 'em differentest of all. Couldn' hardly make out what she was sayin'.

      ○   ○   ○

"Why yes sir, Mister Jem." Calpurnia timidly put her fingers to her mouth. "They were the only books I had. Your grandaddy said Mr. Blackstone wrote fine English—"

"That's why you don't talk like the rest of 'em," said Jem.

"The rest of who?"

"Rest of the colored folks. Cal, but you talked like they did in church. . . ."

That Calpurnia lead a modest double life never dawned on me. The idea that she had a separate existence outside our household was a novel one, to say nothing of her having command of two languages.

"Cal," I asked, "why do you talk nigger-talk to the—to your folks when you know it's not right?"

"Well, in the first place I'm black—"

"That doesn't mean you hafta talk that way when you know better," said Jem.

Calpurnia tilted her hat and scratched her head, then, pressed her hat down carefully over her ears. "It's right hard to say," she said. "Suppose you and Scout talked colored-folks' talk at home—it'd be out of place, wouldn't it? Now what if I talked white-folks' talk at church, and with my neighbors? They'd think I was puttin' on airs to beat Moses."

Anyone acquainted with the problem of standard and nonstandard varieties of English will discern in these passages some of the dimensions of language variation. Perhaps the reader will recognize the first passage as that of Chaucer *(Troilus and Criseyde)*, the poet who not only gave us "God's plenty," but also in these lines the unavoidable fact and trait of language, that is, change or temporal variation. Change is of course the persistent underlying factor that must be dealt with even in the most superficial language studies. The second passage is from John Steinbeck's *The Grapes of Wrath*. It draws the reader's attention to another dimension of language, that of regional variation. The third passage is from Harper Lee's novel *To Kill a Mockingbird*. It reveals still other important dimensions of language, those of social variation and appropriateness. In short, these passages show that language changes as naturally and as steadily as any other human habit does, is not spoken in the same way in all parts of a country, and is an order of dialects correlating in some way with local social status and pretensions and education. The passages also serve to demonstrate that both the lettered and unlettered may detect variation in language.

While the significance of language variation has been recognized in schools and colleges for a long time, the study of language variation, or any aspect of language for that matter, still occupies an ambiguous place in American education. Departments of English are thought to have three main concerns—language, composition, and literature. Among these concerns, it is generally conceded that language matters have received the least attention and have either been isolated or treated as a part of handbook grammar, rhetoric, and literature. Consequently, students enter and leave college, still retaining naive attitudes and misconceptions about the most human of man's behavior—his language.

Anyone familiar with recent articles and books dealing with the English profession will have noted the growing interest in curriculum reform and the suggestion that primacy of language be emphasized in English studies at all levels. This suggestion recognizes, and quite rightly, that knowledge of language matters among college graduates, English majors, and English teachers is distressingly weak. This increasing interest in language must not, however, be interpreted to mean that reformers are suggesting that language should overshadow other concerns of English departments as they have, for years, overshadowed language study. Rather, it means that the English language should be considered as a serious, fundamental study to make students and teachers aware of the fruit of linguistic scholarship as it relates to grammar, dialects and usage, composition, style, literature and the general role of language in human affairs. The aim would not be to require English linguistics as a formal study but rather to emphasize those aspects of language study that will prove helpful for the student during and after his formal education.

Our schools and colleges have always been concerned with standard and nonstandard varieties of English, but unfortunately seldom in a realistic way. The chief interest of English teachers and the general reading public in language seems to be whether a certain form or phrase is "correct" or "incorrect," "good" or "bad," and the like. For them, standard English is "what's in the book and that's that," and all discrepant varieties are described as "corrupt." This attitude leads students to believe that there is a uniformly good way and a uniformly bad way of speaking and writing. But then, as they read and listen to visiting scholars and politicians, other professional people, and even to their own English professors, they note many "bad" features of speech which have been condemned in the English classroom but are commonly used in public speech and in print. The acquisition of standard English appears to be an academic exercise in learning a kind of English that is rarely spoken or written and the English professor seems a caretaker of a form of English that may bear little relation to their daily lives. Thus, this collection is mainly concerned with accurate concepts of and realistic attitudes toward standard and nonstandard varieties of English. The materials have been brought together with the conviction that language touches the human being in a very special way and that an understanding of language variation is a must for the educated man, whatever his interests and ambitions.

Within the last ten to fifteen years, there has been a great increase of interest in standard and nonstandard English. In fact, the acquisition of standard English has become an urgent national concern, not because schools and society generally have become harsher in this egalitarian age and want to upgrade language use in the United States. Rather, the effort has been focused on standard English vis-à-vis nonstandard varieties of regional and social dialects and the generally poor school achievement of speakers of these varieties of English. These speakers are of course the millions of Americans belonging to lower socioeconomic classes—primarily Negroes and Spanish-Americans, but also American Indians, Acadian French and Appalachian Whites.

All these groups share a common experience: They are caught in a vicious poverty cycle which seems inescapable, caused by deprivation, neglect, and social exclusion. The children of these groups also share the common experience of severe learning and reading problems that cause them to lag behind middle-class children and eventually to fail in great numbers. The language problems of these disadvantaged groups have become the focus of federally-sponsored research projects, institutes, workshops, and in-service teaching programs, not to mention subject matter for hundreds of articles in professional journals. This interest follows extensive in-migration of these minority groups to large urban areas, a national commitment to school integration, and recognition of the nationwide failure of minority children to perform adequately on reading and achievement tests.

Educators and psychologists were among the first to tackle the problem and to offer answers. The problem, as they saw it, was cultural deprivation, and the answer was "cultural injection," that is, give them what they need to catch up. Next came the sociologists and anthropologists, who spoke of different expressive styles and cultural diversity and pleaded for understanding. Some educators and psychologists, misunderstanding and misapplying findings of sociologists and anthropologists, began to speak in terms of language deficiency, thus attracting the interest of linguists. Linguistic research soon showed that the concept of language deficiency was groundless, even nonsensical. Language deficiency, the linguists argued, puts the onus on children, perhaps on racial and genetic inferiority and if not this, then on poverty, racial isolation, and oppression. They therefore prefer to speak of linguistic differences, not linguistic deficiencies. The linguist looks upon language as species uniform; that is, all humans develop language, and all languages and dialects are well-ordered systems.

Perhaps the main reason that nonstandard speech has received little attention until very recently has been due to the perspective and state of the art. Linguistics and dialectology had simply not come up with a method adequate to conduct valid and reliable research. The Linguistic Atlas Project, initiated in 1930, gave some attention to social dialects, but its main focus was on language variation in terms of geography, not social stratification, though some attention was given to different educational levels. It was not until the mid-sixties that linguistics came up with an effective combination of sociology and dialectology for conducting research in social dialects. Before the work of Labov, Stewart, Dillard, Bailey, and Shuy and his colleagues in the Sociolinguistic Program at the Center for Applied Linguistics, it was generally assumed that nonstandard Negro speech was the same as uneducated white speech. Hans Kurath observed that Southern Negro speech exhibited "the same regional and local variations as that of the simple white folk," and Raven McDavid wrote that "the range of variants is the same in Negro and White speech." Juanita Williamson in 1961 wrote that the speech of the Negro "does not differ materially from that of the whites of the same economic and educational level of the area in which he has lived the greater part of his life." And finally another reason for the belated interest in Negro speech was the general belief by educated blacks and whites that only Standard English was important and that time should not be wasted on "corrupt forms of speech." They were something to be eradicated.

This collection attempts to bring together some of the most interesting, readable, perceptive and useful linguistic studies of standard and nonstandard varieties of English written by some of the most competent and productive scholars working today. There are three major areas of concern: a description of regional and social variation of American English, the definition of standard English, and the pedagogical treatment of the problems of standard and nonstandard varieties of English. Special features of the book are the sectional introductions by Roger W. Shuy, Philip B. Gove, and Irwin Feigenbaum. Shuy, Gove, and Feigenbaum have done the lion's share of the work for the reader in providing him with a sense of direction. I would like to underscore the importance of reading these introductions, for they are valuable for their interpretation, as explication, and as locaters of crucial points. Another special feature is the bibliography, which is designed to put students and teachers in touch with the most important and useful studies of standard and nonstandard English and relevant linguistic matters.

If the collection seems uneven, it is because research in the field is uneven. It must be noted that the book contains only one essay on lowerclass white speech; nothing suitable on the speech of the Acadian French and American Indians could be found.

With *Contemporary English*, the editor has hoped to provide a book that will serve the needs of college students, prospective teachers and practicing teachers at all levels in the understanding of the problems of language diversity in society. While sections one and two are suitable for students at any level, the book as a whole is designed to be of use to English majors, prospective teachers and those in service. Whether used in the introductory courses or in advanced courses for English majors and teachers, the book can serve to awaken the reader's curiosity about language variation, to deepen his knowledge about standard and nonstandard English, and to establish informed and accurate attitudes and approaches toward language in human affairs.

DAVID L. SHORES
Old Dominion University

Norfolk, Virginia
April 5, 1971

❧ Acknowledgments

As editor I find it difficult to express adequately my appreciation to those who have had something to do with this undertaking. I am of course greatly indebted to the authors and publishers who kindly gave me permission to reprint their essays. Many of the contributors are among the most original, productive, and distinguished linguists now working in the field. I am especially grateful to Roger Shuy, Philip B. Gove, and Irwin Feigenbaum who made excellent contributions to this book through their sectional introductions. I wish furthermore to thank Richard Heffron of J. B. Lippincott Company for his cooperation and help. I must also thank Bonnee Korel, Kathleen Sica, Maggie Malson, and Mrs. Beulah Griffin, departmental secretaries, and Louise DeVere, my graduate assistant, for their helpful assistance. Mention should furthermore be made of Mary Galvan of the Texas Education Agency for her suggestions and of Professor Theresa Love of Southern Illinois University (formerly of Norfolk State College) for providing the opportunity for me to work in this area. I am grateful to Karl Knight, my chairman, for reading portions of the manuscript and suggesting revisions. And finally, I wish to thank David and Keith, my sons, since the book is theirs and my wife, Betty, for being Betty.

❀ Contents

Part I

Standard and Nonstandard English:
Temporal, Regional, and Social Variations

Introduction

ROGER W. SHUY

After years of talking about standard and nonstandard English, we are still lacking a useful, working definition of the terms. One of the reasons for this problem of definition is that language simply refuses to stand still. It is as dynamic and changeable as the people who use it. It exhibits many of the variations that characterize man himself.

Time, geography and societal allegiance are three variables which have attracted the attention of linguists in this century. The major interest of linguists in the early part of our century was in historical matters, the evidence for which was largely from literary texts. In the 1930s and 1940s, these concerns for historical variation were joined by those of linguistic geographers, whose interest in regional variation was tied in closely with migration, internal settlement history and urbanization. The third focus of language variation is the most recent and probably the most complicated of all. Within the last decade, sociolinguists have developed new research strategies and theories which attempt to get at the exciting variation which involves, simultaneously, the intersections of one's social status, education, age, sex,

Roger W. Shuy is director of the sociolinguistic programs at the Center for Applied Linguistics and Georgetown University. He is the author of many articles dealing with social dialects and relevant educational problems. Among his books are *Social Dialects and Language Learning* (editor), *Teaching Standard English in the Inner City* (co-editor), and *Discovering American Dialects*.

race, along with all of the variables connected with purpose, audience, values, mode of expression, sensitivity to group dynamics, and many others.

We now know that the differences between standard and non-standard English cannot be discussed without careful attention to the variables of time, geography and society.

Language change has long been recognized by scholars as a fruitful area for linguistic research. Almost without exception, people know that the speech of their own generation is somehow "different" from the speech of those younger and older than themselves. The most frequently observed differences of this sort are almost always vocabulary. Perhaps this is because people tend to think of vocabulary when they think of language. In any case, it is reasonable to expect people of different age groups to use words which are in common use in their own generation and to scoff at the old fashionedness of older people and at the vulgarity of the younger.

Less obvious to the linguistic layman are the gradual changes which take place in the grammar and pronunciation of his language. For one thing, these changes usually take place very slowly and are related to rather large scale social and political evolution. But even if such variation could be slowed down for careful inspection, the average native speaker tends to edit out small, unessential differences which do not seriously impede his general understanding of what is being said. That is, we generally listen for meaning rather than for those variations by which speech reveals a person as old or young. Evidence of the general tolerance which listeners have for linguistic variation can be seen clearly in the professional acts of ventriloquists and comedians who specialize in double-talk. In the former case, many phonological "near-misses" are clarified by the context of the sentences in which they are used and the substitution of alveolar sounds (t, d, n) for bi-labial ones (p, b, m) keeps the ventriloquist from needing to move his lips. With double-talkers, the logic of the speaker's syntax carries the day and listeners tend to get the impression that they understand what is being said, even though some of the words may be total nonsense. The listener's general focus on meaning, then, is often at war with his conscious awareness of the details of language by which he is judged in terms of age, sex, race, socioeconomic status, education and stylistic appropriateness.

One way to call attention to this highly important aspect of speech is to demonstrate how language change has taken place over a broad period of time. Morton Bloomfield's brief history summarizes many of the major changes that took place in our language over the past centuries, beginning with the earliest written records of English up to modern times.

Another way of observing language change relates to the description of regional dialects as a reflection of settlement history. Since the late 1930s, American linguistic geographers have been working on the mammoth *Linguistic Atlas of the United States and Canada.* Although thousands of individual linguistic interviews have been conducted across the United States, so far the major publications of the *Atlas* have related almost entirely to the data collected in the East. Jean Malmstrom's article describes some of the assumptions and techques of linguistic geography in this country while Raven I. McDavid, Jr., Director of the *Linguistic Atlas of the Southern and Middle Atlantic States* and one of the most prolific fieldworkers and analysts of *Atlas* data, describes the major dialect areas of the United States as revealed by *Atlas* data.

Although *Linguistic Atlas* research focused primarily on regional differences and historical changes in progress, it also recognized the possible effect of social status on language variation by eliciting language data from informants of three designated social classes. A major figure in the recognition of social dialects in this country was McDavid, whose article on social differences as revealed by pronunciation marks a transition to the third emphasis of language variation in American linguistics.

During the 1960s, this shift in attention toward social dialects can be observed in the focus on urban areas (large scale projects were carried out in New York City, Chicago, Detroit, and Washington, for example) rather than the more broad-meshed regional studies that characterized *Atlas* projects. A second characteristic of these studies involved a careful inclusion of urbanites of several socioeconomic classes and particular interest in the speech of Negroes. Ralph Fasold and Walt Wolfram were involved in the research on the speech of Negroes of Washington and Detroit and in their article they summarize, in relatively nontechnical language, some of the major features of the speech of black people in those cities. The grammatical and phonological features which they describe were similar enough in Washington and Detroit to provide such a generalization. Similar data gathered in other northern cities (New York, Chicago and Los Angeles) and at least one rural Southern community (Holmes County, Mississippi) provided ample reason to suppose that there are widespread similarities in the speech of working-class Negroes across the country.

In an effort to account for these generally common characteristics, several linguists who specialize in the process of language called pidginization and creolization turned their attention to the historical change that took place in the English used by Negroes since the time of slavery. William Stewart's contributions to our knowledge of these processes clearly demonstrate the interesting focuses of language variation caused by time and by social concerns.

Other than the data provided by the *Linguistic Atlas of the United States and Canada*, relatively little has been done on the social dialects of other recognizable speech groups in this country. Stewart notes some of the communication problems in his article on Southern Appalachian speech and A. L. Davis does the same for Spanish-Americans of the Southwest.

At the moment, interest in language variation has probably never been greater in this country. During the late 1950s and 1960s great advances in our knowledge of language were made by linguists who took as primary data their ability to discriminate grammatical and ungrammatical sentences. But despite this separation of language from social meaning (however justified it may have been), there is now a movement away from the position which isolates social meaning from linguistic structure, a result, no doubt, of a desire to find a sound empirical base for linguistic theory, to determine the role of language in social concerns, and a new commitment to relate sociolinguistic data to educational problems.

1

A Brief History of the English Language

MORTON W. BLOOMFIELD

Language, like other important patterns of human behavior, slowly but constantly evolves from older forms into newer ones. When different groups of people speaking one language become separated by geographical, political, or social barriers, each group gradually develops its own variety of the language, which we call a dialect. So long as the differences between two varieties do not make mutual comprehension impossible (though they may make it difficult), and so long as the speakers of each do not consider themselves to be speaking a different language, we may say that these varieties are dialects of the same language.

However, the tendency of language throughout the early centuries of human civilization, as tribal groups broke up into subdivisions and migrated, was to split again and again into dialects that in time became mutually incomprehensible. At that point they are recognized as separate languages. Most of the languages spoken today in western Asia and Europe can be traced back to a remote "ancestor" language which we call Indo-European. It was an unwritten language and therefore, of course, no records of it survive. Yet, it can be reconstructed. The character of its words and phrases and of its grammatical structure

Morton W. Bloomfield, a noted medievalist and a student of the English language, is Professor of English at Harvard University. In language, he is best known for his *A Linguistic Introduction to the History of English.*

7

can be inferred by comparative study of the many languages which
are its descendants.

As a matter of fact, the early history of any given descendant has to
be reconstructed too, by essentially the same method, for written records are a relatively recent development. In the case of English, which
is our subject here, we have no written records surviving from earlier
than the eighth century A.D., and they do not become common before
the tenth and eleventh centuries. But by studying the written records
of other languages that clearly show a common ancestry with English
—Dutch and German, for example—and by assuming that evolutionary
changes before the existence of writing were generally similar in kind
to observable changes since, we can make a reasonable guess as to the
vocabulary and structure of the earlier forms of the three sister languages, as well as of their common parent. Thus, for instance, the
Modern English *blue eyes* and the modern German *blaue Augen* are
both traced back to a presumed parent language which we designate
as West Germanic; this in turn is considered to be a major dialect of
Primitive or Common Germanic, in which language the phrase is
reconstructed as *blaewō augona*. All the steps from *blaewō augona* to
blue eyes can be traced or reasonably assumed.

Various kinds of historical evidence indicate that about 1,500 years
ago three closely related tribes, the Angles, the Saxons, and the Jutes,
dwelt beside each other on the North Sea shore in what is today northern Germany and southern Denmark. Their language was a variety of
West Germanic; and when it began to show significant differences
from the other West Germanic dialects spoken around them, we may
say that the English language was born. The speakers of this language
were probably not aware for some time that it was different, but ultimately political and geographical circumstances created such an
awareness. For many decades, however, Old English (as we call it)
must have been very similar to other West Germanic dialects, and
especially to the other North Sea dialects of Old Saxon and Old
Frisian. A modern variant of Old Frisian is still spoken in the northern
Netherlands and the extreme northeast of Germany. Old Frisian and
Old English uniquely share certain sound developments. But gradually Old English became a distinctively different language, even
though it continued to bear, as its modern form still bears, marks of its
Germanic ancestry.

The chief political events that tended toward the development of
Old English as a separate language were no doubt the effects of the
invasion of England by the Angles and the Saxons, which began
around the middle of the fifth century. We do not know exactly what

pressures caused the Germanic invaders to cross the channel, but it seems clear that the ease with which they overcame the native Britons encouraged further invasion and settlement. Britain, of course, had already been subdued by Caesar's Roman legions in the first century, and only the gradual collapse of the Roman Empire, including Roman withdrawal from Britain, made the success of the Germanic tribes possible.

During the next two or three centuries these tribes conquered most of England and parts of Scotland. They drove back the British inhabitants into Wales and Cumberland, killing many and enslaving others. They developed kingdoms and a settled form of life. So complete was their domination of their new land that almost no words have come down to us from the older forms of Celtic, the language of the ancient Britons. Welsh, the language of Wales, is a modern descendant of Celtic, and in more recent centuries there have been borrowings from Welsh. Meanwhile, even as Old English continued to evolve away from its West Germanic sister languages on the continent, it began to develop regional dialects of its own. The evidence indicates that the four main dialects, identified as West Saxon, Kentish, Mercian, and Northumbrian, differed mostly in pronunciation, their syntax and vocabularies remaining more or less similar.

The West Saxon dialect occupies an especially important role in Old English. It is the dialect of most of the documents that have come down to us and was the basis of a kind of standard language which by the tenth century was widely used as the cultural linguistic norm of England. The political dominance of Wessex among the various Anglo-Saxon kingdoms assured the victory of its dialect. A standard language meant that there was a prestigious, relatively fixed form of Old English which was widely understood, and that the scribes who wrote down literary, political, and legal documents were learned in the use of it. Anglo-Saxon England is remarkable in Europe, after the fall of Rome, in having developed a standard literary and official language centuries before all the other European countries. However, as we shall see, this standardization was to be violently upset by political events.

As a Germanic language, Old English had inflectional endings resembling those of modern German. New words were largely formed by compounding and derivation; borrowing from other languages was not frequent, although some Latin and Greek words and a few from other tongues did enter Old English. The language had a much freer word order than Modern English because the inflectional endings indicated grammatical relations which are shown by function words and word order in the language as we speak it today. However, Old Eng-

lish is by no means as free in its word order as Latin, various constraints of linguistic custom operating to restrict its freedom. There is
a kind of compression in its style that gives Old English prose a special
kind of dignity. Old English poetry had a very rich vocabulary, probably partly archaic at the time of its use. The verse was composed in
great measure by formulas, using phrases of fixed metrical pattern
which could be repeated in endless and fascinating variation. As we
have noted, grammatical forms were much like those of modern German, with a number of noun declensions (although in later Old English these tend to fall together), strong and weak adjectives (two sets
of declensions for all adjectives, depending on degree of particularity
wished for), and strong and weak verbs rather like the same categories
in Modern English. Nouns were of the masculine, feminine, or neuter
gender, which determined the form of accompanying adjectives and
the gender (and form) of referential pronouns. One cannot understand
Old English without special study, yet even the most untutored reader
of Modern English can grasp the meaning of some words or phrases.
Here is Mark 12:1 in Old English:

> *Sum monn him plantode wingeard and betynde hine ond dealf anne seath
> and getimbrode anne stiepel and gesette hine mid eorthtilium and ferde
> on eltheodignesse.*

Here is a fairly literal translation of it:

> A certain man planted a vineyard for himself and enclosed it (him) and
> dug a pit and built a tower (steeple) and peopled (set) it (him) with
> farmers (earth-tillers) and went into a foreign country.

Old English is preserved in a rich literature, the oldest of any produced by the Germanic peoples, and in legal documents, inscriptions,
and glosses. Much of this must be credited to the conversion of the
Anglo-Saxon people to Christianity in the seventh and eighth centuries. The clerical scribes learned Latin, the language of their church,
and then began to represent the vernacular language, Old English,
with adaptations of the Roman alphabet. A few early inscriptions are
preserved in the runic alphabet, which is an older form of the Roman
alphabet borrowed by the Germanic peoples from the Romans much
earlier. It is largely because we know rather precisely what sounds the
Latin letters stand for that we can reconstruct the pronunciation of
Old English with considerable certainty.

Some Old English literature is in the form of translations from religious classics; some of it consists of paraphrases and reworkings of

religious stories. There are also original meditations, saints' lives, epics, practical work like collections of charms, and entertaining moralistic works like gnomes and riddles. It is an impressive body of work, and owes much to King Alfred (849–899), who actively encouraged the widespread literary use of Old English. He was himself a writer and translator, and he employed many other scholars at his court.

During much of King Alfred's reign and again early in the 11th century, England was under invasion by Danes and Norwegians—or, as they are often called, the Vikings. The linguistic result of extended Viking occupation of parts of the country was a good deal of exchange and assimilation between the languages of the rival peoples. Since, however, the two were still quite closely related Germanic tongues at this point in their development, this interchange produced no striking shift in the history of English, despite the introduction of some Scandinavian (Old Norse) words and, to a lesser extent, grammatical forms.

A much more drastic change was brought about by the invasion and conquest of England by the Normans from northwestern France in 1066. Originally of Viking ancestry, the Normans had, by the middle of the 11th century, become Frenchified in language and culture; their language is designated as Norman French—a dialect of Old French. The effects of the Norman Conquest were profound in the field of language no less than in other fields. So immense were the changes this event brought about that we give a special name to the period of English after they begin to show themselves, from about 1100: we call the language, from then to about 1500, Middle English.

The replacement of the Anglo-Saxon upper classes by a French-speaking group led to the disappearance of the standard Old English language. As it lost its cultural linguistic center, English fell back completely onto its various dialects and became a language of peasants and laborers—and therefore, largely, unwritten. The early Middle English manuscripts that we have inherited simply represent late Old English, spelled in whatever way seemed to the local scribe (who was likely to be a Norman) to duplicate the sounds of the language as he heard it. This at least has the advantage of giving us clues to the changes that had been taking place in spoken Old English for many decades—changes that to some extent were concealed as long as the scribes used the standardized and relatively fixed literary language.

William the Conqueror and his successors ruled not only England but Normandy, across the English Channel, until 1204. Then France won back the Duchy of Normandy, and the Anglo-Normans, politically detached from the continent, began to regard England as their permanent homeland. One result was the gradual adoption of English as their ordinary form of speech, rather than Norman French. But they brought to English, of course, the influence of Norman French, with its Latin background. Not only did French words come into the English vocabulary in large numbers, but English speech and literary style began to be receptive to borrowings from other languages, particularly Latin.

Middle English, then, comprises the various dialects of late Old English, modified both by evolutionary changes that were already in process and that continued for centuries, and by influences from Norman French. It is clear that English had been steadily losing or reducing its inflections, and consequently was becoming less free in word order; it was also losing its grammatical gender. By the later Middle English period, regardless of the many changes in sound and syntax yet to come, the essentials of Modern English had been created through these evolutionary changes and through the mingling of French and English, with an injection of Scandinavian.

The resurrection of English, in the 13th and 14th centuries, as the universal language of England once again made a standard dialect inevitable. Because London became the capital, its dialect won out over the other dialects of Middle English. Normally we recognize five of these: Northern (descended in the main from Northumbrian), spoken north of the Humber; Midland (descended from Mercian), spoken between the Thames and the Humber and usually divided into East and West Midland; Southern, or South Western (descended from West Saxon), spoken south of the Thames except in Kent; and Kentish, or South Eastern (descended from Kentish), spoken in Kent and its environs.

London was in the East Midland area, and its variety of East Midland as spoken by the court, governmental officials, and university men (both Oxford and Cambridge are in the East Midland area) became the basis for standard English. By the end of the Middle Ages it was victorious and was gradually depressing the other dialects, except for Scottish, which has continued a lively existence as a literary and standard language down to today, though not uninfluenced by the London dialect.

It should be noted that the proper Old English ancestor of standard English is not the Wessex dialect, in which practically all our Old English documents are written, but the Mercian (for London was in Mercia), in which little is preserved. However, in spite of this break, we can still trace our English vocabulary back to Old English with confidence.

The position of the London dialect was further strengthened, though not determined, because it was the language in which Chaucer, Gower, and Lydgate, the major writers of England in the later Middle Ages, wrote. After a lapse of some 350 years, England again had a standard language; but the battle of the vernacular was not yet won.

Middle English in its later forms is recognizably English, and a modern speaker could certainly understand a fair amount of it, although there are traps to be avoided. Some words still used today no longer have the same meaning—for example, *hope* meant "expect," and *edify* meant "build"—and some words have disappeared. Yet the vocabulary is basically familiar. The following passage from Chaucer's Prologue to *The Canterbury Tales*, written about 1387, is not unrepresentative and is clearly English:

> Ther was also a Nonne, a Prioresse,
> That of hir smylyng was ful symple and coy;
> Hir gretteste ooth was but by Seinte Loy;
> And she was cleped [called] madame Eglentyne.
> Ful weel she soong the service dyvyne.

The spelling of Middle English is much more phonetic than that of Modern English, so that the strange orthography often indicates differences in pronunciation from the way we speak today. A final *e*, when not before a vowel, was sounded as a separate syllable, the phonetic value being that of the *a* in Modern English *sofa*. All the consonants were pronounced; for example, the *k* and *gh* in *knight*, and the *l* in *walked*. Yet almost any passage from Chaucer is felt as English, as Old English is not.

A series of major vowel changes from about 1350 to 1550 marks the shift from Middle English to Modern English, and is usually termed the Great Vowel Shift. It is the demarcation between the older stages of the language, strange to modern ears, and the later, which are recognizable as essentially what we speak today. Readers of Shakespeare are aware that his English is not the same as ours, but feel that it is close to our kind of English. The Great Vowel Shift in effect moved the long stressed vowels forward in the mouth and diphthongized long *i* and long *u* to (aī) and (au) respectively, so that Middle English *I*, pronounced (ē), became the Modern English pronunciation of the first person singular pronoun, and Middle English *hous*, pronounced (hōōs), became Modern English *house*. Printing, introduced into England by William Caxton in the midst of this shift, tended to preserve the old Middle English spelling and thus helped to put our orthography into the rather disorganized state from which it has suffered down to our day.

As English was called upon to perform a wider and wider variety of functions, and above all to increase its vocabulary to cope with tasks formerly left to Latin, it modified itself to fit the new needs. The Renaissance period is noted for its great influx of vocabulary, especially from the classical languages, and from French and Italian. Englishmen adopted words right and left; and although some words did not survive, enough did to make the vocabulary of English perhaps the largest of any language. This has created certain difficulties. For example, adjectives and nouns referring to the same thing may be unrelated in root to each other (*oral/mouth; ocular/eye*). But the wide borrowing has produced a rich store of synonyms from different linguistic sources (for example, *royal, kingly,* and *regal*).

A good example of this lexical movement may be seen in Andrew Borde's prologue to his *Breviary of Healthe,* written in 1552: "Egregious doctours and maysters of the Eximiouse and Archane Science of physicke, of your Urbanitie Exasperate not your selfe agaynste me for makyinge of this lytle volume of Phisycke." These "inkhorn" terms, as they were called, provoked some indignation, yet the demands made upon English led to the adoption of many of these words. *Eximiouse* (which meant "excellent") has disappeared, but *exasperate* is a word heard every day, and *egregious* is not rare, although its meaning has shifted from "distinguished" to "flagrant." We now have thousands of long and short, hard and easy, Germanic and Romance (that is, derived from Latin) words in our language, each with its particular powers. Shakespeare can be as moving when he writes "the multitudinous seas incarnadine" as when he writes "to be or not to be." English has extensive resources, both concrete and abstract, everyday and elegant or academic, to satisfy various kinds of users and various goals.

American English is descended from the variety of English brought over to the colonies in the 17th century. It developed on its own to some extent—obviously in the matter of names for new objects, peoples, and flora and fauna—without ever losing contact with its base in England. The American and British varieties of the language have persisted, and seem in this era of mass communications and easy travel to be getting closer to each other. The fate of a language is closely bound up with the political fate of its speakers, and the world role of the United States in the past 30 years has strengthened the position of American English.

The regional dialects of English in America have traditionally been called New England, General American, and Southern; and although there has been some questioning of this categorization in recent years, it still seems more useful than the Northern, Midland, and Southern division some favor. In any event, the mobility of modern life and communication devices such as radio and television are profoundly affecting regional dialects, and they seem on the way to merging with each other. Social dialects, on the other hand, are extremely persistent, especially in England and to some extent in America. We are very much aware of the problem of ghetto and urban dialects today, and consequently of the value of bidialectism as well as of bilingualism. It is sufficient merely to mention the other major dialects of English: Canadian English, Irish English, Australian English, Scottish, Indian English—each, it must be emphasized, with its own subdialects.

In spite of some differences, there has been a basic stability in the rules or inner regulations of English over the centuries. As Professor Ian Gordon has written in *The Movement of English Prose:* "The segmented English sentence, stressed in word-groups, each word-group separated from its neighbour by a boundary-marker, the major stress of each group falling on the semantically important word in the group, the groups occurring in a relatively fixed order, the words in each group generally falling in a precisely fixed order—all this, plus the continuity of the original vocabulary and the preservation of the original structural words, has ensured an underlying stability in English speech, and in the prose which is based upon it."

With the establishment of a standard dialect in the late 14th century and the acquisition of an adequate vocabulary in the 16th and 17th centuries, it was left to the 18th and 19th centuries to create adequate grammars and dictionaries, so that by about 1800 English was fully ready to assume the international responsibility that the cultural, scientific, and political importance of England and America was to thrust upon it. English in 1750 was a language of more or less minor importance in the world; by 1850 it was a world language. Since then it has spread all over the globe and is the international language par excellence. If there are more speakers of some varieties of Chinese than English, a fact not completely established, Chinese does not have the world authority, the geographic spread, the important literature and scientific writings, or the commercial significance of English. English opens gates to great literature and philosophy and makes possible the universality of science. Although this high eminence is not fundamentally because of its innate superiority, it is certainly well fitted for its eminence and for the task of bringing various peoples together and establishing ties rather than severing them.

We have seen, then, how Modern English has developed a vocabulary of great extent and richness, drawn from many languages of the world. Its inflections are few, but its syntactic rules are probably as intricate as those of any language. Its verbal system presents great complexities, making for subtle distinctions. It is both a very concrete and an abstract language. It favors sibilants over other sounds, and yet possesses a wide phoneme repertory. Its spelling is fairly irregular, although not without some patterns and rules. Above all it is a supple and variegated language, which its native speakers should cherish and which provides them with their hold on the past, their contact with the present, and their claim on the future. Finally, it makes possible their view of the world and of themselves.

2

❧ Dialects

JEAN MALMSTROM

Each human being is as individual in speech as in fingerprints. Each person has his own idiolect, his own individual dialect. In physics laboratories, sound spectrographs make sound spectrograms—visible pictures of speech. These pictures show the infinite variations. Actually we cannot repeat a single sound identically even once. Although our naked ears cannot hear the tiny variations, the sound spectrograph senses and records them.

However, these differences are too small to be significant. Idiolects group into dialects. *Dialect* means a variety of language spoken by a distinct group of people in a definite place. A dialect varies in pronunciation, vocabulary, and grammar from other varieties of the same language. People united by dialect form a *speech community*. The members of a speech community share interests, values, ambitions, and communication.

For example, terms like *pattern practice, tape course,* FLES *program,* and *target language* are in-group dialect uniting language teachers into a professional speech community. Families are speech communities, too. Their members share "family sayings," incomprehensible to outsiders. Backyard barbecuers, water skiers, and photographers

Jean Malmstrom is Professor of English at Western Michigan University. She is the author of several articles on usage and dialects and of *Language in Society, An Introduction to Modern English Grammar,* and *Dialects—U.S.A.*

constitute three other speech communities. They use certain words not understood by those who do not share these hobbies. Clearly, everyone speaks more than one dialect. Language teachers may be water skiers; barbecuers may be photography buffs.

Dialects arise because languages change differently in different parts of the world, even though originally they came from the same parent language. Throughout history men have migrated from their homes for economic, political, social, and religious reasons. When they migrated, they took their language with them. Always the transported languages have changed, and in different ways. Edward Sapir, the great anthropological linguist of the 1920's, compared the situation to two men starting on a journey. Each man agrees to depend on his own resources while traveling in the same general direction.

> For a considerable time the two men, both as yet unwearied, will keep pretty well together. In the course of time, however, the varying degrees of physical strength, resourcefulness, ability to orient oneself, and many other factors, will begin to manifest themselves. The actual course traveled by each in reference to the other and to the course originally planned will diverge more and more, while the absolute distance between the two will also tend to become greater and greater.[1]

In this comparison, the two men are two dialects of the same language. After they have left home and "diverge more and more," they become mutually unintelligible. Then they are two separate languages.

Often the line between the dialect and a language is hard to draw. A dialect is enough like another form of speech to be understandable to speakers of the latter. Thus American English and British English are dialects of the same language. Great Russian and White Russian are dialects of the same language. In fact, languages are collections of dialects, and any one of these dialects may eventually become an independent language.

In ordinary conversation, *dialect* often means " a corrupt form of a language." In the light of history, this view puts the cart before the horse. For instance, in the fifteenth century many dialects of English were flourishing in England. The dialect of London won over the other dialects and became the standard for speakers of English because London was the commercial, political, and cultural center of England in late medieval times. Non-Londoners continued to speak their local dialects, which often preserved older forms lost in the standard language. These local dialects did not have the social prestige of the London dialect even though they were as old as it was, if not older.

The German language in Germany, Austria, and Switzerland developed in much the same way. The dialects spoken are all quite different from the High German used in literature, in church, on the stage, and for cultural activity in general. However, these folk dialects go back unbrokenly to the Old High German of early medieval times. The German taught in schools is comparatively new and is the result of one of the Upper Saxon dialects being chosen as standard German. Luther's Bible helped considerably to spread this one dialect as the recognized standard.

More or less the same pattern has occurred in the other national languages of Europe and many other parts of the world. For one reason or another, one of the many local dialects became the approved form of speech within the linguistic community. This approved dialect then became the symbol of culture, and consequently it spread at the expense of the other local dialects.

In the United States, contrariwise, no one dialect of American English became the recognized national standard. In the nineteenth century some people valued a "Harvard accent," the New England dialect of Boston and Cambridge, seats of learning, literature, and wealth. Today such treasures are not concentrated in one place, and no regional dialect predominates as "correct." Consequently, the dialect situation is complex and interesting.

Regional dialects are studied by linguistic geographers, trained to investigate geographic speech communities. Having selected a region that is unified in some way—historically, politically, religiously, sociologically—and using a questionnaire to elicit information about pronunciation, vocabulary, and grammar, linguistic geographers interview selected "informants" of both sexes, young and old, well and poorly educated, urban and rural, from representative parts of the region. Finally, they publish their findings on maps or in tables of figures. Thus today we have the famous linguistic atlases of Georg Wenker in Germany, Jules Gilliéron in France, Jaberg and Jud in Italy, and Hans Kurath in New England. These great linguistic atlases are storehouses of information about geographic dialects.

In the United States, linguistic geographers have discovered three main dialect areas—Northern, Midland, Southern—stretching from east to west across the continent. These dialect areas are clearest on the Atlantic Coast, where they reflect the original patterns of settlement. The farther west we go, the more the dialect areas blend and fuse, mirroring the westward migration of our people. The three dialect areas are defined by consistent differences in pronunciation, vocabulary, and grammar. H. L. Mencken summarizes the situation thus:

The differences in pronunciation between American dialects seldom impede free communication, for a man who converts *pass* to *pahs* or drops the final *r* in *father* is still usually able to palaver readily with one who gives *pass* the *a* of *Dan* and wrings the last gurgle out of his *r*'s. The differences in vocabulary are sometimes more puzzling, but they are not very numerous, and a stranger quickly picks them up. A newcomer to Maryland soon abandons *faucet* or *tap*, or whatever it was that prevailed in his native wilds, and turns to the local *spigot*. In the same way an immigrant to the Deep South is rapidly fluent in the use of *you-all, yonder*, and *to carry* in the sense of to convey. Even the differences in intonation are much less marked between any two parts of the United States than they are between any two parts of England, or than between England and this country as a whole. The railroad, the automobile, the mail-order catalogue, the movie, and above all, radio and television have promoted uniformity in even the most remote backwaters.[2]

In addition to geographic information about dialects in the United States, linguistic geographers uncovered some sociological relationships between education and dialect. Within each region they regularly interviewed college graduates, high-school graduates, and adults with less than a high-school education. Within each region they found the English of each group distinctive.

However, the procedures of linguistic geographers in our country obscured many linguistic facts of prime sociological importance. Though they took geography and education into consideration, linguistic geographers ignored many other social variables, such as race, racial isolation, social class, economic level, occupation, contextual style, group loyalties and values, mobility of population, and urbanization. Moreover, they paid much less attention to grammar than to vocabulary and pronunciation, and so they often missed important connections of words and sounds with grammar. Thus, by design or accident, their syntactic conclusions are often incomplete and unreliable.

Specifically, their language samples were not representative of the populations they studied. No children were included, even though children's speech is highly informative linguistically, especially before they learn to switch dialects to match different situations, as teen-agers regularly do. Moreover, the linguistic geographers preferred to interview elderly adults, considering them the most representative informants within any region. This policy discounts the extreme mobility of our population. Furthermore, Negroes were not adequately represented in the regional surveys. For example, in the Middle and Southern Atlantic States, fewer than two percent of the informants were black, and they were characteristically from the lower working class and so spoke Nonstandard language. The records of the interviews with blacks were not analyzed separately from those with whites. Indeed, they could not be usefully analyzed separately because such a small collection of data could provide only anecdotal, not statistical, information.

Most importantly of all, the linguistic geographers underemphasized our cities. The United States is highly urbanized, and each city is socially stratified in complex ways. The most accurate indicator of social class is one's use of language, but the linguistic features of cities do not yield to broad geographic analysis. As sociologist Glenna Ruth Pickford pointed out in 1956, "The cities remain anomalies of linguistic geography."[3] For example, the speech of New York City does not fit into the dialect of its surrounding region; it reveals no strictly geographical pattern of speech. In Texas, the speech of Dallas differs extensively from that of East Texas around it.[4]

Today, linguists and sociologists are working together to develop new techniques of reliable sampling and valid interviewing in order to illuminate the complex sociolinguistic stratification of large cities like New York, Washington, Chicago, and Detroit. Social classes are determined by regular patterns of linguistic variation. Dialects range from *acrolect* to *basilect*, to use William A. Stewart's terms for describing the topmost (*acro- "apex"* plus *-lect* as in *dialect*) social dialect in Washington, D. C. to the bottom (*basi- "bottom"*) social dialect. A city person speaks several social dialects as he mingles with other city people.

Although acrolect differs also in sounds and words from basilect, grammatical differences between them create the real blocks to communication. For instance, Stewart explains:

> . . . basilect does not normally inflect the verb in any way to show the differences between the simple present and the preterite, e.g., *I see it,* which can mean either "I see it" or "I saw it." On the other hand, basilect has, in addition to a simple perfect construction, e.g., *I seen it* "I have seen it," a completive perfect which has no equivalent in acrolect, e.g., *I been seen it* (with primary stress on been) "I have seen it (already some time ago)."[5]

That the simple present and the preterite both exist as grammatical categories in basilect, however, is clear from the fact that the two are negated differently: *I don't see it* "I don't see it," but *I ain't see it* "I didn't see it." Furthermore, a few basilect speakers do inflect the un-negated simple present with *-s,* e.g., *I sees it* "I see it" beside *I see it* "I saw it."

In New York City William Labov discovered similar social stratification marked by dialects. Patterns are regular; the linguistic norms
defining social strata are clear; each person speaks several social dialects. In addition, Labov found that New Yorkers recognize the social
meanings of dialect differences in the speech of their fellow New
Yorkers. For instance, Standard English speakers in New York City
rarely omit the *r* in words like *guard* and *horse,* and they practically
never say *ting* or *tin* for "thing" or "thin", or *den* and *de* for "then"
and "the". New Yorkers of all classes are quick to hear markers like
these in the speech of other New Yorkers and to recognize the social
meaning of these dialectal signals.

In addition, Labov made the important discovery that younger
Negroes, Puerto Ricans, and lower-class whites avoid the prestige
forms of New York City speech and increasingly use Nonstandard
forms of Southern Negro speech. He comments:

. . . this is due to the influx of Negroes raised in the South, but it also reflects a reversal of the value system held by the older generation, and a
rebellion against the middle class norms.[6]

The Detroit Dialect Study reveals further evidence of "peer-group
pressure" on teen-agers to reject adult norms. Here is a conversation
between a sixteen-year-old Negro boy and an interviewer.

Interviewer: What did he have to do to get in the group?
Informant: He gotta hang around with us more—come to visit; he have to
talk cool, you don't understand.
Interviewer: How do you talk cool?
Informant: Talk hip, man!—you know. Like you don't talk like you sup-
posed to. If you a square you can get out.[7]

At a different social level—for example, among black college students
who speak only Standard English—this group loyalty manifests itself
by ethnic slang and black intonation patterns superimposed on Standard English grammatical patterns.

Comparing Labov's research in New York with the Detroit Dialect
Study, the Chicago Study—"Communication Barriers to the Culturally
Deprived"—and the Urban Language Study of the District of Columbia
reveals remarkable likenesses in the Nonstandard English spoken by
blacks in these widely separated cities.[8] Three frequent patterns are the
"zero copula," "the zero possessive," and "undifferentiated pronouns."
The zero copula means the omission of BE in certain sentence patterns
where Standard English requires it. Examples are *He old* for "He is

old", *Dey runnin'* for "They are running", *She a teacher* for " She is a teacher". The zero possessive means the omission of the possessive suffix as in *My fahver frien'* for "My father's friend". Undifferentiated pronouns appear when the same forms are used indiscriminately for subject and object. That is, where Standard English has "He knows us", Negro Nonstandard has *Him know we, His know us,* and *He know us.* Moreover, possessive and subject forms show undifferentiated use also, varying with Standard use: *He fahver* or *His fahver* for Standard "His father"; *We house* or *Our house* for Standard "Our house".[9]

On the other hand, black Nonstandard differs systematically from white Nonstandard English. For example, in Appalachia, white children who are Nonstandard speakers use both *He's workin'* and *He's a-workin'*, whereas black children who are Nonstandard speakers say both *He workin'* and *He be workin'.* Standard English has only "He is (He's) working"; both Nonstandard varieties make a distinction that is lacking in Standard English. *He's workin'* and *He workin'* both mean that the person is doing a specific task close by. *He's a-workin'* and *He be workin'* mean either that the person has a steady job or that he is away working somewhere.[10]

Another example concerns double and multiple negatives. Such negatives are frequent in both black and white Nonstandard: *He didn't do nothin', We ain't never had no trouble.* But in Detroit certain Nonstandard negatives occur only in Negro Nonstandard: *Nobody didn't do it, Didn't nobody do it,* and *It wasn't no girls couldn't go with us.*

How can we explain both the consistent patterns of black Nonstandard recurring in widely separated parts of the country and also the systematic contrasts between black and white Nonstandard dialects? Some linguists see answers in history.[11] Recent studies of Afro-American dialects suggest that the deep grammar of Negro Nonstandard reflects a creole predecessor developing from an ancient pidgin language. Pidgin languages evolve to meet a communication emergency. When two groups of people speaking different languages are forced to talk together, they invent a pidgin language to communicate with each other. The pidgin is not the native language of either group. It is a mixed language with a simplified version of the grammar of one language into which is inserted the vocabulary of the other language. Pidgin English may have originated on the West African coast where traders mixed slaves from various tribes, each speaking a different African language. Later generations of Negroes in the United States spoke this pidgin language as their creole mother-tongue, their native and only language. The deep structure of the creole is still retained in modern Nonstandard Negro speech and is reflected especially in its verb system, even though its vocabulary is mostly English. Linguistic geographers discovered this English vocabulary since they were more interested in words than in syntax. Yet it is in syntax, not words, that the real relationships appear.

One full-fledged type of creole English still exists today. This is Gullah, the language spoken by Negroes in the Carolina Sea Islands. Gullah was not analyzed by the linguistic geographers, who regarded it as a problem completely separate from the English language of the United States. There is some evidence that Gullah, or a transition dialect between it and Negro Nonstandard English, is still spoken in Charleston, S. C. Here is a set of sentences contrasting Standard English, white Nonstandard, black Nonstandard, and Gullah.

STANDARD ENGLISH—We were eating—and drinking, too.
WHITE NONSTANDARD—We was eatin'—an' drinkin', too.
BLACK NONSTANDARD—We was eatin'—an' we drinkin', too.
GULLAH—We bin duh nyam—en' we duh drink, too.[12]

The four examples pair off syntactically, the white Nonstandard matching Standard English in omitting both the subject pronoun and the auxiliary in the *and* clause. The black Nonstandard and the Gullah repeat the subject pronoun and omit the auxiliary. The word *nyam,* meaning "to eat," is an instance of a Gullah word entirely different from either Standard or Nonstandard English.

Some linguists believe that Negro Nonstandard is a relexification of Gullah.[13] This means that it leaves the Gullah syntax intact but grafts the more traditional English grammatical markers on to what are essentially creole grammatical categories. In the above sentences, for example, *bin duh nyam* is relexified to *was eatin'.* That is to say, not only has the Gullah verb *nyam* been replaced by the English-derived *eat,* but also the past marker *bin* has been replaced by *was,* and the pre-verbal *duh* by the verbal suffix *-in',* all of these changes producing the Nonstandard *was eatin'.* Relexification explains many of the syntactic relationships between black speech and the underlying creole. As Beryl Loftman Bailey says, "... Southern Negro 'dialect' differs from other Southern speech because its deep structure is different, having its origins as it undoubtedly does in some Proto-creole grammatical structure."[14]

During the last century creole markers have all but disappeared from adult Negro speech. However, young children retain these markers, since children characteristically learn more from their peers than from their parents, especially in black society. As black children mature, they give up this "baby talk" or "smallboy talk" as no longer appropriate to their age. This process is called "age-grading".[15] It can help educators judge which features of Nonstandard speech need classroom attention and which will automatically eliminate themselves as the child grows into adolescence and adulthood.

The complex urban dialect situation challenges teachers to absorb sociolinguistic findings into their theory of instruction. In teaching English to speakers of foreign languages, we practice sentence patterns, we use language laboratories to improve pronunciation and comprehension, and we steep students in the culture of our country. These are techniques of modern foreign language teaching. They are based on a contrastive analysis of Standard English and the student's native language. The speaker of Nonstandard English in a modern metropolis is not a speaker of a foreign language. Although his speech is different from the language of the classroom, it is closer to the Standard English of his own city than to any other language. He finds himself in a "quasi-foreign language" situation, as Stewart has said. His teacher needs foreign language techniques to accomplish more than random and piecemeal "correction" that sounds arbitrary to the Nonstandard speaker. No one has told him that "English" in the classroom means Standard English. He is rightly convinced that he too speaks English. He knows that his English is his passport into his most intimate, important groups. Thus a contrastive analysis of the vertical dialect spectrum is much needed. Teachers must know enough about Nonstandard English to make illuminating contrasts with Standard English if they are to pacify the rebels and persuade them to add Standard English to their native dialects.

3

The Principal Dialect Areas of the United States

RAVEN I. McDAVID, JR.

In general, on all levels, one may distinguish, for much of the United States, three major belts of dialects, each with its own characteristics: Northern, Midland, and Southern, Midland being in turn divided into North Midland and South Midland. The map on page 28 shows the dialect areas that have so far been identified. Other recognizable but not clearly set-off areas have been found in the Northern Plains, the San Francisco Bay area, and parts of the Rockies. Clearer subdivisions will be recognized as a result of more extensive analysis of the available data.

The dialect areas, to be sure, are most sharply defined along the Atlantic Coast, where settlement was earliest and patterns have had longest to become stabilized. In fact, even within such an area as the Carolina-Georgia Low Country, it is often possible to tell a Charlestonian from a Savannian. As the lines of settlement move west, local distinctions become increasingly hard to find, and even the boundaries between major areas are not easy to indicate. Moreover, regional words or grammatical forms (less frequently regional pronunciations) which were in the speech of people of all ages and educational levels along the Atlantic Seaboard may survive in the Middle West or the Rocky Mountains only in the speech of the oldest and least sophisticated. In the Mississippi Valley, furthermore, some Northern forms have pushed south of St. Louis, while some South Midland forms occur as far north as Minneapolis or Duluth.

Raven I. McDavid, Jr., is Professor of English and Linguistics at the University of Chicago. Professor McDavid, past President of the American Dialect Society and widely known for his many articles on dialectology, is editor of the *Linguistic Atlas of the Middle and South Atlantic States* and co-author of *The Pronunciation of English in the Atlantic States*.

The analysis of Atlas materials now makes it possible to summarize the characteristics of many of the more distinctive of these speech-areas, especially along the Atlantic Seaboard. Some of the areas, being transition areas, have almost no distinctive characteristics; for others the statement is brief, as that the Delmarva area (14 on the Map) is most easily characterized by *caps* 'corn husks,' *lodge* 'bed on the floor,' and *mongst-ye* as second person pronoun; for still others the analysis of the materials is not yet complete.

The following tables, then, are essentially a conflation of work on the regional distribution of linguistic forms in the United States and Canada. Some parts have appeared in published volumes, like those of Kurath and Atwood; other parts are found in unpublished dissertations like those of Avis, Davis, and Frank; still others appear in articles and reviews; some have been presented only orally. (See bibliography—ed.) Where phonemic data is presented, the transcriptions have been roughly adapted to the system used in other parts of this book. (i.e., *The Structure of American English*—ed.) This adaptation, of course, does not mean that the linguistic geographer feels that his data can be adequately represented by such a system. The structural peculiarities of the Charleston vowel-system, for example, make it impossible to represent it accurately in the nine-vowel-plus-three-semivowel analysis; for other individual Southern and South Midland dialects at least ten vowels and perhaps additional semi-vowels are necessary. Where these difficulties appear most strikingly, phonemicization according to this system has not been attempted, and the data is presented phonetically. In many other places the phonemi-cization is done with extreme diffidence. It is probable that a different set of terms and perhaps a different graphic device (such as reverse slants) will be necessary to represent structural phonological differ-ences between dialects.

The numbers in parentheses after each area designate the dialect areas indicated on the Map. Roman numerals after each item indicate, insofar as it has been determined, the social distribution of the form within the particular area where it is observed. The figures correspond essentially to the social classes of Atlas informants:

    I. Old-fashioned, rustic, poorly educated speakers.
    II. Younger, more modern, better educated speakers.
    III. Cultured, well educated speakers.

When these figures are enclosed in brackets, less currency in that group is indicated.

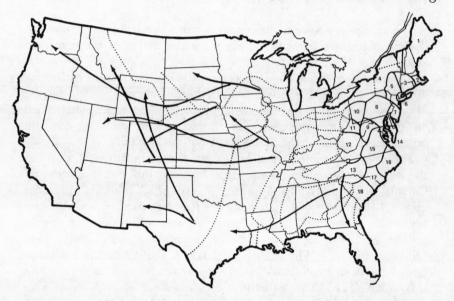

DIALECT AREAS OF THE UNITED STATES

Atlantic Seaboard Areas (after Kurath). Tentative Dialect Boundaries.
Arrows indicate direction of migrations.

THE NORTH

1. Northeastern New England
2. Southeastern New England
3. Southwestern New England
4. Inland North (western Vermont, Upstate New York & derivatives)
5. The Hudson Valley
6. Metropolitan New York

THE MIDLAND

North Midland
7. Delaware Valley (Philadelphia)
8. Susquehanna Valley
10. Upper Ohio Valley (Pittsburgh)
11. Northern West Virginia

South Midland
9. Upper Potomac & Shenandoah
12. Southern West Virginia & Eastern Kentucky
13. Western Carolina & Eastern Tennessee

THE SOUTH

14. Delmarva (Eastern Shore)
15. The Virginia Piedmont
16. Northeastern North Carolina (Albemarle Sound & Neuse Valley)
17. Cape Fear & Peedee Valleys
18. The South Carolina Low Country (Charleston)

Prepared by Mrs. Raven I. McDavid, Jr. for *The Structure of American English,* by W. Nelson Francis Copyright© 1958 The Ronald Press Company, New York. Adapted from Hans Kurath, *A Word Geography of the Eastern United States.* Ann Arbor: University of Michigan Press, 1949.

THE NORTH (1-6)

Pronunciation

/o/ and /ɔ/ (or /oh/ and /ɔh/) distinguished in *mourning:
morning,
hoarse*: *horse, fourteen*: *forty*, etc. I, II, III.
/ɨ/ in unstressed syllables of *haunted, careless,* etc. I, II, III. (Also
South).
[æ] (perhaps an allophone of /æ/ or if lengthened, of /æh/) sometimes used in *stairs, care.* [I], [II], [III]. (Also South).
centralized first element in the diphthong of *fine;* phonetically [ʌɪ]
or [ɐɪ]; phonemically /əy/. I, [II].
centralized first element in the diphthong of *loud;* phonetically [ʌʊ],
or [ɐʊ]; phonemically /əw/. I, [II].
/ð/ regularly in *with.* I, II, III. Possibly receding in Inland Northern.
/-s-/ in *grease* (verb) and *greasy.* I, II, III.
/u/ in *roots.*
/ə/ in *won't.* I, II, [III]. But see New York City.
/uw/, /u/ in *gums.* I, [II]. Receding in Inland Northern.
/bɨləz/ *because.* I, II, III. Also South Carolina-Georgia Low Country.

Vocabulary

pail I, II, III. (Midland and Southern *bucket*).
swill 'garbage' I, II, III. (Midland and Southern *slop*).
clapboards 'finished siding' I, II, III. (Midland and Southern *weather-
boards, weatherboarding*).
brook 'small stream' I, II, III. Rare in Inland North.
(*cherry*) *pit* 'seed' I, II, III.
angleworm 'earthworm' I, II, III.
johnnycake 'cornbread' I, II, III.
whiffletree, whippletree I, II, III.
eavestrough 'gutter on roof' I, II, [III].
spider 'frying pan' I, II. Receding in Inland Northern. (Also South).
fills, thills 'buggy shafts' I, II.
quite (spry) I, II, III. (Midland and Southern *right*).

Morphology and Syntax

dove /dówv/ as preterit of *dive* I, II, III.

sick to the stomach I, II, [III].
all to once [I], [II], receding in Inland Northern.
(he isn't) *to home* I, II, receding in Inland Northern.
hadn't ought 'oughtn't,' I, II.
it wa'n't me I, II. (Also South). Receding in Inland Northern.
see as preterit I, II. (Also South).
clim as preterit of *climb* I, II. (Also South).
be as finite verb (*How be you? Be I going to?*) I. Rare in Inland
  Northern.
/-θs/ or /ðz/ in *troughs* I, [II], [III].
begin as preterit [I], [II]. (Also South).
scairt 'scared' I, II.

EASTERN NEW ENGLAND (1, 2)

Pronunciation

[a] (phonemically /a/) inconsistently in *afternoon, glass, bath, France,*
  etc.; consistently in *barn, yard,* etc. (phonemically /æh/). I, II, III.
/-r/ "lost" except before vowels: *barn, beard, four, Thursday, horse,*
  father, phonemically /bæhn, bihd, foh/, etc. (Also New York City
  and South). Linking and intrusive /r/ are common: *idear of it,*
  /ày ⁺ sɔ́hr ɨm/ 'I saw him,' etc. I, II, III.
/ɔ/ (phonetically [ɒ]) in "short-*o*" words: *crop, lot, on, fog;* often
  no distinction between these words and words like *fought, law,*
  horse, etc. Sometimes the latter group has a higher vowel somewhat
  lengthened: [ɔ·] (phonemically /ɔh/ or /oh/).
/uw/ after /t, d, n/ (rather than /yuw, ɨw, iw/): *Tuesday, due, new.*
  I, II, III. (Also North Midland).
/o/ (a shortened and centralized allophone) in *stone, coat,* etc.
  I, [II], [III]. (Also sporadically in Inland Northern).
/ih/ (with a high allophone of /i/) in *beard, ear,* etc. I, II, III.

Vocabulary

pig-sty 'pigpen' I, II, III.
bonny-clabber, -clapper 'curdled milk' I, II, III.
sour-milk cheese 'cottage cheese' I, [II], [III].
apple dowdy 'deep-dish pie' I, II, III.
buttonwood 'sycamore' I, II, III.

Morphology and Syntax

waked up I, [II], [III]. (Also South).
verb-forms found in northeastern New England (1): preterits *riz*
'rose,' *driv* 'drove,' *div* 'dove' I (also South); participle *gwine*
'going' I.
(I was sitting) *agin* him, . . . *against* him 'next to' I.

INLAND NORTHERN (4)

(This area usually includes all or part of the Northern settlement
areas of the Great Lakes Basin and the Upper Mississippi Valley).

Pronunciation

/-r/ "kept" after vowels in *horse, four, father,* etc. I, II, III. (Also
Midland).
[ɑ] (phonemically /a/) in *on, hog, fog, frog* (but not *dog, log*) I, II,
III. (Also eastern Virginia and North Carolina).
[ɑ˗] or [a] (fronted allophones of /a/) in "short-*o*" words. I, II, III.
/ɪw, iw/ (phonetically [ɪu, ɪʉ]) sometimes in *Tuesday, due, new,
music, beautiful.* I, [II], [III]. Receding in Great Lakes and Upper
Midwest.

Vocabulary

stoop 'porch' I, II, III. (Also New York City and Savannah Valley).
lobbered milk, loppered milk 'curdled milk' I, II, III.
Dutch cheese 'cottage cheese' I, II.
sugar bush 'maple grove' I, II, [III].
stone boat 'sled for hauling stones' I, II, III.

Morphology and Syntax

there are buttons *onto* the coat [I].
we burn coal *into* the stove [I].

NEW YORK CITY AND HUDSON VALLEY (5, 6)

Pronunciation (mostly confined to the immediate vicinity of New
York City)

/-r/ "lost" except before vowels I, II, III. (Also New England and South).

no distinction between *mourning*: *morning, hoarse*: *horse*, etc. I, II, III. (Also North Midland).

/əy/ (phonetically [ɜɪ̯, əɪ̯]) in both *adjourn* and *adjoin*, *curl* and *coil*, etc. I, II. (Also New Orleans).

[e] (phonemically /eh/) in *Mary, dairy* I, II, III. (Also eastern New England. Cf. South).

[ɑ] (phonemically /a/ or /ah/) in *foreign, orange, borrow*; also in *on, hog, frog, fog, log* (not *dog*) I, II, III.

raised allophone of /ih/ in *beard, ear*, etc. I, II, III. (Also eastern New England).

raised and lengthened [æ˔·] (phonemically /eh/) in *pan*, etc. I, II, [III].

raised and lengthened [ɔ˔·] (phonemically /oh/) in *lawn*, etc. I, II, [III].

/uw/ in *won't* I, II, III. (Also Charleston).

/w/ regularly instead of /hw/ in *wheelbarrow*, etc. I, II, III.

[ʔ] (allophone of /t/) in *bottle, mountain*, etc. I, II.

/d/ instead of /ð/ in *this*, etc. I, II, (chiefly in foreignized speech).

/ŋg/ instead of /ŋ/ in *Long Island*, etc. I, II, (chiefly in foreignized speech).

Vocabulary (usually includes Hudson Valley)

Dominie 'preacher' I, II, III.
pot cheese 'cottage cheese' I, II, III.
olicook 'doughnut' I.
hunk 'base' (in tag games) [I] (New York City only).
-kill 'small stream' (proper names only) I, II, III.
barrack 'haystack' I, II (rural only).
suppawn 'corn mush' I, II (rural only).
skimmerton, skimmilton 'mock serenade' I, II (rural only).

Morphology and Syntax

he lives *in* King Street I, II, [III]. (Also Charleston and Canada).
we stood *on* line I, II, III.

MIDLAND (7-13)

Pronunciation

/-r/ "kept" after vowels I, II, III. (Also Inland North).
/ɔ, ɔh, ɔw/ in *on* (also South); in *wash, wasp;* in *log, hog, frog, fog*
  I, II, III.
/e/ (phonetically [ɛ] in *Mary, dairy* I, II, III.
/ə/ in the unstressed syllable of *haunted, careless,* etc. I, II, III.
/ɨ/ in the unstressed syllable of *stomach* I, II.
/θ/ regularly in *with.*
/r/ frequently intrudes in *wash, Washington* I, II.

Vocabulary

blinds 'window shades' I, II, III. (Also Canada).
skillet 'frying pan' I, II, III. Spreading.
snake feeder 'dragon fly' I, II, [III]. Competes with *snake doctor* in
  South Midland.
poke '(paper) sack' I, II, [III]. Not in Eastern Pennsylvania.
sook! 'call to cows' I, II, III.
green-beans 'string beans' I, II, III. Not in Eastern Pennsylvania.
a little piece 'short distance' I, II, III. (Also South Carolina).
to *hull* beans 'shell' I, II, [III].

Morphology and Syntax

clum 'climbed' I, [II].
seen 'saw' I, II. Spreading in North Central States.
you-uns (2nd person plural) I, [II]. Not in Eastern Pennsylvania.
all the further 'as far as' I, II.
I'll wait *on* you ' . . . for you' I, II, [III]. (Also South Carolina).
  Receding in North Central States.
I want off I, II, [III].
quarter *till* eleven I, II, III.

NORTH MIDLAND (7, 8, 10, 11)

Pronunciation

/uw/ after /t, d, n/, as in *Tuesday, new, due,* etc. I, II, III. (Also Eastern
  New England).

no distinction between such pairs of words as *mourning: morning,
hoarse: horse,* etc. I, II, III. (Also Hudson Valley). Such pairs seem
to have /ɔr/ in the Hudson Valley and Eastern Pennsylvania and
/or/ in Western Pennsylvania.
/i/ predominant in *creek.* I, II, [III]. (Also common in North, and
spreading in Inland Northern).

Vocabulary

spouting, spouts 'roof gutters' I, II, [III].
run 'small stream' I, II, III.
smearcase 'cottage cheese' I, II, [III].

EASTERN PENNSYLVANIA (7, 8)

Pronunciation[16]

/a/ in *frog, hog, fog* (not *dog*). [I], II, III. (Also North).
/ɔr/ in *morning, warning;* also *barn, marbles.*
/ɨy/ in *me, be, see,* etc. (especially under primary or secondary stress).

Vocabulary

baby coach 'baby carriage' I, II, [III]. Philadelphia area only.
pavement 'sidewalk' I, II, III.
Germanisms (often scattered through the North Midland):
    paper *toot* (/tut/) 'sack' I, II.
    clook 'setting hen' I.
    ponhaws 'scrapple' I, II.
    fatcakes 'doughnuts' I, [II].
    thick-milk 'curdled milk' I, II.
    spook 'ghost' I, II, III. (Also Hudson Valley).
    snits 'dried fruit' I, II.

Morphology and Syntax

sick *on* the stomach I, II.
Germanisms:
    (the oranges are) *all* 'all gone' I, II.
    got awake 'woke up' I, II.

WESTERN PENNSYLVANIA (10)

Pronunciation

no contrast between *cot*: *caught, collar*: *caller,* etc. I, II, III.
/u/ in *food* I, II.
/uw/ in *drouth* I, [II].

Vocabulary

hap 'comforter' I, [II].
cruds, crudded milk 'curdled milk' I, II.
mind 'remember' I, II, [III]. (Also South Carolina).
hay doodle 'haycock' I, II. Expanding in North-Central area.
grinnie 'chipmunk' I, II.
carbon oil 'kerosene' I, II.
baby cab 'baby carriage' I, II.

SOUTH MIDLAND (9, 12, 13)

Pronunciation

[a·], [a·ə] for /ay/ before voiceless and voiced consonants, as in *nice time* I, II.

Vocabulary

french harp 'harmonica' I, II, [III].
pack 'carry, tote' I, II.
clabber milk 'curdled milk' I, II, III.
redworm 'earthworm' I, II.
sugar tree 'sugar maple' I, II, [III].
fireboard, mantelboard 'mantel' I, II.
milk gap 'cow pen' I, [II].

Morphology and Syntax

dogbit 'bitten by a dog' I, II. (Also South Carolina).
(the sun) *raised* I, [II].

drinkt (preterit and participle) I.
shrinkt (preterit and participle) I.
swim (preterit) I.
sot down 'sat' I.
/-n/ forms of second possessive: *ourn, yourn,* etc.
I ran *on* him I, [II].

THE SOUTH (14-18)

Pronunciation

/r/ 'lost' except before vowels [I], [II], III. (Also eastern New England and New York City). Linking and intrusive /r/ usually do not occur in the South.
/ey/ in *Mary,* etc. I, II, III.
/i/ in unstressed syllables of *haunted, careless,* etc. I, II, III. (Also North).
/-il, in/ in *towel, funnel; mountain* I, II, [III]. (Also eastern New England).
/ey/ in *bleat* I, II, [III].
palatal allophones of /k-, g-/ in *car, garden* I, II, [III].
/z/ in *Mrs.* [I], II, III.

Vocabulary

lightwood 'fatty kindling' I, II, [III].
low 'moo' I, II, III.
tote 'carry' I, II.
carry 'take, escort' I, II, [III].
chittlins 'edible intestines' I, II, III.
co-wench! 'call to cows' I, II, III.
hasslet 'liver and lungs' I, II, III. (Also North).
snap beans, snaps 'string beans' I, II, III. Spreading.
harp, mouth harp 'harmonica' I, II, III. Not in Charleston area.
turn of wood 'armload' I, II, [III].
fritters I, II, III.
Confederate War 'Civil War (1861–65)' I, [II], [III].

Morphology and Syntax

it wan't me I, II, [III]. (Also North).
he belongs to be careful I, II.

heern tell I. (Also northeastern New England).
he *do* 'does' I.
what *make* (him do it?') 'makes' I.
is I . . . ? I.
gwine 'going' I. (Also northeastern New England).
he fell *outn* the bed I.
(I like him) *on account of* (he's so funny). I, [II].
all two, all both 'both' I, [II].

EASTERN VIRGINIA (14-15)

Pronunciation

[əu, ʌu] (phonemically /əw/) before voiceless consonants (*house, out*) against [æʊ] (phonemically [æw/) before voiced (*down, loud*). I, II, III. (Also Charleston area and Canada).
/a/ in *pasture* and a few other words; also in *stairs*. I.
[əi, ɐi] (phonemically /əy/) before voiceless consonants (*white, nice*) against [a̱, a·ɛ], etc., before voiced (*time, ride*). I, II, III. (Also Charleston area and Canada).
/u/ in *home* I.
/e/ in *afraid* I, II, III.

Vocabulary

batter bread 'spoonbread, soft cornbread' I, II, III.
lumber room 'store room' I, II, III.
croker sack, crocus sack 'burlap bag' I, II, [III]. (Also South Carolina).
cuppin 'cow pen' I.
corn house 'corn crib' I, II. (Also South Carolina).
hoppergrass 'grasshopper' I.
goobers 'peanuts' I, II, [III].

Morphology and Syntax

clome 'climbed' I.
see (preterit) I, II. (Also North).
I ran *up on* him I, II.
he did it *for purpose* I, [II].

SOUTH CAROLINA-GEORGIA LOW-COUNTRY (18)

Pronunciation

[əu, ʌu] (phonemically /əw/) and [əi, ɐi] (/əy/) before voiceless
consonants in *house, night.* I, II, III. Tidewater communities only.
(Also eastern Virginia and Canada).

[ɝ] occasional in *bird,* etc. [I], [II], [III]. Not homophonous with
Boyd.

centering diphthongs: [oˑə] in *road, post,* and [eˑə] in *eight, drain.*
I, II, III. Syllabics of *beet, boot, bought* less often in-gliding
diphthongs, often monophthongs, very rarely up-gliding diphthongs.

/w/ in *whip, wheelbarrow,* etc. [I], [II], [III]. (Also Hudson Valley
and eastern Pennsylvania).

/ɔ/ in *pot, crop, oxen.* I, II, III. (Also eastern New England).

[u, ʊ] in *won't* [I], [II], [III]. (Also Hudson Valley).

only one front vowel phoneme before /-r/: homophony of *ear: air,
fear: fair,* etc. I, II, III. Rare above tidewater.

/-b/ in *coop* I, II. (Also eastern North Carolina).

/θ/ in *with, without.* I, II, III. (Also Midland).

/æh/ in *pa, ma, palm, calm* I, II, [III].

Vocabulary

fatwood 'fatty kindling' I, II, [III]. Tidewater in South Carolina, further inland in Georgia and Florida.

press, clothespress 'movable wardrobe' [I], [II], [III]. Chiefly in
Santee Valley.

stoop 'small porch' [I], [II], [III]. Chiefly in Savannah Valley. (Also
in North).

cripple 'scrapple' [I], [II], [III]. Savannah Valley.

spring frog 'small green frog' I, II, III.

groundnuts 'peanuts' I, II, III.

joggling board 'springing board anchored at both ends' I, II, III.

awendaw ['oˑm̩dɔ] 'spoon bread, soft cornbread' [I], [II], [III].
Charleston County only.

savannah 'grassland' I, II, III.

mutton corn 'sweet corn' I, II, [III].

corn dodgers 'dumplings' I, II.

Africanisms of various spread:
    bloody-noun 'large bullfrog' I, II, III.

cooter 'turtle' (with /u/ on coastal plain, /uw/ further inland).
  I, II, III.
pinders 'peanuts' I, II, [III].
yard-ax 'untrained preacher' [I]. (Widely known, but generally
  labeled a Negroism).
pinto 'coffin' [I]. Chiefly from Negro informants.
buckra 'white man' I, II, III.

Morphology and Syntax (forms current in Negro speech, occasionally
  in old-fashioned white speech).
he come over *for* tell me [I].
Uninflected preterits and participles [I].

SOUTH AND SOUTH MIDLAND (9, 12-18)

Pronunciation

/yuw/ after /t, d, n/ in *Tuesday, due, new,* etc. I, II, III.
[a·ɛ, a·], etc., in *five, my,* etc. I, II, III.
/o/ and /ɔ/ contrasting before /r/ in *mourning: morning, hoarse:
  horse, fourteen: forty,* etc. I, II, III. (Also North).
/æw/ predominant in *mountain, loud,* etc. I, II, III. Not common in
  Charleston area.
/æ/ in *stairs, care, chair.* I, II, III. (Also North).
/o/ in *poor, your,* etc.
/u/ in *coop, cooper.*
/uw/ as a high-central monophthong or diphthong, [ʉ, ʉʉ]. I, II, III.
  Not universal in Charleston area.
/u/ as a high-central rounded vowel, [ʉ], [I], [II], [III]. Not in
  Charleston area.
/ə/ in *put.* I, [II].
/u/ in *bulk, bulge, budget.* I, II, [III]. Not in Carolina–Georgia
  coastal plain.
/ɨ/ frequent in *sister, dinner, scissors, pretty, milk, mirror,* etc.

Vocabulary

light bread 'white bread' I, II, III.
clabber 'curdled milk' I, II, III.
corn shucks 'husks' I, II, III.

pallet 'bed on floor' I, II, III.
jackleg preacher 'unskilled preacher' I, II, [III].
snack 'light lunch between meals' I, II, III. (Also New York City).
pulley bone 'wishbone' I, II, III.
snake doctor 'dragon fly' I, II, III. Not on Carolina–Georgia coast.
ha'nts, haunts 'ghosts' I, II, [III].
disremember 'forget' I.
hay shocks 'haycocks' I, II, III.
branch 'small stream' I, II, III.

Morphology and Syntax

you-all (second person plural) I, II, III.
I might could I, II. (Also Pennsylvania German area).
I'm not for sure I, II.
seed 'saw' (preterit of see) I.
a apple I, II. Apparently spreading.
I taken 'took' [I], II.
tuck (participle of *take*) I, [II].
holp 'helped' I, [II].
riz 'rose' I. (Also northeastern New England).
div 'dived' I. (Also northeastern New England).
mought 'might' I.
/-ɨz, -əz/ in plural ending of *fits, posts, costs* I.
perfective use of *done*, as in *I('ve) done told you that* I, II.
bought bread I, II.
use to didn't I, II.

CANADA (CHIEFLY ONTARIO)

Pronunciation[17]

/əy/, /əw/ before voiceless consonants, as in *nice, house*. I, II, III.
  (Also eastern Virginia and tidewater South Carolina).
/a/, /ɔ/ in *shone*.
/u/, /uw/ in *won't*. (Also Hudson Valley and South Carolina).

Vocabulary

chesterfield 'sofa.' (Also northern California).
county town 'county seat' I, II, III.

reeve 'township officer' I, II, III.
warden 'county officer' I, II, III.
dew worm 'large earthworm' I, II, III.
tap 'faucet' I, II, III.
serviette 'table napkin' [I], II, III.
stook 'pile of sheaves' I, II, [III].

Morphology and Syntax

He lives *in* King Street. (Also New York City and Charleston).

4

❧ Some Social Differences

in Pronunciation

RAVEN I. McDAVID, JR.

When we compare varieties of American English, we generally assume that differences in grammar reflect social differences, and that differences in vocabulary or pronunciation reflect regional differences. Yet we must often modify this useful practical rule. The word *bastard* occurs everywhere, but everywhere it seems to be a cruder term than *illegitimate child*. In all regions where *jacket* and *vest* are synonymous, *jacket* is apparently more rustic and old-fashioned. Conversely, Atwood's monograph shows that the differences in status between the preterits *dove* and *dived*, *woke up* and *waked up*, *sweat* and *sweated*, are more regional than social.[18] Moreover, though /klɪm, kləm, klom, klæm, klam, klum/ all have less prestige as preterits than *climbed*, at least three of these forms occur in definite regional patterns: /klɪm/ in the North and South, /kləm/ in the Midland, /klom/ in eastern Virginia.[19] Even /ɛt/ as the preterit of *eat*—a social shibboleth to many speakers—turns out to be the socially elegant form in Charleston, South Carolina, where the use of /ɛt/ (and of *ain't* in informal speech) sets off those who belong to the best Charlestonian society from those who would like to belong but don't.

We should therefore not be surprised if some pronunciations carry connotations of social prestige or lack of it. We can discuss a few of these pronunciations by examining the evidence collected for the Linguistic Atlas of the United States and Canada. This evidence has been collected in the field by trained investigators using a finely graded

42

phonetic alphabet and a questionnaire of selected items dealing with everyday experience. The persons interviewed are strongly rooted natives of their communities, typical of various age or social groups. Usually there is one person, as unsophisticated as possible, from the oldest generation, and another either younger or more sophisticated or both. Besides, there are enough cultured informants to indicate the local or regional standards. For the Atlantic seaboard states alone, the field workers for the Atlas interviewed over 150 cultured informants—a greater number of cultured informants than even the largest standard dictionary has utilized for the entire United States.

Besides the relative status of informants in their own communities (indicated by the field worker after he has completed the interviews), one must evaluate communities, or groups of communities, against the whole body of American English. Previous work in linguistic geography, especially Kurath's *Word Geography of the Eastern United States*, enables us to judge pronunciations by the type of dialect areas in which they occur.

Focal areas are those areas whose economic, social, or cultural prestige has led to the spread of their linguistic forms into other areas. Examples are eastern New England (Boston), eastern Pennsylvania (Philadelphia), the Hudson Valley (New York City), the Virginia Piedmont (Richmond), and the South Carolina Low-Country (Charleston). Pronunciations characteristic of focal areas are likely to have prestige, especially when used by the younger and more sophisticated speakers.

Relic areas, on the other hand, are those whose geographical or cultural isolation, and relative lack of prestige, has caused the retention of older forms or prevented the spread of forms characteristic of these areas. Examples are northeastern New England, the eastern shore of Chesapeake Bay, and eastern North Carolina. Pronunciations characteristic of relic areas are likely to lack prestige, especially if they are chiefly used by the older and less sophisticated speakers.

A third problem we must consider is the attitude of speakers towards particular pronunciations—whether we call them "secondary responses" with Bloomfield or "metalinguistic details" with Trager. Here, incidental comments of the informants are of great value. For instance, the American *vase* /ves/ is a /vaz/ in Southern British Received Pronunciation. We might expect /vaz/ to have prestige in the United States, especially in those areas of New England and the Old South where British customs are admired and British speech forms are often adopted into local cultured speech. However, not only is /vaz/ rare as a spontaneous pronunciation, but the frequent comments of informants that "if it costs over $2.98 it's a /vaz/" suggest that many people who say /vaz/ are judged as parvenus who have acquired the pronunciation during a recent exposure to culture and who wish to use it to impress their neighbors. Judgments that pronunciations are characteristic of less privileged social groups—Negroes, unsuccessful farmers, recent immigrants—indicate for such pronunciations a lack of prestige in the community, regardless of their status elsewhere or their occurrence in the informant's unguarded conversation.

Finally, some informants may deliberately stick to pronunciations they know are considered old-fashioned, unprivileged, or simply peculiar. New Yorkers generally consider it substandard to pronounce a *curl* of hair and a *coil* of rope the same way, yet I know at least one prosperous and well-educated New Yorker of colonial stock who does not distinguish such pairs. The most sophisticated informant interviewed in Charleston proclaimed that she personally said /tə'mætəz/, though she knew other people said /tə'metəz/ or /tə'matəz/—"because Grandmother H--- always said /tə'mætəz/, and what Grandmother H--- said is good enough for me." One cultured informant near Galt, Ontario consistently says /bul, pul/ for *bull, pull*, instead of /bʊl, pʊl/ because these pronunciations have come down in his Scotch-Canadian family. Such examples of "rugged individualism," family pride, or personal stubbornness do not give us patterns of prestige, but they warn us to go slow in condemning what we do not say ourselves.

As Kurath has often pointed out, there are three types of differences in pronunciation:

(1) Differences in the pronunciation of the individual phonemes.

(2) Differences in the occurrence of the individual phonemes.

(3) Differences in the system of phonemes.[20]

Differences in the pronunciation of the individual phonemes are hardest to detect and evaluate. Some of these pronunciations are fairly striking, and do denote social status:

1. The ingliding diphthongal pronunciation of *date* and *boat*, as [deət] and [boət] is generally confined to the Charleston area.

2. The fronted [ʉ] in *two, boot* is very common in the Midland and the South.

3. The monophthongal or near monophthongal variety of /ai/ occurring finally and before voiced consonants in *high, hide*. This type of pronunciation is chiefly found in Southern and South Midland dialects. Though sometimes ridiculed by speakers from other regions, it is rarely considered an unprivileged form in the areas where it occurs—and then only if the speaker does not differentiate *high* from *hah, blind* from *blond, hide* from *hod* or *hard*.

4. The fronted beginning of /au/ ([æu, ɛʊ]) in such words as *cow* is found in northern New England and the New England settlement area, and in the South and South Midland. In the North they are generally considered old-fashioned or rustic, and are disappearing. They are very common in the Richmond area and seem to be spreading nearly everywhere in the South except in South Carolina.

5. The centralized beginning of /ai, au/ ([əɪ, əʊ]) in *rite, ride, lout, loud*. Sometimes this occurs only when the diphthong is followed by a voiceless consonant, sometimes in all positions. In the inland North the centralized beginning may occur regardless of the consonant following the diphthong, but in this region the centralized beginning is often considered somewhat old-fashioned and rustic, though it is used by many cultured informants. The centralized beginning when the diphthong is followed by a voiceless consonant, but not otherwise, is characteristic of the speech of three well-defined areas: Canada (especially Ontario), the Virginia Piedmont, and the Atlantic Tidewater area from Georgetown, South Carolina, to St. Augustine, Florida. In view of the social prestige of the Richmond and Charleston areas, the pronunciations of *light* and *lout* as [ləɪt, ləʊt] probably have privileged status.

6. An ingliding vowel with a rather high beginning sometimes occurs for /æ/ in such words as *calf, bad* [æ˙ə, ɛə] or for /ɔ/ in *law* [ɔˑə, oˑə]. These pronunciations are most common in such cities as New York, Philadelphia, and Baltimore. They are especially common in families with a central or eastern European background, and the more extreme varieties are often considered substandard.

There are relatively few differences in the system of phonemes that all students would agree upon.

1. For some speakers the "New England short *o*," /ŏ/, occurs alongside /o/ in such words as *coat, road, home, whole.* It probably is found everywhere in the New England settlement area since it has been recorded as far west as Montana. On the other hand, even in New England it is losing ground, since it is found chiefly in smaller and relatively isolated communities and in the speech of the older and less sophisticated informants.

2. A falling diphthong /iu/ occurs alongside /yu/ (or /u/) in such words as *puke, beautiful, music, tube, due, new, suit, sumach, grew, blew.* It is found chiefly in the New England settlement area, but also occurs along Chesapeake Bay and the Carolina and Georgia coast. It is slightly old-fashioned, especially in the North (it occurs most frequently in *puke*, which does not have a "schoolroom pronunciation"); yet it still occurs in cultured speech.

3. In the Pittsburgh area the vowel /a/ occurs only before /-r/, with both *cot* and *caught, collar* and *caller* having /ɔ/. This feature also seems to occur frequently in western Canada and in the Minneapolis area. If anything, it seems to be spreading among younger and better educated speakers.

Differences in the occurrence of individual phonemes are most common and easiest to evaluate. They may be grouped according to several social types, though we must remember that these groupings are only tentative ones.

1. Some differences are purely regional:

In such words as *whip, wharf,* and *whoa,* some speakers have /hw-/, others /w-/.

For *humor,* the pronunciation /hyumər/ occurs sporadically and chiefly in the Northern area, though elsewhere there are indications it is being sponsored by the schools as a spelling pronunciation. /yumər/ is far more common, at all levels of usage. For other words of this group, however, (though the evidence is less adequate) the forms with /yu-/ seem to be less widespread and somewhat lacking in prestige.

For *without,* the middle consonant may be either /θ/ or /ð/ at any social level. In the North and eastern North Carolina /ð/ is overwhelmingly predominant; in Canada, the Midland area, eastern Virginia, South Carolina, and Georgia /θ/ is very frequent.

Ewe is /yo/ in most of the country where people have knowledge of sheep. Since this pronunciation is never heard from those who have not lived where sheep were raised, it may be considered an occupational pronunciation among sheep herders.

Bleat, the cry of a calf, is prevailingly /blæt/ in the North and /blet/ in the South, being replaced by *bawl* in the Midland; /blit/ is almost exclusively a city pronunciation.

Because is frequently pronounced /bɪˈkəz/ in the North and in South Carolina, but rarely in other regions. Where this pronunciation occurs it is used by speakers of all degrees of sophistication.

The unstressed vowel of *without* is always /ɪ/ in the North and the South, but usually /ə/ in the Midland.

Beside the usual /ču-/, Massa*chu*setts is often /ju-/ in New England, but /tyu-/ or /tu-/ in the South and south Midland.

Instead of /wɔnt/ (or the common Southern /wɔʊnt/) *want* is very often /want/ in Massachusetts and Vermont, /wənt/ in New Jersey and Western Pennsylvania. Both of these pronunciations occur sporadically in western areas settled ultimately from New England.

Words such as *orange, Florida, borrow,* and *tomorrow* may have either /a/ or /ɔ/ before /-r-/. In the Atlantic seaboard states /ɔ/ is most likely to occur in these words in northern New England, western Pennsylvania, and the Charleston area. For such words as *Florida* and *oranges*, /ɔ/ is practically universal in the North Central States and westward, but in these same areas /a/ or /ɔ/ may occur in *borrow* and *tomorrow*.

For *bulge, bulk,* and *budget,* both /ʊ/ and /ə/ occur: /ə/ in the North and North Midland, /ʊ/ in the South Midland, eastern Virginia, and the Piedmont of the Carolinas and Georgia, /ə/ again along the southern coast south of Chesapeake Bay.

For *won't,* /wont/ occurs everywhere. In addition there are four forms with regional distribution: (1) /wənt/ in the North, outside of the Hudson Valley; (2) /wɔnt/ in North Carolina; (3) /wunt, wʊnt/ in Canada, New York City, the Hudson Valley, Chesapeake Bay, eastern North Carolina, and the Charleston area. All of these forms occur in cultured speech.

For many of the words derived ·from Middle English /o:/—and some borrowings that have fallen into the pattern—both /u/ and /ʊ/ occur, without social distinction but with sharply differing regional patterns. This is true of *coop, cooper, hoop, goobers, room, broom, root, cooter, food, hoof, roof, spooks,* and probably others. For instance, I—a native of upper South Carolina—normally have /u/ in *root, cooter, food, roof, spooks,* and *goober,* /ʊ/ in *coop, cooper, hoop,* and either /u/ or /ʊ/ in *room, broom, hoof.*

For such words as *tube, dew, new,* we find /iu/ in the North and occasionally along the southern coast, although it is somewhat old-fashioned in both areas. In the South and South Midland, /yu/ is predominant. It occurs as a prestige form in some communities in the North and North Midland. In northeastern New England, the Hudson Valley, and the North Midland, /u/ is almost universal and is spreading in other parts of the North.

Such pairs as *horse* and *hoarse, morning* and *mourning, border* and *boarder* are usually distinguished in the North, the South, and the South Midland, but not in the North Midland. In many parts of the Inland North and in Canada the distinction is disappearing.

2. A few pronunciations seem to lack prestige everywhere. *Italian* as /ˌai ˈtælyən/ is generally looked down upon; /dif/ (instead of /dɛf/) for *deaf* and /ˈwaundɪd/ (instead of /ˈwundɪd/) for *wounded* are generally considered old-fashioned.

3. Other pronunciations lack prestige, but occur in limited regions.
Along Chesapeake Bay, *fog* and *hog* occasionally have /o/.
Rinse is rarely /rmč, rĕnč/ in the North, but these pronunciations are common in the Midland and the South. They are slightly old-fash-

ioned, but not uncommon in cultured speech. The hyper-form /rmz/ is less common, limited to the same areas, and chiefly found in the speech of the half educated.

Coop occurs with /-b/ on Delaware Bay and along the southern coast south of Chesapeake Bay. This pronunciation is not common in cities, is slightly old-fashioned, but is used by many cultured speakers.

In parts of the South Midland and the South (but not in the Virginia Piedmont) *took, roof,* and *hoof* frequently have /ə/ in uneducated speech.

In much of the South and South Midland, the less educated speakers have /ə/ in *put,* to rime with *cut.*

For *loam* and *gums,* the pronunciations with /u, ʊ/ are confined to the New England settlement area, with /ʊ/ more common in Maine and New Hampshire than elsewhere. Although generally lacking in prestige, /gʊmz/ and /lʊm/ sometimes occur in cultured speech in Maine and New Hampshire. In other areas cultured speakers occasionally say /gumz/ and /lum/.

Two pronunciations of *can't*—/kent/ and /kæmt/—occur chiefly in parts of the South and South Midland. Although both pronunciations seem to have spread from the Virginia Piedmont, /kent/ seems to be the older and /kæmt/ the more recent form. Consequently, although both forms occur in the speech of all types of informants, /kent/ is often considered just a little more old-fashioned.

4. Several pronunciations may lack prestige in one region but be acceptable in another:

In the South and South Midland the pronunciation of *creek* as /krɪk/ is usually considered very quaint and lacking in prestige, since it is largely confined to the uneducated Negroes of the Carolina and Georgia coast. Even in the South, however, /krɪk/ may occur in the speech of cultured Charlestonians. In the North both /krik/ and /krɪk/ occur, with some pressure from the public schools to enforce /krik/ as a spelling pronunciation. However, /krɪk/ is very common in northern cultured speech. In the North Midland, especially in Pennsylvania, /krɪk/ is practically universal.

In the Atlantic seaboard states, *farm* and *form* are rarely homonymous, and where this homonymy occurs, as occasionally in South Carolina and Georgia, it is only in uneducated speech, and consequently frowned upon. In parts of Louisiana and Texas, however, this homonymy is normal among all classes of speakers.

Soot is most frequently pronounced as /sət/, except in Pennsylvania. In many parts of the country /sət/ is looked upon as old-fashioned, rustic, or uneducated. In the South, however, it is the pronunciation used by a majority of cultured speakers.

Many scholars, even C. C. Fries, have labeled the pronunciation of *catch* with /ɛ/ as lacking in prestige. However, /kɛč/ is overwhelmingly the normal pronunciation, for the nation as a whole and for all regions except southern New England, the Hudson Valley, Pennsylvania, and the city of Charleston, where /kæč/ is the majority usage. In the areas where /kæč/ is the usual pronunciation, it is naturally preferred by educated speakers. In Virginia, and to some extent in North Carolina, /kæč/ is a prestige pronunciation, used by a majority of the cultured informants but by few others. In other parts of the country, however, a majority of the cultured informants say /kɛč/.

5. For some words, one pronunciation may have prestige in one region and another pronunciation have prestige somewhere else.

For *raspberries*, the "broad *a*" pronunciation with /a/ seems to have some prestige in eastern New England, and to a lesser extent in New York City and eastern Virginia. In other parts of the country, however, —particularly in the Inland North—the pronunciation with /æ/ is socially preferred, and the /a/ pronunciation considered old-fashioned or rustic.

For such words, as *hog* and *fog*, pronunciations with /a,ɔ,ɔʊ/ have been recorded from speakers on all social levels. The /a/ pronunciation seems to have social prestige in Boston, New York City, Philadelphia, Charleston, Richmond (but not in smaller communities in the Virginia Piedmont), western North Carolina, northwestern South Carolina, and northern Georgia. In other southern communities the cultured informants have /ɔ,ɔʊ/. It is probable that /ɔʊ/ is an older prestige pronunciation that has spread from the Virginia Piedmont, with /a/ replacing it in cultured Richmond speech and in the cultured speech of other metropolitan centers.

Almost everyone knows that the two pronunciations of *greasy* sharply divide the eastern United States, with /-s-/ more common in the North and North Midland but /-z-/ usual in the South and South Midland. In some areas where both pronunciations occur, they are associated with different social levels or social contexts. Trager has frequently pointed out that among his boyhood playmates in Newark the /-z-/ pronunciation was confined to such derogatory phrases as a *greasy grind*. In South Carolina and Georgia the /-s-/ pronunciation is regular among the Gullah Negroes but almost never occurs in the speech of whites.

6. Occasionally a pronunciation may have social prestige in one area but elsewhere be only one of several acceptable pronunciations. For instance, *office* with /a/ has social prestige in eastern Pennsylvania and eastern Virginia; in other areas /a/ or /ɔ/ or /ɔʊ/ may occur without any implication of social distinction.

7. Some pronunciations have prestige in the limited areas in which they occur.

The pronunciation of *can't* with /a/ is the socially preferred form in eastern New England, and to a lesser extent in New York City, Philadelphia, and eastern Virginia. Elsewhere it is extremely rare.

The pronunciation of *soot* as /sut/ is largely confined to the northern areas. Wherever it occurs, it is likely to be found in the speech of the moderately or better educated.

The lack of constriction of post-vocalic /-r/ (the socalled loss of /r/") in *burn, barn, beard* occurs mostly in eastern New England, New York City, and the South Atlantic States. In the areas where it occurs, it is most likely to appear in the speech of the younger and better educated informants. In some communities in the South Atlantic States the rustic and uneducated white speakers preserve the constriction of /-r/, while Negroes and the more sophisticated whites lack constriction. In such communities visitors from the Inland North or the North Central States, where the constriction of /-r/ occurs in the speech of all classes, are likely to be at a social disadvantage. Conversely, in some Inland Northern communities, the only residents who lack constriction of /-r/ are the Negroes who have come from the South in the last generation. In these communities, Southern students have had difficulty securing rooms. In telephone conversations, landladies may identify the lack of constriction of /-r/ as a Negro characteristic and announce that no rooms are available.

8. A few pronunciations are always somewhat prestigious since they occur most frequently in cities and in the speech of the younger and better educated informants. However, if the group of informants using such a pronunciation is very small, the prestige of the pronunciation may be lost since the pronunciation will be interpreted as a mark of conscious snobbery.

The pronunciation of *soot* as /sut/ always has social prestige, not only in Pennsylvania where /sut/ is the usual pronunciation but in the North where /sut/ is a common pronunciation among educated speakers and in the South where /sət/ is the usual pronunciation among speakers of all classes.

The pronunciations of *vase* as /vez/, (less frequently /vaz/) and of *nephew* as /'nɛvyə,-yu/ (much less commonly (/'nɛvi/) are largely confined to cultured informants—chiefly in Southern Ontario, Boston, New York City, Philadelphia, Richmond and Charleston, where British speech forms are likely to have prestige. Inland informants who say /vez/ or /'nɛvyə/ usually have strong family or cultural ties to one of those centers.

The pronunciation of *sumach* with /su-/ instead of the more common /šu-/ is also largely confined to the larger coastal cities and to a relatively few inland cultured informants.

Such words as *suit, blew, threw* are normally pronounced with /u/. Although the pronunciations with /yu/ have social prestige in England they are extremely rare in this country, occurring almost exclusively in the North. Most Americans consider them unnatural and affected.

9. Sometimes the pronunciation of a word may involve a number of intricately related cultural, historical, and political facts. One of the most complex of these is *Negro*, where the pronunciations involve not only the status and the attitudes of those who use them, but the reactions of those the pronunciations designate. The historical pronunciation /'nɪgər/ is by far the most common, and in many communities it is the normal pronunciation used by speakers of both races. However, since it is used by many people as a term of contempt, it is actively resented by Negro spokesmen—regardless of the intent behind it. The spelling pronunciation /'nigro/ is comparatively new, but it has been actively sponsored as a polite pronunciation and is so used by most cultured speakers of the North and North Midland. However /'nigro/ is very rare south of the Mason-Dixon line, partly because it is recognized as a Northern pronunciation of a word about which most Southerners have strong prejudices, partly because it violates the normal Southern tendency to have /ə/ in unstressed syllables. The pronunciation /'nigro/ is also a common polite form in the North and North Midland, but relatively uncommon in the South. The normal polite form in the South (and occasionally in other sections) is /'nɪgrə/. Most cultured informants in the South do not use /'nɪgər/, which they feel is both derogatory to the Negro and characteristic of poor white speech. The difference in status and implication of /'nɪgrə/ and /'nɪgər/ is very sharply maintained in the South, though frequently outsiders do not understand the distinction and wonder why the Southerner does not say /'nigro/, which to the Southerner seems unnatural.

Even such a limited approach to the problem of social differences in pronunciation indicates that it is very complex and that the person who attempts to label the status of a pronunciation must have information about such social forces as trading areas, educational practices, and community structure. Nor will it be a simple matter for teachers to apply the knowledge gained from studies such as this. Yet one may suggest certain procedures.

Those who teach English in the public schools should be fully aware of the socially preferred pronunciations in the communities in which they are teaching. They should not waste time and energy attempting to force exotic pronunciations upon their students, regardless of how desirable or elegant such pronunciations seem. They should also be aware that other types of pronunciation may be acceptable in other communities. Such awareness will not only make it easier for teachers to deal with the student who has moved to the community from another region, it will also make it easier for them to teach in communities outside their own dialect area.

Teachers of English to foreign students must also recognize this problem. In universities with a cosmopolitan student body, the instructors and drillmasters may speak any one of several varieties of American English. Even if it is possible to choose instructors and drillmasters from one dialect area, or require them to use something like a uniform dialect in their classes, as soon as the foreign student goes into his regular classes he will hear other types of pronunciation from the professors and his fellow students. The problem would be less difficult at smaller colleges where the faculty and the student body are predominantly from one region. Even here, however, the students will occasionally encounter other varieties of English. The longer they are in the United States and the broader their contacts—by travel, movies, radio, or television—the more frequently they will hear other pronunciations than those they have learned. How much attention the teacher should pay to variant pronunciations is a matter of practical pedagogy, depending on circumstances—it is much more important for the student to master one American pronunciation of *can't* than to learn a little about several pronunciations—but certainly the advanced students should know that speakers may differ markedly in the details of their pronunciation, and yet all speak socially acceptable American English.

5

❈ Some Linguistic Features

of Negro Dialect

RALPH W. FASOLD AND
WALTER A. WOLFRAM

There are essentially three sources of information on the features of Negro dialect.[21] First, there are detailed technical linguistic analyses which are difficult for nonspecialists to read. Another source of information is in the form of lists which usually sacrifice adequacy in favor of simplicity. A third source of information is articles about the history of Negro dialect in which certain features are emphasized, but in which no comprehensive analysis is attempted. Our purpose here is to present the information currently available on the linguistic features of Negro dialects in non-technical language, but in sufficient detail to be useful, if not to teachers themselves, at least to those who would like to write teaching materials but do not feel secure in their knowledge of the features involved. The details of the analysis being presented are based on careful research.

Before discussing the features themselves, it is necessary to clarify

Ralph W. Fasold is a Senior Linguist in the Sociolinguistics Program at the Center for Applied Linguistics and Associate Professor of Linguistics at Georgetown University. Professor Fasold, a researcher on inner-city dialects, has published articles on social dialects and linguistic variability. He is co-author of *Teaching Standard English in the Inner City*.

Walter A. Wolfram, a Senior Linguist in the Sociolinguistics Program at the Center for Applied Linguistics and Professor of Communication Sciences at Federal City College, is well-known for his fieldwork in social dialects and his *A Sociolinguistics Description of Detroit Negro Speech*.

several facts about Negro dialect. First, it should be understood that not all Negroes speak Negro dialect. There are many Negroes whose speech is indistinguishable from others of the same region and social class, and there are many whose speech can be identified as Negro only by a few slight differences in pronunciation and vocal quality. Second, Negro dialect shares many features with other kinds of English. Its distinctiveness, however, lies in the fact that it has a number of pronunciation and grammatical features which are not shared by other dialects. It is important to realize that Negro dialect is a fully formed linguistic system in its own right, with its own grammar and pronunciation rules; it cannot simply be dismissed as an unworthy approximation of standard English. In fact, there are some grammatical distinctions which can be made more easily in Negro dialect than in standard English. Negro dialect, then, as the term is used here, is a cohesive linguistic system which is substantially different from standard American English dialects. It is spoken by some, though not all Negroes, particularly those of the lower socioeconomic classes. Furthermore, as will be brought out in the discussion, almost all the features associated with Negro dialect alternate with standard English forms in actual speech. To avoid forming a distorted picture of how speech is actually used in the lower socioeconomic black community, this variation or alternation should be kept in mind when reading the descriptions which follow.

There are two possible reasons for the distinctiveness of Negro dialect, one being the fact that the linguistic history of the dialect is partly independent from the history of the rest of American English. It has been postulated that several of the features of the dialect are traceable, not to British dialects, but to African languages via the Caribbean Creole languages. Even if this is not the case, the persistent segregation patterns of our society are sufficient cause for Negro dialect to develop its own character. Dialects develop when speakers of a common language are separated from each other, either by geographical or social distance. The social distance between white and black Americans must be cited as a contributing factor to the maintenance and development of distinct dialect features.

PRONUNCIATION

It is important to keep separate the two kinds of differences between standard English and Negro dialect. Some of these features, like the pronunciation of *then* as *den,* are the result of differences in the pronunciation systems of two kinds of American English. Other differences, like the use of "double" or multiple negatives, are grammatical in nature. Sometimes it is not obvious which kind of feature is involved. For example, we will see that the rule which causes speakers of Negro dialect to say *He go* where standard English speakers say *He goes* is a grammatical rule. On the other hand, the rule by which speakers of Negro dialect say *He walk* where standard dialect speakers say *He walked* is a pronunciation rule. Some of the reasons for this conclusion and for the importance of the distinction between the two types of rules will be given in the description to follow.

Word-final Consonant Clusters

1. *General.* Standard English words ending in a consonant cluster or blend often have the final member of the cluster absent in Negro dialect.[22] As we shall see, the reduction of some clusters which are formed by the addition of the -*s* suffix can be attributed to a grammatical difference between standard English and Negro dialect (see pp. 70, 80-82). Other types of cluster "reductions," however, do not result from grammatical differences, but are the product of pronunciation differences in final consonant clusters. In Negro dialect, words such as *test, desk, hand,* and *build* are pronounced as *tes', des', han',* and *buil'* respectively. Because of this, we find that pairs of words such as *build* and *bill, coal* and *cold,* and *west* and *Wes* have identical pronunciations in Negro dialect.

It is important to distinguish two basic types of clusters which are affected by this sort of reduction. First of all, clusters in which both members of the cluster belong to the same "base word" can be reduced, as in *tes', des', han',* and *buil'.* But reduction also affects final *t* or *d* which results when the suffix -*ed* is added to the "base word."[23] In all varieties of English, the -*ed* suffix has several different phonetic forms, depending on how the base word ends. If it ends in *d* or *t,* the -*ed* suffix is pronounced something like *id* (e.g. *wantid, countid*); otherwise it is pronounced as *t* or *d.* When the word ends in a voiced sound, it is pronounced as *d,* so that words with -*ed* like *rubbed* or *rained* are actually pronounced as *rubd* and *raind* respectively. Consonants like *b, n,* and *g* are pronounced with vocal chords vibrating, that is, they are voiced. If the base word ends in a voiceless consonant, the cluster ends in *t,* so that *messed* and *looked* are actually pronounced as *mest* and *lookt,* respectively. Consonants such as *s, k,* and *f* are pronounced without the vibration of the vocal chords, that is, they are voiceless. In Negro dialect, when the addition of the *-ed* suffix results in either a voiced or voiceless cluster, the cluster may be reduced by removing the final member of the cluster. This affects *-ed* when it functions as a past tense marker (e.g. *Yesterday he move' away*), a participle (e.g. *The boy was mess' up*) or an adjective (e.g. *He had a scratch' arm*), although its association with the past tense is the most frequent. The list of clusters affected by this process and the examples of the two types of consonant cluster reduction are given in the following table: Type I represents clusters which do not involve *-ed* and Type II represents clusters which result from the addition of the *-ed* suffix.

Note that in the table, such clusters as [mp] (e.g. *jump, ramp*), [nt] (e.g. *count, rent*), [lt] (e.g. *colt, belt*), [ŋk] (e.g. *crank, rank*), and [lp] (e.g. *gulp, help*) are not included. The reason is that the reduction rule operates only when both members of the cluster are either voiced or voiceless. Words like *mind, cold,* or *rained* (pronounced *raind*) end in two voiced sounds, *n* and *d*. On the other hand, words like *jump, count, belt, crank,* and *help* end in one voiced and one

TABLE 1

Consonant Clusters in which the Final Member
of the Cluster may be Absent

Phonetic Cluster	Examples*	
	Type I	Type II
[st]	test, post, list	missed, messed, dressed
[sp]	wasp, clasp, grasp	
[sk]	desk, risk, mask	
[št]		finished, latched, cashed
[zd]		raised, composed, amazed
[žd]		judged, charged, forged
[ft]	left, craft, cleft	laughed, stuffed, roughed
[vd]	·	loved, lived, moved
[nd]	mind, find, mound	rained, fanned, canned
[md]		named, foamed, rammed
[ld]	cold, wild, old	called, smelled, killed
[pt]	apt, adept, inept	mapped, stopped, clapped
[kt]	act, contact, expect	looked, cooked, cracked

*Where there are no examples under Type I or II, the cluster does not occur under that category.

voiceless sound; *m, n, l* and the [ŋ] sound are voiced, while *t, k* and *p* are voiceless. Since final consonant clusters can be reduced only when both consonants are voiced or when both consonants are voiceless, these words ending in one of each kind of consonant never have reduced clusters.

In some ways, the absence of the final member of the consonant cluster in Negro dialect is like a process which can also be observed in standard English; in other ways, however, it is quite different. In standard English, the final member of the cluster may be absent if the following word begins with a consonant, so that *bes' kind, col' cuts,* and *wes' side* are common and acceptable in spoken standard English. In standard English, however, this reduction can take place only when the following word begins with a consonant. While *col' cuts,* does not violate the pronunciation rules of standard English, *col' egg* does. In Negro dialect, this reduction not only takes place when the following word begins with a consonant, but it may also take place when it is followed by a vowel or a pause of some type. Thus *wes' en', bes' apple,* or *col' egg* are all acceptable according to Negro dialect rules of pronunciation. Items such as *Yesterday he was mess' up* occur because of this pronunciation rule and not because past tense is absent in Negro dialect. In standard English it is not at all unusual to hear a sentence such as *Yesterday I burn' my hand,* since the potential cluster in *burned* is followed by a word beginning with a consonant. But a sentence such as *It was burn' up,* acceptable in Negro dialect, would not be acceptable in standard English since the potential cluster is followed by a word beginning with a vowel.

2. *Plural formation.* Related to the reduction of final consonant clusters in Negro dialect is a particular pattern of pluralization involving the *-s* and *-es* plural forms. In all varieties of English, there are several different phonetic forms for the plural suffix. If the word ends in an *s*-like sound (i.e. a sibilant such as *s, sh, z, zh*), the plural suffix is formed by adding *-es;* phonetically, this is pronounced something like *-iz.* Thus *bus, bush,* and *buzz* are pluralized as *buses, bushes,* and *buzzes* respectively. If the word does not end in an *s*-like sound, then *-s* is added; phonetically this is *z* after voiced sounds and *s* after voiceless sounds. Thus, the plural of *pot, coat, bud,* and *pan* is *pots, coats, buds* (phonetically *budz*) and *pans* (phonetically *panz*) respectively. In Negro dialect, words ending in *s* plus *p, t* or *k* add the *-es* plural instead of the *-s* plural.[24] Thus, words like *desk, ghost, wasp,* and *test* are pluralized as *desses, ghoses, wasses, and tesses.* Because the *p, t,* and *k* are so often removed by the rule discussed above, these plurals are formed as if *desk, test,* and *wasp* ended in *s,* instead of *sk, st,* or *sp.*

It is essential to understand that this is a regular pluralization pattern due to the status of final consonant clusters in Negro dialect.

Attempting to learn standard English pluralization patterns, speakers will sometimes pluralize words like *desk* and *test* as *deskes* and *testes* respectively. These forms result from the failure to eliminate Negro dialect pluralization after realizing that words like *test* and *desk* are to be pronounced with a cluster. Technically, this is known as "hypercorrection".

3. *The status of word-final clusters.* Because consonant clusters occur so infrequently at the end of words in Negro dialect, one might ask whether these word-final clusters can be considered an integral part of the Negro dialect system. That is, are speakers of Negro dialect at all familiar with what words may and what words may not end in clusters? This question is crucial for teaching, since clusters must be taught as completely new items if Negro dialect speakers are completely unfamiliar with them. On the other hand, if clusters are a part of the dialect and simply different from standard English because they can undergo reduction in certain contexts where reduction is not possible in standard English (e.g. when the following word begins with a vowel), the teaching problem is of a different nature. What must be taught in the latter case, is the contexts in which cluster reduction is not possible in standard English but is possible in Negro dialect, while the lists of standard English words ending in clusters must be taught as completely new items if clusters are not an integral part of the dialect.

This question can be answered most clearly by observing what happens when suffixes beginning with a vowel are added to a base word ending in a cluster in standard English. This includes *-ing* as in *testing* or *scolding*, *-er* as in *tester* or *scolder* and *-est* as in *coldest* or *oldest*. If a consonant cluster is present in such constructions (e.g. *testing*, *tester*), we may assume that the speaker is fully acquainted with the cluster, but that it can be reduced in places where it is not possible in standard English. For the vast majority of Negro dialect speakers in the North, this is exactly how the rule concerning consonant clusters operates. These speakers may reduce the cluster in the context of *tes' program* or *tes' idea,* but retain the cluster in *tester*. There is, however, also a group of Negro dialect speakers, most typically Southern children, who not only show the absence of the final member of the cluster in *tes' program* or *tes' idea,* but in *teser* as well. For these speakers, the teaching of standard English must start with the list of standard English words which end in consonant clusters.

We may summarize our observations about the word-final consonant clusters in the following table, which represents how standard English and the two varieties of Negro dialect function with respect to final consonant clusters. The three contexts mentioned above are: (1) the following word begins with a consonant, (2) the following word does not begin with a consonant, and (3) a suffix beginning with a vowel follows.

TABLE 2

Consonant Cluster Reduction

	(1)	(2)	(3)
	——#C	——#	——-V
Standard English	tes' program	test idea	testing
Negro dialect 1	tes' program	tes' idea	testing
Negro dialect 2	tes' program	tes' idea	tes'ing

On the basis of this table, we can draw some general conclusions about the social significance of consonant cluster reduction. We see, for example, that Negro dialect is very much like standard English when the following word begins with a consonant; a reduction of the cluster therefore has little social significance in this context. When not followed by a consonant, however, it is socially stigmatized. Absence of the cluster is most stigmatized when a suffix beginning with a vowel is added.

The th-Sounds

1. *General.* In standard English, the letters *th* actually represent two different types of sound. First, they represent the voiced sound in words such as *the, they,* and *that* (i.e. a voiced interdental fricative). Second, they represent the voiceless sound as in words like *thought, thin,* and *think* (a voiceless interdental fricative). In Negro dialect, the regular pronunciation rules for the sounds represented by *th* are quite different. The particular sounds which *th* represents are mainly dependent on the context in which *th* occurs. That is, the sounds for *th* are dependent on where *th* might occur in a word and/or what sounds occur next to it.

2. *Word-initial.* At the beginning of a word, the *th* in *the* is frequently pronounced as a *d* in Negro dialect, so that words such as *the, they,* and *that* are pronounced as *de, dey,* and *dat* respectively. It has been pointed out that a limited amount of *d* for *th* is also charac-

teristic of standard English in the most casual or informal speech style. In Negro dialect, however, it is much more frequent so that the pronunciation *de* for *the* is the regular pronunciation. It is important to note here that the pronunciation of *d* for *th* in Negro dialect is not simply an error in pronunciation, but the result of a regular and patterned rule.

In the case of *th* in words such as *thought, think* or *thin* (the voiceless interdental fricative), *th* is sometimes pronounced as *t,* so that *thought, think* or *thin* are pronounced as *tought, tink* and *tin* respectively. However, most Negro dialect speakers who pronounce *thought* as *tought* will also sometimes pronounce it as *thought.* That is, both the *th* and *t* pronunciations for *thought* are appropriate for Negro dialect. If *th* is followed by *r* as in *throat* or *three* still another pronunciation is possible. These words may be pronounced with an *f,* so that *three* and *throat* can be pronounced as *free* and *froat* respectively. This means that items such as *three* and *free* may be pronounced the same in Negro dialect.

3. *Within a word.* In the middle of the word, there are several different pronunciations for *th* in Negro dialect. For the voiceless sound as in *nothing, author,* or *ether,* most frequently it is pronounced as *f.* Thus, *nothing, author,* and *ether* are pronounced as *nuf'n, ahfuh,* and *eefuh* respectively. For the voiced sound, as in *brother, rather* or *bathing, th* is pronounced as *v* in some varieties of Negro dialect, so that these words are pronounced as *bruvah, ravah,* and *bavin',* respectively.

In addition to *f* and *v* for *th* in the middle of a word, several other pronunciations may occur. When *th* is followed by a nasal sound such as *m* or *n, th* may be pronounced as *t.* Thus *'ritmetic* for *arithmetic, nut'n* for *nothing* or *montly* for *monthly,* are patterns frequently used in Negro dialect. There are also several items in which no consonant at all is found. For example, *mother* may be pronounced as *muh* (with a lengthened vowel) and *brother* may be pronounced as *bruh.* This pattern, however, is relatively infrequent and only takes place when the vowel sounds preceding and following *th* are similar.

4. *Word-final.* At the end of a word, *f* is the predominant pronunciation of *th* in words such as *Ruth, tooth,* and *south,* which are pronounced as *Ruf, toof,* and *souf,* respectively. Whereas most speakers fluctuate between the pronunciation of *f* and *th* in the middle of the word, some speakers exclusively use *f* and *v* at the ends of these words. In addition to *f* and *v* at the ends of these words, several other sounds may be represented by *th,* dependent upon the sounds which precede it.[25] When the preceding sound is the nasal sound *n, t* may occur so

that *tenth* and *month* are pronounced as *tent'* and *mont'*, respectively. The stop *t* or *d* may also be used with the preposition *with,* so that it is pronounced as *wit* or *wid.* Next to the nasal *n,* it is also possible to have no consonant at all present. This means that *month* and *tenth* may be pronounced as *mon'* and *ten'.*

r and l

1. *After vowels.* The pronunciation rule for *r* and *l* in Negro dialect operates in a way quite similar to white speech in certain parts of the South. At the beginning of a word, *r* and *l* are always pronounced, as in *run, lip, rub,* or *lamp.* In other positions, however, *r* and *l* are sometimes reduced to a vowel-like quality pronounced something like *uh.* The most important context to recognize in discussing the so-called "loss" of *r* and *l* is when they follow a vowel (technically called "postvocalic"). In such items as *steal, sister, nickel,* or *bear,* only a "phonetic vestige" of *r* or *l* is pronounced, so that we hear *steauh, sistuh, nickuh,* and *beauh* respectively. Preceding a consonant in a word (e.g. *wart, tart*) some speakers do not have any phonetic vestige of *r* or *l;* this means that *help* and *hep* and *taught* and *torte* may be pronounced identically by these speakers. In some areas of the South, Negro dialect may also reveal no vestige of *r* following the vowels *o* or *u.* For these speakers, *door* and *doe, four* and *foe,* and *sure* and *show* may be pronounced alike. Although it has been suggested that *l* may also be completely absent at the end of a word following *o* or *u,* there seems to be some small phonetic vestige so that *toll* and *toe* or *mole* and *mow* do not sound exactly alike in Negro dialect.

In some "r-less" American English dialects the word which follows *r* or *l* is important in determining whether or not *r* and *l* loss may take place. For example, in the *r*-less dialect of New England, *r* is consistently absent when the following word begins with a consonant, as in *brothuh Mike* or *fouh people;* when followed by a word that begins with a vowel, the *r* is consistently present, as in *brother Ed* or *four apples.* In Negro dialect, however it may be absent in both types of contexts, although it is more frequently absent when followed by a word beginning with a consonant (e.g. *fouh people*) than when followed by one beginning with a vowel (e.g. *fouh apples*).

2. *Between vowels.* Not only may *r* or *l* be absent when followed by another word beginning with a vowel, but *r* absence is occasionally observed between two vowels within a word. Thus, it is possible to get *Ca'ol, sto'y* or *ma'y* for *Carol, story* and *marry* respectively.

3. *Effect on vocabulary and grammar.* The consistent absence of *r* at the end of a word has led to several "mergers" of vocabulary items. That is, because of the similarity of two words after a particular pronunciation rule has taken place, one word has assumed the function of what was originally two words. For example, when the phonetic vestige which replaces the *r* is removed, there is only a small difference which separates *they* from *their* or *you* from *your*. The forms *they* and *you* can be used as possessive as in *It is they book* or *It is you book* in Negro dialect as a result of this merging process (cf. Undifferentiated pronouns, p. 81).

Like *r*, the loss of *l* may have important implications for grammatical functions. The most crucial of these deals with the loss of *l* on a contracted form of the future modal *will*. We may get a sentence such as *Tomorrow I bring the thing* for *Tomorrow I'll bring the thing*, where *will* becomes *'ll* and then is lost completely. This pronunciation process accounts for the use of *be* in Negro dialect as an indicator of future time, as in *He be here in a few minutes*. The pronunciation rule for the loss of the contracted form of *l* takes place most frequently when the following word begins with *b, m,* or *w* (i.e. labial sounds).

4. *After initial consonants.* Before leaving our description of the rules for *r* and *l* in Negro dialect, we must note that in certain words, *r* may be absent when it follows a consonant. Two main types of contexts can be cited to account for this phenomenon. First, *r* may be absent when the following vowel is either *o* or *u*, so that we get *th'ow* for *throw*, and *th'ough* for *through*. Second, *r* may be absent in unstressed syllables, so that *protéct* and *proféssor* are pronounced as *p'otéct* and *p'oféssuh*, respectively.

5. *Social stigma.* On the whole, *r* and *l* absence has not been as socially stigmatized as many other grammatical and pronunciation rules of Negro dialect. This is probably due to the fact that certain types of *r* absence are generally recognized as legitimate regional characteristics of some dialects of standard English. Because of the relatively slight stigmatization, the rule for *r* and *l* absence is often found in the speech of middle class Negroes living in regions characterized by the presence of *r* and *l*.

Final b, d, and g

1. *Devoicing.* At the end of a syllable, the voiced stops *b, d,* and *g* (and, to a lesser extent, all voiced consonants except nasals *r, l, w* and *y*) are often pronounced as the corresponding voiceless stops, *p, t,*

and *k*, respectively. This means that words such as *pig*, *bud*, and *cab* end in *k*, *t*, and *p*, respectively. Before concluding that *pig* and *pick*, *bud* and *butt*, and *cab* and *cap* sound identical in Negro dialect, it is essential to note that they are still distinguished by the length of the vowel. English vowels are held slightly longer when the following sound is voiced (i.e. the vowel in *bud* is held slightly longer than the vowel in *butt*). In the case of Negro dialect, the vowel is lengthened before sounds such as *d* in *bud*, even though the *d* is actually pronounced *t*. As a result, *bud* does not sound the same as *butt* because the *u* is "stretched out" a little in *bud* but not in *butt*.

In some varieties of standard English, "devoicing" can take place in an unstressed syllable, so that we can get *salat* for *salad*, *hundret* for *hundred*, or *acit* for *acid*. Negro dialect not only has the rule for devoicing in unstressed syllables, but stressed syllables as well, so that we hear *mut* for *mud*, *goot* for *good* and *loat* for *load*.

The *-ed* suffix, when attached to verb bases ending in a vowel, is represented by *d* in all varieties of English. The devoicing rule applies to this *d* as well as the *d* of *mud*, *good*, and *load*. For this reason, *played* is sometimes pronounced *playt* in Negro dialect.

2. *Deletion of d.* In addition to the devoicing rule, there are some speakers who may have the complete absence of the stop *d*, although this is not nearly as frequent as devoicing. This results in pronunciations such as *goo' man* and *ba' soldier*. The rule for the absence of *d* occurs more frequently when *d* is followed by a consonant than when followed by a vowel (e.g. *goo' soldier* is more frequent than *goo' egg*); *d* absence is most common before *s* or *z*. For this reason, the addition of an *-s* suffix often results in pronunciations such as *kiz* for *kids*, and *boahz* for *boards*.

d-absence is also possible when *d* represents the *-ed* suffix with verbal bases ending in vowels. It is possible to observe sentences like *Yesterday he play it* and *He had play it the day before*. However, since this rule is much less frequently applied than the rule eliminating the second member of a consonant cluster, there are many more cases of sentences like *Yesterday he miss it* than *Yesterday he play it*.

Nasalization

There are several different aspects of the nasals *m*, *n*, and *ng* (phonetically [ŋ]) which must be discussed with reference to Negro dialect. Some of these are quite characteristic of all nonstandard English dialects, others are characteristic of Southern standard as well as nonstandard dialects, and still others are unique to Negro dialect.

1. *The -ing suffix.* The use of the *-in* suffix for *-ing* (e.g. *singin'*, *buyin'*, *swimin'*) is a feature which is characteristic of all socially stigmatized varieties of English. Because of the spelling of [ŋ] as *ng* this is sometimes referred to as a "dropping of the *g*". Although *in* in such words as *singin'*, *comin'* and *doin'* occurs in all socially stigmatized varieties of American English, its frequency is somewhat greater in Negro dialect than in other nonstandard dialects. In fact, there may be some speakers who do not use the *-ing* form at all. This form is one of the most stereotyped phonological features of nonstandard speech in the American language.

2. *Nasalized vowels.* Another feature which is found in Negro dialect is the use of a nasalized vowel instead of the nasal consonant. Generally, this only takes place at the end of a syllable. In words like *man, bun,* or *bum* the final consonant is sometimes not pronounced, but a nasalization of the preceding vowel is found similar to the type of nasalization of vowels that is found in a language such as French. This means that words such as *rum, run,* and *rung* might all sound alike in Negro dialect (that is, they may all be produced as [r̃ə] phonetically where [˜] stands for nasalization). As many other features in Negro dialect, this feature does not occur categorically. That is, there is always fluctuation between the use of the nasalized vowel and the nasal consonant.

3. *The influence of nasals on i and e.* Finally, we should mention the influence that nasal consonants have on the vowels *i* and *e*. Before a nasal consonant, *i* and *e* do not contrast, making words such as *pin* and *pen* or *tin* and *ten* sound identical. This pronunciation rule of Negro dialect is quite like some standard varieties of Southern speech, and only has social significance in a Northern context.

Vowel Glides

In some parts of the South, the vowel glides represented as *ay* (e.g. *side, time*) and *oy* (e.g. *boy, toy*) are generally pronounced without the glide. Thus, *side* and *time* may be pronounced as *sahd* and *tahm* and *boy* and *toy* as *boih* and *toah*. This feature of some Southern standard as well as nonstandard dialects has been adopted as an integral part of Negro dialect. The absence of the glide is much more frequent when it is followed by a voiced sound or a pause than it is when followed by a voiceless sound. This means that the absence of a glide is much more likely in words such as *side, time,* or *toy* than it is in *kite, bright,* or *fight.* Many speakers never have a glide when followed by voicing but always have one when followed by a voiceless sound (e.g. they always have *tahm* for *time* but never have *kaht* for *kite*). Because the rule for vowel glides is found among middle class speakers in the South its social significance is limited to Northern areas, where it is associated with class and race. Even in Northern areas, however, its stigmatization is minimal.

Indefinite Articles a and an

In standard English, when the following word begins with a vowel, the indefinite article *an* is used as in *an apple* or *an egg;* when it is followed by a word beginning with a consonant, *a* occurs as in *a boy* or *a dog.* In Negro dialect, as in some varieties of white Southern speech, the article *a* is used regardless of how the following word begins. With a selected group of words (of more than one syllable) which may begin with a vowel similar to *a* (phonetically [ə]), the article may also be completely absent (or, at least, "merge" with the vowel); this results in sentences such as *He had eraser* or *He had erector set.* Less frequently, and mostly among younger children, this article may be absent in other types of constructions (e.g. *I have pencil*), but this type of absence seems to be a grammatical rather than a pronunciation feature.

Stress

Stress or accent in Negro dialect operates quite like the stress patterns of standard English with several exceptions. One exception can be found when standard English words of more than one syllable have their stress on the second syllable rather than the first. In Negro dialect, some of these words may be stressed on the first rather than the second syllable. This only affects a small subset of words such as *políce, hotél,* or *Julý,* which in Negro dialect are pronounced as *pólice, hótel* and *Júly.*

Another difference which can be traced to stress is the absence of the first syllable of a word when the first syllable is unstressed. For example, we find *'rithmetic, 'member, 'cept* or *'bout,* respectively. Because this pattern results in the absence of certain types of prefixes, some speakers may occasionally "overuse" the prefix *re-.* This overuse of *re-* may result in formations such as *revorce* or *remorial* for *divorce* and *memorial,* according to William A. Stewart.

Other Pronunciation Features

In addition to the systematic patterns which have been mentioned above, there are several features which are quite restricted. One such feature is the pronunciation of *ask* as *ax,* so that it sounds like *axe.* This feature, which is quite prominent in some speakers of Negro dialect, can be related to an Old English pronunciation which has been preserved in Negro dialect as well as white Appalachian speech.

Another rule which is quite limited is the absence of *s* in a word which ends in *x* (phonetically [ks]). This pattern results in the pronunciation of *box* as *bok* and *six* as *sik* (homophonous with *sick*). For the most part, this feature is limited to a few items ending in *x* and is more frequently found in Southern speakers of Negro dialect than it is in Northern speakers.

Finally, we may mention rules for the *str* clusters in such words as *string* and *street,* which may be pronounced as *skring* and *skreet,* respectively. At the end of a word, *st* may also be changed to *sk,* so that *wrist* and *twist* are occasionally pronounced as *wrisk* and *twisk* when speakers are trying to approximate a standard English norm.

There are, of course, other restricted types of differences between the pronunciation rules of Negro dialect and standard English which might be mentioned. Other examples, however, are either so limited in terms of the numbers of items affected or so unobtrusive in terms of their social significance, that it is sufficient for the teacher to have a firm understanding of the pronunciation features which we have described above. Indeed, the teacher who fully understands and respects the pronunciation rules of Negro dialect discussed here will have taken a necessary step in the effective teaching of standard English.

GRAMMAR

Other features of Negro dialect are due to the fact that some of the rules of Negro dialect grammar are different from grammatical rules in standard English. These rules deal with the verb system, with negation, with noun suffixes, with question formation, and with pronouns. Some of the features in the following section, however, are technically pronunciation features, but are described as grammatical features because they are usually perceived as such.

VERBS

Many of the most significant features of Negro dialect are to be found in its verb system. The differences in the verb structure of Negro dialect as compared to standard American English are mainly found in the tense systems of the two dialects and in their treatment of the verb *to be*.

Past Forms

1. *The -ed suffix.* As we have seen already, the *-ed* suffix which marks past tense and past participial forms, as well as derived adjectives, is sometimes not pronounced in Negro dialect because of pronunciation rules (pp. 56 and 63). When *-ed* is added to a verb base ending in a consonant, as in *missed,* it can be removed by application of the consonant cluster reduction rule. When *-ed* is added to a verbal base which ends in a vowel, it can be removed by the rule for deletion of syllable-final *d.* As we have already pointed out, the *d*-deletion rule applies much less often than the consonant cluster reduction rule, so that *-ed* is much more frequently absent from bases ending in a consonant which is not *t* or *d* than from bases ending in a vowel.

When *-ed* is added to a base ending in *t* or *d,* it is pronounced something like *id,* as we have mentioned before.[26] In this form, it is rarely absent in Negro dialect. However, this *id* form can be reduced to *d* alone in Negro dialect and also in standard English by some fairly complex, but very regular rules. In casual speech, the words *want* and *start* are the most frequently occurring verbs which are eligible for these rules. If they apply, the *i*-sound of *id* can be eliminated. The verb then ends in *dd* or *td* which is simplified to *d.* These operations result in sentences like *He stard crying* (from *He started crying*) and *He wanda go* (from *He wanted to go*). Such sentences are common in all varieties of American English and are not considered nonstandard. In the case of *stard,* Negro dialect (but not standard English) has a rule for the elimination of the remaining *d,* especially when the verb occurs before a gerund, as in *He sta crying* (the *r* of *start* is absent for reasons we have already discussed). The verb *started* is virtually the only verb to undergo this process.[27]

These rules are pronunciation rules. This means that the missing *-ed* suffix does not reflect a grammatical difference between Negro dialect and standard English. The suffix is a part of the grammar of both kinds of English. Any attempt to teach the *-ed* suffix as a grammatical entity, then, will be superfluous.

Another important implication is that children who speak Negro dialect should not be required to learn the careful pronunciation of -*ed* where speakers of standard English usually do not pronounce it. When -*ed* is phonetically *t* or *d* and is the second member of a consonant cluster, and when the next word begins with a consonant, as in *Yesterday I burned my hand,* Negro dialect speakers should be allowed to pronounce *burned* as *burn',* the way standard English speakers do.

2. *Irregular verbs.* Verbs which form their past tenses in an irregular way distinguish present and past forms in the overwhelming majority of cases in Negro dialect. The occurrence of sentences like *Yesterday he give it to me* are rare. However, some verbs which have irregular past forms in standard English have the same form for past and present tenses in Negro dialect. There are also such verbs in standard English (*They hit him yesterday; They hit him every day*). A few verbs, notably *say,* behave like *hit* for some speakers of Negro dialect, giving, for example, *He say it every day; He say it yesterday.* In the case of *say,* the situation is complicated by the fact that some speakers who actually use *said* will be heard by speakers of standard English as having said *say* because the *d* of *said* has been removed by the word-final *d*-elimination rule.

Perfective Constructions

1. *General.* The perfective constructions in Negro dialect discussed below are first illustrated in Table 3.

TABLE 3

The Perfective Constructions in Negro Dialect and Standard English

	Negro Dialect	Standard English
Present Perfect	I have walked I('ve) walked	I have walked I've walked
Past Perfect	I had walked	I had walked I'd walked
Completive	I done walked	
Remote Time	I been walked	

2. *Omission of forms of have.* In standard American English, the present tense forms of auxiliary *have* can be contracted to '*ve* and '*s,*

giving sentences like *I've been here for hours* and *He's gone home already*. In Negro dialect, the contracted forms *'ve* and *'s* can be removed, giving *I been here for hours* and *He gone home already*. Rules for removing the remnants of contraction account for at least three of the most noticed features of Negro dialect, as we shall see. The frequent operation of this rule, together with the relatively infrequent use of the present perfective tense can lead to the conclusion that *have* + past participle is not part of Negro dialect. It is true that the present perfect tense is quite infrequent. But the past perfect construction with *had* is, if anything, even more common in Negro dialect narratives than in narratives by speakers of standard American English. Sentences like *He had found the money* appear strikingly often in story-telling. Negro dialect speakers do not select the present perfect as often as do speakers of standard English, but they select the past perfect more often than standard English speakers. As with the *-ed* suffix, pronunciation rules have removed forms which are present grammatically.

3. *The past participle*. While it is quite clear that the tenses formed grammatically with *have* and *had* are part of Negro dialect, it is less clear whether or not there are past participles in its grammar. In standard English, most past participles are formed with the *-ed* suffix and so are identical with the past tense form. But there are a number of semi-regular and irregular verbs for which the past participle and past tense are formally distinguished (e.g. *came* versus *has come; ate* versus *has eaten,* etc.). In Negro dialect, however, it seems that there may not be any irregular verbs for which the past tense and past participle are distinct. Sometimes the standard English past participle form is generalized to serve both functions (*He taken it; He have taken it*), but more commonly the simple past form is used in both kinds of constructions (e.g. *He came; He have came*). For a few verbs, some Negro dialect speakers generalize one form while others generalize the other (e.g. *He done it; He have done it; He did it; He have did it*). It is possible, then, that the Negro dialect equivalents of the present and past perfect tenses are not formed with forms of *have* plus the past participle, but rather with a form of *have* plus a general past form.

4. *The completive aspect with done*. Where standard American English has only two aspectual contrasts of the perfective type, Negro dialect has four. With standard English, Negro dialect has perfective tense (or aspect) constructions with *have* and *had*. In addition, Negro dialect has a completive construction and a remote time construction. The completive aspect is formed from the verb *done* plus a past form of the verb. Because of the uncertain status of the past participle in

the grammar of the dialect, it is difficult to determine whether this form is the past participle or not. This construction occurs in sentences like *I done tried hard all I know how* and *I done forgot what you call it*.

5. *The remote time construction with been.* A similar construction with *been* indicates that the speaker conceives of the actions as having taken place in the distant past. The remote aspect is used in *I been had it there for about three or four years* and *You won't get your dues that you been paid*. Often, the *been* construction is used with emphatic stress to doubly emphasize the total completion of an action, although it is not always used in this way. Unlike the *done* construction, the *been* construction is used only in Negro dialect. Both constructions are rather rare, at least in Northern cities.

The Third Person Singular Present Tense Marker

1. *General.* In standard American English, the suffix *-s* (or *-es*) is used to identify the present tense of a verb if the subject of that verb is in the third person singular. The paradigm is:

Singular	*Plural*
I walk	we walk
you walk	you walk
he walks; the man walks	they walk; the men walk

In a sense, the use of the *-s* suffix to mark present tense with third person singular subjects is an irregularity, since no suffix is used to mark present tense with other persons. The paradigm in Negro dialect is more regular:

Singular	*Plural*
I walk	we walk
you walk	you walk
he walk; the man walk	they walk; the men walk

It is important to realize that the *-s* suffix is not carelessly "left off" by speakers of Negro dialect. This suffix is simply not part of the grammar of the dialect.

2. *Auxiliary don't.* The verb *do* is used as an auxiliary in negative and other kinds of sentences. In Negro dialect, the *-s* suffix is absent from the auxiliary *don't* in the present tense when the subject is in the third person singular, just as it is from other third person singular

present tense verbs. The equivalent of the standard English sentence *He doesn't go*, then, is *He don't go*. Some other nonstandard dialects of English lack the *-s* suffix only with auxiliary *don't*. Speakers of such dialects rarely or never use sentences like *He walk*, but frequently use such sentences as *He don't walk*. The use of *don't* for *doesn't* in Negro dialect does not apply only to auxiliary *don't*, but is part of a general pattern involving all present tense verbs with subjects in the third person singular.[28]

3. *Have and do.* The verb *have* in standard English is unique in that the combination of *have* and the *-s* suffix results in *has* rather than *haves*. Similarly, when the *-s* suffix is added to *do*, the vowel quality changes and the result is *does*, not *dos*. Since the *-s* suffix does not exist in the verb system of Negro dialect, the verbs remain *have* and *do* with third person singular subjects in the present tense. For this reason, we observe sentences like *He have a bike, He always do silly things*, and *I don't know if he like you, but I think he do*.

4. *Hypercorrect forms.* The absence of the *-s* suffix in Negro dialect causes a real language learning problem when Negro dialect speakers come in contact with standard English. They observe that speakers of standard English have a suffix *-s* on some present tense verbs. But the grammatical rules restricting its use to sentences with third person singular subjects is just like a rule in the grammar of a foreign language. Like a foreign language learner, Negro dialect speakers begin to use the feature, but do not restrict it according to the rules of the new dialect. The result is that the *-s* subject is sporadically used with present tense verbs with subjects other than third person singular. This accounts for sentences like *I walks, you walks, the children walks*, etc., as well as the appropriate standard English *He walks*. Occasionally, the suffix is also added to non-finite forms, giving sentences like *They want to goes*. No Negro dialect speakers, however, add the *-s* suffix to all present tense verbs with non-third person singular subjects.

The use of sentences like *I walks* has a quite different status from the use of sentences like *He walk*. A speaker of Negro dialect uses *walk* instead of *walks* with a subject like *he* because this is the correct form according to the grammatical rules of his dialect. He uses *walks* with subjects like *I*, not because this grammar calls for this form but because of a partial learning of the grammar rules of a different dialect.

Future

1. *Gonna.* A very frequent future indicator in Negro dialect, as in

other dialects of English, is the use of *gonna*. The rule for deleting *is* and *are* (see below) operates very frequently when *gonna* follows, giving sentences like *He gonna go* and *You gonna get in trouble*. So rarely is a form of *be* used with *gonna* that it may seem that *gonna* is not related to standard English *be going to*, but is an auxiliary in its own right. However, the behavior of *gonna* as compared with true auxiliaries like *can* shows that this is not the case. In questions and in abbreviated sentences, *can* and *gonna* function quite differently (*Can he go?* but never *Gonna he go?; He can sing, I know he can* but *He gonna vote for you, I know he is,* not *I know he gonna*). As Labov and his associates have pointed out, the phonetic form of *gonna* can be reduced in a number of ways in Negro dialect which are different from its reductions in standard English. When the subject of the sentence is *I* in standard dialects of American English, *gonna* can be reduced to *ngna* (*I'ngna go*). In Negro dialect, there are three reductions not possible in standard English, *mana* (*I'mana go*), *mon* (*I'mon go*) and *ma* (*I'ma go*). When the subject is something other than *I*, Negro dialect may give the reduced form *gon* (*He gon go*).[29]

2. *Will*. The use of *will* to indicate future time reference is also part of both Negro dialect and standard English. As in the case of *has* and *have*, *will* can be contracted (to *'ll*). This contracted form, like *'ve* and *'s*, can be eliminated, as we have seen, especially if the next word begins with a labial consonant, as in *He miss you tomorrow*. This makes it appear that the future is sometimes indicated by the use of the main verb alone.

Invariant Be

1. *General*. When the verb *to be* is used as a main verb in standard English, it appears as one of the five variant inflected forms *is, are, am, was* or *were,* depending on the verb tense and the person and number of the subject. In Negro dialect, the form *be* can be used as a main verb regardless of the subject of the sentence as in *I be here this afternoon* and *Sometimes he be busy*. This use of invariant *be* in Negro dialect has two explanations; deleted *will* or *would* and distributive *be*.

2. *Will be or would be*. Since *be* begins with a labial consonant, the *'ll* contraction of *will* is often absent before *be*. This is fairly common in Negro dialect, but also happens occasionally in standard English, giving sentences like *He be here pretty soon*. The contracted form of *would* is *'d*, which can merge with the *b* of *be* or be removed by the final *d* elimination rule. This process is another source for invariant *be*

and is quite common in standard English as well. A sentence like *If you gave him a present he be happy* is possible both in standard dialects and in Negro dialect.

It may seem that an intolerable number of ambiguous sentences would result from the removal of the remnants of contraction. But the context usually makes the intended meaning clear. The same sort of thing happens in standard English, not only in the occasional removal of *'ll* and *'d*, but in the contraction of *'d* of both *had* and *would*. The sentence *He'd come home* is ambiguous by itself. But in contexts like *He'd come home before I got there* or *He'd come home if he could,* the meaning is clear.

3. *Distributive or non-tense be.* The other source for invariant *be* is very different. This type of invariant *be* occurs because *to be* is possible in Negro dialect without tense specification with a meaning something like "object or event distributed intermittently in time." This use of *be*, as in *Sometime he be there and sometime he don't,* occurs only in Negro dialect and is usually misunderstood by standard English speakers. It is common for standard English speakers to take non-tense *be* as a deviant form of *am, is,* or *are,* when in fact it contrasts with these forms. To say *I'm good* is to assert a permanent quality of oneself. To say *I be good* means that the speaker is good only intermittently. Unlike the cases of invariant *be* which are derived from *will be* or *would be,* non-tense *be* usage is highly stigmatized socially. Because there are three sources for invariant *be* in Negro dialect, any positive statement containing invariant *be* is potentially three-ways ambiguous. In the sentence *If somebody hit him, Darryl be mad,* if the use of *be* is taken as coming from *would be,* it is a hypothesis about how Darryl might act if he were hit. If *will be* is understood, it is a prediction as to how Darryl will react. If distributive *be* is the interpretation, it is a statement of Darryl's reaction to a certain kind of intermittent event. The sentence is only ambiguous because it is a positive statement. In negative sentences, contraction of *will* and *would* is not possible. The three interpretations above would each be denied in a different way. The hypothesis would be denied by *Darryl wouldn't be mad,* the predication by *Darryl won't be mad,* and the statement by *Darryl don't be mad.*

Absence of Forms of To Be

1. *General.* When the *is* or *are* forms of *to be* are expected in standard English, Negro dialect may have no form at all. When the subject

is *I,* and the expected standard English form is *am,* however, *am* or its contraction *'m* is almost always present. For most varieties of Negro dialect, the absence of forms of *to be* represents the elimination of the contracted forms *'s* and *'re* of *is* and *are,* much as the contractions of *have, has, will* and *would* are removed. Just as in these cases and in the case of the *-ed* suffix, the *to be* forms are grammatically present and are known to the speaker, but have been removed by a pronunciation rule. It is not necessary to teach the present tense forms of *to be* to speakers of Negro dialect, but they will need to learn to contract these forms without also deleting the remnants of contraction.

2. *Is.* As we have seen, the absence of *is* is common before *gonna.* Some Southern dialects of English besides Negro dialect show the absence of *is* in this context. In Negro dialect, unlike other English dialects, *is* can be absent wherever it can be contracted in standard English. We observe sentences like *He a man, He running to school, That dude bad,* as well as *He gonna go.* When the subject of a sentence is *it, that, or what,* the next word is *is,* an *s*-sound is usually heard. This is not the *'s* from the contraction of *is,* however. The *s* in such sentences is the result of the following process. First, *is* is contracted to *'s.* Then, the *t* of *it, that* and *what* is transformed into *s* under the influence of the *'s* from *is.* This leaves *is's, thas's,* and *whas's.* But these forms are never heard because the *'s* from *is* is then eliminated as it almost always must be when it follows a sibilant. This leaves the pronunciations *iss, thas* and *whas* for these three words. Apparently something similar happens in the case of *let's* (pronounced *les*) even though the *'s* comes from *us* rather than *is.*

3. *Are.* The form *are* is present less often than the form *is* in the speech of Negro dialect speakers. *Are* is also absent in white Southern dialects of English which do not allow the absence of *is,* including some which are socially standard. The English contraction rule provides for the removal of all but the final consonant of certain auxiliaries (*are* to *'re, will* to *'ll, have* to *'ve,* etc.). In dialects which lack *r* after most stressed vowels, *are* has no final consonant (i.e. it is pronounced *ah*). Regular pronunciation rules of English reduce this *ah* to *uh.* Applying the contraction rule to this pronunciation eliminates the word *are* entirely, without utilizing the Negro dialect rule for removing the consonant. Because of this there are speakers who have *are* absence but do not have *is* absence.

4. *Agreement with forms of to be.* Some speakers show no person-number agreement when full forms of *to be* are used. The past tense form is *was* regardless of the subject, giving sentences like *They was there, You was there,* etc. When the full forms of the present tense

form are used, *is* is used by these speakers for all persons, e.g., *The boys is there, You is there,* etc. However, some Southern speakers of Negro dialect occasionally use *are* or even *am* as the general form of the present tense of *to be* (*There she are, You am a teacher,* etc.).

NEGATION

The Use of Ain't

Due to a series of phonetic changes in the history of English, the negative forms of *is, are, am,* and auxiliary *have* and *has* became *ain't.* Although *ain't* is used by educated speakers in casual conversation in some parts of the country, the use of *ain't* in this way is one of the clearest and universal markers of nonstandard speech of all kinds. In some varieties of Negro dialect, *ain't* also corresponds to standard English *didn't.* This probably developed from rather recent phonetic changes. In Negro dialect, negative forms of auxiliary *do* can lose the initial *d* in casual speech. This gives, for example, *I 'on't know* for standard English *I don't know.* In the case of *didn't,* the second *d* can merge with the following *n.* The result of these two developments is the pronunciation *int* for *didn't.* This form is so similar in pronunciation and function to the already existing *ain't* that the two forms merged. For speakers of Negro dialect who have this use of *ain't,* there are sentences like *He ain't do it* as well as *He ain't done it* (or *He ain't did it*) and *He ain't there.* The unfamiliarity of this usage to speakers of standard English often leads to misunderstanding between speakers of the two dialects. A Negro dialect speaker may say *He ain't touch me* which should be translated as *He didn't touch me* in standard English but be understood as having meant *He hasn't touched me* (with the *-ed* suffix supplied by the hearer). *Ain't* is often used with multiple negation, leading to sentences like *He ain't nobody, He ain't did nothing* and *He ain't go nowhere.*

Mutiple Negation

1. *General.* "Double negatives" or, more accurately, multiple negation is another very common feature of nonstandard dialects. A frequent misconception about multiple negation is that it leads to misunderstanding because "two negatives make a positive". For example, it is often said of a sentence like *He doesn't know nothing* that the in-

tention of the speaker is reversed because if he doesn't know *nothing*, he must know *something*. But in actual usage, sentences with multiple negatives are always understood as the speaker intends them, by other speakers of nonstandard English and usually by speakers of the standard dialects as well. The reason is that there is basically only one negative in *He doesn't know nothing* which is expressed in more than one place in the sentence. Standard English allows negatives to be expressed only once; nonstandard dialects have no such restriction. Yet there are strict grammar rules in nonstandard dialects of English which govern precisely at which places in a sentence a negative can be expressed.

2. *Three negative placement rules in standard English.* To understand these facts, it is necessary to introduce a new concept of grammar rule. We will conceive of all sentences as starting out at an abstract level with an abstract structure which is not actually pronounced. What grammar rules do is to take this unpronounceable abstract structure and convert it, step by step, into an ordinary sentence which can actually be spoken. These rules are partly the same for all dialects of English, but partly different. These differences account for the fact that the same basic structure can be expressed in different ways in different dialects.

As an example, we will see what happens when the abstract structure of the sentence *Nobody knows anything* is operated on by the rules of standard English. At the abstract level, we can think of the structure of *Nobody knows anything* as: NOT + ANY-BODY + DOE-S + KNOW + ANY-THING. The element NOT is to be understood as denying the truth value of the rest of the sentence. All dialects of English have a rule which requires that this NOT be placed into any noun phrase containing the indefinite element ANY, if that noun phrase comes before the main verb. Because of this rule, the first rule of negative placement, there are no dialects of English which have such sentnces as *Anybody doesn't know anything* or *Anybody knows nothing*. We can symbolize the fact that NOT has been incorporated into ANY by changing the first plus sign to a dash. This means that the element NOT is now part of the same word as ANYBODY. The result is: NOT-ANY-BODY + DOE-S + KNOW + ANY-THING. Since standard English allows the basic negative element NOT to be expressed only once, this is the only negative placement rule which can be applied to this sentence. Later on, there will be a rule to convert cases of NOT-ANY into *no*. There is another rule which removes DO in sentences like this one and attaches the -S to main verbs like KNOW. The final result is *Nobody knows anything*.

In the sentence *He doesn't know anything,* there is no ANY in the noun phrase which comes before the verb. The abstract structure would be NOT + HE + DOE-S + KNOW + ANY-THING. Because there is no ANY before the verb, the first negative placement rule does not operate. NOT must be placed by the second negative placement rule in this sentence. This rule stipulates that the element NOT will be attached to the main verb phrase, if the first rule is not applicable. The effect on our abstract structure is: HE + DOE-S + NOT + KNOW + ANY-THING. There is a later rule which contracts *does not,* giving *doesn't.*

In formal styles of standard English speech, it is possible to use sentences such as *He knows nothing.* This sentence results from the third negative placement rule, which may be applied, but is not required. This rule allows a negative to be removed from the main verb phrase and be attached to the first ANY which follows the verb phrase. This rule operates on the result of the second negative placement rule. As we know, the structure which results from the application of this rule is HE + DOE-S + NOT + KNOW + ANY-THING. If the third negative placement rule is selected, the structure of HE + DOE-S + NOT + KNOW + ANY-THING is converted to HE + DOE-S + KNOW + NOT-ANY-THING. After the rules for removing DO and converting NOT-ANY to NO have been applied, HE + DOE-S + KNOW + NOT-ANY-THING becomes *He knows nothing.*

3. *The three negative placement rules in nonstandard English.* In standard English, the three negative placement rules operate under the general restriction that the negative element NOT can be expressed in the final version of any sentence only once. If the first rule applied, the second and third rules do not. If the conditions for the use of the first rule are not met, the second rule applies. In some styles of speech, it is possible to use the third rule, but if it is used, NOT is removed from the position given it by the second rule. In nonstandard dialects, the second and third rules are copying rules, not placement rules in the strictest sense. These rules make a copy of the original NOT somewhere else in the sentence, but leave the first NOT in its original position. Let us examine the abstract structure NOT + ANY-BODY + DOE-S + KNOW + IT, which would be expressed in standard dialects as *Nobody knows it.* The first negative placement rule, as we have seen, operates in all dialects of English. In any variety of English, the result of the first rule is NOT-ANY-BODY + DOE-S + KNOW + IT. In standard English, the second and third rules are not allowed to operate if the first rule has been applied. In some kinds of nonstandard English, including Negro dialect, the second negative placement

rule is allowed to apply to NOT-ANY-BODY + DOE-S + KNOW + IT as a copying rule. That is, it makes a copy of NOT in the main verb phrase of the sentence, but leaves the original NOT where it is. The result is: NOT-ANY-BODY + DOE-S + NOT + KNOW + IT. When the rules which convert NOT-ANY to *no* and contract *not* have been applied, the sentence comes out as *Nobody doesn't know it.*[30] At this point, it is essential to keep in mind that *Nobody doesn't know it* comes from exactly the same abstract structure as the standard English *Nobody knows it* and means the same thing. The *n't* of *doesn't* is a mere copy of the *no* of *nobody*. Unlike most kinds of multiple negation, sentences to which both the first and second rules have been applied are likely to be misunderstood by speakers of standard English. Standard English speakers would not expect *Nobody doesn't know it* to have a negative meaning.

The third negative placement rule operates differently in nonstandard dialects from the way in which it operates in standard dialects. Like the nonstandard use of the second rule above, the third rule in nonstandard English acts as a copying rule. Consider the following structures: NOT + ANY-BODY + DOE-S + KNOW + ANY-THING + ABOUT + ANY-THING (the basis for standard English *Nobody knows anything about anything*), and NOT + HE + DOE-S + KNOW + ANY-THING + ABOUT + ANY-THING (the basis for standard English *He doesn't know anything about anything* or *He knows nothing about anything*). The first negative placement rule converts NOT + ANY-BODY + DOE-S + KNOW + ANY-THING + ABOUT + ANY-THING to NOT-ANY-BODY + DOE-S + KNOW + ANY-THING + ABOUT + ANY-THING, incorporating NOT into ANY-BODY. In standard English, the second and third placement rules can never apply if the first rule applies. We have seen that the second negative placement rule can apply in some nonstandard dialects as a copying rule, even if the first rule has already operated. In most nonstandard dialects, whether or not the second rule is allowed to operate as a copying rule, the third rule is allowed to operate as such. In this form, the third rule stipulates that NOT may be copied with every ANY in the sentence, but also must be left in its original position. When this rule applies in these nonstandard dialects, it converts NOT-ANY-BODY + DOE-S + KNOW + ANY-THING to NOT-ANY-BODY + DOE-S + KNOW + NOT-ANY-THING + ABOUT + NOT-ANY-THING. After the rule about NOT-ANY and the rule about DOES have operated, the result is: *Nobody knows nothing about nothing.* Again it is imperative to keep in mind that the sentences *Nobody knows anything about anything*, *Nobody knows nothing about nothing* and *Nobody doesn't know nothing about nothing* are all equivalent in meaning. The multiple negative expressions are simply different ways of copying the one basic sentence-negating NOT.

If we take the structure, NOT + HE + DOE-S + KNOW + ANY-THING + ABOUT + ANY-THING, we notice that the first rule does not apply, since the first noun phrase does not contain ANY. If the first rule does not apply, all dialects of English require that the second rule apply, which places the NOT in the main verb phrase. The result is HE + DOE-S + NOT + KNOW + ANY-THING + ABOUT + ANY-THING. The third negative placement rule can apply, but does not necessarily have to, in standard English. If it does apply, it removes the NOT from the verb phrase and attaches it to the first ANY. The ultimate result is *He knows nothing about anything.* In nonstandard dialects, there are two differences. First, the rule is a copying rule, so the original NOT remains in the main verb phrase. Furthermore, the NOT is copied with every ANY in the sentence, so that the resulting structure is HE + DOE-S + NOT + KNOW + NOT-ANY-THING + ABOUT + NOT-ANY-THING, and the ultimate sentence is *He doesn't know nothing about nothing.*

For some speakers of Negro dialect, the third rule must apply to every sentence with ANY after the main verb phrase. For these speakers, there are no such sentences as *Nobody knows anything about anything* and *He doesn't know anything about anything;* the grammar of this variety requires *Nobody knows nothing about nothing* and *He doesn't know nothing about nothing.* Another way of putting it is that the word *any* can never appear in the spoken form of a negative sentence.

4. *Multiple negation in two clauses.* The nonstandard applications of the second and third negative placement rules above only apply within a single clause. There is another type of multiple negation, which is possible for some Negro dialect speakers, in which negation may be marked in two different clauses. These speakers use sentences like *Nobody didn't know it didn't rain* meaning *Nobody knew it rained.* But such sentences are extremely rare.

5. *Multiple negation with negative adverbs.* Negation can be expressed with negative adverbs, as well as in verb phrases and by incorporation into ANY. Multiple negation can be expressed by a negative adverb and also by one of these other methods in the same sentence. The result is the utterance of sentences like *He doesn't hardly come to see us any more,* or more commonly, *He doesn't come to see us any more, hardly.* Standard English speakers who never use other kinds of multiple negation sometimes use sentences like the above. In Negro

dialect, the marking of negation in the verb phrase or with ANY in sentences which contain *hardly* is the rule rather than the exception. Negro dialect, along with other nonstandard English dialects, also allows negation to be multiply expressed when the same sentence contains the adverbs *never* and *neither*.

6. *Negativized auxiliary pre-position.* If a sentence has an indefinite noun phrase containing a negative marker (*nobody, nothing, no dog*) before the verb, the negativized form of the verbal auxiliary (*can't, wasn't, didn't*) may be placed at the beginning of the sentence. The result is sentences like *Can't nobody do it, Wasn't nothing wrong,* and *Didn't no dog bite him.* Although these sentences appear to be questions in their written form, the intonation of the spoken form in Negro dialect makes it clear that they are statements. If the noun phrase before the verb does not contain a negativized indefinite, pre-position of the auxiliary is not possible, so that a sentence like *Don't the man do it* will not occur as a statement.

-s SUFFIXES

Possessive

1. *With common nouns.* Where the 's possessive appears in standard English, Negro dialect indicates possessive by the order of the words. The phrase *The boy hat* corresponds to *The boy's hat* in the standard dialect. In Northern urban Negro dialect, apparently no one uses the zero form of the possessive exclusively; it alternates with the 's form. In Southern varieties of Negro dialect it seems possible to find speakers who do not use 's for possessive at all. There is some reason to believe that the presence of the 's possessive suffix is more common at the end of a clause (i.e. in absolute position, as in *The hat is the boy('s)* than in the attributive possessive (*The boy('s) hat*). It has been claimed that the 's in this situation is regularly present. However the absence of the 's suffix in the absolute possessive suffix has been observed with some frequency in the speech of Northern urban Negro dialect speakers and has been found to be extremely common in Southern Negro dialect data. Pedagogically, it would seem wise to deal with both kinds, but to emphasize the attributive construction.

2. *With personal names.* Because the position of the 's possessive is somewhat unstable in the grammar of Negro dialect, some speakers use the 's suffix inappropriately with personal names when attempting to speak standard English. In standard English, of course, the rule is

that the 's suffix is attached to the surname when the possessor is identified by his full name (*Jack Johnson's car*). Occasionally, a Negro
dialect speaker will attach the 's suffix to both names (*Jack's Johnson's
car*) or to the first name (*Jack's Johnson car*). This feature is not part
of the grammar of Negro dialect but is a hypercorrection in attempting to use standard English (cf. the hypercorrections in connection
with the -s third person singular present tense marker on p. 71).

3. *Mines.* Some speakers of Negro dialect use the form *mines* for
mine in the absolute possessive construction (never in the attributive
construction) giving sentences like *This mines.* This is a regularization in Negro dialect of the absolute possessive form of the first person pronoun to conform to the other pronoun forms which end in *s*
(*his, hers, its, yours, ours, theirs*).

4. *Undifferentiated pronouns.* Some speakers of Negro dialect use
the standard English nominative or accusative forms of personal pronouns for possession in attributive constructions (*he book, him book,
we book,* etc.). This feature, which is probably to be ascribed to the
lingering influence of the grammar of Caribbean Creole languages in
Negro dialect, is extremely rare in the North but apparently somewhat more common in the speech of young children in the South.

Plural

1. *Absence of the plural suffix.* The -s (or -es) suffixes which mark
most plurals in standard English are occasionally absent in the speech
of Negro dialect speakers. This results in sentences like *He took five
book* and *The other teacher, they'll yell at you.* The absence of the
plural suffix in Northern urban Negro dialect occurs considerably less
often than the absence of the possessive suffix and far less than the
absence of the third person singular present tense marker.[31] There is
no question that most Northern speakers of Negro dialect have the
use of the plural suffix as part of their grammar. Much of the absence
of the plural suffix is due to a difference in the classification of certain
nouns in Negro dialect from standard English. A few nouns do not
take the plural suffix at all in standard English (*one sheep, two
sheep*). Words which are so classified in Negro dialect, but which
take the regular -s plural in standard English include *cent, year,* and
movie. It is possible that the absence of the plural suffix in words like
cent and *year* is because the grammar of Negro dialect allows the optional absence of the plural marker with nouns of measure. Such a
rule is also part of the grammar of a number of white regional dialects.

For some speakers of Southern Negro dialect, particularly young children, the plural suffix is almost always absent and may well not be part of the grammar of their dialect at all. The occasional claim that the plural suffix may only be absent when the plural noun is preceded by a quantifier (*two, several,* etc.), and not otherwise, is invalid. There are a great many examples of plural nouns not preceded by a quantifier which lack the plural suffix.

2. *Regular plurals with irregular nouns.* Some nouns in standard English form plurals by a vowel change (*one foot, two feet*), or with no suffix at all (*one deer, two deer*). For many Negro dialect speakers, these nouns take the regular -*s* suffix (*two foots, two deers*). This is another example of a classification difference between the two kinds of English.

3. *Double plurals.* Where standard English forms plurals irregularly, Negro dialect may add the -*s* suffix to the irregular plural (*peoples, childrens*). A possible historical reason relates to an earlier stage of Negro dialect in which the plural category was not part of the grammar.[32] In learning standard English, speakers of the dialect tended to add the -*s* suffix to words which were already pluralized in an irregular way. These doubly pluralized words became fossilized and are preserved to the present. Words most frequently affected are *childrens, peoples,* and *mens.*

QUESTIONS

Inversion

The form which questions take in standard English depends on whether the question is direct or indirect. If the question is direct, word-order inversion takes place, but if the question is indirect, the basic word order is retained. Inversion affects the questioned element, if any, and the verbal auxiliary or copula, transferring them to the beginning of the sentence. The statement *He went somewhere* can be content questioned or yes-no-questioned. To form the content question, *somewhere* is replaced by *where,* the auxiliary *did* is added and both are moved to the head of the sentence, giving *Where did he go.* The yes-no question simply requires the insertion of the auxiliary *did* and its transfer to the head of the sentence, giving *Did he go somewhere.* The indirect question involves the transfer of the questioned element to the head of the clause only. In the case of yes-no questions, *if* or *whether* is used in the construction. Examples of the two types of indirect questions corresponding to *He went somewhere* would be *I want to know where he went* and *I want to know if (whether) he went somewhere*. In Negro dialect spoken in the North, the inverted form of the question is used for both direct and indirect questions and the words *if* and *whether* are not used to form indirect yes-no questions. The direct questions for *He went somewhere* are the same as the standard English examples given above. But the two indirect questions would be *I want to know where did he go* and *I want to know did he go somewhere*. The Negro dialect grammar rules for question formation are more regular than the standard English rules, since they apply in the same way to both kinds of questions.[33] Some speakers, on the other hand, have the uninverted form for direct questions, at least in content questions. These speakers use questions like *What that is?* and *Where the white cat is?*.

A historical process something like the following may explain this state of affairs. The uninverted construction is probably the older one. As Negro dialect began to approximate standard American English more closely, its speakers noticed that the standard dialect had inverted direct questions. Since there was no distinction in Negro dialect between direct and indirect questions, inversion may have been generalized to both types.

The Absence of Preposed Auxiliaries

In inverted direct questions, the auxiliary or copula form of the main verb phrase is moved to the front of the sentence, as we have seen. In this position, some of these elements are especially vulnerable to deletion. This gives questions like *He coming with us?* (deletion of *is*), *Where you been?* (deletion of *have*), and *You understand?* (deletion of *do*). Although this is frequently cited as a feature of nonstandard dialects, deletion of these auxiliaries in direct questions is very common in spoken standard English. Therefore, attempting to eliminate this kind of auxiliary deletion from the speech of inner-city Negro children would be a low-priority task.

PRONOUNS

A number of usages involving personal, demonstrative and relative pronouns are sometimes cited as examples of nonstandard dialect usage. We will discuss only two of them here.

Pronominal Apposition

A well-known, but little understood feature of nonstandard English dialects including Negro dialect, is pronominal apposition. Pronominal apposition is the construction in which a pronoun is used in apposition to the noun subject of the sentence. Usually the nominative form of the pronoun is used, as in *My brother, he bigger than you* or *That teacher, she yell at the kids all the time.* Occasionally, the objective or possessive pronoun is used in apposition as well, as in *That girl name Wanda, I never did like her* or *Mr. Smith, I got one F in his class one time.* It was discovered in a study of Detroit speech that pronominal apposition was used by all speakers whether they were speakers of standard English or not. It seems likely that the length of the modifying material which intervenes between the noun and the pronoun has an effect on acceptability; the more intervening material, the more acceptable the pronoun in apposition. For example, pronominal apposition in a sentence like *That man that I met on the train to Chicago last week, he turned out to be a Congressman* is more acceptable than in a sentence such as *My mother, she's here now.* But the exact restrictions on the acceptable usage of pronominal apposition have yet to be discovered. Negro dialect speakers who use the stigmatized kinds of pronominal apposition do not use it in every sentence. It has been suggested that the use of pronominal apposition is related to the entry and re-entry of participants in a narrative, but this hypothesis has not been thoroughly investigated.

Existential It

Where standard English uses *there* in an existential or expletive function, Negro dialect has *it.* This results in sentences like *It's a boy in my room name Robert* and *Is it a Main Street in this town?* where standard English would have *There's a boy . . .* and *Is there a Main Street . . . .* This difference in the choice of one word in a single construction, affects the understanding of a considerable number of sentences in ordinary speech. For example, a television advertisement for a brand of powdered soup contained the line *Is it soup yet?* This was intended to mean something like *Has it become soup yet?* and was no doubt so understood by the standard English speaking audience, except possibly in parts of the South. But speakers of Negro dialect might well understand the same sentence as something like *Is there any soup yet?*

CONCLUSION

It should be clear from our approach to the features discussed here that we are not using the terms "grammar rule" and "pronunciation rule" in the traditional sense. As in the physical sciences, in which laws are discovered by observing natural phenomena and are not imposed on nature by scientists, so grammar rules and pronunciation rules are discovered by observing actual usage rather than taken as given and imposed on people's speech. For this reason, we can speak meaningfully of the grammar and pronunciation rules of a nonstandard dialect. For this reason also, some of the rules cited for standard American English will appear startling. In both cases, the rules are discovered from careful observation of usage. It is proper to refer to "rules" because in no speech (except possibly in the speech of the mentally ill or brain-damaged) are words randomly put together. Negro dialect and other nonstandard linguistic systems operate under rules just as do socially favored dialects. But the rules are different.

Because this is the nature of the rules of language, it is therefore important to uphold real spoken standard English as a model to inner-city children rather than an artificially precise language based on an arbitrary prescriptive norm of what is "correct." A good rule of thumb for a teacher to follow is to carefully and honestly reflect on his own usage in casual conversation and not to insist on any usage on the part of his pupils which he does not find in his own casual speech. Children, and perhaps especially Negro children, are quick to detect hypocrisy and will soon lose all motivation if they see that they are being taught "better" English than their teacher actually uses himself.

The grammatical aspects of Negro dialect which have been outlined here are by no means the only ones which differ from standard American English. Yet, we have said something about all the most crucial features. Hopefully, an accurate understanding of some of the grammar of the dialect will contribute to the more efficient teaching of standard American English as an alternative way of speaking.

6

※ Sociolinguistic Factors
in the History
of American Negro Dialects

WILLIAM A. STEWART

Within the last few years, the increased national commitment to bettering the lot of socially and economically underprivileged groups of Americans—the so-called "disadvantaged"—has caused educators to consider ways in which the schools may involve themselves in this task. Of the many possibilities, certainly one of the most obvious is to deal with the chronic language problems associated with many of the disadvantaged. Yet, although there is a general awareness that certain of the disadvantaged do have language problems, there is at the same time a lack of agreement as to what these problems entail, and therefore what to do about them. Some investigators (often educational psychologists) have maintained that the disadvantaged characteristically do not use verbal communication to the extent that members of the middle class do, and are thus impoverished in "communicative skills". To alleviate this situation, they have recommended programs aimed at encouraging the use of verbal communication of a variety of kinds by disadvantaged pupils. A few investigators have theorized that members of disadvantaged groups may even engage less in abstract thinking than do middle-class persons. For this there have been suggested programs designed to teach more perception and conceptualization on the part of the disadvantaged pupils.

William A. Stewart, a noted creolist and co-director of the Education Study Center (Washington, D.C.) is well-known for his important work in Negro dialect history. He is the author of *Non-Standard Speech and The Teaching of English*.

On the other hand, linguists have tended to emphasize one other type of language problem which some disadvantaged groups often have, and for which evidence is quite accessible—being encountered every.day in the nation's classrooms. This is the purely structural conflict between on the one hand the patterns of a non-standard dialect which an individual may have learned at home or in peer-group interaction, and on the other hand the equivalent patterns of standard English—the language of modern technology and of the middle class. This is one kind of problem which many of the nation's schools ought to be ready and willing to cope with. One indication of the readiness of the schools is the fact that traditional English teachers are rapidly abandoning the older "sloppy speech" and "lazy tongue" views of non-standard speech in favor of a realization that it usually represents the speaker's use of some language system which, though it may differ from standard English in form and sometimes even in function, is nevertheless logical, coherent, and (in its own way) grammatical. Another indication of the readiness of schools to cope with the problem of dialect differences is the growth of a cadre of specialists in the teaching of English to speakers of other languages. With them, there has come into being a set of new techniques for teaching English to persons coming from a different language background.

Just as they are ready, America's schools certainly ought to be willing to deal with dialect-based problems, since there are a number of ways in which, by themselves, they can render a non-standard speaker dysfunctional in exchanges with standard-English-speaking members of the middle class. One way is for minor pronunciation differences between a non-standard dialect and standard English—each one perhaps trivial by itself—to pile up in an utterance to such an extent that the non-standard version becomes unintelligible to a middle-class listener, even though in grammar and vocabulary it may be quite similar to its standard equivalent. Thus, a non-standard version of "I don't know where they live" might, in one dialect, become cryptic to the standard-speaking listener, merely because of its being pronounced something like *Ah 'own know wey 'ey lib*. Or, a standard English speaker may misunderstand a non-standard utterance, even though he thinks he has deciphered it correctly, because it contains non-standard grammatical constructions which are unknown to him. For example, a middle-class listener may take a non-standard sentence *Dey ain't like dat* to mean "they aren't like that", when it really means "They didn't like that". The standard-English speaker is simply unaware that *ain't* is this particular dialect's way of negating verbs in the past tense, as he is unaware that the usual equivalent in the same dialect of "They

aren't like that" would be either *Dey not like dat* or *Dey don't be like
dat* (the two variants indicating a difference in meaning which is not
easily expressed in standard English). Of course, similar breakdowns
in intelligibility may also occur in the other direction, when the non-
standard speaker tries to understand standard English. Finally, even
when he does succeed in making himself understood by his middle-
class listeners, the non-standard speaker may still fall victim to the
difference in social prestige between his dialect and standard English.
In other words, although middle-class persons may understand what
he is saying, they may still consider him uncouth for saying it the way
he does.

Professionally able though the schools may now be to embark on
programs which would deal effectively with this kind of problem, the
likelihood of their actually doing so in the near future is certainly not
increased by the unwillingness of many educators and even some
applied linguists to approach the problem in any but the most general
terms. For, unfortunately, the technical know-how necessary to teach
standard English to speakers of non-standard dialects is simply not
embodied in an awareness of the problem at the level of "Some children should probably be taught standard English as a second dialect"
—no matter how true such statements may be. The necessary know-
how will begin to be adequate when and only when applied linguists
can give, and educators will take seriously, details of the type "The
verb system of such-and-such a non-standard dialect operates in such-
and-such a way, and the verb system of standard English operates in
such-and-such a way, so that structural interference is most likely to
occur at points *a, b,* and *c*. Therefore, the following lessons and drills
in the standard English verb system is what children who speak this
non-standard dialect will need."[34]

One reason why there is little remedial English now being taught
based upon a systematic comparison of the differences between non-
standard dialects and standard English is that information about one
of the pedagogically most important features of non-standard dialects
—their grammatical systems—is still largely lacking. This lack is due in
great part to the fact that American dialect studies have traditionally
emphasized differences in pronunciation and vocabulary, at the expense of information on systematic grammatical differences.

Now that linguists have begun to fill this information gap, however,
they are finding their observations on language variation among the
disadvantaged received with uneasiness and even hostility by many
teachers, administrators, and community leaders. The reason for this
is undoubtedly that the accurate description of dialect variation in
American communities—particularly in urban centers—is turning out

to show a disturbing correlation between language behavior on the one hand and socio-economic and ethnic stratification on the other.[35] The correlation is particularly controversial insofar as it involves the speech of large numbers of American Negroes, since at the present time Negro leadership (and this includes most Negro educators) is probably more achievement-oriented than any other. Because of this orientation Negro elites tend not to welcome any evidence of uniform or stable behavioral differences between members of their own group (even lower-class ones) and those of the white-dominated middle class. Yet the fact is that Negroes account for most of the most pedagogically problematic non-standard dialect speakers in the larger cities, and also include within their group speakers of the most radically non-standard dialects of natively-spoken English in the entire country.[36] Furthermore, because *de facto* segregation in housing has caused non-standard-dialect-speaking Negroes to predominate in many schools and because these Negroes appear in many cases to have different kinds of problems with standard English than non-standard-dialect-speaking whites have (even in the same area), the sweeping, for political purposes, of Negro dialect descriptions under the white-oriented geographic dialect rug would probably be more detrimental to disadvantaged Negro children than it would be advantageous to Negro elites.[37]

On the other hand, linguists should realize that the fears and anxieties of Negro leaders about public discussion of ethnically correlated behavioral differences may have some foundation. It is possible, for example, that quite objective and innocently-made statements about dialect differences between whites and Negroes might be interpreted by white racists as evidence of Negro cultural backwardness or mental inferiority, or even seized upon by black racists as evidence of some sort of mythical Negro "soul". Linguists should not censor their data, but they should make sure that their statements about Negro-white differences are not divorced from an awareness of the historical, social, and linguistic reasons why such differences may have come into existence and been maintained. Perhaps it would serve that end to point out here some of the sociolinguistic factors involved in the evolution of American Negro dialects, factors which explain why certain kinds of American Negro dialects are both different from the non-standard dialects of American whites, and more radically deviant from standard English.

Although the linguistic history of the Negro in the United States can be reconstructed from the numerous literary attestations of the English of New World Negroes over the last two and a half centuries, and by comparing these with the English of Negroes in the United States, the Caribbean, and West Africa today, this has never been done for the English teaching profession. In presenting a historical sketch of this type, I realize that both the facts presented and my interpretations of them may embarrass or even infuriate those who would like to whitewash American Negro dialects by claiming that they do not exist —that (in spite of all sorts of observable evidence to the contrary) they are nothing but Southern white dialects, derived directly from Great Britain. I will simply make no apologies to those who regard human behavior as legitimate only if observed in the white man, since I feel that this constitutes a negation of the cultural and ethnic plurality which is one of America's greatest heritages. On the other hand, I do regret that such a historical survey, although linguistically interesting, may at times conjure up out of the past memories of the Negro-as-slave to haunt the aspirations of the Negro-as-equal.

Of those Africans who fell victim to the Atlantic slave trade and were brought to the New World, many found it necessary to learn some kind of English. With very few exceptions, the form of English which they acquired was a pidginized one, and this kind of English became so well established as the principal medium of communication between Negro slaves in the British colonies that it was passed on as a creole language to succeeding generations of the New World Negroes, for whom it was their native tongue.[38] Some idea of what New World Negro English may have been like in its early stages can be obtained from a well-known example of the speech of a fourteen-year-old Negro lad given by Daniel DeFoe in *The Family Instructor* (London, 1715). It is significant that the Negro, Toby, speaks a pidginized kind of English to his boy master, even though he states that he was born in the New World.

A sample of his speech is:

Toby.   Me be born at Barbadoes.
Boy.   Who lives there, Toby?
Toby.   There lives white mans, white womans, negree mans, negree womans, just so as live here.
Boy.   What and not know God?
Toby.   Yes, the white mans say God prayers,—no much know God.
Boy.   And what do the black mans do?
Toby.   They much work, much work,—no say God prayers, not at all.
Boy.   What work do they do, Toby?
Toby.   Makee the sugar, makee the ginger,—much great work, weary work, all day, all night.

Even though the boy master's English is slightly non-standard (e.g. *black mans*), it is still quite different from the speech of the Negro.

An idea of how widespread a pidginized form of English had become among the Negro population of the New World by the end of the Seventeenth Century can be gathered from the fact that it had even become the language of the coastal plantations in the Dutch colony of Surinam (i.e., Dutch Guiana), in South America. In an early description of that colony, the chapter on the Negro ends with a sample conversation in the local Negro English dialect. The dialogue includes such sentences as *Me bella well* "I am very well", *You wantee siddown pinkininne?* "Do you want to sit down for a bit?", and *You wantee go walka longa me?* "Do you want to take a walk with me?"[39] In these sentences, the use of the enclitic vowel in *wantee* recalls the same in DeFoe's example *makee*. Also, the speaker, like Toby, uses *me* as a subject pronoun. In the first Surinam sentence, we see an early example of a construction without any equivalent of the standard English verb "to be". Toby also would probably have said *Me weary*, since the *be* in his first sentence was in all likelihood a past-tense marker (as it is in present-day West African Pidgin English)—the sentence therefore meaning "I was born in Barbadoes". In the last Surinam sentence, a reflex of English *along* is used with the meaning of standard English "with". It may or may not be accidental that in the Gullah dialect, spoken by the Negroes along the South Carolina coastal plain, the same phenomenon occurs, e.g., *Enty you wanuh walk long me?* "Do you want to take a walk with me?" Some Gullah speakers even still use *me* as a subject pronoun, e.g., *Me kyaan brukum* "I can't break it", and enclitic final vowels seem to have survived in such Gullah forms as *yerry, yeddy* "to hear".

Early examples of Negro dialect as spoken in the American colonies show it to be strikingly similar to that given by DeFoe for the West Indies and by Herlein for Surinam. In John Leacock's play, *The Fall of British Tyranny* (Philadelphia, 1776), part of the conversation between a certain "Kidnapper" and Cudjo, one of a group of Virginia Negroes, goes as follows:

Kidnapper.   . . . what part did you come from?
Cudjo.   Disse brack man, disse one, disse one, disse one, come from Hamton, disse one, disse one, come from Nawfok, me come from Nawfok, too.
Kidnapper.   Very well, what was your master's name?
Cudjo.   Me massa name Cunney Tomee.
Kidnapper.   Colonel Thompson—eigh?

Cudjo.   Eas, massa, Cunney Tomsee.
Kidnapper.   Well then I'll make you a major—and what's your name?
Cudjo.   Me massa cawra me Cudjo.

Again, the enclitic vowels (e.g., *disse*) and the subject pronoun *me*
are prominent features of the Negro dialect. In the sentence *Me Massa
name Cunney Tomsee* "My master's name is Colonel Thompson", both
the verb "to be" and the standard English possessive suffix -*s* are absent. Incidentally, Cudjo's construction is strikingly similar to sentences like *My sister name Mary* which are used by many American
Negroes today.

One possible explanation why this kind of pidginized English was
so widespread in the New World, with widely separated varieties resembling each other in so many ways, is that it did not originate in the
New World as isolated and accidentally similar instances of random
pidginization, but rather originated as a *lingua franca* in the trade
centers and slave factories on the West African coast.[40] It is likely that
at least some Africans already knew this pidgin English when they
came to the New World, and that the common colonial policy of mix-
ing slaves of various tribal origins forced its rapid adoption as a plantation *lingua franca*.

In the course of the Eighteenth Century, some significant changes
took place in the New World Negro population, and these had their
effect on language behavior. For one thing, the number of Negroes
born in the New World came to exceed the number of those brought
over from Africa. In the process, pidgin English became the creole
mother-tongue of the new generations, and in some areas it has remained so to the present day.[41]

In the British colonies, the creole English of the uneducated Negroes
and the English dialects of both the educated and uneducated whites
were close enough to each other (at least in vocabulary) to allow the
speakers of each to communicate, although they were still different
enough so that the whites could consider creole English to be
"broken" or "corrupt" English and evidence, so many thought, of the
mental limitations of the Negro. But in Surinam, where the European
settlers spoke Dutch, creole English was regarded more objectively.
In fact, no less than two language courses specifically designed to
teach creole English to Dutch immigrants were published before the
close of the Eighteenth Century.[42]

Another change which took place in the New World Negro population primarily during the course of the Eighteenth Century was the
social cleavage of the New World-born generations into underprivi-

leged fieldhands (a continuation of the older, almost universal lot of the Negro slave) and privileged domestic servant. The difference in privilege usually meant, not freedom instead of bondage, but rather freedom from degrading kinds of labor, access to the "big house" with its comforts and "civilization", and proximity to the prestigious "quality" whites, with the opportunity to imitate their behavior (including their speech) and to wear their clothes. In some cases, privilege included the chance to get an education and, in a very few, access to wealth and freedom. In both the British colonies and the United States, Negroes belonging to the privileged group were soon able to acquire a more standard variety of English than the creole of the field hands, and those who managed to get a decent education became speakers of fully standard and often elegant English. This seems to have become the usual situation by the early 1800's, and remained so through the Civil War. In Caroline Gilman's *Recollections of a Southern Matron* (New York, 1838), the difference between field-hand creole (in this case, Gullah) and domestic servant dialect is evident in a comparison of the gardener's "He tief one sheep—he run away las week, cause de overseer gwine for flog him" with Dina's " 'Scuse me, missis, I is gitting hard o' hearing, and yes is more politer dan no" (page 254). A more striking contrast between the speech of educated and uneducated Negroes occurs in a novel written in the 1850's by an American Negro who had traveled extensively through the slave states. In Chapter XVII, part of the exchange between Henry, an educated Negro traveler, and an old "aunty" goes as follows:

'Who was that old man who ran behind your master's horse?'
'Dat Nathan, my huban'.'
'Do they treat him well, aunty?'
'No, chile, wus an' any dog, da beat 'im foh little an nothin'.'
'Is uncle Nathan religious?'
'Yes, chile, ole man an' I's been sahvin' God dis many day, foh yeh baun! Wen any on 'em in de house git sick, den da sen foh 'uncle Nathan' come pray foh dem; 'uncle Nathan' mighty good den!'[43]

After the Civil War, with the abolition of slavery, the breakdown of the plantation system, and the steady increase in education for poor as well as affluent Negroes, the older field-hand creole English began to lose many of its creole characteristics, and take on more and more of the features of the local white dialects and of the written language. Yet, this process has not been just one way. For if it is true that the speech of American Negroes has been strongly influenced by the speech of whites with whom they came into contact, it is probably also true that the speech of many whites has been influenced in some way by the speech of Negroes.[44]

Over the last two centuries, the proportion of American Negroes who speak a perfectly standard variety of English has risen from a small group of privileged house slaves and free Negroes to persons numbering in the hundreds of thousands, and perhaps even millions. Yet there is still a sizeable number of American Negroes—undoubtedly larger than the number of standard-speaking Negroes—whose speech may be radically non-standard. The non-standard features in the speech of such persons may be due in part to the influence of the non-standard dialects of whites with whom they or their ancestors have come in contact, but they also may be due to the survival of creolisms from the older Negro field-hand speech of the plantations. To insure their social mobility in modern American society, these non-standard speakers must undoubtedly be given a command of standard English; that point was made in the early part of this paper. In studying non-standard Negro dialects and teaching standard English in terms of them, however, both the applied linguist and the language teacher must come to appreciate the fact that even if certain non-standard Negro dialect patterns do not resemble the dialect usage of American whites, or even those of the speakers of remote British dialects, they may nevertheless be as old as African and European settlement in the New World, and therefore quite widespread and well-established. On various occasions, I have pointed out that many speakers of non-standard American Negro dialects make a grammatical and semantic distinction by means of *be*, illustrated by such constructions as *he busy* "He is busy (momentarily)" or *he workin'* "he is working (right now)" as opposed to *he be busy* "he is (habitually) busy" or *he be workin'* "he is working (steadily)", which the grammar of standard English is unable to make. Even this distinction goes back well over a century. One observer in the 1830's noted a request by a slave for a permanent supply of soap as "(If) Missis only give *we*, we be so clean forever", while *be* is absent in a subsequent report of someone's temporary illness with "She jist sick for a little while".[45]

Once educators who are concerned with the language problems of the disadvantaged come to realize that non-standard Negro dialects represent a historical tradition of this type, it is to be hoped that they will become less embarrassed by evidence that these dialects are very much alike throughout the country while different in many ways from the non-standard dialects of whites, less frustrated by failure to turn non-standard Negro dialect speakers into standard English speakers overnight, less impatient with the stubborn survival of Negro dialect features in the speech of even educated persons, and less zealous in proclaiming what is "right" and what is "wrong". If this happens, then applied linguists and educators will be able to communicate with each other, and both will be able to communicate with the non-standard-speaking Negro child. The problem will then be well on its way toward a solution.

7

❋ Continuity and Change in American Negro Dialects

WILLIAM A. STEWART

In a previous article on the history of American Negro dialects (in this volume see pp. 86-95) I cited examples of the kind of literary and comparative evidence which exists for determining earlier stages of these dialects, and which practically forces the conclusion that the linguistic assimilation of the Afro-American population to the speech patterns of English-speaking American whites was neither as rapid nor as complete as some scholars have supposed.[46] Of the Negro slaves who constituted the field labor force on North American plantations up to the mid-nineteenth century, even many who were born in the New World spoke a variety of English which was in fact a true creole language—differing markedly in grammatical structure from those English dialects which were brought directly from Great Britain, as well as from New World modifications of these in the mouths of descendants of the original white colonists.[47] And, although this creole English subsequently underwent modification in the direction of the more prestigious British-derived dialects, the merging process was neither instantaneous nor uniform. Indeed, the non-standard speech of present-day American Negroes still seems to exhibit structural traces of a creole predecessor, and this is probably a reason why it is in some ways more deviant from standard English than is the non-standard speech of even the most uneducated American whites.

For the teacher, this means that such "Negro" patterns as the "zero copula", the "zero possessive", or "undifferentiated pronouns"[48] should not be ascribed to greater carelessness, laziness or stupidity on the part of Negroes, but rather should be treated as what they really are —language patterns which have been in existence for generations and which their present users have acquired, from parent and peer, through a perfectly normal kind of language-learning process.[49]

Since the main purpose of the earlier article was to document the use of creole English by native-born American Negroes during the colonial and ante-bellum periods, almost nothing was said about the course of Negro dialects since Emancipation. But, as anyone can see who compares written samples of Negro dialect from around the Civil War with Negro dialect today, there have been changes. And, equally interesting, one can also see that there are still many similarities between the two. An overview of the interacting processes of continuity and change in American Negro dialects as they relate to one important aspect of language variation—grammatical structure—will help educators to put the classroom language problems of today's disadvantaged Negro children into a clearer perspective.

One of the more important changes which have occurred in American Negro dialects during the past century has been the almost complete decreolization of both their functional and lexical vocabulary. Although this process actually began long before the Civil War (particularly in areas with a low proportion of Negroes to whites), the breakdown of the plantation system apparently accelerated it considerably, even in the coastal areas of South Carolina and Georgia. In the process, overt creolisms which were so common in early attestations of slave speech, such as *been* for marking past action (with no basic distinction between preterite and perfect), undifferentiated pronouns for subject and object (e.g., *me, him,* and *dem* also as subject pronouns and *we* also as an object pronoun), a single subject pronoun form (usually *him* or *he*) for masculine, feminine and neuter in the third person singular, *-um* (or *-am*) as a general third person (all genders and numbers) object suffix, *no* as a verbal negator, and *for* as an infinitive marker became quite rare in even the more nonstandard speech of Negroes born after Emancipation.[50]

However, the speed and thoroughness with which the plantation fieldhand dialects were thus made more "proper" varied both according to the region and according to the social characteristics of the speakers themselves. Because people learn most of their language forms from others, the change took place more rapidly and completely in areas where speakers (white or Negro) of more-or-less standard varieties of English were present in numbers than it did in areas with a high concentration of field laborers. On the other hand, because children generally are more affected by the language usage of other children than by that of grownups, and because lower-class child peer groups tend to remain rather isolated from the stylistic innovations of adult discourse, the change took place more slowly and less thoroughly in the speech of young children than it did in that of adolescents and adults.

The result of this uneven "correction" of the older plantation dialects was that, while they seemed to have died out by the end of the nineteenth century (particularly outside the South Atlantic coastal area and the Mississippi Basin), juvenile versions of them actually continued to survive in many Negro speech communities as "baby talk" or "small-boy talk".[51] That is, the older non-standard (and sometimes even creole-like) dialect features remained in use principally by younger children in Negro speech-communities—being learned from other young children, to be given up later in life when "small-boy talk" was no longer appropriate to a more mature status.[52] And even though the adult dialects which these child dialects were ontogenetically given up for were also structurally non-standard and identifiably Negro in most cases, they were still more standard—enough, at least, so that conspicuous retentions of child-dialect forms in the speech of an adult could sometimes result in the accusation that he or she was "talking like a child" or simply "talking bad".[53]

Interestingly enough, the use of an older, more conservative form of Negro dialect as child speech was not always limited to Negroes. In the Old South, many upper-class whites went through a similar linguistic metamorphosis from the non-standard dialect of their Negro playmates to the relatively standard English of their adult station in life. As John Bennett described the situation for the Charlestonian aristocracy of his day:

> It is true that, up to the age of four, approximately, the children of the best families, even in town, are apt to speak an almost unmodified *Gullah*, caught from brown playmates and country bred nurses; but at that age the refinement of cultivation begins, and "the flowers o' the forest are a' weed awa!"[54]

It was undoubtedly in this manner that such white southern writers as Joel C. Harris and Ambrose E. Gonzales first acquired their knowledge of the Negro dialects which they immortalized in print.[55]

Today, genteel Southern whites no longer learn non-standard Negro dialects as children, since the social conditions which once prompted them to do so have now become part of history. In their pre-school childhood, however, many Negroes still learn and use such dialects, and although they may modify these in later life, few ever attain anything like the elegant standard English which was the familial and social heritage of the older white aristocrats. Yet, when they enter the standard English milieu of the school, Negro children from this kind of language background are expected to compete linguistically with children (usually white) who have known and used standard English all their lives. Of course, a few of these Negro children do succeed, not because of good teaching, but because of their own exceptional abilities. But a far greater proportion of these children—the average ones, as well as the few who are truly below average—fail conspicuously. And, because there is obviously some sort of ethnic correlation between pupil success and failure in newly-integrated school situations, the embarrassed educational establishment and the frustrated public enter into a crisis relationship. Some whites charge (privately, at least) that the schools are being given the impossible task of teaching unteachable Negroes. And some Negroes charge (not so privately) that white educators are involved in a conspiracy to deliberately keep Negro children from learning. Parents protest blindly, and school administrators run helter-skelter, holding councils of despair with colleagues who understand the problem no better.

A basic reason why so many Negro children fail in school is not that they are unteachable, but that they are not being taught efficiently or fairly. And this fact may have little or nothing to do with a white conspiracy against integrated schools. Rather, it may be the result of a far less deliberate yet equally devastating insensitivity of the educational process to the social and cultural characteristics of the school population. This is probably nowhere more striking than in the area of language since, as speakers largely of non-standard dialects which are among the most deviant from standard English now being used in America, many Negro children are burdened at every turn with achievement barriers in the form of extra (and uncompensated for) language learning requirements. For example, all children are expected to learn how to read in school. But, for many Negro pupils, the problem is made more difficult by the fact that they are unfamiliar, not only with the sound-spelling-meaning correspondences of many of the words, but even with the grammatical patterns which these words make up in their reading lessons. Consequently, the reading achievement of these children becomes dependent upon their own success in deciphering standard English sentence structure. And the same type of problem is reflected in other subject areas in the schools. The irony, here, is that the traditional educational system is itself creating much of the pedagogical disadvantagement of its linguistically-different pupils by requiring them to accomplish, on their own, as much again as middle-class pupils from a standard English background are expected to accomplish with expert help.

In many ways, the plight of the Negro child who enters school speaking a non-standard dialect is similar to that of a foreign-language-speaking child entering an American school. And, while it can be argued that no Negro dialect is as different from standard English as is, say, Spanish, this does not necessarily mean that the linguistically-different Negro's task is that much easier. For, while the boundaries between a full-fledged foreign language and English are usually clear-cut (the Spanish-speaking child, for example, will usually know at any given point whether Spanish or English is being used, and so will the teacher), the many similarities between any Negro dialect and standard English makes it difficult to tell exactly where one leaves off and the other begins.[56] Thus, even the linguistic similarities between a non-standard dialect and standard English can be pedagogically and psychologically disadvantageous, since they can camouflage functional differences between the two linguistic systems. Furthermore, while a wealth of linguistic knowledge and pedagogical know-how is currently brought to bear on the language problems of the child who speaks a foreign language such as Spanish, no similar competences have yet been developed to help the child who speaks a non-standard dialect, although his needs are just as great—and his numbers greater. Considering his educational prospects as they stand at present, the linguistically-different Negro child might well say "I look down de road an' de road so lonesome."

Although English teachers, speech therapists and other language-oriented educators are now dedicating themselves more than ever to the task of helping disadvantaged children—and especially disadvantaged Negro children—acquire proficiency in standard English, very few of these dedicated professionals have demonstrated any real understanding of the language characteristics of the communities from which these children come. For their part, teachers of English to Spanish-speaking Mexican, Puerto Rican or Cuban children know that an understanding of the structure of Spanish will give insights into the problem which such children have with English, and these teachers would be shocked by any suggestion that a comparative approach to the language of the school and the language of the child is unnecessary. In contrast, teachers of English to disadvantaged Negro children have generally remained aloof from the serious study of non-standard Negro dialect.

This lack of interest on the part of many English teachers in the non-standard language of Negro children is in large part the product of a normative view of language which has long been the mainstay of traditional teacher training. Either overtly or by implication, the teacher-to-be is taught that the kind of usage which is indicated in grammar books, dictionaries and style manuals, (and which is presumably followed by educated speakers and writers) represents a maximum of structural neatness, communicative efficiency, esthetic taste and logical clarity. Once this normative view has been inculcated in the prospective teacher (and it must be admitted that popular beliefs about "correct" and "incorrect" language practically guarantee this) then the teacher will quite naturally regard departures from the norms of standard English as departures from structure, clarity, taste, and even logic itself.[57]

Of course, there have always been exceptional teachers who have seen that chronic deviations from standard English usage on the part of their pupils may indicate simply their normal use of some other variety of English, with its own structure and logic. William Francis Allen was an early example of a teacher who not only discovered this, but came to realize that even apparent "ignorance" in coping with logical or experiential problems could sometimes be traced to mere difficulty with the language in which the problems were posed. He recorded the following incident, which occurred while he was teaching Gullah Negro children on Port Royal Island, South Carolina, during the Civil War.

> I asked a group of boys one day the color of the sky. Nobody could tell me. Presently the father of one of them came by, and I told him their ignorance, repeating my question with the same results as before. He grinned: "Tom, how sky stan'?" "Blue," promptly shouted Tom.[58]

But in attempting to teach standard English to children who speak a non-standard dialect, even those teachers who understand that there is a language conflict involved, and who would accordingly like to borrow techniques from foreign-language teaching methodology, are likely to find their efforts hampered by too limited a knowledge of the structural characteristics of whatever non-standard dialect the children speak. For, in all too many cases, the best pedagogical grasp of the structural features of a particular non-standard dialect will consist of little more than a list of certain "folk" pronunciations and an awareness of the use of such grammatical shibboleths as *ain't* and the double negative. Unfortunately, this kind of superficial knowledge

of the structural details of the speech of disadvantaged children will
not only prevent the teacher or therapist from understanding the reasons for many of these children's "mistakes" in standard English, but
it is also likely to lead to an inadvertent lumping together of children
who speak different dialects (and therefore who have different kinds
of problems with standard English) under a generalized remedial
English approach which would not take these differences into account.
In the likely event that both Negroes and whites make up the disadvantaged student population of a school system, this egalitarian approach to their language problems may prove almost irresistible in the
face of a particularly unsophisticated kind of social liberalism, currently in vogue among educators, which regards it as a manifestation
of racism to entertain even the most well-qualified hypothesis that
differences in ethnicity (such as being "white" or "Negro" in America)
might possibly correlate with differences in behavior (in language
usage, for example). In fact, so strong is the hold upon today's educators of this sociologically simplistic philosophy, with its "all children
are the same" credo, that many educators and teachers even find un-
comfortable the anthropologist's contention that correlations between
ethnicity and behavior are not only possible but probable, when one
considers that ethnicity is more of a social phenomenon than a physiological one, and that so much of human behavior is socially conditioned rather than genetically determined. And instead of seeing the
chronic failure of disadvantaged Negroes in integrated school situations as a strong indication that this "sameness" credo is inadequate
and counter-productive in terms of the real goals of education, many
educators let such unpleasant realities force them into clinging all the
more blindly and tenaciously to their simplistic views of the matter.

But the failure to perceive structural differences between the non-
standard dialects of American Negroes and those of American whites
has not been unique to English teachers and speech therapists. Some
prominent dialectologists also have claimed that Negro dialects represent, at the most, a minor statistical skewing of white dialect features.
And still others have passed over the subject altogether.[59]

One further reason why both language teachers and dialectologists
have failed to appreciate the extent to which non-standard Negro dialects may differ from non-standard white dialects (even in the Deep
South) may simply be that such differences now remain mostly in
syntax (i.e., grammatical patterns and categories) rather than in
vocabulary or lexicophonology (i.e., word forms), and are thus not
normally uncovered by the word-comparison techniques which dialectologists and non-linguists rely on so heavily. Yet, a comparison of

the grammatical details of white and Negro non-standard dialects suggests a very different kind of historical relationship than is evident from a comparison of words alone. This can be illustrated by the comparison of a standard English (STE) conjunctive sentence like "We were eating—and drinking, too" together with its equivalents in representative varieties of Southern white non-standard basilect (WNS), Negro non-standard basilect (NNS), and Gullah Basilect (GUL)[60]:

STE: We were eating—and drinking, too.
WNS: We was eatin'—an' drinkin', too.
NNS: We was eatin'—an' we drinkin', too.
GUL: We bin duh nyam—en' we duh drink, too.

If one compares only the forms of the equivalent words in these sentences, NNS (Negro non-standard) appears to be virtually indentical to WNS (white non-standard), with both of them about equally different from STE (standard English).[61] Judged by the same criteria, GUL (Gullah) appears to be radically different from all the others, including NNS.

Because of such word-form similarities and differences, many dialectologists have concluded that, while Gullah itself may be a creolized form of English (rather than a direct descendant of any British dialect or dialects), there is no evidence that other kinds of American Negro speech are related to it in any direct way.[62] For, according to the same kind of word-form comparisons, these represent little more than the use by Negroes of dialect patterns which are also used by (and presumably borrowed from) whites in the Deep South.

However, a comparison of the sentence structure of these dialects shows a somewhat different kind of relationship. In the foregoing equivalent sentences, this is evident in the treatment of the subject pronoun and the tense-marking auxiliary (or copula). For, although STE, WNS, NNS, and GUL can all repeat the subject pronoun and auxiliary in a conjunctive clause (e.g., STE "We were eating—and we were drinking, too"), this is not generally done in any of them. Instead, one or both will usually be omitted (provided, of course, that the subject and temporal referents remain the same). But in terms of what they omit, these dialects split along lines which are different from those indicated by word-form similarities and differences. Both STE and WNS normally omit both the subject pronoun and the auxiliary in a conjunctive clause, although the tense-marking auxiliary must be present if the subject is not omitted. But NNS, like GUL, often repeats the subject pronoun in a conjunctive clause while omitting the auxiliary—even when this indicates past tense.[63]

An example of the same phenomenon in American Negro speech at the beginning of the nineteenth century is to be found in A. B. Lindsley's play *Love and Friendship* (New York: 1807). A Negro says: "I tink dey bin like sich a man de bess, for dey like for be tumel 'bout." Side by side with *dey bin like* in the first clause is *dey like* in the second one, even though the context makes it reasonably clear that both mean "they liked".

If, in such features as the omission of a redundant auxiliary, (while retaining the redundant subject pronoun, Gullah and other non-standard Negro dialects part company with standard English and non-standard white dialects (of both America and Great Britain), they do have counterparts in a number of pidgin and creole forms of English which, though used far from the shores of the United States and in widely separated places, are all the legacy of the African slave trade. To illustrate how much these forms of English resemble Gullah and other non-standard Negro dialects with respect to auxiliary omission, the same equivalent sentences are given in Jamaican Creole (JMC), Sranan (SRA), the creole English of Surinam in South America, and West African Pidgin English (WAP)[64]:

JMC: We ben a nyam—an' we a drink, too.
SRA: We ben de nyang—en' we de dringie, too.
WAP: We bin de eat—an' we de dring, too.

In addition to the grammatical correspondences, the word-form similarties of these languages with Gullah will be apparent.[65]

These correspondences are much too neat to be dismissed as mere accident. Rather, they seem to indicate that at least some of the particular syntactic features of American Negro dialects are neither skewings nor extensions of white dialect patterns, but are in fact structural vestiges of an earlier plantation creole, and ultimately of the original slave-trade pidgin English which gave rise to it.

This kind of evidence—existing in abundance for those who will admit it—calls for a complete reassessment of the relationships between British dialects, white American dialects, Negro American dialects (including Gullah), and the pidgin and creole English of Africa and the Caribbean. In particular, a new and more careful look at the question of American Negro dialects needs to be taken by those working within orthodox American dialectology—most of all by those who have made an almost exclusive use of American Dialect Atlas materials and techniques. High on the list of priorities for determining Negro and white dialect relationships should be: 1) the relationship between Gullah and other Negro dialects, and 2) the relationship between Negro dialects (other than Gullah) and white dialects. In such a reassessment, many new insights into the history of these relationships will be gained from studies of the syntax, not only of present-day dialects, but also of literary attestations of early Negro and white non-standard dialect, and by comparative studies of European, pidgin, and creole dialects of English.

All-in-all, it looks very much like the word-form similarities between non-standard Negro dialects and non-standard white dialects are the result of a relatively superficial merging process, in which creole-speaking Negroes tried to make their "broken" (i.e., creole) English become more like that of the whites by means of minor pronunciation changes and vocabulary substitutions. But the creole grammatical patterns of these Negroes' speech, being less amenable to conscious manipulation, remained more resistant to this substitution process.[66] In an earlier article on urban Negro dialect in Washington, D.C., I pointed out how Negro children who reach school age speaking a radically non-standard dialect often modify it in the direction of standard English in a similarly superficial fashion as they grow older. It is interesting to consider that, in the language-socialization process of their individual lifetimes, many American Negroes may actually repeat something of the larger process of Negro dialect history.

Now, the pedagogical implications of a historical relationship of this kind between Negro and white non-standard dialects and, more particularly, between non-standard Negro dialects and standard English ought to be clear. For, if American Negro dialects have evolved in such a way that structural similarities with other dialects of American English (including standard English) are greatest at the superficial word-form level, then it is possible for these similarities to mask any number of grammatical differences between them. And the teacher, concentrating on the more obvious word-form differences, is quite likely to miss the grammatical differences in the process—thereby leaving them to persist as apparent malapropisms, awkward turns of phrase, and random "mistakes" in speech and composition through grade school, high school, and frequently even through higher education.

As the grammatical study of non-standard Negro dialect progresses, it is quite probable that many more differences will be found between Negro and white speech patterns, and it may well turn out that at least some of these will also be traceable to a creole English, pidgin English, or even African language source. Of course, such discoveries are bound to cause embarrassment to those superficially liberal whites who will accept the Negro for what he is only if his behavioral patterns prove to be as European as their own, and they will be disquieting to those racial image-conscious Negroes who are so often preoccupied with the question "What will the white folks think?" But quite apart from whether he thinks they are a help or a hindrance in integration, good or bad for the Negro's racial image, the dedicated educator should welcome the discovery and formulation of such ethnically correlated dialect differences as do exist. For, only when they are taken into account in the teaching process will the linguistic cards cease to be stacked against the disadvantaged Negro pupil in the nation's classrooms.

8

🌿 Language and Communication Problems in Southern Appalachia

WILLIAM A. STEWART

INTRODUCTION

When used in its broadest sense, the term *Appalachia* usually refers to an immense portion of the mid-Eastern United States—one which includes all of West Virginia, the eastern thirds of Kentucky and Tennessee, and adjacent parts of Pennsylvania, Ohio, Maryland, Virginia, North Carolina, Georgia, and Alabama. Yet, in spite of the fact that the Appalachian region is dissected by a number of state boundaries, there are still at least two good reasons for considering it a single entity. The first reason is geographic; the region consists of a continuum of virtually uninterrupted mountain chains and hills.[67] The second reason is cultural; there exists within these mountains and hills a special kind of American, usually referred to as the Southern Highlander, or Southern Mountaineer. A common geographic and national origin before migration to Appalachia, plus the effect of similar ecological factors throughout the area of settlement, has led to the maintenance of a rather uniform mountain culture which, even today, results in striking similarities between individuals living as far apart as the coal mines of western Pennsylvania and the hills of northern Alabama.[68] Although for over a century and a half there had been little if any contact between mountaineers living in different parts of Appalachia, their cultural similarity was such that with the advent of technology and, with it, more efficient means of communication, citizens throughout the region were able to develop and become part of the Appalachian-wide networks of cultural exchange. For example, the radio contributed the technological means by which a country-music network, centering in Nashville, was able to extend over the entire territory.

But while geographic isolation was largely responsible for the mountaineer's preservation of similar life-ways throughout Appalachia, it was also largely responsible for an increasing amount of cultural divergence between those of the mountaineer and the rest of the American population. For the difficulties of travel and transportation in Appalachia prevented the introduction of many of the cultural and technological changes which took place in "Outland" America—particularly in the large cities on the East Coast and the Mid West—during the course of the nineteenth century. By the end of the last century, differences in attitudes and life-ways between these mountaineers and other Americans had become so pronounced that misunderstandings and conflicts between the two were commonplace whenever they came into contact; the mountaineer was regarded by the outsider with amusement and even contempt, while the outsider was viewed by the mountaineer with suspicion. It is largely because of such differences that, even today, Appalachian mountaineers often have serious adjustment problems when—as is becoming more and more the case—economic blight forces them to leave their ancestral "hollers" and move to the big cities on either coast or around the Great Lakes. Of course, both this out-migration of the mountaineer and the adjustment problems which he is likely to encounter in his new environment pose special problems for public education in Appalachia, which must prepare the region's inhabitants not only for the progress at home, but also for the eventuality of a highly competitive existence in some far-off city.

Even apart from the problem of preparing young people for out-migration, Appalachian education must still deal with a number of complications in the educational process which have been created by recent changes, either in the nature of the Appalachian population itself, or in the avowed obligations of education to that population. One of the main changes in the Appalachian population which has occurred—mostly since the Civil War period—is the addition, to the mountaineer, of sizeable numbers of other kinds of persons. For example, there are today urban dwellers in Appalachia. Although the territory has obviously been less affected by urbanization than most other parts of the United States, cities have nevertheless grown up within Appalachia. None of them are really big cities, by national standards, yet many are big enough and old enough to have already developed distinctly urban cultural patterns, and to have attracted, over the decades, persons of a variety of types from outside the region. This has been especially true of the Appalachian cities like Charleston (West Virginia), Knoxville and Chattanooga (Tennessee), and Asheville (North Carolina). Even many mountaineers have left their rural hollers to settle down in such cities, and they have also contributed to Appalachia's growing urban population. The descendants of these mountaineers-turned-townsmen have produced a uniquely Appalachian kind of city culture—one which represents a transitional stage between the values and life-ways of rural mountaineers and those of urbanites in the more cosmopolitan cities of the nation.

Another factor which has contributed to an increase in cultural complexity of the Appalachian population is the in-migration, particularly during the first part of the present century, of foreign groups, such as Italians, Poles, Germans, etc. They have moved, not only into the area's cities, but also into the more rural districts where mining activities and lumber mills have offered opportunities. Although the Appalachian-born descendants of these foreign in-migrants have assimilated to the local culture in many ways, they still tend to remain distinct from the more traditional mountaineer. In recent years, with the development of technical industries in some Appalachian cities (for example, the chemical industry in Charleston and the electrical industry in Chattanooga), well-educated and highly trained technicians have been attracted and they have usually brought their families with them. Coming as they usually do from big coastal cities, these people have created in some Appalachian cities a new élite which is more closely in contact with American life outside of the region than the more traditional Appalachian educated class usually is. Although the members of this new group are still relatively uninvolved with other Appalachians—and still largely unaccepted by them—the fact that there is now, within the area, a highly prestigious segment of the population which behaves in terms of outland norms is bound to have an effect on all the inhabitants in the future.

Finally, the place of the Negro in Appalachia certainly deserves much more consideration than it has generally been given to date. Although the Negro accounts for a much smaller percentage of the total population of the region than in the southern lowlands, the Negro/white ratio in many Appalachian cities attains (and in Chattanooga exceeds by far) the national Negro/white ratio. There are even rural settlements of Negroes in some of the mountain counties of all the states extending into the section. Often from a family line which has been in Appalachia for generations, the rural Negro is increasingly forced into local cities by a lack of opportunity in the countryside. In these cities, the Negro's lot becomes much the same as in other American cities. Race-caste phenomena keep him distinct from the rest of the population and make his poverty more endemic than that of the poor white. Thus, the Appalachian Negro continues, for generation after generation, to constitute a distinct cultural group within his region—behaving in terms of cultural norms which are in many ways quite different from those of the local whites. Consequently, the Appalachian Negro's needs are often rather different from those of the mountaineer. Yet, because the prototype of Appalachia is the white mountaineer, and because in comparison the Negro constitutes an embarrassingly different but (from the white point of view) unpicturesque minority, his needs are seldom given adequate consideration by local power structures.

Although the recognition of these ecological, sociological and ethnic differences within Appalachian society certainly adds complexity to the traditional view of it, as yet no comprehensive educational program for the region will be effective unless it takes account of these differences. This is certainly the case with language teaching, since all of these variables, and others, have a direct correlation with language usage and language variation. A number of such correlations will be pointed out below. It should be made clear, however, that they are only rather general ones; much more detailed knowledge is still needed, and it will come only with carefully planned and executed investigation and research.

LINGUISTIC VARIATION AND LANGUAGE LEARNING IN APPALACHIA

With the settlement of Appalachia by pioneers of English-Scotch-Irish descent, English became virtually the only language used in the region.[69] Some Indians (mostly Cherokees) preserved their original language, to be sure, but this did not happen on any significant scale. Nor was the later arrival of foreign language speaking immigrants in some parts of Appalachia substantial enough to affect the dominance of English. Yet, the English spoken in Appalachia today is by no means uniform. Rather, a number of varieties (or dialects, as the linguist calls them) are used. An understanding of the reasons for this and of the circumstances under which the different dialects of English are used is important in assessing the language teaching problems which Appalachian education must face today, and in the future.

Among the kinds of English used in Appalachia, that which undoubtedly has the greatest historical association with the region is

Mountain Speech, so-called. Technically speaking, this term refers to a family of several closely related dialects, rather than to a single one. But, since they are structurally more like each other than they are like other dialects of American English, and since all are used by rural mountaineers living in adjacent areas, it is justifiable to refer to them collectively as Mountain Speech.

For the most part, Mountain Speech is the linguistic legacy of the folk speech of the early settlers, most of whom came into Appalachia from Pennsylvania, Maryland, Virginia, and the Carolinas during the latter part of the eighteenth century. Although it has undoubtedly changed since that time, Mountain Speech seems to have done so less than the folk speech of other regions of America. The relatively archaic character of present-day Mountain Speech is manifested by the survival in it of speech-forms otherwise known primarily from Shakespearean literature, and has given rise to a popular idea that Mountain Speech is "pure Elizabethan English". It is really not, of course, since by the time the settlement of Appalachia had begun, English had already changed considerably from what it had been in Elizabethan times, a century and a half before.[70]

Today, for better or for worse and in spite of its regional seniority, Mountain Speech is no longer accepted by most Appalachians as a generally respectable way to talk. While many older mountaineers can undoubtedly still be found who use a more-or-less "pure" form of rural dialect, the younger ones have begun to reject the more rustic speech patterns in favor of standard English ones which they learn in school and hear on television and the radio. Of those who have given up Mountain Speech in the course of their education, some continue to harbor a private affection for their childhood dialect, and may even drop back into it occasionally when talking with rural neighbors or kin. Publicly, however, these same individuals are likely to pay lip service to deprecating stereotypes of rural dialect as imprecise, ungrammatical, and even comical.

The tragedy of the growing rejection of Mountain Speech is not so much that it is causing the rural dialects to die out (since, after all, no dialect survives or remains unchanged forever), but rather that the form it is taking is bound to cause the mountaineer to despise his own origins—and unjustifiably so. For, from a linguistic point of view, no language or dialect (and this includes Mountain Speech) is inherently inferior to any other in its potential communicative efficiency. Some languages or dialects are rich and expressive in some ways, and others are equally rich and expressive in other ways. If a particular language or dialect has been used more than others for talking or writing about a particular subject, then it is likely to have developed a specialized vocabulary for dealing with that subject—one which other languages or dialects may not have. However, this kind of communicative efficiency or "preciseness" is a result of adaptation to need, not of inherent characteristics. Furthermore, all languages, as well as all dialects within a language have their own grammatical structure (i.e., meaningful sentence-structure patterns), so that none is truly "ungrammatical". Therefore, a given dialect may be said to be "ungrammatical" only in the sense that its grammatical patterns have not been set forth formally in a grammar book or manual of style.

Virtually every spoken language exists in more than one variety, or dialect, the differences between which may be in pronunciation, grammatical patterns, or vocabulary.[71] Sometimes different dialects of a language may be separated from each other by geographic or political boundaries. In such cases, the dialects may have fairly equal status— one being considered just as "good" as another. This is so, for example, with standard American English and standard British English. There are other cases, however, in which two or more dialects of the same language are used side by side within a single geographic or political domain. When this is the case, it is rare for them to have equal status. Instead, one dialect may come to be much more generally accepted than another. There are a number of reasons, sometimes interrelated, why one particular dialect may come to be regarded as "better" than others. For instance, it may have started out as the native speech of a socially or politically dominant group—consequently, may have been chosen for producing the language's first literary works—thereby becoming the basis for a standard written language—in turn serving as the model for a normative grammatical tradition. An example of a dialect with such a history is standard British English as opposed to, say, Cockney dialect in London. Over the years, the former has been increasingly studied, analyzed, described, codified, taught, learned, and pontificated upon, while the latter has been increasingly condemned and ridiculed. Yet it is essentially because of the difference in treatment, rather than any difference in inherent linguistic superiority that standard British English is held to be "elegant", "precise", and "grammatical" while Cockney is said to be "coarse", "sloppy", and "faulty". One might compare such popular misconceptions about differences between dialects with ones about differences between members of social classes, castes, or ethnic groups in markedly stratified societies. In both cases, the cited characteristics of each are more likely to be a product of the ranking process than an explanation of it.

Social downgrading, in accommodation to an encroaching dialect of higher prestige, seems to have been the fate of Mountain Speech in Appalachia. As long as mountain life remained relatively well-isolated from the cosmopolitan ways and standardized speech of the big cities, Mountain Speech enjoyed general acceptance as the medium of oral communication.[72] But as contact between Appalachia and the "Outland" increased, and as cities grew up within the region, new influences began to exert themselves on mountain life. Among these was standard English, which began to replace or modify Mountain Speech to the extent that at least the older, more rustic and non-standard varieties began to disappear. Yet, the influence was not entirely one-way. For, while standard English affected Mountain Speech, standard English in Appalachia was in turn given a mountain flavor—particularly in pronunciation. Thus, the English of educated natives of Charleston, West Virginia, while quite acceptably standard, is still unmistakably Appalachian in sound.

The mountaineer who leaves his hill or holler to take up residence in an Appalachian city is faced with a linguistic adjustment problem. He is expected to modify his Mountain Speech patterns further in the direction of standard English than would be necessary in a rural community. But since the standard English of Appalachian cities uses essentially the same sound system as Mountain Speech, and even some of the same idiomatic constructions, the transition may be a relatively painless one—involving substitutions in grammatical patterns and vocabulary for the most part. Furthermore, any linguistic difficulties which the mountaineer might experience are eased by the fact that Appalachian urbanites are accustomed to, and tend to be tolerant of, compromises between city English and Mountain Speech. The situation will be altogether different, however, when the mountaineer moves instead to one of the large Outland cities. There the urban English will not even have a sound system which is similar to Mountain Speech, so that the in-migrant mountaineer will brand himself as a "hillbilly" with every utterance.

Although Mountain Speech is undoubtedly the variety of non-standard English most widely used in Appalachia, it is not the only one. For most of the region's less educated Negroes speak a type of non-standard English which, for practical purposes, one may call Negro Dialect. However, it should be understood that, as in the case of Mountain Speech, this term refers not to one dialect, but rather to several closely related ones.

Because of its non-standard nature, Negro Dialect is generally considered to be "ungrammatical", just as Mountain Speech is. However, since Negro Dialect is spoken by persons who have traditionally been

relegated to low rank in the American race-caste system, it has even
less social status than Mountain Speech—so much less, in fact, that
many of those who are associated with Negro Dialect (either as
speakers of it, or simply as Negroes) go so far as to deny its very
existence. Some do this by maintaining that the speech of uneducated
Negroes is no different from that of uneducated whites. Yet, although
this may or may not be true for some areas of the United States, it is
certainly not the case in Appalachia. There, Negro Dialect differs
from both the Mountain Speech of the rural whites and the city speech
of the urban whites in many details of pronunciation, grammar and
vocabulary.[73] Others who would not deny that some Negroes do speak
a distinct dialect still object to the designation "Negro Dialect", point-
ing out that the kind of speech it refers to is not used by *all* Negroes.
This is certainly true, but it is interesting that the analogous objection
is never raised about Mountain Speech—that it is not used by *all* mountaineers. Of course, what justifies the designation "Mountain Speech"
is not that it is used by all mountaineers, but rather that it is used
almost exclusively by mountaineers. By the same token, the "Negro"
in "Negro Dialect" refers to its virtually exclusive use by Negroes, not
to universal use by Negroes.

There are many reasons why Negro Dialect is different from Mountain Speech in Appalachia, and none of them have anything to do
with physiological or mental differences—real or imagined—between
Negroes and whites. Instead the differences have to do in great part
with different migration patterns; while whites came into Appalachia
largely from Midland and Northern territories of the East, the region's
Negroes came in largely from the South Atlantic plantation area. Thus,
Negro Dialect differs from Mountain Speech partly in that it has more
Southern dialect features. Furthermore, Negro Dialect also differs
from Mountain Speech in having structural traces of the older plantation creole English from which it in part derives.[74] While the speech of
some whites in the Deep South may also have some creole features
(due to prolonged contact between whites and Negroes in the plantation area), this is generally not the case with white Appalachian mountaineers.

Just as the speech of Appalachian whites differs between mountaineers and city dwellers, Negro Dialect has both rural and urban
varieties—the urban variety being somewhat closer to standard English, at least in vocabulary. Finally, there is a numerically small but
socially important group of urban Negroes in Appalachia who do not
speak any kind of non-standard dialect. Their English figures among
the most standard found in the region.

The foregoing discussion of linguistic variation in Appalachia has concentrated on two variables: ecology (rural/urban) and ethnicity (white/Negro). Cutting across these (although partly affected by them) are three other variables which influence linguistic variation and language learning. These are age, sex, and education.

Differences in the age of the speakers are matched by difference in language usage in virtually all societies. In the very early years (roughly the first four or five), many of the special characteristics of a child's speech are manifestations of first-language acquisition—that is, the interaction between the neurological development which allows a human being to learn a language for the first time, and the social process of actually acquiring it. After this developmental period is over, the differences between child and adult language are almost entirely social in nature, and often derive from the fact that children in many societies associate more with other children their own age than they do with older persons. One interesting Appalachian social phenomenon which has to do with this is that Negro children seem to be oriented more toward age-graded peer groups of this type, while white children tend to be oriented more toward family units.[75] Even in cases where children are family-oriented, other social factors may operate to make their speech different from that of their parents. For example, children may be more under the care of their grandparents, and thus preserve older dialect features which their parents might have given up.

Differences in language usage between the sexes at virtually all ages are probably much less the product of hormones than they are of social differentiation. In almost every human society, males and females are taught to behave differently, and this usually includes the ways of speaking.

Finally, the educational process itself can have a decided effect on an individual's language behavior—particularly if it is reinforced by high educational standards at the family or neighborhood level. But the role of education alone in affecting the language habits of an individual, a community, or a region must not be oversimplified. It interacts with other social factors, such as social structure and individual goals, in complicated and little-understood ways. For example, archaic or radically non-standard dialect features may be preserved, by means of age-grading, in the speech of generation after generation of preschool children, even though formal education may discourage or eliminate such features in the speech of such children when they enter school and become adults.

Another linguistic phenomenon which presents problems for the

Appalachian schools is the retention by older children (some even in their early teens) of non-standard speech features which must have started out as developmental ones (i.e., as "baby-talk") since they are a part of no well-formed English dialect. Such features include a lack of distinction between pre-vocalic *l, r,* and *w* sounds (e.g., a pronunciation of *weed* for *lead* and *read,* as well as *weed*), the failure to produce normal consonant clusters (e.g., a pronunciation *krait* for *straight*), etc. This phenomenon seems to be far too widespread among white mountaineer children in Appalachia to be regarded as simply random fixation in a baby talk stage by some individuals, and the fact that it is relatively uncommon among white city and Appalachian Negro children makes it seem obvious that its causes must lie in some relationship between language learning, social structure and formal education.[76] What may well be the case is that developmental phenomena are eliminated less by peer group imitation in the family-oriented white mountaineer child than in the peer group-oriented urban white or Negro child. For some mountaineer children, actual physical isolation may reinforce this social isolation from other youngsters outside the family. At the same time, age-grading in mountain society discourages the mountaineer child from imitating his elders to any full degree until he is ready to become an adult himself. Reinforced by a lack of formal education, age-grading also inhibits correction by adults of developmental features in their offspring ("That's jist the natcherl way fer young-uns to talk").

LANGUAGE TEACHING PROBLEMS IN APPALACHIA

During the past decade, there has been a great deal of national attention focused on such problematic aspects of Appalachian life as geographic and cultural isolation, endemic poverty, and technological backwardness. While undoubtedly motivated by the best of intentions, this public airing of what many Appalachians probably consider to be their "dirty laundry" has frequently combined too much zeal in the search for problems with too little analysis of them once they are found. The result has been to create misunderstanding, where understanding was the goal, by giving the nation an overly pessimistic picture of just what Appalachian life is really like. For example, an outland educator could easily get the impression that formal education in the region is characteristically antiquated and inept. Although this may be somewhat the case with the more isolated rural schools (usually of the "one room" type), it is no more true for Appalachia's urban schools than it is for urban schools in other parts of the nation. The schools in such cities as Charleston, Knoxville, Clinton and Chatta-nooga are usually well run, and staffed with imaginative and highly motivated teachers. In fact, this is even true of some of Appalachia's rural schools as well. Where inadequate instruction does exist, it is more likely to be the result of a lack of resources, or of the training necessary to deal with special problems, than it is to be the result of a lack of motivation.

Because the national assessment of the state of Appalachian educa-tion puts matters in such an unfavorable light, the region's educators often become excessively defensive, focusing even more on achieve-ments and overlooking failures even more than is usually the practice with teachers. Understandable though this defensive reaction may be, however, it can easily do the cause of Appalachian education more harm than good. For the sweeping-under-the-rug of chronic failures in the classroom can easily blind one to the basic problems which give rise to such failures—problems which could eventually be dealt with if only faced up to and accounted for. For example, in a locality where most of the population speaks a non-standard dialect of Eng-lish, an understandable pride on the part of the teacher and the com-munity in the success of those few pupils who somehow do learn standard English may draw attention away from the unpleasant fact that such success is exceptional—that the majority of pupils never do acquire, either in the classroom or outside of it, an acceptable com-mand of the standard language. In this way, the problem of actually turning the majority of pupils into educational successes may be post-poned indefinitely.

Complicated as educational improvement may be by regional defen-siveness, it may be even further complicated by ethnic defensiveness in certain cases. For example, no matter how true it may be, the obser-vation that many if not most Appalachian Negroes talk more like Negroes in other parts of the United States than they do like Appa-lachian whites may sound dangerously like racial stereotyping to many social-conflict-wary teachers. Consequently, they might insist upon applying the same corrective techniques to Negro Dialect speakers as to those who use Mountain Speech, with the predictable result that Negro failures in the English classrooms of Appalachia would not decrease to any significant degree. In such a case, commitment to a well-meant but superficial concept of "togetherness" could actually help to prolong deep-seated ethnic inequity.

Distracting as they are, regional and ethnic defense mechanisms are not the only obstacles to effective language teaching in Appalachia. More problematic still are some very common misunderstandings about the nature of the educational problems of socio-economically "disadvantaged" youngsters, both in Appalachia and in other parts of the nation. Many teachers, relying heavily on the traditional philosophy of their profession for an understanding of what they are doing, actually believe that they are teaching Truth. Accordingly, the language and cultural norms which they teach, and which are embodied in innumerable textbooks, are regarded as being maximally well-formed and logical. From this point of view, the child who deviates from classroom expectations seems to be failing to understand or appreciate natural order or basic good sense. It then follows that the way to help such children is simply to expose them to more intensive doses of the classroom norms, until they finally see the light. All in all, this approach to teaching the disadvantaged is pathetically similar to the linguistic technique of the unsophisticated traveler abroad who believes that foreigners will understand his own language if only he shouts it loudly enough.[77]

What is more likely to be the case is that socio-economically disadvantaged children have social behavioral patterns which are well-formed and "logical" in their own terms, but that these differ from those taught in the classroom and expected from all who would enter the mainstream of American life. The fact that the disadvantaged should often turn out to be culturally different (from middle-class Americans) ought not to be too surprising, since one of the main reasons why a particular segment of the national population may be economically underprivileged is that it has been excluded from mainstream life, either by the barriers of a race-caste system (as in the case of the American Negro) or by geographic isolation (as in the case of the Appalachian mountaineer). This social or geographic isolation would have encouraged the development and maintenance of social norms (both in language and in other kinds of cultural behavior) which might be unique to the particular group, and thereby set its members off from other people even further.

Once this is understood to be so, the process of teaching the disadvantaged child takes on an entirely different character. Instead of being considered inattentive, lazy, malicious, or mentally deficient, the disadvantaged child who chronically fails in the classroom can be seen to be confused by two conflicting (but often somewhat similar, and therefore not easily distinguishable) norms of behavior. In terms of language teaching, this means that the problematic child is not so much likely to be verbally destitute as he is to be confused by the differences between his own non-standard dialect and the standard English taught at school. Precisely because his non-standard dialect is a variety of English, similarities between it and standard English may make it especially difficult for the child (and, in fact, for the teacher as well) to be sure where one leaves off and the other begins. It should therefore be clear that, for teaching standard English to speakers of non-standard dialects (such as Mountain Speech or Negro Dialect), the best techniques will be those which are specifically designed to teach the patterns and habits of standard English to persons (of whatever age) who already know a different set of language patterns and habits. Such techniques have already been developed for teaching English as a foreign language to speakers of other languages, and an increasing number of linguists and educators are now recommending that such techniques, adapted to deal with the specific linguistic differences involved, be used for teaching (standard) English to the disadvantaged.

When first encountered, the idea that the disadvantaged child may have a language and culture of his own can be terribly threatening to the teacher who assumes that there is only one way of talking English, or only one way of being American. For it not only goes against the American Dream of cultural unity, which she probably teaches in Social Life class (a myth predicated on fantasy and intolerance, if ever I saw one), but it also robs her of the strongest crutch she has for teaching English—an appeal to some sort of absolute, universal order and logic. Yet, the really bright and dedicated teacher will not take long to see the advantages of an approach which gives some insight into what is going on in the child's mind, which explains the reasons for his otherwise unreasonable mistakes, and which allows for a considerable amount of control over the teaching process. One good example should illustrate these advantages.

It is well known by Appalachian teachers that many of the children who come to school speaking a non-standard dialect will experience chronic difficulty in the "correct" use of many standard English patterns. Among these is the present durative form of the verb, e.g., *he is working* (or its contracted form, *he's working*). Many teachers have noticed that these children do not necessarily produce the same "incorrect" form all the time, and the particularly observant teacher may even have noticed that the variant patterns produced differ somewhat between children who know Mountain Speech and those who know Negro Dialect. A listing of variant forms equivalent to standard English *he (i)s working* to be heard from such children in a first grade classroom would be:

Mountain Children	Negro Children
he's workin'	*he workin'*
he's a-workin'	*he be workin'*

Now, since all of these patterns are used where only the one pattern (*he (i)s working*) would be used in standard English, it is easy to see how the teacher could come to the conclusion that the speech patterns of such children are inconsistent, and perhaps even imprecise. Once this interpretation is accepted, it is only natural for the teacher to assume that the children's verbal behavior can be changed by teaching the children to articulate and express themselves more clearly. Unfortunately, such an approach is destined to have only random success in eliminating the use of "incorrect" forms; for the most part, it will fail. What is tragic about such failure is not only that it frequently besets experienced teachers, in good schools, teaching bright children, but also that it is so easy to eliminate—once it becomes understood what the children's real problem is, and what the teacher should do about it.

A good linguist would approach such a problem, first by assuming that the average child's speech is probably well-formed, consistent and meaningful—no matter how non-standard it may be. In other words, it is probably a perfectly well-developed linguistic system, like adult speech is. Of course, the linguist is aware that a child five, or six, or seven years old has simply not had the learning experiences (including those involving the use of language) that a full-grown adult has had, so that the child's full language may be somewhat less elaborate than that of an adult. However, the linguist knows that this difference mostly involves specialized vocabulary and unusual sentence patterns, and that the basic language patterns of a child (at least after the fifth or sixth year) are likely to be much like those of an adult. At the same time, the linguist also knows that different languages (or different dialects) are to a certain extent arbitrary in what they do or don't do, so that even if a child has as well-formed a basic linguistic system as the adult has, the child's language may have a different structure than the adult's language. This is especially likely to be the case if the child is a speaker of non-standard dialect while the adult is a speaker of standard English, or vice-versa. The implication of this fact for the English teaching problem just mentioned is rather profound, for it means that if a pupil uses two different patterns where standard English uses only one, it may well be that his language behavior is not inconsistent, but rather that his dialect makes a distinction which standard English does not make at all. It is because of such possibilities that the linguist starts by taking the child's speech on its own grounds, observing and analyzing it to see how it functions.

What the linguist finds when he examines the Appalachian dialect situation is precisely what was suggested—that both Mountain Speech and Negro Dialect make grammatical distinctions within the range of the durative construction of standard English, e.g., *he is working*. In Mountain Speech, the distinction is indicated by the presence or absence of a verbal prefix *a-*. This prefix shows that the action of the verb is indefinite in space or time, while its absence implies that the action of the verbs is indefinite in space or time. Thus, *he's a-working'* in Mountain Speech means either that the subject has a steady job, or that he is away (out of sight, for example) working somewhere. On the other hand, *he's workin'* in Mountain Speech means that the subject is doing a specific task, close by.[78] A similar, (though not identical) grammatical distinction is indicated in Negro Dialect by the verbal auxiliary *be*.[79]

Since these grammatical distinctions seem just as necessary, natural and logical to the non-standard speakers as, say, the distinction between past and present tense seems to a speaker of standard English, the former are simply not prepared for the possibility that the kind of English they are hearing in the classroom makes no such distinction. Consequently, upon seeing or hearing standard English *he (i)s working*, the Mountain child will equate it only with his *he's workin'* (and will continue to use *he's a-workin'* as well), while the Negro Dialect child will equate it only with his *he workin'* (and will continue to use *he be workin'* as well). For his or her part, the teacher will wrongly consider the different dialect forms to be cases of random variation, since they all correspond to a single pattern in standard English.

Borrowing from foreign language teaching techniques, a much more effective way of teaching the standard English durative construction to users of Mountain Speech or Negro Dialect, would be one which would take specific account of the structural differences between these dialects and standard English. In this case, the pupils would be taught to collapse the non-standard grammatical distinction (shown by the presence and absence of *a-* and *be*) when speaking English. This would be done by drilling them on using the same standard English pattern both for the meaning of non-specific space or time and specific space or time, e.g.,

he's working right here—he's working somewhere.
he's working right there—he's working down the river.
he's working right now—he's working every day.
he's working today—he's working all next week.

In some cases, the teacher might even explain the difference between the non-standard dialect and standard English to the pupils.

If the foregoing example were to be multiplied many times over, to account for the numerous structural differences between the nonstandard dialect of the mountain or Negro child and the standard language which he is expected to learn in school, one can get some idea of the pressing need for further dialect studies in Appalachia, and for the incorporation of the findings of such studies into improved language teaching methods and teacher training programs.

When it becomes clear how different a non-standard dialect may be from standard English, and yet how masked these differences may be by superficial similarities between the dialects, it will be much easier to appreciate the extent to which structural conflicts between the language of the child and the language of the school can contribute to poor learning and poor teaching. And the problem is not restricted to the acquisition of standard oral English; it affects learning to read, and even the learning of other subjects as well.

When a standard English speaking child learns to read, his task is essentially one of decoding the graphic representation of a language which is very much like the one he already uses. For him, the reading problem is basically just that—a reading problem. However, when a child who has not learned how to speak standard English is asked to learn to read in it, his task will be infinitely more difficult—and perhaps even senseless. For even if he succeeds in decoding the written forms of individual words, such a child may find that they do not go together in any (to him) familiar or meaningful pattern.[80]

Finally, it may well be the case that many of the learning difficulties which the disadvantaged characteristically have with such "non-language" subjects as mathematics and science are also due to dialect differences. For it must be remembered that mathematics and science courses are taught in standard English. Therefore, even a child with high natural ability in these fields may experience difficulty in understanding classroom instruction in these subjects, and in articulating what he does understand, if that child does not know standard English. Thus, what looks at first like a lack of technological aptitude on the part of the disadvantaged child might turn out to be more a language problem than anything else.[81]

9

✿ English Problems of Spanish Speakers

A. L. DAVIS

The Spanish-speaking child faces many problems in the learning of English. Besides the strictly linguistic difficulties, the child often lives in a different culture, which may little resemble that of the affluent middle-class. In some large cities and in large parts of the nation the child lives in a completely Spanish-speaking neighborhood; English is the language of the schools and of the outside world. This environment can have an adverse effect on motivation compared to the high motivation college students, foreign and immigrants, have to learn the language.

In this section we will discuss some of the linguistic difficulties to aid the teacher in understanding the most noticeable mistakes the Spanish-speaker makes when he is learning English.

THE SOUNDS

The learner of a foreign language will at first hear the language through his own phonemic system, ignoring contrasts which he does not make and hearing contrasts where the target language has none.

A. L. Davis, co-director of the Center for American English at Illinois Institute of Technology, is the author of many articles on regional and social dialects and relevant educational problems and the editor of *On the Dialects of Children*.

We will first examine the Spanish sounds and contrast them with English.[82]

Spanish has only five vowel phonemes:

	Front	Central	Back
High	i		u
Mid	e		o
Low		a	

The child must learn to discriminate vowels not distinguished in Spanish. The five Spanish vowels nearly cover the ranges of the English vowels, with the high and mid vowels often lowered in syllables ending in a consonant. No Spanish vowel is exactly equivalent to any English vowel, the closest match being /a/. /i, e, o, u/ are not diphthongized as English /iy, ey, uw, ow/.

The consonant system also has important differences from English. The stop series /p, b, k, b, d, g/ in Spanish is not aspirated. t and d are made with tongue farther forward touching the upper teeth and all are made with a somewhat less vigorous articulation.

/b/ is a stop only in phrase initial position (or following juncture) or when following m. Otherwise it is a bilabial fricative [β] made with the lips slightly parted. In Spanish orthography both the letters b and v are used for this phoneme. Examples: *vino* [bino] 'wine,' *bastante* [bastante] 'enough,' *Cuba* [kuβa], *hombre* [ombre] 'man.'

/d/ and /g/ are also stops only in phrase initial (or following juncture), with stop [d] following [n] or [l] and stop [g] following [ŋ].

The fricative allophone of /d/ [ð] is similar to English ð but more weakly articulated. In final position it may be lost altogether and in intervocalic position as well. Examples: *donde* [donde] 'where,' *crudo* [kruðo] 'raw,' *verdad* [berðad, berða] 'true,' *soldado* [soldaðo, soldao] 'soldier.'

The fricative allophone of /g/ is [ɣ] made with the tongue close to the velum. Examples: *ganar* [ganar] 'to win,' *tengo* [teŋgo] 'I have,' *hago* [aɣo] 'I do,' *salgo* [salgo] 'I leave.' Before w it may be lost as in *agua* [aɣwa, awa] 'water.'

With the exception of /d/ which may be lost, none of the stops occurs in final position except in rare foreign words.

/f/ is a labio-dental fricative somewhat more lightly articulated than English /f/. It should be noted that the corresponding voiced sound of English /v/ is absent, the bilabial [β] being an allophone of /b/. (Surely, labiodental articulation, but it is nevertheless, an allophone of Spanish /b/.)

[/θ/ is typical of Castilian Spanish (of Madrid). It enjoys great prestige among speech teachers. It has a voiced allophone, an interdental ð. The sound is spelled c and z. In other dialects it is /s/.]

/s/ is farther forward than English s. It has a voiced allophone [z] before voiced consonants. In some dialects (sub-standard?) it may be reduced to a weak [h] in preconsonantal and final positions. Examples: *cinco* [siŋko] 'five,' *mismo* [mizmo, miʰmo] 'same,' *soldados* [soldaðos, soldaoʰ], *estos* [estos, eʰtoʰ] 'these.'

/x/ is a voiceless velar fricative. Examples: *gente* [xente] 'people,' *jota* [xota] the letter 'j', *rojo* [roxo] 'red,' *reloj* [relox] 'watch.' The orthographic h is not pronounced except sometimes before w *hueso* [weso, ɣweso] 'bone.'

/y/ is a palatal with or without friction (the latter like English y) or an affricate like ǰ, causing *yellow* and *Jello* to sound alike to some Spanish-speakers. The palatal l of Castilian, [ʎ], is [y] in other dialects. Examples: *llamo* [yamo] 'I call,' *hierba* [yerba] 'grass,' *voy* [boy] 'I go,' *oigo* [oygo] 'I hear,' *aire* [ayre] 'air.'

/č/, a voiceless affricate, is like English ch in *China, church* with a little less friction. Examples *chico* [čiko] 'little,' *muchacha* [mučača] 'girl.'

/m/ the voiced bilabial nasal is like English m. Examples: *mucho* [mučo] 'much,' *calma* [kalma] 'calm.'

/n/ varies from labio-dental to velar depending upon its environment. It does not appear before p and b (becoming /m/); it is labio-dental before f, dental or alveolar before vowels and finally (depending upon dialect; some dialects have ŋ finally), velar [ŋ] before k, g, x. Examples: *enfermo* [eɱfermo] 'ill,' *donde* [donde] 'where,' *ron* [ron, roŋ] 'rum,' *cinco* [siŋko] 'five,' *en casa* [eŋkasa] 'at home,' *tengo* [teŋgo], *monja* [moŋxa] 'nun.'

/ñ/ is a palatal nasal occurring between vowels (very rarely initially). Example *mañana* [mañana] 'tomorrow.' In some dialects it may be a combination of /n/ and /y/.

/r/ and /rr/ are almost in complementary distribution. Initially only /rr/ occurs with r in final position. They contrast in intervocalic position. /r/ may be a fricative in final position or at the end of a syllable. Examples: *rojo* [rroxo] 'red,' *pero* [pero] 'but,' *perro* [perro] 'dog,' *cantar* [kantar] 'to sing.' /r/ is an alveolar flap or fricative and /rr/ an alveolar trill.

/l/ the lateral is dental before a dental consonant, otherwise alveolar. It is more 'clear' in final position than is English l. Examples: *largo* [largo] 'long,' *tal* [tal] 'how,' *alto* [alto] 'high.'

/w/ is a rounded consonantal counterpart of /u/ and in this resembles /y/. It is written u,o. *Oaxaca* [waxaka], *bueno* [bweno] 'good,' *bacalao* [bakalao] 'codfish,' *aula* [awla] 'classroom.'

The distribution of these phonemes may be summarized.

Stops: non-final except for /d/ which is fricative. The voiced stops are fricatives in intervocalic positions. Not aspirated as in English.

Fricatives: /f/ non-final.

Affricate: /č/ non-final.

Nasals: /m/ non-final. /n/ has allophone [ŋ] in some dialects in final position.

/r/ and /rr/ -rr initial, r final either intervocalically.

Consonant clusters: initial stop + 1 or r: *plato*, 'dish,' *primo* 'first,' *blanco* 'white,' *broma* 'jest,' *tratar* 'to try,' *drama* 'drama,' (no tl- or dl-) *clima* 'climate,' *crema* 'cream,' *gloria* 'glory,' fl- *flor* 'flower,' fr- *freno* 'brake.' Clusters with w include *puente* 'bridge,' *bueno, tuerto* 'one-eyed,' *duende* 'ghost,' *cuatro* 'four,' *guante* 'glove,' *fuente* 'fountain,' *suerte* 'luck,' *luego* 'afterwards,' *muerte* 'death,' *nueve* 'nine,' *ruido* 'noise.' Clusters with y include *pierna* 'leg,' *bien* 'well,' *tienda* 'shop,' *diente* 'tooth,' *quien* [kyeŋ] 'who,' *fiesta, siete* 'seven,' *miedo* 'fear,' *nieve* 'snow,' *riesgo* 'risk.'

No final clusters are possible in Spanish and the only consonants which occur are (d), s, l, n, r and x.

Medially the 'initial clusters' occur; and p,t,k,b,d,g,m,n,l,r,s, plus another consonant. Three consonant groups include p,k,b,g,m,n,l,r,s, plus the initial clusters; voiced consonant plus s plus consonant. Four consonant groups include b,d,n,r plus s plus the initial clusters.

In comparison with English then, all vowels will give some difficulty, especially the /iy:i, uw:u, ey:e, ow:o/ contrasts; /æ/ which will be heard as /e/ or /a/ (usually a) and /ə/ which will also be /a/ (sometimes /o/). In weak stressed syllables where English has reduction to /ɨ/ and /ʃ/ for most vowels, Spanish retains the pronunciation of the loud stress (this gives trouble to English speakers learning Spanish). Final consonants non-occurring in Spanish will be omitted, followed by an -/e/, or a permitted final will be substituted: *top* [ta], *cake* [keke] *home-run* [xoŋroŋ]. Initial clusters frequently have an /e/- preceding: *sport* [espor]. Final clusters are formidable: *bounced* /bawntst/ becomes [bawnse(d)] etc.

For teaching these sounds and combinations the instructor must be prepared to demonstrate the placement of vocal organs and to drill until the physical tricks of the new sounds are mastered. Some of the cluster problems can be helped by making use of the permitted medial consonant combinations. It should be kept in mind that mere physical drill will not suffice—the new phonemic system must become internalized.

The speech rhythm of Spanish differs from English in many ways. One is the tempo. Spanish syllables in phrases are more even in length, whereas English speeds up and slows down within a phrase. The result is that Spanish may sound more staccato. Within English phrases plus junctures tend to break up the phrase. In Spanish the phrase may seem to be pronounced as "one word." Repetition drills with lengthening of phrases is helpful. "I'm a student—I'm a good student—I'm a very good student" etc.

Syllable division in Spanish follows the permitted sequences. An intervocalic consonant goes with the following vowel, and an 'initial cluster' in medial position with a following vowel *ca-sa, Pe-dro*.

Spanish intonation and stress varies from dialect to dialect as does English. Some linguists set up three stresses and three pitches for Spanish, and three terminal junctures (rising, falling, sustained). Intonations are /121 (1211)/ with fall common for statements, /1231/ with fall in yes-no questions; and some kind of emphases. /122/ with rise with yes-no questions, and /11/ with fall in vocatives; they contrast with English /231/ with fall on statements and questions beginning with question words, /211/ with fall showing annoyance or lack of interest, /241/ with fall emphatic.

King and Bowen set up two stresses: strong and weak. According to King if two strong stresses in a phrase occur the second is loudest, if more than two then the first and last are primary; tertiary and weak are allophones of weak stress.

Although the rhythm features are hardest to describe they are of greatest importance for understanding. Even if the segmentals are not pronounced accurately, understanding is better than if segmentals are accurate while the supra-segmentals are not.

GRAMMAR

English makes use of four primary devices to signal grammatical meanings, that is, to mark such meanings as subject-verb-object, what is modifier or modified, singular-plural, tense and mood, whether a statement, question, or command is being uttered. The order of words in a phrase or sentence, the use of special endings or word forms, the use of function words such as prepositions and conjunctions, and supra-segmental stress, juncture and intonation are these devices.

Word order, so obvious to the native speaker of English that it is often omitted from elementary treatments of grammar, is so important in grammatical signalling that the hearer will often interpret it as the over-riding device. A sentence such as "him doesn't see I," probably

never said by a native speaker, would ordinarily be recast by the
hearer as "he doesn't see me," in spite of three morphological markers:
the cases of the pronouns and the verb form.[83]

The special endings and word forms set off morphological classes.
Nouns have special plural or possessive endings: *boy -'s -s, man men
men's*. Verbs have third person singular, present, past, and participial
endings: *walk walks walked walking, ring rings rang rung ringing*.
Adjective-adverbs have comparison: *small smaller smallest; fast faster
fastest*. Pronouns form a special class, some having accusative (or
objective) case forms: *he his him, they their them, who whose whom*.
Words which have *no* inflection belong to an uninflected class. *Deer*
has no plural form, or is undifferentiated from the singular. Because
nearly all other count-nouns have a plural inflection: *pen pens*, linguists set up a *zero* plural for *deer*, since it has the possessive suffix
deer's. People on the other hand has no singular—except with meaning
change—but has a possessive. Some mass nouns are seldom used in
the plural or possessive, the plural showing meaning change as in
natural sugars. The same applies to some abstract nouns e.g. *readiness*
(possibly plural in Educationalese). Although the latter enters into
the compound, réading+rèadiness, it would be only classed as a *morphological noun* on this basis and on its derivational suffix. Words
which cannot fit *morphologically* are classed with the uninflecteds.

Words may also be classed *syntactically* that is, on the basis of their
position and function in phrases. The common statement patterns are
subject-verb-(indirect object)-(object) (adverbial/time, place, man-
ner/): "They gave him their contribution yesterday at the office reluctantly," with some variation in the adverbial sequences. The above
seems to the writer most "normal" when all three are used when there
is no intonation break. Words which fit into the patterns are classified
together: *Gladys, they* gave *Mrs. Smith, her, him,* their *contributions,
checks, money,* at *the office,* at *work, yesterday, last pay-day,* very
reluctantly, with regret. The substitutions with similar meanings can
be multiplied. The words fitting into the subject, indirect object, direct
object slots are NOMINALS. Those which would fit into the verb slots
are SYNTACTIC VERBS (or verbals—this is not used here because of the
traditional use of verbal for participial, infinitive, and gerund forms).
At the office, at work, yesterday, last night, reluctantly, with regret
are adverbials. *Their* and *last* are ADJECTIVALS (substitute *meager,*
and *next,* with tense change). Words like *at* (*in, on, by* etc.) are
PREPOSITION(AL)s which combine with nominals to form adjectivals
and adverbials: The man *in the store,* the house *by the river, in the
morning* etc. Notice that the noun 'yesterday' is adverbial. CONJUNC-

TION(AL)s may be illustrated by "the man *and* woman," "He wrote *or* said," "He came *when* she called," "*As* tall *as* he is etc." *The, a, an,* are DETERMINERS and *very* is an INTENSIFIER. *It* in "it's going to rain," *there* in "there is much wealth," *one* in "two red ones" are fillers. They complete the pattern but seem to have no other function. The modals (can, may, shall, will, should, could, would, must, might, ought) are used with infinitive forms—except for ought not marked by *to*—and have no distinctive third person singular present. *Could, should, would* are related to *can, shall, will* in some uses. The forms of *be, have* and *used* with *to* and infinitive, *be, get* and *keep* with the present participle e.g. "is going," "got going," "kept going," *be* and *get* passives "was hit," "got hit," *have* with past participle, "has gone," etc. *To* with the infinitive form is a special prepositional use. All of these C. C. Fries calls *function words.*[84] In English simple modifiers of nominals generally precede the word modified:

"He is *a very fine* student," with complex modifiers

"The man *in the park*" following.

The suprasegmentals are used as grammatical signals in differentiating questions from statements when no other signal is present: 'Jòhn cómǐng' with /2-3-3 ||/ = ?, Jòhn cómǐng /2-3-1 #/ = ., to indicate utterance continuance—a signal that the hearer should not break in—where single-bar /|/ or /|||/ may be used instead of /#/, and for indicating compounds e.g. súgar+bòwl. They also indicate brusqueness—politeness and other meanings carried in the paralanguage.

Spanish uses the same kinds of grammatical devices as English—word order, inflections, function words and suprasegmentals. Unfortunately, for the learner, they do not completely match.

The inflections of Spanish occur on the noun, pronoun, verb, and adjective. The noun is marked by singular and plural endings and it has grammatical gender. Males are masculine, females are feminine but all nouns are either masculine or feminine: *señor—señores, señora—señoras* 'sir—sirs,' 'lady—ladies' *padre—padres, madre—madres* 'father—fathers,' 'mother—mothers,' *muchacho—muchachos, muchacha—muchachas* 'boy—boys' 'girl—girls,' *vez—vezes* 'time—times,' *sombrero—sombreros* 'hat—hats,' *pluma—plumas* 'pen—pens.' The plural ending is *-s,* or *-es/-s, -es/.* Some of the list are marked as masculine by *-o* or feminine by *-a.* There is no logical reason for *hat* being masculine while *time* and *pen* are feminine, except that it is part of the history of the language. There is no possessive suffix, Spanish using the function word *de* (of).

The adjective is also masculine or feminine, singular or plural to agree with the noun it modifies: *el hombre malo* 'the bad man,' *los hombres malos* 'the sick men,' *la calle nueva, las calles nuevas* 'the new street, the new streets.' Some adjectives *grande* 'big,' *azul* 'blue' have no gender marked, merely adding the plural marker for agreement. Note that the gender is not inherent for adjectives but is merely a matter of the noun modified. The adjective as we see follows the noun in the above examples. It may precede: *un buen hombre* 'a good man.' Adjectives in series follow the noun. *Una señora feliz y gorda* 'a happy fat woman.' The determiner *el-la-los-las* 'the,' *un-una* 'a, an' (*unos-unos* 'some') is also an adjective agreeing in gender and number with the noun.

The pronoun has the forms:

yo—I
tu—you (familiar singular)—*usted*, formal
él—he
ella—she
nosotros—we *nosotras*, feminine
ustedes—you, formal but general
ellos—they, masculine *ellas*, feminine
me—me
te—you
lo le—him
la—her   used with second singular formal also
nos—us
los—them, masculine
las—them, feminine   used with the second person plural also
mí (used with preposition)
tí (used with preposition)
le (indirect object him or her)
les (indirect object them)
se (reflexive third person) me, te, nos are reflexive also.

There is a neuter form used *esto* 'this,' *eso* 'that' *aquello* 'that' but it is not used in modifying position. The other demonstratives have -*e*, -*a*, zero, -*os*, -*as*, endings.

Additional forms are possessive adjectives *mi, mío, mía; mis, míos, mías* 'my, mine;' *tu, tuyo, tuya, tus, tuyos, tuyas* 'your' (singular familiar antecedents); *su, suyo, suya, sus, suyos, suyas* (third person singular and plural and second person formal antecedents) *nuestro, -a, -os, -as* 'our, ours.'

The verb forms are quite complex and cannot be included here. The verb is inflected for person and number, has present, imperfect, preterit (past), and future tenses, indicative, subjunctive, and conditional moods, infinitive, present and past participle forms. In addition many of the verbs are irregular. The reader may wish to consult a Spanish grammar for these forms.

For the learner of English the pitfalls are that the Spanish system is more extensive and he must learn how to match up the forms. Other devices must be mastered, as for example the use of auxiliary verb forms which parallel his own forms. Juan *hablaba*, John was talking; Juan *hablará*, John will talk. These parallels will not be exact—he must learn the new system as a system.

Spanish word order is similar to English but the subject may be omitted, if clearly understood "*Juan tiené carro. Es rico.* 'John has a car. He's rich.'" *No es nada* 'It's nothing.' (double negative normal for Spanish). The adjective following the noun has been illustrated.

The kinds of grammatical errors produced by learners are often caused by contrasts in the language structures. The following partial list is adapted from *Teaching English to Puerto Rican Pupils in Grades 1 and 2* published by the New York City Board of Education (1956, 1963). Older students make the same errors.

1. Omission of pronoun subject:
   Is big. Is teacher. (Article omitted also.)
2. Not before verb:
   Mariá not is here. (Also Mariá no is here, Mariá no here.)
3. Adjective following noun:
   The dress yellow; the dresses yellows with agreement in number (final /s/).
4. The comparative forms used with *more, most* where English uses *-er, -est*:
   It is more big. He is most fat of the boys.
5.
   a. Dropping of -s inflection on third person singular verbs:
      He go to school.
   b. Dropping of -s inflection on plurals:
      The book are here.
   c. Dropping of past tense inflection:
      The boy play.
   d. Omission of *will* in future tense:
      The boy play.

In 4—Spanish uses *más* (more), *el más, la más, los más, las más* (most). In 5 the Spanish inflections differ so much in form from English that omission takes place. Some of the English forms require unusual consonant clusters also. Besides, most language learners find out that they can simplify the verb forms using time words to get their meanings across: *I go yesterday,* etc.

6. Use of *go* with *to* for future:
   He go to sing = He's going to sing
7. Use of *no* for *don't* in commands:
   no run (not run).
8. Use of simple present where English uses progressive:
   He sleep now.
9. Omission of article with nationality, profession, etc.:
   Is American. Is teacher.
10. Use of *the* for possessive in parts of the body, and personal articles:
    The foot hurts me.
    The coat (of him) is blue.
11. Titles used with definite article:
    The Mr. Jones.
12. *In* used for *on, at:*
    In the table, in Michigan Avenue, in 1515 Michigan Avenue. Prepositions in English are extraordinarily difficult, in fact, prepositional usage in any new language will present extraordinary difficulties!
13. Use of *have* for *be:*
    I have hunger. He have six years = He's six years old.
14. Avoidance of inversion in questions:
    Juan can go? Juan like(s) this? (Spanish does not use the *do* function word-verb form) Also, How come they to school? (or How they come to school?)
15. Noun-compounding not used or order in error:
    The wife-house, the wife of the house.

In vocabulary there is no complete match from language to language. We see this even in the same language as British *vest* is American *undershirt.* Words must be learned in all their semantic ranges, their degrees of formality, their related forms. A Spanish-English speaker may say "God" as he says Diós in Spanish but the Spanish meaning as an interjection is far milder; 'bye-bye' is used with children or familiarly, *fish* is *pez* in Spanish when alive but *pescado* is fish on the table. Vocabulary is only partly learned by vocabulary list translations. We learn the vocabulary of the language through situational contexts including the culture.

Idioms are usually defined as combinations of words peculiar to a language. In English houses burn down but small things burn up. Idiom study manuals, often lists of verb-adverb combinations, are understandably popular with foreign learners.

Complete mastery of the pronunciation, grammar, vocabulary and styles are impossible for the native learner. What the learner of a foreign language should aim for is mastery at the social competence level which he will fit into. The true bilingual is exceedingly rare, as is the person equally at home in two cultures.

In the past, schools have failed to understand the size of the problem because children 'pick up the language so easily.' While children apparently learn new language habits more readily than adults, the age difference is not so important as it might seem, provided the language training is of top quality. What often happens is that part of the language is learned: the learner's language may be relegated to family use, or the new language used only in relationships with English speakers.

It seems hardly likely that the schools will overestimate the problem by committing the resources necessary in time and funds. There may be a *danger* that some school systems will use the size of the problem as an excuse not to provide the proper language training.

10

❧ Sense and Nonsense About American Dialects

RAVEN. I. McDAVID JR.

In my boyhood—more years ago than I care to remember—we used to define an expert as "a damned fool a thousand miles from home." Since I am considerably less than a thousand miles from where I grew up, and stand but a few minutes from my residence in Hyde Park, it behooves me to avoid any claim to expertness about the problems faced in practical situations where the dialect of the school child is sharply divergent from what is expected of him in the classroom. For many of these situations, neither I nor any other working dialectologist knows what the local patterns actually are; for some, there has been no attempt, or at best a partial and belated one, to find out the patterns. Nevertheless, the implications of dialectology for the more rational teaching of English in the schools—and not only in the schools attended by those we currently euphemize as the culturally disadvantaged—are so tremendous that I am flattered to have John Fisher ask for my observations. The problems are not limited to Americans of any race or creed or color, nor indeed to Americans; they are being faced in England today, as immigrants from Pakistan and the West Indies compete in the Midlands for the same kinds of jobs that have drawn Negro Americans to Harlem and the South Side, and Appalachian whites to the airplane factories of Dayton. In fact, such problems are faced everywhere in the world as industrialization and urbanization take place, on every occasion when people, mostly but not exclusively the young, leave the farm and the village in search of the better pay and more glamorous life of the cities. In all parts of the world, educators and politicians are suddenly realizing that language differences can create major obstacles to the educational, economic, and social advancement of those whose true integration into the framework of society is necessary if that society is to be healthy; they are realizing that social dialects—that is, social differences in the way language is used in a given community—both reflect and perpetuate differences in the social order. In turn, the practicing linguist is being called on with increasing frequency to devise programs for the needs of specific groups—most often for the Negroes dwelling in the festering slums of our northern and western cities; and generous government and private subsidies have drawn into the act many teachers and administrators—most of them, I trust, well meaning—who not only have made no studies of dialect differences, but have ignored the studies and archives that are available, even those dealing with their own cities.

Perhaps a data-oriented dialectologist may here be pardoned an excursion into the metaphors of siegecraft, recalled from the time when under the tutelage of Allan Gilbert I learned something of the arts of war and gunnery, if not all their Byronic applications. In confronting our massive ignorance of social dialects, the professional students of the past generation have been a forlorn hope—burrowing into a problem here, clawing their way to a precarious foothold of understanding there, seizing an outwork yonder. Like many forlorn hopes, they have been inadequately supported, sometimes ignored, even decried—not only by their literary colleagues, with the usual patronizing attitude toward anything smacking of affiliation with the social sciences, but also by their fellow linguists who are interested in international programs for teaching English as a second language, in machine translation, in formulaic syntax, or in missionating to convert the National Council of Teachers of English. It is small wonder that some students of dialects have withdrawn from the assault to participate in these better-heeled campaigns; it is a tribute to the simple-minded stubbornness of the survivors that they have not only persisted but advanced. Today their work, their aims, are embarrassingly respectable, as legions spring from the earth in response to the golden trumpet sounding on the banks of the Pedernales. It is inevitable, perhaps even fitting, that the practical work in social dialects should be directed by others than the pioneers in research. But it is alarming that many of those now most vocally concerned with social dialect problems not only know nothing about the systematic work that has been done, about the massive evidence (even if all too little) that is available, but even have a complete misconception about the nature and significance of dialects. At the risk of drawing the fire of the House Un-American Activities Committee, I would agree with my sometime neighbor James H. Sledd that our missionaries should at least know what they are talking about before they set out to missionate.

I have a particular advantage when I talk on this subject: I am one of those who speak English without any perceptible accent. I learned to talk in an upper-middle-class neighborhood of Greenville, South Carolina, among corporation lawyers, bankers, textile magnates, and college presidents, among families with a long tradition of education and general culture. Many of my playmates, like myself, represented the sixth generation of their families in the same county. It never occurred to any of us to tamper with our language; our only intimate acquaintaince with non-standard grammatical forms in writing came from stories in literary dialect or from the quaint and curious exercises that infested our textbooks—though we knew that less privileged forms of speech than ours were found in our community, and were not above imitating them for rhetorical effect. Not a single English teacher of an excellent faculty—our superintendent had his doctorate, not from Peabody or from Teachers College, Columbia, but from the University of Berlin in 1910—made a gesture of tampering. Nor have I ever heard anything in the exotic dialects of the Northeast or the Middle West that would make me feel less content with a way of speaking that any educated person might want to emulate. And yet, a few years ago, my younger sister, who has remained in the South Carolina upland, told me over the telephone: "Brucker, you've been North so long that you talk just like a Yankee." Even though I doubt if I would fool many real Yankees, I know that something has rubbed off from my travels and teaching to make me talk a little different from the boys I grew up with. Still, whenever I go back and start talking with them again, I find myself slipping into the old ways; it is natural for us to shift our way of talking, according to the people we are talking with. In fact, it is the people we talk with habitually who give us our way of talking. Here, in essence, is the way dialects originate. And until everybody lives in a sterile, homogenized, dehumanized environment, as just a number on the books of an all-powerful state, we can expect differences in environment to be reflected in those differences in speech that we call dialects.

An appreciation of this fact would avoid a lot of nonsense expressed in categorical statements in educational literature. Two amusing if distressing examples are found in *Language Programs for the Disadvantaged: Report of the NCTE Task Force,* a booklet released at the

1965 convention of the NCTE. These statements, the more distressing because so much of the report is magnificently phrased, probably arose from the inevitable wastefulness of haste (the Task Force was in the field only last summer) and from the imbalance of the Task Force itself: there was only one linguist and not a single sociologist or anthropologist or historian in a group heavily loaded with supervisors and (to coin a term, which is probably already embalmed in educationese) curriculologists:

> Most disadvantaged children come from homes in which a nonstandard English dialect is spoken. It may be pidgin, Cajun, Midland, or any one of a large number of regional or cultural dialects. Many preschool teachers are concerned about the dialect of their children and take measures to encourage standard pronunciation and usage. (p. 70)
>
> . . . the general feeling is that some work in standard English is necessary for greater social and job mobility by disadvantaged students with a strong regional or racial dialect. (p. 89)

Among the bits of nonsense to be found in these two statements we may notice:

1. A belief that there is some mystical "standard," devoid of all regional association. Yet the variety that we can find in cultivated American English, as used by identifiable informants with impeccable educational and social credentials, has been repeatedly shown in works based on the American Linguistic Atlas, most recently and in greatest detail in Kurath's and my *Pronunciation of English in the Atlantic States* (Ann Arbor: University of Michigan Press, 1961).

2. A belief that there are "racial" dialects independent of social and cultural experiences.

3. A snobbishness toward "strong" dialect differences from one's own way of speaking. Would Bobby Kennedy, politically disadvantaged after the Atlantic City convention, have run a better race in New York had he learned to talk Bronx instead of his strong Bostonian?

4. A glib juggling of terms, without understanding, as in the parallelism of "pidgin, Cajun, Midland." *Pidgin* denotes a minimal contact language used for communication between groups whose native languages are mutually unintelligible and generally have markedly different linguistic structures; typical examples are the Neo-Melanesian of New Guinea and the Taki-taki in Surinam. However scholars may debate the existence of an American Negro pidgin in colonial days, speakers of pidgin constitute a problem in no Continental American classroom, though it would be encountered in Hawaii and the smaller Pacific islands. *Cajun* properly describes the colonial varieties of

French spoken in southwestern Louisiana and in the parts of the Maritime Provinces of Canada from which the Louisiana Acadians were transported; even if by extension we use the term to describe the varieties of English developing in the French-speaking areas of Louisiana and the Maritimes, the problems of teaching English in these areas are really those of teaching English as a second language. *Midland* is a geographical designation for those dialects stemming from the settlement of Pennsylvania and embracing a broad spectrum of cultural levels. At one extreme, we may concede, are the impoverished submarginal farmers and displaced coal miners of Appalachia; at the other are some of the proudest dynasties of America—the Biddles of Philadelphia, the Mellons of Pittsburgh, the Tafts of Cincinnati, and their counterparts in Louisville and in St. Louis, in Memphis and in Dallas—people it were stupid as well as impractical to stigmatize in language like that of the Task Force Report. So long as such glib generalities are used about social dialects, we must conclude that our educators, however well intentioned, are talking nonsense.

And regrettably, such nonsense is no new phenomenon in American culture; it has long been with us. Much of it, fortunately, runs off us like raindrops off a mallard's back. But enough lingers in the schoolroom to do positive harm. My friend Bob Thomas, the anthropologist—a Cherokee Indian and proud of it, though with his blond hair and blue eyes he looks far less like the traditional Cherokee than I do—tells of his traumata when he moved to Detroit from Oklahoma at the age of fourteen. Although Cherokee was his first language, he had picked up a native command of Oklahoma English. Since he had always lived in a good neighborhood, and his family had used standard English at home, he had no problems in grammar; through wide reading and a variety of experiences he had acquired a large and rich vocabulary. But his vowels were Oklahoma vowels; and some benevolent despot in Detroit soon pushed him into a class in "corrective speech." The first day the class met, he looked around the classroom and noticed everybody else doing the same. As eyes met eyes, it became apparent that the class in "corrective speech" contained no cleft palates, no stammerers, no lispers, no foreign accents, not even any speakers of substandard English—for again, the school was in a good neighborhood. The only thing wrong with the boys and girls in the class was that they had not learned English in Michigan, but in Oklahoma, Arkansas, Missouri, Kentucky, Tennessee, West Virginia, Mississippi, and Alabama. "We all realized immediately," Bob told me years afterward, "that they were planning to brainwash us out of our natural way of speaking; and it became a point of honor among us to sabotage the program." To this day, Bob flaunts his Oklahoma accent belligerently; if the teachers had let him alone, he might have adapted his pronunciation to that of the Detroit boys he played with, but once he felt that the school considered his home language inferior, nothing could make him change. The first principle of any language program is that, whatever the target, it must respect the language that the students bring with them to the classroom.

Another kind of nonsense was demonstrated by the head of the speech department at the University of Michigan during my first Linguistic Institute. Impelled by the kind of *force majeur* that only a four-star general can exert, I had compromised with my scientific interest in linguistics to the extent of enrolling in a course in "stage and radio diction," only to find myself bewildered, frustrated, and enraged from the outset. Typical of the petty irritations was the panjandrous insistence on the pronunciation /'pradjus/, though all my friends who raised fruits and vegetables for market, many of them gentlemen with impeccable academic credentials, said /'prodjus/. But far more distressing were the pronunciations advocated in the name of elegance. We were advised to reject the Middle Western and Southern /æ/, not only in *calf* and *dance* and *command,* but even in *hat* and *ham* and *sand,* for an imitation of the Boston /a/ in environments where Bostonians would never use it, so that we would say /hat/ and /ham/ and /sand/, pronunciations legitimate in no American dialect except that of the Gullah Negroes of the South Carolina and Georgia coast. A few departmental underlings even went all out for an equally phony British [ɑ], again in the wrong places, yielding [hɑt] and [hɑm] and [sɑnd], and all of them plumped for replacing the Midwestern [ɑ] of *cot* and *lot* with an exaggerated [ɔ]. Of course, Midwesterners ordering [hɔt hɑm 'sɑndwɪčɪz] are as suspect as counterfeit Confederate $3 bills. It is possible that some compulsive aspirants to social elegance docilely lapped up this pap; but those of us who were seriously concerned with English structure and usage laughed the program out of court and left the course, never to return. A second principle can be deduced from this experience: to imitate a dialect sharply different from one's own is a tricky and difficult assignment. A partial imitation is worse than none, since the change seems an affectation to one's neighbors, and the imperfect acquisition seems ridiculous to those whose speech is being imitated. Any attempts at teaching a standard dialect to those who speak a nonstandard one should be directed toward an attainable goal, toward one of the varieties of cultivated speech which the student might hear, day after day, in his own community.

At this point, perhaps, some of you may be muttering, "But what do these experiences have to do with dialects? I always thought that a dialect was something strange and oldfashioned." Many will share your opinion, especially in such countries as France and Italy, where an academy accepts one variety of the language as standard and casts the rest into outer darkness. In such countries the word *dialect* implies a variety of the language spoken by the rustic, the uneducated, the culturally isolated. To say that someone "speaks a dialect"—as one Italian professor patronizingly described one of the best soldiers working with me on our Italian military dictionary—is to exclude him forever from the company of educated men. For a dialect, to such intellectuals, is a form of the language they had rather be found dead than speaking.

True, there are other attitudes. Germans and Austrians make a distinction between the standard language—literary High German—and the dialects, local and predominantly rural forms of speech. But educated Germans do not always avoid dialect speech forms; in some areas, such as the Austrian Tyrol, an educated person will take particular pains to use some local forms in his speech, so as to identify himself with his home. The attitude may be a bit sentimental, but it does help to maintain one's individual dignity in a homogenizing world.

A more extreme attitude was prevalent in the Romantic Era. If the Augustans of the seventeenth and eighteenth centuries looked upon dialects as corruptions of an originally perfect language, the Romantics often alleged, in Wordsworth's terms, that people in humble and rustic life used "a purer and more emphatic language" than that to be met with in the cities. In this viewpoint, the dialects represent the pure, natural, unchanging language, unencumbered by the baggage of civilization. This attitude has long prevailed in Britain; even today the English Dialect Survey is heavily slanted toward archaic forms and relics and ignores modern innovations.

Nor are Americans wholly free from this attitude that a dialect is something archaic and strange. Time and again, a fieldworker for our Linguistic Atlas is told, "We don't speak no dialect around hyur; if you want *rale* dialect you gotta go down into Hellhole Swamp"—or up into Table Rock Cove, or at least across the nearest big river. To many of us, as my student Roger Shuy put it, a dialect is something spoken by little old people in queer out-of-the-way places.

When we become a little more sophisticated—as we must become on a cosmopolitan campus—we realize that cities as well as rural areas may differ in the ways in which their inhabitants talk. Thus we next conclude that a dialect is simply the way everybody talks but us and the people we grew up with; then, by force of circumstance, we realize that we speak a dialect ourselves. But at this point we still feel that a dialect is something regional or local. When we notice that people of our own community speak varieties of English markedly different from our own, we dismiss them as ignorant, or simply as making mistakes. After all, we live in a democratic society and are not supposed to have class markers in our speech. It is a very sophisticated stage that lets us recognize social dialects as well as regional ones—dialects just as natural, arising out of normal, everyday contacts.

By this time we have elaborated our definition of a dialect. It is simply a habitual variety of a language, regional or social. It is set off from all other such habitual varieties by a unique combination of language features: words and meanings, grammatical forms, phrase structures, pronunciations, patterns of stress and intonation. No dialect is simply good or bad in itself; its prestige comes from the prestige of those who use it. But every dialect is in itself a legitimate form of the language, a valid instrument of human communication, and something worthy of serious study.

But even as we define what a dialect is, we must say what it is not. It is different from slang, which is determined by vogue and largely distinguished by transient novelties in the vocabulary. Yet it is possible that slang may show regional or social differences, or that some regional and social varieties of a language may be particularly receptive to slang.

A dialect is also different from an argot, a variety of the language used by people who share a common interest, whether in work or in play. Everyone knows many groups of this kind, with their own peculiar ways of speaking and writing: Baptist preachers, biophysicists, stamp collectors, model railroad fans, Chicago critics, narcotic addicts, jazz musicians, safecrackers. But in the normal course of events a person adopts the language of such subcultures, for whatever part of his life it may function in, because he has adopted a particular way of life; he uses a dialect because he grows up in a situation where it is spoken. Again, some argots may show regional or social variations; the term *mugging*, to choose one example, is largely found on the Atlantic Seaboard; the sport has different designations in the Great Lakes region and on the Pacific Coast.

Nor are dialect differences confined to the older, pre-industrial segments of the vocabulary. Here European and American attitudes differ sharply. The late Eugen Dieth chided the editors of the *Linguistic Atlas of New England* for including such vocabulary items as window shades, the razor strop, and the automobile, such pronunciation items

as *library* and *postoffice* and *hotel,* on the ground that these are not
genuine dialect items. Yet if they have regional and social variants, as
all of these have in North American English, they warrant inclusion.
In my lifetime I have seen the *traffic circle* of the Middle Atlantic
States become the *rotary* of Eastern New England; the *service plaza*
of the Pennsylvania *Turnpike* become the *oasis* of the Illinois *Toll-
way;* the *poor boy* of New Orleans—a generous sandwich once confined to the Creole Gomorrah and its gastronautic satellites—appearing
as a *grinder* in upstate New York, a *hoagy* in Philadelphia, a *hero* in
New York City, a *submarine* in Boston. Nor will dialect terms be used
only by the older and less sophisticated: a Middle Western academi-
cian transplanted to MIT quickly learns to order *tonic* for his children,
not *soda pop,* and to send his clothes to a *cleanser.* And though some
would consider dialect a matter of speech and not of writing, one can
find regional and local commercial terms on billboards and television
as well as in the advertising sections of local newspapers.

Finally, dialect terms are not restricted to sloppy, irresponsible
usage—a matter of personality type rather than of specific vocabulary
items. And though regional and local terms and usages are likely to
appear most frequently in Joos' casual and intimate styles, the example of William Faulkner is sufficient evidence that they may be trans-
muted into the idiom of the greatest literature.

All of these comments are the fruit of centuries of observation, at
first casual and anecdotal, later more serious and systematic. The grim
test of the pronunciation *shibboleth,* applied by Jephthah's men to the
Ephraimites seeking to ford the Jordan, the comic representations of
Spartan and Theban speech by Aristophanes, the aspiration of the
Roman cockney Arrius-Harrius, immortalized by Horace, the Northern
English forms in the Reeves Tale—these typify early interest. With the
Romantic search for the true language in the dialects came the growth
of comparative linguistics, and the search for comparative dialect evidence in translations of the Lord's Prayer and the proverb of the
prodigal son. The search for comparable evidence led, in the 1870's, to
the monumental collections for Georg Wenker's *Deutscher Sprachatlas,*
later edited by Ferdinand Wrede and Walther Mitzka—44,251 responses, by German village schoolmasters, to an official request for
local dialect translations of forty-four sentences of Standard German.
Designed to elicit fine phonetic data, the collections proved notably
refractory for that purpose, but the sheer mass of evidence corrected
the unevenness of individual transcriptions. More important, the discovery that questions designed for one purpose may yield a different
but interesting kind of evidence—as *Pferd* proved useless for the

/p:pf/ consonant alteration in dialects where the horse is *Ross* or *Gaul*—was reflected in greater sophistication in the design and use of later questionnaires. Less happy was the effect on German dialectology, with later investigations, such as Mitzka's *Wortatlas,* sticking to correspondence techniques, a short questionnaire, an immense number of communities, and an expensive cartographic presentation of the data. But the *Sprachatlas* and *Wortatlas,* and the Dutch investigations modeled upon them, provided us with the evidence on which to determine their own defects.

A valuable innovation was made at the turn of the century in the *Atlas linguistique de la France,* directed by Jules Gilliéron. Correspondence questionnaires gave way to field interviews on the spot, in a smaller number of selected communities (some six hundred in this instance) with a longer questionnaire; a trained investigator interviewed a native of the community in a conversational situation and recorded his responses in a finely graded phonetic alphabet. As with the German atlas, however, the communities chosen were villages; larger places were first investivated in the Atlas of Italy and Southern Switzerland, under the direction of the Swiss scholars Karl Jaberg and Jakob Jud, who also introduced the practice of interviewing more than one informant in the larger communities. With certain refinements, then, the basic principles of traditional dialect study were established by World War I. Some subsequent investigations have followed Wenker, others Gilliéron; some, like the current Czech investigations, have combined both methods, relying primarily on field interviews but using correspondence surveys in the early stages, so that the selection of communities can be made most effectively. Only the British Isles have lagged, perhaps because Joseph Wright's *English Dialect Dictionary,* with its claim to have recorded ALL the dialect words of English, has erected a Chinese Wall worthy of Mr. Eliot's scorn. Not till the 1950's did any kind of field work get under way in either England or Scotland; in both countries it was handicapped by a shortage of funds and fieldworkers, and in England by an antiquarian bias that over-emphasized relics, shunned innovations, and neglected opportunities to provide data comparable to that obtained in the American surveys. Yet both Harold Orton in England and Angus McIntosh in Scotland have enriched our knowledge of English.

Perhaps because American linguists have kept in touch with European developments, the *Linguistic Atlas of New England,* launched in 1930, drew on the lessons of the French and Italian atlases. Although the transition from casual collecting to systematic study was not welcomed by all students, nevertheless—even with the Hoover Depres-

sion, World War II, the Korean intervention, and the tensions of the
Cold War—a respectable amount of progress has been made toward a
first survey of American English. *The Linguistic Atlas of New England*
was published in 1939-43; scholars are now probing for the changes
that a generation has brought. For four other regional surveys, field
work has been completed and editing is under way: (1) the Middle
and South Atlantic States, New York to central Georgia, with outposts
in Ontario and northeastern Florida; (2) the North-Central States:
Wisconsin, Michigan, southwestern Ontario, and the Ohio Valley; (3)
the Upper Midwest: Minnesota, Iowa, Nebraska, and the Dakotas;
(4) the Pacific Southwest: California and Nevada. Elsewhere, field
work has been completed in Colorado, Oklahoma, Washington, and
eastern Montana; respectable portions have been done in several
other states, Newfoundland, Nova Scotia, and British Columbia; with
a slightly different method the late E. Bagby Atwood produced his
memorable *Regional Vocabulary of Texas*. In all of these surveys the
principles of European dialect investigations have been adapted to
the peculiarities of the American scene. Settlement history has been
studied more carefully before field work, since English-speaking settlement in North America is recent, and its patterns are still changing.
At least three levels of usage are investigated—partly because cultivated American speech has regional varieties, just like uneducated
speech, and the cultivated speech of the future may be foreshadowed
in the speech of the intermediate group; partly because until very
recently general education has been a more important linguistic and
cultural force in the United States than in most of the countries of
Europe. Urban speech as well as rural has been investigated in each
survey, and intensive local investigations have been encouraged. The
questionnaires have included both relics and innovations. All of these
modifications were suggested by Hans Kurath, first Director of the
Atlas project, who is currently drawing on his experience in developing a new theory for the interpretation of dialect differences.

Just as warfare is still decided ultimately by infantrymen who can
take and hold territory, so dialect study still depends on competent
investigators who can elicit and record natural responses in the field.
The tape recorder preserves free conversation for later transcription
and analysis, and permits the investigator to listen repeatedly to a
response about whose phonetic quality he is in doubt; but the investigator must still ask the right questions to elicit pertinent data. He
must remember, for instance, that *chicken coop* is both a vocabulary
and a pronunciation item—that the pronunciation in the American
North and North Midland is /kup/, in the South and South Midland

/kvp/, that *coop* in the North designates the permanent shelter for the whole flock, in the South a crate under which a mother hen can scratch without an opportunity to lead the little ones off and lose them in the brush. The full record for such an item may require three or four questions, which only a human interviewer can provide.

But if the fieldworker remains essential, the objects of his investigation may change. Recent studies have turned increasingly to urban areas, urbanizing areas, and minority groups. To a long list of impressive early investigations one can now add such contributions as Lee Pederson's study of Chicago pronunciation and Gerald Udell's analysis of the changes in Akron speech resulting from the growth of the rubber industry and the consequent heavy migration from West Virginia. Among special groups investigated in detail are the Spanish-American bilinguals in San Antonio by Mrs. Janet Sawyer, the American Norwegians by Einar Haugen, the New York City Greeks by James Macris, the New England Portuguese by Leo Pap, the Chicago Slovaks by Mrs. Goldie Meyerstein, the Gullah Negroes by Lorenzo Turner, and the Memphis Negroes by Miss Juanita Williamson. In all of these studies the emphasis has been on the correlation between linguistic and social forces.

Another significant development has been the investigation of the way language attitudes are revealed by the choice among linguistic variants under different conditions. The most impressive work of this kind has been done by William Labov of Columbia University, in his study of the speech of the Lower East Side of New York. Limiting himself to a small number of items—the vowels of *bad* and *law,* the initial consonants of *think* and *then,* the /-r/ in *barn* and *beard*—phonological details that can be counted on to appear frequently and in a large number of contexts during a short interview, Labov gathers specimens of linguistic behavior under a wide range of conditions. At one end of the spectrum is the reading of such putatively minimal pairs as *bed* and *bad;* at the other is the description of children's games or the recounting of an incident when the informant thought he was going to be killed. The difference between pronunciations in the relaxed situation and those when the informant is on what he considers his best linguistic behavior is an index of his social insecurity. Almost as revealing is the work of Rufus Baehr with high-school students in the Negro slums of the Chicago West Side. It is no surprise that in formal situations the students with greater drive to break out of their ghetto reveal striking shifts of their speech in the direction of the Chicago middle-class norm. This kind of discovery should give heart to all who believe that a directed program of second-dialect teaching can make at least a small dent in our problems of providing a wider range of economic and educational opportunities for the aspiring young Negro.

Out of all these investigations two patterns emerge: (1) a better understanding of the origin and nature of dialect differences; (2) a set of implications for those who are interested in providing every American child with a command of the standard language adequate for him to go as far as his ability and ambition impel him.

No dialect differences can, as yet, be attributed to physiology or to climate. Perhaps anatomists will discover that some minor speech-differences arise from differences in the vocal organs; but so far there is no evidence for any correlation between anatomy and dialect, and the burden of proof is on those who propose such a correlation. As for climate: it is unlikely that nasality could have arisen (as often asserted) both from the dusty climate of Australia and the dampness of the Tennessee Valley. And though it is a favorite sport among Northerners to attribute the so-called "Southern drawl" to laziness induced by a hot climate, many Southerners speak with a more rapid tempo than most Middle Westerners, and the Bengali, in one of the most enervating tropical climates, speak still more rapidly. For an explanation of dialect differences we are driven back, inevitably, to social and cultural forces.

The most obvious force is the speech of the original settlers. We should expect that a part of the United States settled by Ulster Scots would show differences in vocabulary, pronunciation, even in grammar from those parts settled by East Anglians. We should expect to find Algonkian loans most common in those regions where settlers met Algonkian Indians, French loans most frequent in Louisiana and in the counties adjacent to French Canada, Spanish loans most widespread in the Southwest, German loans clustering in cities and in the Great Valley of Pennsylvania, and indubitable Africanisms most striking in the Gullah country.

Speech forms are also spread along routes of migration and communication. The Rhine has carried High German forms northward; the Rhone has taken Parisian forms to the Mediterranean; in the United States, the same kind of dissemination has been found in the valleys of the Mississippi, the Ohio, and the Shenandoah.

If speech forms may spread along an avenue of communication, they may be restricted by a physical barrier. As Kurath has observed, there is no sharper linguistic boundary in the English-speaking world than the Virginia Blue Ridge between the Potomac and the James.

The tidal rivers of the Carolinas, the swamps of the Georgia coastal plain, have contributed to making the Old South the most varied region, dialectally, in the English settlements of the New World.

The economic pattern of an area may be reflected in distinctive dialect features. *Fatwood,* for resin-rich kindling, is confined to the turpentine belt of the Southern tidewater; *lightwood,* with a similar referent, to the Southern coastal plain and lower Piedmont. *Case weather,* for a kind of cool dampness in which it is safe to cut tobacco, occurs over a wide area, but only where tobacco is a money crop. *To run afoul of,* a maritime phrase in the metaphorical sense of "to meet," seems to be restricted to the New England coast.

Political boundaries, when long established, may become dialect boundaries; in the Rhineland, pronunciation differences coincide strikingly with the boundaries of the petty states of pre-Napoleonic Germany. In the New World, on the other hand, political boundaries have seldom delimited culture areas. Yet *county site,* for the more usual *county seat,* is common in Georgia but unknown in South Carolina, and Ontario Canadians speak of the *reeve* as chief officer of a township, the *warden* as chief officer of a county, and a *serviette* instead of a table napkin—terms unfamiliar in the United States.

Each city of consequence may have its distinctive speech forms. The grass strip between the sidewalk and the curb, undesignated in South Carolina, is a *tree belt* locally in Springfield, Massachusetts (and hence unlabeled in *Webster's Third New International Dictionary*), a *tree lawn* in Cleveland, a *devil strip* in Akron, and a *boulevard* in Minneapolis and St. Paul. And only Chicagoans naturally refer to political influence as *clout,* or to a reliable dispenser of such influence as a *Chinaman.*

Nor are differences in the educational system without their effect. Where separate and unequal education is provided to particular social groups, we can be sure that a high-school diploma or even a college degree will be no indication by itself of proficiency in the standard language. That this problem is not confined to any single racial or cultural group has been shown by institutions such as West Virginia State College, which have undergone the process of reverse integration. This particular school, which once drew an elite Negro student body, is now eighty percent white, with the white students mostly from the disadvantaged mountain areas along the Kanawha. Since the teachers in the mountain schools are not only predominantly local in origin, but often have had little education beyond what the local schools offer, and then, since most of them habitually use many nonstandard forms, it has been difficult for the college to maintain its academic standards in the face of increasing white enrollment, however desirable integration may be.

Most important, perhaps, is the traditional class structure of a community. In a Midwestern small town, it is still possible for one brother to stay home and run a filling station, and another to go off and become a judge—and nobody mind. But in parts of the South there is a social hierarchy of families and occupations, so that it is more respectable for a woman of good family to teach in an impoverished small college than to do professional work for the government at twice the salary. Here, too, an aristocratic ideal of language survives, and the most cultivated still look upon *ain't* as something less reprehensible than incest—but use it only in intimate conversation with those whom they consider their social equals. Here too we find the cultural self-assurance that leads an intelligent lawyer to ask the linguistically naive question: "Why is it that the educated Northerner talks so much like the uneducated Southerner?"

If social differences among the WASP population are reflected in linguistic differences, we should not be surprised if similar differences among later immigrants are reflected in the extent of linguistic borrowing from particular foreign-language groups, or even from the same foreign-language group at different times. Our longest continuous tradition of borrowing with probably the largest and most varied kinds of words, is that from various kinds of German. Even the bitterness of two world wars cannot prevent us from seeing that of all foreign-language groups the Germans have been most widely distributed, geographically and socially, throughout the United States—as prosperous farmers, vaudeville comedians, skilled craftsmen, merchants, intellectuals. In contrast, the hundreds of thousands of Italian- and Slavic-speaking immigrants of the last two generations have left few marks on the American vocabulary; most of them were of peasant stock, often illiterate, and settled in centers of heavy industry as basic laborers.

Even more striking is the change in the incidence of Texas borrowings from Mexican Spanish. In her study of the bilingual situation in San Antonio, Mrs. Sawyer has shown that although early Spanish loans were numerous, quickly assimilated, and widely spread—*canyon, burro, ranch, lariat, broncho, silo* are characteristic examples—there have been few such loans in the last seventy years. The explanation is the drastic change in the relationships between Anglos and Latins. When English-speaking settlers first moved into Texas, they found the hacienda culture already established, and eagerly took over culture and vocabulary from the Latins who constituted the local elite. Anglo and Latin, side by side, died in the Alamo 4 March 1836 and conquered at San Jacinto seven weeks later. But since 1890 the Texan has encountered Mexican Spanish most often in the speech of unskilled laborers, including imported braceros and illegally entered wetbacks; derogatory labels for Latins have increased in Texas English, and loans from Spanish have declined. We borrow few words from those we consider our inferiors.

We can now make a few clear statements about the facts of American dialects, and their significance:

1. Even though much work remains to be done, we can describe in some detail most of the principal regional varieties of American English and many of the important subvarieties; we can indicate, further, some of the kinds of social differences that are to be found in various dialect areas, and many of the kinds that are to be found in some of the most important cities.

2. We can be sure that in many situations there are tensions between external norms and the expectations of one's associates. These tensions, most probably, are strongest in the lower middle class—a group anxious to forget humbler backgrounds but not sure of their command of the prestige patterns. Since the teaching profession, on all levels, is heavily drawn from the lower middle class, we can expect—as Marjorie Daunt found years ago—that anxiety is the characteristic attitude of the English teacher toward variations in usage. There is a strong urge to make changes, for the sake of making changes and demonstrating one's authority, without stopping to sort out the significance of differences in usage. This attitude is reflected in the two most widely known programs for teaching better English to the disadvantageed: a socially insignificant problem, such as the distinction between *Wales* and *whales,* is given the same value as the use of the marker for the third singular in the present indicative. Future programs should use the resources of the dialect archives, at least as a start, even though more detailed and more recent information may be necessary before one can develop teaching materials. The inevitable prescription in a pedagogical situation can be no better than the underlying description.

3. There is evidence that ambitious students in slum areas intuitively shift their speech patterns in the direction of the prestigious local pattern, in situations where they feel such a shift will be to their advantage. Some actually achieve, on their own, a high degree of functional bidialectalism, switching codes as the situation demands. In any teaching program it would seem intelligent to make use of this human facility.

4. The surest social markers in American English are grammatical forms, and any teaching program should aim, first of all, at developing a habitual productive command of the grammar of standard English—with due allowance for the possiblilty that the use of this grammar may be confined to formal situations in which the speaker comes in contact with the dominant culture.

5. Relatively few pronunciation features are clear social markers, though in many Northern cities there is a tendency to identify all Southern and South Midland pronunciations as those of uneducated rural Negroes. How much one should attempt to substitute local pronunciations for those which are standard in regions from which migrants come would probably depend on the extent to which variations in standard English are recognized and adapted in the community: Washington, for instance, may be more tolerant than New York. In any event, programs to alter pronunciation patterns should concentrate on those pronunciations that are most widely recognized as substandard.

6. Few people can really identify the race of a speaker by pronunciation and voice quality. In experiments in Chicago, middle-class Middle Westerners consistently identified the voice of an educated urban white Southerner as that of an uneducated rural Negro, and many identified as Negro the voice of an educated white Chicagoan. Similar experiments in New York have yielded similar results. And many white Southerners can testify to personal difficulties arising from this confusion in the minds of Northerners. In Ithaca, New York, I could not get to see any apartment advertised as vacant until I paid a personal visit; over the telephone I was always told that the apartments had just been rented; James Marchand, a Middle Tennessean now on the Cornell faculty, must carefully identify himself as "Professor Marchand," if he wants a garageman to come and pick up his car. And the telephone voice of my Mississippi-born chairman, Gwin Kolb, is racially misidentified with alarming regularity.

7. There can be no single standard in programs for the disadvantaged; the target dialect must vary according to the local situation. In Mississippi, the same program can be used for Negroes and whites, because they share most of the same grammatical deviations from the local standard, and share phonological patterns with that standard; in Cleveland, grammatical features in writing are sufficient to distinguish Negro college applicants from white better than ninety percent of the time, and deviations from local standard pronunciation are far more striking and numerous among Negroes than among locally-born disadvantaged whites.

8. To the suggestion that Southern Negroes should not be taught

local standard pronunciation, but some external standard—the hypothetical variety some call "network English"—there is a simple answer in the form of a question: "Do you want integration in the South?" The Southern patterns of race relations have suffered too long from too many separate standards for Negro and white; it would be ironical if those speaking most loudly in behalf of the aspirations of the Southern Negro should create new obstacles to those aspirations. The language problems of the uneducated Southern Negro are the language problems, even to fine detail, of the uneducated Southern white in the same community; the South may well solve the language problems in its schools before Detroit does. Once the races are brought into the same classroom, a community will need only one intelligent program based on a solid body of dialect evidence.

9. While we are planning language programs for our disadvantaged, we must educate the dominant culture in the causes and significance of dialect differences: it is particularly urgent that we educate teachers on all levels, from kindergarten through graduate school. The disadvantaged will have enough to do in learning new patterns of language behavior; the dominant culture must meet them part way, with greater understanding, with a realization that dialect differences do not reflect intellectual or moral differences, but only differences in experiences. Granted that this reeducation of the dominant culture is bound to be difficult, we should not be so cynical as to reject it, on the ground that it cannot take place. In an age when we are turning the heat off under the melting pot and accepting the cultural contributions of Americans with ancestral languages other than English, in an age when we are learning the art of peaceful coexistence with a variety of economic and political and cultural systems, it should not be difficult to extend this acceptance to fellow Americans of different cultural backgrounds and linguistic habits, and especially to recognize that cultured American English may be found in many regional and local varieties. It is a poor cultural tolerance that would accept all cultivated speech except that in other parts of our own country.

With my deep-ingrained horror of patent-medicine salesmen, I would not leave you with the impression that we already have all the answers, or even all the evidence we need to arrive at those answers. We need many more kinds of investigation, and we should like to think that John Fisher, with his unlimited license to stalk money-bearing animals, might help us conduct some of them. We are still to do even the preliminary surveys in such parts of the country as Tennessee and Arkansas; we need many more studies of the actual patterns of social dialects in most American cities. We really have no serious evidence on regional and social differences in such prosodic features as stress and pitch and juncture. The recognition of paralanguage— the non-linguistic modulation of the stream of speech—is so recent that we have no idea as to the kinds of regional and social rhythm, in range of pitch and stress, in drawl and clipping, in rasp and nasality and mellifluousness. We have not even begun to study regional and social variations in gesture and other kinds of body movement. But we do have a framework which we can fill in detail, continually building our teaching programs on solid research into the ways in which Americans communicate in various localities, and into the attitudes of specific speakers toward those whose usage differs from their own. In comparison with the immensity of our social problems, our linguistic knowledge is as a little candle in the forest darkness at midnight; let us not hide that candle under a basket, but put it in a lantern and use it to find our way.

Part II

Standard English: The Problem of Definition

Introduction

PHILIP B. GOVE

The third definition of the term *standard English* in *Webster's Third New International Dictionary* is: "the English that with respect to spelling, grammar, pronunciation, and vocabulary is substantially uniform though not devoid of regional differences, that is well-established by usage in the formal and informal speech and writing of the educated, and that is widely recognized as acceptable wherever English is spoken and understood." The first and second definitions are valid but narrow. They do not refer to the kind of English considered in this introduction and may be dismissed at once. The first reads "the English taught in schools," sometimes known as academic English, schoolroom English, or even schoolmarm English. This may be called a nineteenth-century notion of English, although there are still so many people who limit their understanding to it that it must be accepted as a definition, however inapplicable to the problem today. The second definition, "English that is current, reputable, and national," is an early twentieth-century handbook definition, setting up three criterions by which student composition may be tested. It does not help with any of the points needed to be made in the 1970s.

The third definition, however, reaches out to cover a language made up of many dialects and varieties. Professor Joos, in his article following, says "I speak Wisconsin dialect [in context, a dialectal variety

Dr. Philip B. Gove, author of numerous articles on usage and lexicography, is the Editor-in-Chief of the Merriam-Webster Dictionaries, G. & C. Merriam Company.

of standard English], with many borrowings from other dialects."
Practically all the names of the states of the United States and of the
shires and counties of Great Britain as well as the provinces of Canada
and the states and territories of Australia can modify the word *dialect*
in the same way. Sometimes the geographic designations include more
than one state; sometimes only a part. I can say, for example, that I
speak the dialect of New Hampshire, having been born and reared
there, but I am more likely to say that I speak Eastern New England
dialect, or even just Eastern, among those who I know would understand me.

It takes many different kinds of English to add up to standard English. No single dialect is coextensive with standard English and no one
person can command either in speaking or writing (or in both) all the
words and locutions of standard English. No individual is the community. Yet many a teacher of English has set up his own dialect—his idiolect—as something better than the standards of the community. And
many a literary pundit has made some forms of expression debatable
that are not, according to the evidence of usage, debatable at all. Either
one communicates successfully, that is, with responsibility, as Professors Joos and DeCamp explain this dimension of English, or he doesn't
communicate. There is no message. Since no one encompasses standard English, the purist (whether teacher or pundit) in self-protection
frowns upon many words and expressions that belong to the standard
English of others, that is, to a different dialectal variety. For example,
everyone has a tolerable informal synonym for the stuffy word *inebri-
ated*, say *tipsy* or *loaded* or *tight*. Since in our society being drunk is
usually connected with some kind of unpleasantness (reprehensible
lack of control) many words which aptly describe this condition are
considered unpleasant. One perspicacious critic pretended to be horri-
fied at finding that over a dozen of these synonyms for *drunk* are not
labeled *slang* in *Webster's Third* and, after setting them down one
after another in the same sentence, could come up with only an ineloquent *odzooks* followed by an equally ineloquent exclamation mark.
At that point he couldn't be sure what hat he was wearing.

Frowning on colloquialisms should have been stopped half a century
ago by a remark (whether apocryphal or not) of Harvard's great philol-
ogist, George Lyman Kittredge: "I myself speak 'colloke' and often
write it." The base of standard English is gradually widening to admit
more variety in language. As the number of native speakers of English increases and as the number of those completing high school inevitably climbs in percentage as well as in actual figures, standard
English includes more and more of what's possible.

There is a fourth definition of standard English in *Webster's Third* not yet quoted: "all words entered in a general English language dictionary that are not restricted by a label (as *slang, dial, obs, biol, Scot*)." (The label *dial* here refers to a different sense of the word than in such phrases as "Wisconsin dialect.") This raises the question of why dictionary makers have traditionally entered and defined words which they then restrict and condemn in some way. Professor Joos implies one answer when he says of *ain't* that it "has a home in English even if only a disadvantaged home." The editors of *Webster's Third* in the 1950s felt, on the basis of written quotations, that *clam up* meaning "become silent," that *bunch* meaning "a close-knit group of friends," and that *bug* meaning "to bother, annoy, irritate" have a home in English but slapped them down with a *slang* label. Now in the 1970s it is clear to a professional observer of language that the label should be removed from all three and from dozens more like them. A decade is hardly long enough for observing significant change in language but that observation does not justify the handbooks' repeating the same usage advice for half a century, at least. If you used in college a popular handbook of a generation or more ago, you might be surprised to discover that thirty or forty years later it is not much changed with respect to usage pronouncements. Spelling and grammar do change more slowly but some changes in word usage can easily be observed from decade to decade. It can be predicted that some slang words will become standard but which ones? There is no easy answer beyond saying that if a word is used significantly in the presence of standard English, it belongs in a dictionary of standard English, probably without a label. It may not be absurd to argue that standard English is to most of its ideally observable users—those who are unaware of their usage, those whose usage is a neuromuscular response—the language which a native user makes himself understood in as clearly as the situation requires. It may not always be good English, but good English and standard English are not always the same thing.[85]

Nor is the prestige dialect of the handbooks and of teachers trained by them always standard English. Professor Joos writes: "Every small child knows that this *may* (in *may I leave?*) is correct but not standard." It has not always turned out to meet the requirements of standard English. It has been bypassed by so many millions of educated— including college-educated—users of English that it, except in very limited situations, is almost a rarity. You can seldom find it consistently employed in magazines, newspapers, or books edited for educated readers. The verbal habits of students today do not always accord with the prestige dialect. The requirements for being included among the educated, as far as standard English dictates go, are not literary or formal or polite. Anyone who graduates from high school and gets out of it what high school is intended to give is likely to be one of the educated. Shortly before his death Ford Madox Ford wrote: "By the nineties, in fact, not only had the literary language become unusable by the common man the world over; it had become nauseous when it was not grotesque" (*Portraits from Life,* Cambridge, 1937, p. 210). Perhaps terms like "formal writing" should be abandoned, especially when the criterions are the stylebooks and the handbooks. There are formal people and informal people. The former cannot help being formal and usually make themselves look foolish when they try not to be. The informal should not be downgraded for not being formal.

None of the authors of the five articles which follow needs an introduction by me, and it ill becomes me to endorse their every remark about *Webster's Third.* They are all well-known published professional observers of language behavior. The late John S. Kenyon came to realize in the 1940s that he and many other language students had been confusing levels of speech with functional varieties. Few afterwards could ignore his published admission and reanalysis. Also he was among the first to call attention to what may now be called the radio-TV announcer problem: overemphasis on spelling pronunciation. From nearly every station you can hear a five-syllabled *controversial* or a *February* with an intrusive *r* in the second syllable. Professor Pyles ridicules gently but tellingly some of the linguistic folklore that guides well-known critics in "consistent avoidance of certain *pro*scribed constructions . . . and consistent employment of certain *pre*scribed ones," truck that is not needed for teaching the language of today. Any linguistic folklore that implies that the language of Walter Cronkite, Chet Huntley, Tom Wicker, John Chancellor, Eric Sevareid, Hugh Downs, Edwin Newman, Frank McGee, David Susskind, Harry Reasoner, or William F. Buckley, Jr., is superior to the language of Cab Calloway, Pearl Bailey, Ethel Merman, Dean Martin, Leslie Uggams, Harry Belafonte, Dionne Warwick, Art Linkletter, John Wayne, Jonathan Winters, or Bill Cosby is unrealistic. Whether a panel of "a hundred, even a thousand, self-appointed sages" can have any significant role in the making of a dictionary is a question every reader of this book can answer in his own way, perhaps with an assist from Professor Kilburn. If you are unable to read the sixty-two pages of Professor Joos' *Five Clocks,* a next best choice is his article on the community language, where you can become familiar with his ingenious five-step scales. Joos will tell you wherein a language is like a loaf of bread, will give you new light for distinguishing between the language of a member of the community and the community language, will explain to you lucidly why "the job of a standard is simply to be a standard" based on the analogy of a tipsy sailor, and will give you a new and unexpected definition of *education*. (What Joos says—in the fifth paragraph—about the wrong way to understand the "dimensions" of language does not invalidate the intent of DeCamp's title.) Finally, Professor DeCamp's article, the longest of these five, summarizes this complicated question of what standard English is and fills in something of the historical background. He suggests one ideal solution: "we should make Johnny bidialectal." But if all children were brought up to be bidialectal—or multidialectal—there would still be no single universally accepted dialect of standard English.

1

❦ English Usage:

The Views

of the Literati

THOMAS PYLES

There are few touchier subjects in the world than English usage. Those who think about it at all, if they are not professional linguists, are likely to feel almost as strongly about it as they do about God and the American Way of Life; and even a few professionals are from time to time subject to states of incalescence induced by what one would expect to be, after all, only their bread and butter. The lay observer, who may be, and nowadays frequently is, otherwise well educated, almost invariably fancies himself competent to make *ex cathedra* pronouncements concerning the speech which he speaks, writes, reads, and listens to almost constantly. Most professional students of language, by the time they have acquired a modicum of maturity, have learned not to question such pronouncements when they occur, as they often do, in ordinary social contexts. There is no more effective way of losing friends and alienating people than by knowing more about language than they do, particularly the language which they themselves speak and write. It is the better part of wisdom under such circumstances to avoid the subject as one would avoid religion, politics, and the cozier aspects of sex.

But occasionally one slips up, as even the late, great Leonard Bloom-

Thomas Pyles, Professor of English and Linguistics at Northwestern University, has written many articles on the English language and is the author of *Words and Ways of American English* and *The Origins and Development of the English Language*.

160

field did upon being informed by a "physician of good general background and education" that the Chippewa language had only a few hundred words. The doctor had acquired this information from a Chippewa Indian hunting guide, who really ought to have known, since his ancestors had almost certainly spoken the language fluently. Bloomfield, who, as everyone knows, was a distinguished student of American Indian languages, tried—to use his own ironic choice of words—to state the diagnostic setting," whereupon the physician "briefly and with signs of displeasure repeated his statement and then turned his back to me. A third person, observing this discourtesy, explained that I had some experience of the language in question. This information had no effect."[86] One wonders how the doctor of the story would have responded to a layman's diagnosis of some illness or other which might have been afflicting him—for it is a fact within my own sad experience that the medical diagnoses of laymen are just about as likely to be wrong as the linguistic lore of doctors. Without specialized training it is quite easy to diagnose influenza as poliomyelitis and vice versa; the fact is that I have been guilty of doing both.

Seldom does the lay linguist, who may incidentally be quite a distinguished writer, have any sort of rationale. "Good English" may be, from his point of view, quite easy of attainment, since it involves only the consistent avoidance of certain *pro*scribed constructions—split infinitives, dangling modifiers, terminal prepositions, and the like—and the consistent employment of certain *pre*scribed ones: the supposedly proper *shall-will* distinction, "the reason is that" rather than the somewhat commoner and more idiomatic "the reason is because," and the like. This is very democratic, in that it puts good speech within the reach of every man intelligent enough to master a few simple rules. It becomes even easier in view of the patent fact that many who sit in judgment on the speech of their neighbors are addicted to only a few such prescriptions; they have usually forgotten the others learned in high school and in English 1. What they have remembered, however, furnishes a bludgeon with which to belabor those who in their opinion use "bad English." In other words, not every *only*-snooper—to use Sir Ernest Gower's apt phrase for those who set out to pillory every instance of what they suppose to be a misplaced *only*—is also a split-infinitive sleuth; and many a *due to* bloodhound is quite impervious to the supposed bad grammar of split infinitives—he may in fact split them wide open himself without being aware of any relapse from the strictest principles of linguistic hygiene. As I have pointed out elsewhere C. S. Forester characterizes as a vulgar fellow a certain copy writer to whom "split infinitives and 'different to's' meant nothing," but himself uses in the same novel "cannot help but" (p. 124), "Everyone . . . fidgeted in their chairs" (p. 127), and "why his voice changed was because he was not at all sure that [his decision] was a wise one" (p. 151)—all constructions which are stigmatized by school grammars and handbooks of good English.[87]

Indeed the lay linguist—and those who are themselves writers are naturally likely to be more vociferous than the less articulate—is quite likely to deliver jeremiads over his particular linguistic *bête noire,* like the well-known diatribe of Professor Sheridan Baker in *College English* against a harmless and historically quite respectable contraction of *am not* which is to him an especially dirty four-letter word.[88] Attitudes toward language being thus permeated—and they usually are—with the same sort of emotionalism as pertains naturally to God, the home, the American mother, and the flag, it has become practically impossible for the professional observer of language to make a factual statement about a given locution without its being misunderstood as either a recommendation or, less frequently, a condemnation of the locution in question. In the opinion of so brilliant a scholar and writer as Professor John Nash Douglas Bush, those of us who do so belong to "a tribe of linguistic scholars who proclaim that there is no such thing as good or bad English: whatever is used is right," going on to say that "This ultra-democratic gospel was supported a few years ago by a new edition of Webster; there were some persons who vehemently denounced the abandonment of any standard, but their voices did not carry very far"—which seems to me to be the prize understatement of the year.[89] If the linguist so much as points out that "he, she, it don't" occurs quite frequently in the speech of cultivated speakers in the works of George Bernard Shaw, W. S. Gilbert, and other writers of an earlier period, this is taken as indicating a conviction on his part that present-day schoolchildren should be indoctrinated and drilled in the use of third-person singular *don't.* Actually, the student of usage is quite cognizant of the widespread unreasoning prejudice against this alternate contraction of *does not,* and merely intends to make the point that, though now old-fashioned, the form cannot be considered "bad English."

It is obvious from a good many pronouncements on language scattered throughout his *The Last Puritan* (New York, 1936) that even so sophisticated and learned a writer as George Santayana gave himself a good deal of concern over purity and impurity as linguistic characteristics. There is, for instance, Dr. Peter Alden's wish that his son's English should be "fundamentally pure"; he goes on to say: "Did it ever strike you how little we are affected by the servants' way of talking, though we hear it every day of our lives? It's because we recognise it for a dialect apart, which is not our own. That's the way anyone to whom good English is not natural must regard the common speech of the day" (p. 80).

In other words, Dr. Alden, whose linguistic judgments can fairly be taken to reflect those of his distinguished creator, believed that educated speech was pure, common speech impure. If *pure* means 'conservative, uncontaminated,' as I take it to mean here rather than being merely an endorsement of the type of speech Dr. Alden (and Santayana) happened to prefer, then it is noteworthy that from the point of view of the historical linguist precisely the opposite is true. For the folk, if they but knew the facts and were in the least interested in defending themselves from the charge of having messed up the language by adding supposed impurities of one sort or another—a charge which most of them would doubtless humbly accept as true—might with a good deal of reason point out that they have retained many characteristics of the earlier and presumably "pure" English of Alfred, Chaucer, Shakespeare, and Milton which we who speak the current Standard have lost. Every student of dialect is well aware of the fact that the folk have made very few innovations, and that it is the taboo against nonstandard constructions which is usually the innovation rather then the constructions themselves.

Subservience to, or at least faith in, the traditional school discipline in English is a very notable and potent characteristic of American English. Teacher knows best in such matters as correct grammar, though she may be regarded as a complete booby and a crashing bore in all other departments. Witness this statement of Mr. J. Donald Adams concerning the present deplorable state of the language and his remedy for it:

> Some of the editors in our leading publishing houses are apparently as ignorant of the fundamentals of good English as the writers over whose copy they labor. If you think this an unfounded assertion, open at random, as I often do, a batch of newly hatched books, particularly those known as "creative writing," and read a few pages carefully. Often they would not have passed muster by the nineteenth-century schoolmarm of the little red schoolhouse enshrined in American memory. . . . For one Maxwell Perkins, to name the already classic example of a literate book editor, there are at least two or three men or women holding editorial posts who should be sent to night school. Those who exhibit some knowledge of and regard for good English are not unlikely the beneficiaries of the training provided by some exacting newspaper editor who himself had the benefit of an instructor free of hifalutin theories.[90]

Mr. Adams has long been a crusader for what he considers the good English of the little red schoolhouse. Elsewhere he has indicated the desirability of an "armed uprising among the Parent-Teacher Associations all over the United States" which would "demand and get the scalps of those so-called educators whose indefensible doctrines are rapidly producing a generation of American illiterates." These murderers of grammar, the so-called educators referred to by Mr. Adams, are doubtless to be identified with the "structural linguists" so vigorously lambasted by Mr. Dwight Macdonald in his notorious review of *Webster's Third* in the *New Yorker* of March 10, 1962. Those who in former days would have brandished their hickory sticks and their blue-backed spellers in "the little red schoolhouse enshrined in American memory " have been demoralized most, Mr. Adams feels, by the National Council of Teachers of English, which he believes to be the official organ of the grammar-murderers. The attitudes and activities of this subversive organization, he declares, "constitute one of the chief threats to the cultivation of good English in our schools."[91]

By virtue of the fact that they supply the data on which the scholar's conclusions about usage are based, one would expect successful literary men and women to take a somewhat cavalier attitude toward the matter of correctness. (I leave out of the question the semiliterate writers mentioned by Mr. Adams; I seldom, if ever, come upon their books.) On the contrary, many seem to regard it as the be-all and end-all of good writing. They are, in fact, even more puristic than most teachers nowadays, for even the backwoods ma'am, if there still be any such, must have felt some impact of the scholarly study of usage; or, as Mr. Adams would interpret the matter, even she has to some extent been corrupted by the National Council of Teachers of English.

Let us examine a few other linguistic pronouncements from well-known professional writers, though actually some of these dicta would be more accurately termed stylistic than linguistic. All, however, are concerned with what the writers would think of as "good English."

Thus Edmund Wilson, who self-righteously declares "I never use Webster," apparently referring to *Webster's Third*, takes a writer severely to task because "he habitually uses 'transpire' as if it meant 'occur,'" though the word has meant just that, among other things, for the better part of two hundred years. The fact that the newer meaning arose from misunderstanding is quite irrelevant as far as its present status is concerned, for many unquestionably standard constructions began as blunders. Whether or not one chooses to use *transpire* in this sense is one's own affair, and hardly a gauge of one's ability as a writer. I may say parenthetically that I have never so used it and never intend to; but my eschewal is purely a personal and stylistic matter, having no validity in lexicography or in linguistics. Word choice is, after all, a matter of style.

It is not surprising that Wilson should share the horror of many other lay linguists over *disinterestedness* in the sense 'lack of interest.' This is a usage which I personally have no more love for than do Dean Jacques Barzun and Professor Mario Pei, but it does seem to have been used by a good many distinguished people, including the hapless author who is Wilson's reviewee—a former ambassador to the Soviet Union, visiting professor at Oxford, member of the Institute for Advanced Studies at Princeton, and president of the National Institute of Arts and Letters—whose knuckles Wilson duly raps.[92]

Professor Mark Schorer, who is of considerable eminence as both teacher and writer, has declared, in reference to *Webster's Third:* "I frankly prefer the old dictionary, speaking not only as a teacher, but as a writer. Granted, language changes. But I don't see any great advantage in trying to hurry it along that way. They accept anything, because it is used."[93] As for Mr. Schorer's magnanimous acceptance of the fact of linguistic change, one is reminded of what Carlyle, or Emerson, or Thoreau, or some other good gray person is reported to have said to Margaret Fuller when she vouchsafed the information that she accepted the universe: "By gad, Margaret, you'd better." As for the preference for the "old dictionary," that is, the *New International* of 1934, Professor Bergen Evans has well said, "Anyone who solemnly announces . . . that he will be guided in matters of English usage by a dictionary published in 1934 is talking ignorant and pretentious nonsense."[94]

Let us examine a few more specimens from my florilegium of linguistic pronouncements by professional writers. The critic Brendan Gill, reviewing in the *New Yorker* a motion picture dealing with the life of Christ, has this to say: "My respect for Christianity and good grammar obliges me to call attention to the fact that among the phrases . . . put into the mouth of Christ is the barbarism 'different than.'"[95] Leaving the mouth of Christ out of the question, this particular barbarism has, according to the *OED,* also issued from the pens of Fuller, Addison, Steele, DeFoe, Richardson, Goldsmith, Fanny Burney, Coleridge, Southey, DeQuincey, Carlyle, Thackeray, Newman, Dean Trench, and others of comparable distinction in English literature who, unlike Brendan Gill, were unaware that it was a barbarism.

Equally magisterial is Miss Dorothy Parker, who has declared that "any one who, as does [Henry] Miller, follows 'none' with a plural verb . . . should assuredly not be called writer."[96] The usage in question is first recorded in the ninth century in the writings of Alfred the Great. More recent occurrences cited by the *OED*, which points out that the plural usage is "now the commoner . . . the sing.[ular] being expressed by *no one*," are from the writings of such nonwriters as Dryden, Goldsmith, Burke, and Southey; and Otto Jespersen adds occurrences from St. Thomas More, Shakespeare, Dr. Johnson ("None are wretched but by their own fault"), Scott, Charlotte Brontë, Ruskin, Morris, Shaw, Stevenson, and Kipling.

It is noteworthy that both Mr. Gill and Miss Parker have managed to out-Fowler Fowler, whose *Dictionary of Modern English Usage* echoes the comment of the *OED* regarding plural *none* and adds that "It is a mistake to suppose that the pronoun is singular only and must at all costs be followed by singular verbs etc."[97] As for what ought to follow *different,* Fowler says unequivocally—though in so doing he misplaces *only* by all decent little red schoolhouse standards—"That d[*ifferent*] can only be followed by *from* & not by *to* is a SUPERSTITION" (1st ed., p. 113), *to* being in this construction perhaps somewhat more usual than *than* in current British English. Fowler's reviser, however, adds that "*different than* is sometimes preferred by good writers to the cumbersome *different from that which* etc. . . ." (2nd ed., p. 621). It is to be hoped that my disclosure of these grammatical defections of H. W. Fowler and Sir Ernest Gowers will not lay them open to the charge of being "permissive."

That good writers like Professor Schorer, Professor Bush, Mr. Wilson, Mr. Gill, and Miss Parker should believe so sincerely in the linguistic folklore which they promulgate is not really surprising to the linguist, who is quite aware of lay attitudes toward his craft and its ineffable mysteries—even if the lay commentators are talented creative writers and hence, in my candid opinion, far more important than mere linguists. Certainly Miss Parker, to cite an example, must often have encountered plural *none* in the writings of those whose claims to be called writers she would, it is hoped, readily admit to be at least equal to her own; and Mr. Brendan Gill must likewise often have come upon *different than* and *different to* in what he would consider nonbarbaric writing. The fact seems to be—for I can think of no other reasonable explanation—that, unlike the scholarly drudge, who has been trained to observe such phenomena, they simply fail to notice carefully much of the time. But, even if they were indeed careful observers of the facts of English usage, it is likely that the traditional arbitrary appeal to some sort of supposed grammatical logic (*than* goes with compartives, and *different* is no comparative) or to history and etymology (*none* was in the beginning singular and ought still to be) would impress them more strongly than the evidence of their own eyes and ears; so that it is probably just as well that they are unaware of the currency in high places of most of the constructions which they set out to discredit.

It is, I suspect, highly doubtful that anyone writes anything worth reading just by following rules, or that the difference between good writing and bad writing is anything so simple as this. Nevertheless, some of our literati would seem to think so. Mr. Clifton Fadiman, for instance, in a piece of direct-mail advertising sent out by the Book-of-the-Month Club offering Fowler's aforementioned *Modern English Usage* as a "book-dividend," has testified that the book in question, characterized as "the final arbiter of our language," "shows me how bad a writer I am, and encourages me to do better."

Now, no one could deny that Clifton Fadiman has been a prolific and highly successful writer, and most people, including myself, would think of him as a rather good one as well. Perhaps he is here overawed by the Fowlerian charisma; perhaps he is unconsciously reflecting the humility of the New York *Times* as quoted in the same advertisement: "The most practiced writer will only too often find himself convicted of sin when he dips into Fowler."

The need for what is thought of as authority—a need which, as we have just seen, is filled in part by works like Fowler's and in part by Mr. J. Donald Adams's Miss Fidditch fiddling away in her little red schoolhouse—is the motivation for many of the ill-informed attacks upon *Webster's Third.* This monument of American scholarship has been so much in the news since its publication in 1961 that I shall here limit myself to a single, but highly typical, reaction other than that of Professor Schorer, which has previously been alluded to. The reactor in this instance is Dr. Max Rafferty; the *Dr.* always precedes his name in the byline of his newspaper columns dealing with educational topics of one sort or another. Dr. Rafferty has been Superintendent of Public Instruction for the State of California since 1963. His concept of lexicography is one which not even Samuel Johnson, who never called himself doctor, would have approved, but it is still very widespread: "If a dictionary doesn't exist to set standards and maintain them, what possible use can it have? I don't know about you, but when I go to a dictionary I want to know what's right. I already know what folks ARE saying; what I want to know is what they SHOULD be saying." What Dr. Rafferty regards as the current "trend toward lexicographical futility" is, in his opinion, "just one phase in the decline of our language." (Florida Times-Union, June 7, 1965, p. 6.)

Such notions as those of Dr. Rafferty may be linguistically untenable, but none of us can deny that they are tenacious. It is obvious that the good doctor believes in some absolute, God-given set of standards which have nothing in particular to do with actual usage, that is, with "what folks ARE saying." (Incidentally, I would not have said *folks* if I had meant just people—not because I regard the word as "incorrect," but because I regard the concept of folksiness as both corny and phony. But this is purely a personal matter appertaining to style, and I voice no criticism of Dr. Rafferty's use of the term. If that's what he wanted to say, that's what he should have said.) Apparently Dr. Rafferty also believes that certain folks—namely, dictionary folks— know what other folks ought to say, and that the dictionary folks are shirking their duty—nay, their responsibility—when they don't let him in on their private information, presumably derived from a linguistic Jahveh with whom they have been fortunate enough or gifted enough to establish contact.

Because the world is so full of a number of people who have presumably acquired their knowledge of linguistics either by afflatus or by osmosis, the lot of the professional student, traditionally a neck-shaven drudge who finds it necessary to do a great deal of home-work, is oftentimes hard. Though he does not presume to instruct engineers, naturopaths, or for that matter creative writers for whom he may have tremendous respect in their respective crafts, he can hardly be blamed for his discouragement over the fact that they seem to know, or at least are given credit for knowing, so much more about language than he does, and can speak so much more authoritatively concerning it than he can.

In condemning what Sterling Andrus Leonard called "the old purist junk," we are not beating a dead dog. Antiquated attitudes based on arbitrary appeals to logic, reason, and often traditional prejudice are still very much with us; indeed, they seem to me to be very viable. "Yet the old schooling sticks," as Browning's Fra Lippo Lippi complained. Furthermore, as we have seen, such attitudes are by no means confined to the badly educated and the *petit bourgeois;* as often as not, they are held as tenets of linguistic faith by the highly literate and in some instances by the brilliantly creative and talented.

Because he is usually, at least externally, a calm fellow with little capacity for passion over matters of usage, the linguist is likely to be accused of assuming an Olympian attitude, of being "permissive" (one of the most damning of adjectives in this glorious era of our Great Republic), or of maintaining that, as far as the English language goes, anything goes. The fact is, I believe, that those of us not gifted either by afflatus or osmosis are not likely to learn much that is really worth knowing about man's greatest accomplishment—that is, language—if we succumb to the allurement of making vague, glamorized, pseudo-philosophical generalizations about English usage. To do so in sufficiently authoritative tones is the surest route to linguistic mahatmadom, as Dean Barzun, Professor Pei, Mr. Dwight Macdonald, the late Wilson Follett, and other popular pundits have discovered. Nevertheless, the supposed obtuseness of the professional grammarian is such that he will doubtless go on adding one to one in his unglamorous way; and, though he may never contribute anything of much importance to the Great Society in which we are privileged to live, let alone settling *hoti's* business or unraveling the mysteries of the enclitic *de,* he will doubtless stubbornly insist upon going on in his own way, with all his human limitations, examining the evidence on what folks—to use Dr. Rafferty's darling homespunism—say and write. What they ought to say and write must be decided by those who are presumably more gifted than he. As we all know, their name is Legion.

2

❧ Cultural Levels and Functional Varieties of English

JOHN S. KENYON

The word *level,* when used to indicate different styles of language, is a metaphor, suggesting higher or lower position and, like the terms *higher* and *lower,* figuratively implies 'better' or 'worse,' 'more desirable' or 'less desirable,' and similar comparative degrees of excellence or inferiority in language.

The application of the term *level* to those different styles of language that are not properly distinguished as better or worse, desirable or undesirable, creates a false impression. I confess myself guilty of this error along with some other writers. What are frequently grouped together in one class as different levels of language are often in reality false combinations of two distinct and incommensurable categories, namely, *cultural levels* and *functional varieties.*

Among *cultural levels* may be included, on the lower levels, illiterate speech, narrowly local dialect, ungrammatical speech and writing, excessive and unskillful slang, slovenly and careless vocabulary and construction, exceptional pronunciation, and, on the higher level, language used generally by the cultivated, clear, grammatical writing, and pronunciations used by the cultivated over wide areas. The different cultural levels may be summarized in the two general classes *substandard* and *standard.*

John S. Kenyon, late Professor of the English language at Hiram College, served as a consulting editor for the Merriam-Webster Dictionaries and was the co-author of the important book *A Pronouncing Dictionary of American English.*

Among *functional varieties* not depending on cultural levels may be mentioned colloquial language, itself existing in different degrees of familiarity or formality, as, for example, familiar conversation, private correspondence, formal conversation, familiar public address; formal platform or pulpit speech, public reading, public worship; legal, scientific, and other expository writing; prose and poetic belles-lettres. The different functional varieties may roughly be grouped together in the two classes *familiar* and *formal* writing or speaking.

The term *level*, then, does not properly belong at all to functional varieties of speech—colloquial, familiar, formal, scientific, literary language. They are equally "good" for their respective functions, and as classifications do not depend on the cultural status of the users.

The two groupings *cultural levels* and *functional varieties* are not mutually exclusive categories. They are based on entirely separate principles of classification: *culture* and *function*. Although we are here principally concerned with the functional varieties of standard English (the highest cultural level), yet substandard English likewise has its functional varieties for its different occasions and purposes. Thus the functional variety colloquial English may occur on a substandard cultural level, but the term *colloquial* does not itself designate a cultural level. So the functional variety formal writing or speaking may occur on a lower or on a higher cultural level according to the social status of writer or speaker, and sometimes of reader or audience. It follows, for instance, that the colloquial language of cultivated people is on a higher cultural level than the formal speech of the semiliterate or than some inept literary writing.

Semiliterate formal speech is sometimes heard from radio speakers. I recently heard one such speaker solemnly announce, "Sun day will be Mother's Day." Because the speaker, in his ignorance of good English, thought he was making himself plainer by using the distorted pronunciation *sun day* instead of the standard pronunciation *sundy,* he was actually misunderstood by some listeners to be saying, "Some day will be Mother's Day." About forty years ago the great English phonetician Henry Sweet used this very example to show that "we cannot make words more distinct by disguising them."[98] He was referring to the use, as in this instance, of the full sound of vowels in unaccented syllables where standard English has obscure vowel. On the same page Sweet gives another example of the same blunder: "Thus in the sentence *I shall be at home from one to three* the substitution of tuw for tə [ə = the last sound in *sofa*] at once suggests a confusion between the preposition and the numeral." This was also verified on the radio. Not long ago I heard a radio speaker announce carefully, "This program will be heard again tomorrow from one two three." I have also recorded (among many others) the following such substandard forms from the radio: *presidEnt* for the standard form *presidənt*, the days of the week ending in the full word *day* instead of the standard English syllable *-dy*, *ay man* for the correct *ə man*, *cahnsider* for *cənsider*, *tooday* for *təday*, *too go* for *tə go*. *Coalumbia* for *Cəlumbia*, etc. This is merely one sort among many of substandard features in the formal speech of the semiliterate.

To begin my strictures at home, in *American Pronunciation* (9th ed., 4th printing, p. 17), I use the page heading "Levels of Speech." This should be "Functional Varieties of Standard Speech," for the reference is solely to the different uses of speech on the one cultivated level. Similarly, in the Kenyon-Knott *Pronouncing Dictionary of American English* (p. xvi, § 2), I carelessly speak of "levels of the colloquial" where I mean "styles of the colloquial," as three lines above. For though there are different cultural levels of colloquial English, the reference here is only to standard colloquial.

S. A. Leonard and H. Y. Moffett, in their study, "Current Definition of Levels in English Usage", say (p. 348): "The levels of English usage have been most clearly described in Dr. Murray's Preface ["General Explanations, p. xvii] to the *New English Dictionary*.[99] I have varied his diagram a little in order to illustrate better the overlapping between the categories." It appears to me that Leonard and Moffett have so varied the diagram as to obscure Murray's intention. For he is not here primarily exhibiting levels of speech but is showing the 'Anglicity,' or limits of the English vocabulary for the purposes of his dictionary. The only topical divisions of his diagram that imply a cultural level are "slang" and "dialectal," and the only statement in his explanation of the diagram that could imply it is, "Slang words ascend through colloquial use." This may imply that slang is on a lower cultural level than "colloquial, literary, technical, scientific, foreign." We may also safely infer that Murray would place "Dialectal" on a lower level than colloquial and literary if he were here concerned with cultural levels. Murray's diagram rests consistently on the same basis of classification throughout ('Anglicity'), and he emphasizes that "there is absolutely no defining line in any direction [from the central nucleus of colloquial and literary]." Moreover, Murray's exposition here concerns only vocabulary, with no consideration of the other features that enter so largely into "levels" of language—grammatical form and structure, pronunciation, spelling, and meaning—of styles, in short, only so far as they are affected by vocabulary. These he treats of elsewhere but without reference to levels.

It is not quite clear just how far Leonard and Moffett intend their grouping "literary English," "standard, cultivated, colloquial English," and "naïf, popular, or uncultivated English" to be identical with what they call Murray's "levels," his description of which they commend. But it is clear that they call their own grouping "three levels of usage" (p. 357) and classify them together as a single descending scale (cf. "the low end of the scale," p. 358). The inevitable impression that the average reader receives from such an arrangement of the scale is: Highest level, literary English; next lower level, colloquial English; lowest level, illiterate English; whereas, in fact, the first two "levels" are functional varieties of the one cultural level standard English, while the third ("illiterate or uncultivated," p. 358) is a cultural level.

Krapp has a chapter on "The Levels of English Speech," in which he reveals some awareness of the confusion of cultural levels with functional varieties. He says:

> Among those who pay any heed at all to convention in social relationships, a difference of degree is implicit in all use of English. This difference of degree is usually thought of in terms of higher and lower, of upper levels of speech appropriate to certain occasions of more formal character, of lower levels existing, if not necessarily appropriate, among less elevated circumstances. These popular distinctions of level may be accepted without weighting them too heavily with significance in respect of good, better, and best in speech. A disputatious person might very well raise the question whether literary English, ordinarily regarded as being on a high level, is really any better than the spoken word, is really as good as the spoken word, warm with the breath of the living moment.[100]

At the risk of having to own the hard impeachment of being disputatious, I must express the fear that the logical fallacy in treating of levels, which Krapp rather lightly waves aside, is having a serious effect on general ideas of speech levels, and especially of the significance of colloquial English in good usage. Krapp's grouping, frankly on a scale of "levels" throughout, constitutes a descending scale from the highest, "Literary English," through "Formal Colloquial," "General Colloquial," "Popular English," to the lowest, "Vulgar English." Here the fallacy is obvious: Literary English, Formal Colloquial, and General Colloquial are not cultural levels but only functional varieties of English all on the one cultural level of standard English. The last two, Popular English and Vulgar English, belong in a different order of classification, cultural levels, without regard to function.

So in his succeeding discussion *level* sometimes means the one, sometimes the other; now a functional variety of standard English, and now a cultural level of substandard or of standard English. It is functional on page 58 ("a choice between two levels") and on page 60 ("level of general colloquial"), cultural on page 62 ("popular level" and "cultivated level") and on pages 63–64 ("popular level," "level of popular speech"), functional on page 64 ("general colloquial level"), cultural again on the same page ("popular level," "still lower level"), cultural on page 67 ("vulgar . . . level of speech," "applying the term 'vulgar' to it at certain levels"), cultural on page 68 ("its own [popular] level"), cultural and functional in the same phrase on page 68 ("speakers from the popular and the general colloquial level meet and mix"), and so on most confusingly to page 75.

The same kind of mixture of cultural levels and functional varieties is thrown into one apparently continuous scale by Kennedy: "There is the formal and dignified language of the scholarly or scientific address or paper. . . . The precision and stateliness of this uppermost level . . . is a necessary accompaniment of thinking on a high plane." Next in order he mentions colloquial speech, which he refers to as "the second level, . . . generally acceptable to people of education and refinement."[101] Clearly this is not a cultural level but a functional variety of standard English, like the "uppermost level." The third level is, however, a cultural one: "the latest slang," workmen's "technical slang and colloquialisms which other persons cannot comprehend," "grammatical solecisms." "The speech of this third level can fairly be ranked as lower in the social scale." His fourth level is also cultural: "At the bottom of the scale is the lingo, or cant, of criminals, hobos, and others of the lowest social levels."

Finally, Kennedy fixes the false mental image of a continuous and logically consistent descent from "the cold and lonely heights of formal and highly specialized scientific and scholarly language" to "the stupid and slovenly level of grammatical abuses and inane slang." In reality there is no cultural descent until we reach his third "level," since "formal and dignified language" and "colloquial speech" are only functional varieties of English on the one cultural level of standard English.

In Perrin's excellent and useful *Index,* under the heading "Levels of Usage," he names "three principal levels": "Formal English" (likened to formal dress), "Informal English" (described as "the typical language of an educated person going about his everyday affairs"), and "Vulgate English."[102] From his descriptions it appears clearly that Formal and Informal English are functional varieties of standard English, while Vulgate is a substandard cultural level. A similar classification appears in his table on page 365.

On page 19 Perrin uses *level* apparently in the sense of functional variety, not of cultural level: "Fundamentally, good English is speaking or writing in the level of English that is appropriate to the particular situation that faces the speaker or writer. It means making a right choice among the levels of usage." His advice, however, involves two choices: (1) choice of a standard cultural level and (2) choice of the appropriate functional variety of that level.

A clear instance of the inconsistent use of the term *level* is found in Robert C. Pooley's *Teaching English Usage* (New York, 1946), chapter iii, "Levels in English Usage." He names five levels: (1) the illiterate level; (2) the homely level; (3) standard English, informal level; (4) standard English, formal level; and (5) the literary level. In (1) and (2) *level* has an altogether different meaning from that in (3), (4), and (5). In the first two *level* plainly means 'cultural level'; in the last three it just as plainly means 'functional variety of standard English,' all three varieties being therefore on the one cultural level of standard English. So *level* in the two groups belongs to different orders of classification. All misunderstanding and wrong implication would be removed from this otherwise excellent treatment of levels if the last three groups were labeled "Standard English Level, Informal Variety"; "Standard English Level, Formal Variety"; and "Standard English Level, Literary Variety." Pooley's groups contain three cultural levels (illiterate, homely, standard) and three functional varieties of the standard cultural level (informal, formal, literary).

The misapplication to colloquial English of the term *level*, metaphorically appropriate only to cultural gradations, is especially misleading. We often read of English that is "on the colloquial level." For example, Krapp writes: "*Who do you mean?* . . . has passed into current spoken use and may be accepted on the colloquial level."[103] This implies that colloquial English is on a different cultural level from formal English (literary, scientific, etc.), and a too frequent assumption, owing to this and other misuses of the term *colloquial*, is that its cultural level is below that of formal English. This supposition, tacit or explicit, that colloquial style is inferior to formal or literary style, leads inescapably to the absurd conclusion that, whenever scientists or literary artists turn from their formal writing to familiar conversation with their friends, they thereby degrade themselves to a lower social status.

This misuse of *level* encourages the fallacy frequently met with of contrasting colloquial with standard English, logically as fallacious as contrasting white men with tall men. For instance, Mencken writes:

"'I have no doubt *but* that'. . . seems to be very firmly lodged in colloquial American, and even to have respectable standing in the standard speech."[104] This contrast, not always specifically stated, is often implied. For example, Kennedy writes: "Colloquial English is, properly defined, the language of conversation, and especially of familiar conversation. As such it may approximate the standard speech of the better class of English speakers, or it may drop to the level of the illiterate and careless speaker."[105] *May approximate* should be replaced by *may be on the level of*.

Similarly, on page 440: "Some measure words [are] still used colloquially without any ending in the plural . . . ; but most of these are given the *s* ending in standard English usage." Here *standard* is confused with *formal*.

Kennedy (pp. 534, 616) several times contrasts colloquial English with "standard literary English." This implies that colloquial English is not standard, while literary English is. If he means to contrast standard colloquial with standard literary, well and good; but I fear that most readers would understand the contrast to be of colloquial with standard.

The term *colloquial* cannot properly designate a substandard cultural level of English. It designates a functional variety—that used chiefly in conversation—and in itself says nothing as to its cultural level, though this discussion, and the dictionary definitions, are chiefly concerned with cultivated colloquial, a functional variety of standard English. When writers of such standing as those I have mentioned slip into expressions that imply lower cultural status of colloquial English, it is not surprising that some teachers fall into the error. One teacher expressed the conviction that colloquialisms should not be represented as standard American speech. But the context of the statement indicated that its author was using colloquialism in the sense of 'localism.' I could hardly believe how frequent this gross error is, until I heard it from a well-known American broadcaster.

The best dictionaries, at least in their definitions, give no warrant for the various misuses of *colloquial, colloquially, colloquialism, colloquiality*. I urge the reader to study carefully the definitions in the *Oxford English Dictionary*, with its many apt examples from standard writers, and in *Webster's New International Dictionary, Second Edition*, with its quotations from George Lyman Kittredge. Kittredge's views on the standing of colloquial English are well known. It is said that somebody once asked him about the meaning of the label "Colloq." in dictionaries. He is reported to have replied, "I myself speak 'colloke' and often write it." I cannot verify the story, but it sounds authentic.

It seems to me inevitable that the frequent groupings of so-called "levels" such as "Literary, Colloquial, Illiterate," and the like, will lead the reader to suppose that just as Illiterate is culturally below Colloquial, so Colloquial is culturally below Literary. While I can scarcely hope that my humble remonstrance will reform all future writing on "levels of English," I believe that writers who confuse the meaning of the term *level* must accept some part of the responsibility for the popular misunderstanding of the true status of colloquial English; for I cannot avoid the belief that the popular idea of colloquial English as something to be looked down upon with disfavor is due in part to the failure of writers on the subject to distinguish between *cultural levels of English* and *functional varieties of standard English*.

3

❧ The Gentlemen's Guide
to Linguistic Etiquette

PATRICK E. KILBURN

Until a few years ago, even among those who commonly dismiss the Bible as a collection of quaintly poetic ancient myths, there still reigned a species of Holy Writ: the dictionary. Sophisticates knew that there were dictionaries and then there were dictionaries, but no one questioned the Merriam-Webster product of Springfield, Mass.—*Webster's Unabridged*. That work packed such scholarly might that it occupied a quasi-legal status: its definitions were cited in court opinions as the final word on words.

Practically speaking, this situation still obtains in all but the most linguistically sophisticated of circles. Discussions of word meaning or usage are settled by looking it up in "the dictionary" (translate: the dictionary at hand, of whatever age, publisher, or editorial respectability); "the dictionary" settles the issues and satisfies all parties. As if there were no differences among dictionaries. As if all dictionaries were alike.

Dictionaries, of course, have never been alike, any more than cars have been alike: they are similar in gross outline but differ widely to the critical eye; they are more scholarly and independent or less so; more reliable or less so; and so on. Even though "Webster's dictionaries" are as ephemeral as the mayfly in their brief lives on drug- and

Patrick E. Kilburn, a student of lexicography and the author of several articles on usage, is Professor of English at Union College, Schenectady, New York.

dime-store shelves (the current *Books in Print* lists 28 "Webster's" dictionaries from 10 publishers), the innocence of belief in "the dictionary" reigned nearly unchallenged in the general mind until the sixties. Then, all quietly, with relatively little fanfare, the third edition in this century of *Webster's Unabridged* appeared in 1961.

Although the official publication date was not until Sept. 28, the *New York Times,* the *Chicago Tribune,* and the *Chicago Sun-Times* on Sept. 7 carried greetings whose tone is indicated by the title of the *Tribune* piece: "Saying Ain't Ain't Wrong: See Webster." Through September the hubbub mounted and in the months that followed became a very hullabaloo, culminating in an eruption by Wilson Follett in the *Atlantic* for January 1962, called "Sabotage in Springfield," and a long and determined attack by Dwight Macdonald in *The New Yorker* for March 10, 1962, called "The String Untuned." The substance of this anvil chorus of dispraise was that the new dictionary was unsatisfactory on three counts: 1) it dropped "colloquial" from its list of monitory labels; 2) it was too "scientific" in its definitions—*scientific* in this dispute became anathema as denoting qualities alien to persons of good sense, taste, and feeling; and 3) it paid too much attention to current usage. It had thereby, it was charged, opened the gates to the barbarians, who, being given sanction by the very bastion of power, would sweep in and do whatever hordes of barbarians are supposed to do. Occasional demurrers to the general outcry appeared, but they were lost in the uproar. The battle was joined largely between denouncing journalists on the one hand and defending academics on the other.

In the midst of it all, James Parton of *American Heritage* called the new dictionary "an affront to scholarship" and announced a move to buy up Merriam-Webster stock, presumably to take over the company in order to produce a dictionary for people of taste, culture, and learning. The move failed since "leading stockholders and officers of Merriam . . . advised the management that they were 'not interested' in the offer." Then Parton, down but not out, set up his own organization, and, under the joint sponsorship of *American Heritage* and the Houghton-Mifflin Company, published amidst a blizzard of advertising *The American Heritage Dictionary of the English Language* (the AHD). The sponsorship of AHD suggests that this is the dictionary Parton would have produced if he had succeeded in taking over G. & C. Merriam. Perhaps it is fair to look at it in that light to see if the publishers' claims of advances in lexicography have been made good.

First of all, in size the new volume belongs in that class called the

"college" dictionary, the largest of the "abridged" dictionaries, repre-
senting an editor's guess at what are the most useful words in the
language, yet making no pretense of completeness. This is the largest
of the class in my collection, weighing six pounds against an average
of three to four pounds. A substantial amount of the increase in heft,
I should guess, is taken up in larger than average type and a very
generous side margin, to which the illustrations are relegated. One
of the ads claimed 155,000 entries in the body of the dictionary, and
this number is about standard for college dictionaries. Except for the
size and weight, however, it fits well among the college dictionaries
which appear with shelf-bending regularity.

The advertising enters on one gimmick, the Usage Panel, which
deserves special comment. This Panel is really the only thing that
distinguishes this dictionary from nearly a dozen college dictionaries
on the market today, but the hoopla has echoed so loudly that one
ought to examine the principle to determine whether it is the great
advance in dictionary making it is claimed to be.

The publishers

> asked a panel of 100 outstanding speakers and writers a wide range of ques-
> tions about how the language is used today, especially with regard to
> dubious or controversial locutions. After careful tabulation and analysis
> of their replies . . . [they] . . . prepared several hundred usage notes to
> guide readers to effectiveness in speech and writing. As a consequence,
> this Dictionary can claim to be more precisely descriptive, in terms of
> current usage levels, than any heretofore published—especially in offering
> the reader the lexical opinions of a large group of highly sophisticated
> fellow citizens.

This procedure represents a major departure from the usual methods
of lexicography. From Dr. Johnson's *Dictionary* of 1755 on down, lexicographers recruited teams of readers, not writers, who collected quotations (called "cites" in the trade) illustrating usage of words *in
context,* from which a definer would write a definition, oftentimes
quoting the word as it appeared in the cites as illustration. Dr. Johnson
himself did the whole job of defining, as did Noah Webster, whose
Dictionary of 1828 was the last major one-man effort. Since that time
even the college dictionaries have mushroomed in size beyond the
powers of a single man and are now produced by a swarm of scholars
presided over by an editor-in-chief who lays down policy. The essential
difference is that previous dictionaries have relied upon research for
their findings; the AHD places its faith in a process of introspection by
a panel of pundits who ruled upon the credentials of a word or usage
deemed scruffy in its lineage.

In fact, they came to think of themselves as an Academy of linguistic dictators to rule, dispose, and order the mighty flow of the English language, ridiculous as that may seem. For example, the advertising quotes—even, apparently, takes pride in—Dwight Macdonald's cry regarding *enthuse:* "By God, let's hold the line on this one!"

Gad, what a scene! The whole thing rises before me like a vision: a lonely embattled little band, threatened by a horde of bloodthirsty savages, unseen, menacing, bent on destruction of All That We Hold Dear—theme music from *Beau Geste,* punctuated by a ghostly drum beat—and through the dusty air rasps the hoarse voice of Dauntless Dwight Macdonald, "By God, let's hold the line on this one!" One swallows a lump and brushes a tear from his eye, murmuring over and over the spunky line, which could, in time, become as hallowed as "Let's win one for the Gipper."

If I seem to be poking fun, it is because I am only following the wisdom of Dr. Johnson in this matter. Johnson, who individually wielded more linguistic influence than the whole of AHD's instant Academy, "flattered" himself at the outset of his project, he said, that he might "put a stop to those alterations which time and chance have hitherto been suffered to make in [the language] without opposition." But he mournfully concluded that "with . . . justice may the lexicographer be derided, who . . . shall imagine that his dictionary can embalm his language, and secure it from corruption and decay." AHD raises a great hue and cry over *enthuse* but lists *reminisce* and *grovel* without comment, and yet all three words are of a piece: all are back-formations made by people who did not know that *enthusiasm* and *reminiscence* and *groveling* did not come from shorter verb forms. So, while the insignificant barricade is raised at *enthuse,* the tide of the language goes around both ends and finally inundates the whole. The notion that the vaporings of a hundred, even a thousand self-appointed sages might affect the flow of language perceptibly is ludicrous in the extreme.

In his *New Yorker* article, Macdonald showed that he knew the principles of language, but he is a man who knows more than he is willing to understand. Intellectually, he knows—as I am sure that many on the Usage Panel must have known—that his rallying cry of "Hold the line" is preposterous; he is a man hoist on his own metaphor. He knows that usage is never settled finally, that meaning derives from usage, that the language is more like a mighty river than a battle between opposing forces, a river which, as long as the language is spoken by native speakers and thus is still a living language, is quite undammable, quite irreversible in its movement, constantly flowing, ever changing, into which, like the river of Heraclitus, one cannot step twice, for in the interim between steps it has become a different river. Macdonald knows this, but in his heart of hearts, he believes that these are really matters that God has ordained; that God said, "Let there be light," and there was the English language (to be precise, the American language).

And this is a hidden assumption—in some cases not so hidden—of this dictionary. For instance, the Introduction goes out of its way to repeat that old chestnut about the English language, that it "is still the richest, most rewarding language in the world"—a proposition to which, of course, 48 million Frenchmen would instantly assent, to which 225 million Russians would fall down in abject adoration. That is a proposition, in short, which is patent nonsense, of which few people in the world are qualified to judge in even its most limited aspects (that is, whether English is or is not superior, *for that person,* to another language) and of which literally no one is properly qualified to judge since no one knows more than the tiniest fraction of the 3,000 or so recorded languages in the world. Political or military importance of the speakers of the language has nothing to do with the question, and as a matter of fact, Morton W. Bloomfield, who contributed "A Brief History of the English Language" to the introductory material, says of English that its present "high eminence is not fundamentally because of its innate superiority," but the editor-in-chief seems not to have got the message. Benjamin Whorf, the linguist and semanticist, some years ago concluded that the Hopi Indian language was superior to English for expression of the ideas of relativity. If it were so blindingly clear that English is obviously superior to all other languages, what has kept the rest of the world in its benighted state? Is it sheer willfulness, stupidity, or just cross-grained cantankerousness that has kept it from discovering this remarkable fact and forthwith becoming a one-language world? Why, I wonder, should the Nobel Prize winner Samuel Beckett, who was born in Ireland and whose native tongue is English, or still to be precise, the Irish variety of it, have chosen to write in French? Why, for example, should Vladimir Nabokov, who has written successively in Russian, French, and English, have said that his great novel, when it is written, must be in Russian? Perhaps one may argue that such statements as that the English language is "the richest, most rewarding language in the world" are a mere sop to the prejudices of the linguistic Neanderthals. But that is precisely my objection; such people don't read introductions. Even if they did, dictionaries should not give sops to prejudices; they are a place for straight talk about language.

While we are about it, many things about this dictionary are irritating. Why should the publishers have gone out of their way to emphasize that this is a dictionary of the *English* language? It is no more English than New York City is English. It has three or four deracinated Englishmen, like Alistair Cooke, on its Usage Panel, but beyond that, it is American. AHD pays little attention to British usage, and when it does list such an item, it usually labels it *British* (as *bonnet:* "*British.* The hood of an automobile"). On the other hand it defines *hood* as "The hinged metal lid over an automobile engine," and attaches no *American* label to the definition. It lists *windshield, pay station, barbershop* with no label, but it does not list the British forms, *windscreen, telephone box,* or *barber's shop.* Incidentally, AHD shares this failing with its archenemy, Merriam-Webster's *Third New International Dictionary of the English Language,* which, on its appearance in 1961, was quite properly criticized by a number of British reviewers for calling itself a dictionary of the "English language" and yet displaying a blatant American bias. The Third's little brother, *Webster's Seventh New Collegiate Dictionary,* sidesteps the problem, as do several of the other collegiate dictionaries, by not saying what it is a dictionary of, and this is probably a better solution than misstating the case.

Since Johnson's time, lexicographers have been humbler creatures, who recognized the inevitable and accepted the universe. They have sought only to describe the practice of writers, knowing that in a spinning world, full of uncertainty, it is folly to believe men's professions. It is safe only to believe that men say what they actually record in print. It seemed obvious to them, as it should seem obvious to even the most obtuse, that preaching does not match practice, even among the gurus of the Usage Panel. This point, too, seems to have been lost on the AHD's editors.

The Usage Panel is only a gimmick, a linguistic guide to pinky-pointing, for what it comes down to in actuality is that each of the pundits is asked, in essence, "Do you use this word or expression? Are you offended when you hear the expression or read it in print?" And then, God save the mark, since there was unanimity on only one usage ("in disfavor of *simultaneous* as an adverb"), the results are reported in percentages, which must represent the absolute triumph of useless information reported in numbers. (Are you in favor of adultery, Mrs. O'Leary? Ninety-six per cent of the time I am against it.) And then, to compound confusion thrice confounded, they ignore the advice of their own Usage Panel in writing their Usage notes: 42 per cent of the panel would restrict *alternative* "to a choice involving only two."

But their Usage note at *so-called* tweaks the noses of the 42 per cent: ". . . *these so-called friends.* An alternative construction is *these 'friends.'* So called (without a hyphen) may be used in still another alternative: *these friends, so called.*" This is like the grammar book that advised, "A preposition is a bad thing to end a sentence with." Therefore, the claim that this dictionary is "more precisely descriptive . . . than any heretofore published" is sheer balderdash; the Usage Notes are "precisely descriptive" of nothing but the state of the pundits' navels.

And a sagging bunch of navels they are, too, to report on the state of the living language of 1970. I have not been able to ascertain the birth dates of all the panel, but 28 were born in the nineteenth century—are seventy or more years old; 32 are in their sixties, 29 are in their fifties, and out of 95 whose ages I have been able to discover, only *six* are under fifty years old! I have nothing against age—I have a substantial amount of it myself—but the old are as rigid in their language as they are in their joints. Sixty out of the ninety could tell me much, perhaps, about the language of Flaming Youth and bathtub gin, but what could such a huddle of arthritic ancients tell me about the language of 1970—beyond, that is, displaying an understandable touchiness about such terms as "senior citizen" (a locution condemned by over half the panel as "a euphemism associated with the worlds of politics and advertising." This pronouncement, as well as anything that could be cited, displays in a merciless intensity, the silliness of the method. What, for sweet reason's sake, has the fact that it is a euphemism to do with usage? It may be trite, it may be a euphemism, one may prefer "old man" to "senior citizen," but when has purging the language of euphemisms ever been any part of a dictionary's task? Was there no one on the panel with a saving ounce of logic to protest that classifying euphemisms was not a proper matter for a dictionary?).

A more noticeable departure of the AHD from the other college dictionaries is its heavy reliance on photographs as illustrations, with occasionally one of the familiar line drawings. The decision to use photographs opened a possibility denied the drawing: portraits. Portraits, lots and lots of them, are a distinctive feature of this dictionary. It is a surprise, in this day of hairy radicalism, to see the splendid set of burnsides sported by the Grand Pooh-bah of censorship, Anthony Comstock, which eclipse those worn by the originator of the style, Gen. Ambrose Burnside, and to compare them with the clean-shaven old radical, John Brown, who looks as if his portrait might have been taken after they hung him [According to the AHD, in this context, *"hung* is acceptable, as an alternative to *hanged,* to only 31 per cent of the Usage Panel."—Ed.] instead of before. The choice of portraits, though, is sometimes whimsical, to say the least. For instance, it is a puzzle to discover the criteria which chose John L. Sullivan, the boxer, over either Sir Arthur Sullivan, of Gilbert and Sullivan, or Louis Sullivan, the American architect whom Frank Lloyd Wright called "the Master." Why Jane Seymour and not Shakespeare, or Dick Whittington and not Walt Whitman? Why Chaucer and not Milton (there is plenty of room in the margin, and even if there were not, Milton is a shade more important in the history of human thought than "Marcel Marceau as his character Bip" which appears at *mime*)? Why Emily Dickinson and not Mark Twain? And why on earth *two* photographs of the said Gen. Burnside (at *Burnside* and *sideburns*) and none of Robert Burns, or Aaron Burr or Vannevar Bush?

Many of the pictures, however, have an interest of their own. I would not willingly do without the astounding photograph of *contortionist,* and the "Campaign button used in Theodore Roosevelt's 1904 Presidential campaign" makes a nice point about the origin of the term *teddy bear.* However, there is a fine line of gradation here that often got lost in putting this book together. The Germans have a useful distinction between *Wörter* (words) and *Sachen* (things, events, circumstances, facts). Properly speaking, a dictionary is concerned with *Wörter* only, with words, not with *Sachen,* which are matters for an encyclopedia. Granted, many dictionaries treat *Sachen* in biographical appendices and gazetteers and sometimes, as AHD does, in the body of the alphabet, but AHD gets mired in the *Sachen* of its pictures as pictures. For example, at *columbine,* we get not only what looks like an old-fashioned botany textbook drawing (why not a photograph?) of a columbine in flower, but also a "Marginal illustration from *The Hours of Catherine of Cleves.*" Although I have nothing against either Catherine of Cleves or flowers, I find it hard to square the inclusion of her columbine with the editor's profession that "The pictures have been chosen as much as possible in an attempt to add genuine meaning to the subjects they illustrate." Including it meant also that the portrait of Samuel Colt, of revolver fame, is shouldered on to the page opposite where his name is entered, and this dislocation is common: the illustrations are so haphazardly placed that, although the margins form a pleasant picture-book, they are often separated so much from the text that they do not properly illustrate it at all.

Relegating the illustrations to the margins was probably a bit of a trap. The chance of the alphabet—the fact that the dictionary must go through all the ac's before it can go on to the ad's—sometimes opened an offensive naked space, the sight of which to a compositor's eye brought on an acute attack of illustrator's itch, an allergy eased only by finding a picture of something, *anything,* to darken the unseemly white of the margin. Combine this with a passion for peddling information, no matter how irrelevant as long as it is specific and accurate—sometimes not so accurate: in early printings, the captions for the portraits of the assassin John Wilkes Booth and his actor-brother Edwin were reversed—and the result is pedantry run amok.

Consider the case of *unleavened.* Offhand, one would say there was nothing much to illustrate in *unleavened,* unless, by a curious twist, one pictured the fungi which are *not* at work in unleavened bread. Such a line of reasoning would fail to reckon with illustrator's itch, which not only produced a picture for *unleavened* but threw in a prize of more information about that particular engraving than I care to know. Another illustration showing the virulence of the mania for spreading information, any information, is at *cat's cradle.* Was there no one on the staff with even a rudimentary sense of relevance? Apparently not. Or take the "Nineteenth-century poster" at *nostrum.* Or take *telescope;* out of the photograph of the Mt. Palomar installation emerges only a tangle of struts and beams; it tells nothing to one who does not already know what a telescope is (and that person, remember, is the one for whom the illustration is presumably included). Or *Dutch oven,* where the focal point of the picture is at the kneading trough in front and not at all on the oven. Or *caparison,* or *depth charge.* The book is full of illustrations that do not illustrate.

On the face of it, photographs would seem an improvement over line drawings until one remembers that the camera eye is a faithful recorder of all that is placed before it. It has no intelligence to filter out the extraneous in the interests of clarity—something the line drawings which were made specifically to illustrate a point do superbly. The photographs make a better looking book, but the *Sachen* of the woodcuts and engravings, which are included for their historical interest and rarely illustrate what they are supposedly included for, detract from the book as a dictionary, a *Wörterbuch.*

In the blizzard of advertising surrounding the appearance of this book, one of the items assured the public that on the day of its publication, AHD had rendered obsolete no less than "61 million" other dictionaries. Perhaps one should not stick at the febrile fancies of a publisher's flack, but that 61 million is a bit much, unless the reader can swallow half the story, in which case I will manfully try to swallow my half of it. Otherwise, the case seems not proved. AHD is an adequate college dictionary, not notably different from a number of others already on the market. The touted Usage Panel is only a gimmick, and a poor one at that.

The best advice would be, don't throw out your old *Webster's Third*. It's not really obsolete. If your dictionary is obsolete, the passage of time made it so, not the AHD.

4

❧ Standards in the Community Language

MARTIN JOOS

This topic is one of those provided for in the editor's plan, but the wording of the title is my own. The words were chosen and arranged to provide enough starting-points for the various things that need saying.

What is a language? It is a habit-structure and an institution. These are two names for one thing, and the choice between them depends only on whether we are thinking of one person or of many. The equivalence means that the one person is *a member of* the community. The two must not be misunderstood as suggesting that the institution somehow is better, higher, stronger than the habit-structure in the single speaker, or misunderstood as meaning that the habit-structure within the one speaker is somehow better than the institution. These two misunderstandings are both dangerous fallacies. The first fallacy is the popular misunderstanding about language that dominates our traditional schooling; the second fallacy is common among reformers.

The language is basically spoken. Writing and print are secondary phenomena, derived and dependent phenomena. But they are not derived from speech alone, nor dependent on speech alone. There are

Martin Joos is Professor of Linguistics and Director of the Centre for Linguistic Studies at the University of Toronto. Professor Joos has written extensively in scholarly journals and is the author of *Acoustic Phonetics, The English Verb: Form and Meaning,* and *The Five Clocks.*

188

other factors determining them. Speech is only their indispensable determiner, not their only one. This makes writing and print harder to discuss than the spoken language and makes it necessary to delay discussing them until enough has been said about speech. This necessity has led many linguists to say that there is no language other than speech, and that writing is ideally a faithful reflection of speech. I do not agree. Let that suffice for now.

The institution, then, is basically an institution that is equivalent to the structure in the speech-habits of community members. It is not the sum of their speech-habits; it is the structure in those habits. It is not simple; it is complex in a number of different ways. The language is complex in a number of dimensions. There is a right way and at least one wrong way to understand this remark.

The wrong way would be to say that the language "has" several dimensions, for then we would be tempted to slice it like a loaf of bread. That would destroy the coherence between slice and slice, the tenacious webs and threads that hold the whole loaf together; and that would destroy more than is preserved. Why more? Because those webs and threads are structure, and a language is nothing if it is not structure. And why is that? Because of the whole mission of language: what it is for. Its job is to connect: to connect person with person, to connect sound with sense, to connect senses with each other, to connect items and events with each other and connect them to personal statuses and roles, and so on and on seemingly without end. The result is that any slicing of language, though it may have a legitimate purpose towards our understanding, is inimical to any understanding of what it is.

For example, we may want to slice it into local varieties. The technical name for them is "dialects." (Among professional people, this is not a bad word. I speak Wisconsin dialect, with many borrowings from other dialects.) Now a dialect is a dialect only in comparison to other dialects; by itself, it is the language, and so is each other dialect by itself. Dialects are important only when their differences make a difference in the way people react to each other, in the way they interact in cooperating for general human purposes. Therefore, the consequential differences between two dialects constitute all that matters about each of them. Do the dialects, that is to say the differences between two of them, have a real value to us? Do they have a positive social function, so that we would be poorer without them? Unquestionably. Demonstrably. There will be room, later on here, for some of the demonstration.

Nevertheless, we have to do a good deal of slicing in order to dis-

cuss at all. That is the difference between two kinds of understanding:
1) the way a member of the community, as a member (not as a
sociologist or a linguist), understands what other members say to him
and what he says to them; 2) the understanding that depends on linguistic or sociological discussion. It is worth remarking that what a
linguist says about the community language is necessarily uninterest-
ing to normal community members unless he speaks as a sociologist,
and that is what I mean to do here.

In this double capacity, the discusser of the community language
distinguishes, or slices, between two kinds of structure: 1) internal;
2) external. The internal structure is what holds the language together
within itself; the external structure relates it, in many ways, to its community service. The internal and the external structure overlap constantly in any discussion of standards; therefore the discussion of
standards has to be both cautious and elaborate, because it must repair
the damage caused by the slicing.

As a pure linguistic scientist (not in the least a sociologist), a linguist is essentially concerned with the internal structure of the language; and this is so fascinating by itself that few linguists allow
themselves to be concerned with the external structure at all. This
normal behavior of linguists is what has given the impression that linguists have nothing to say about standards and even that they deny
that standards exist. They are quoted, for example, as having said that
ain't is good English. Now it is true that many a linguist, when baited
with sufficiently vehement nonsensical statements, has said that *ain't*
is just as English as *aren't,* or even gone so far as to say that it has
just as good a claim to be an English word, defiantly heedless of the
way his statement is always misunderstood by a non-linguist. (He has
said only that it is a word, as the other party also said, and that it has
a home in English even if only a disadvantaged home.)

For normal people, the only question about *ain't* is whether it is
good or bad. I am not going to say that this is a foolish question. It is a
reasonable question, but a good deal more background is needed before it can be answered: several more pieces of background, and my
problem is to present them in a suitable sequence even though they
are backgrounds of different kinds.

What is a standard for? What is its social function? Simply the fact
that it is a standard: the job of a standard is simply to be a standard.
An analogy: Sailors have a standard knot for mooring a small boat.
Why? So that when a shore-leave party, along towards midnight on a
dark and rainy evening, races to the landing-place with the local
gendarmerie in hot pursuit, the first sailor to get to the boat can untie

that knot instantly without looking to see what knot another sailor used: the difference between a successful shore-leave and a night in jail. The sailor will tell you that this knot, one out of many dozens used for various purposes, is the best possible knot for mooring a small boat. Nonsense. There are a dozen others that would serve equally well, as far as keeping the boat moored is concerned, or swift tying and swift untying. What makes the standard knot the right one is simply that it is the expected knot and thereby keeps him out of jail. This purpose of the standard is *to fulfill expectations.*

But this is only half the story. Take a frequent scene aboard the sailing vessel, perhaps aloft in the rigging and perhaps on deck, but in any case dark and rainy; this is the equivalent of *noise* that almost makes speech unintelligible. The sailor comes to a place where two or more lines are made fast to the same cleat, and he wants to untie the right one and leave the others tied; his sense of touch, even with one hand, is enough to tell him which of the different knots is the one he wants, and he unties it confidently. This time, the purpose of the standard is *to generate expectations.*

I use the term "text" for speech as well as for print; and a text may be very short: the shortest text is what is spoken between one major pause and the next one. Now the generating and fulfilling of expectations takes place within a text too. The simplest knot analogy is furnished by the sheepshank knot, a pair of half-hitches used for shortening a rope. Neither half-hitch will hold without the other; each generates an expectation of the other and also fulfills the expectation generated by the other.

Quite simliarly, portions of a text generate and fulfill expectations to and from other portions of the same text. For example, the English word *the* calls for a noun to follow without much delay; and each noun generates a much weaker expectation that a *the* preceded it not too long before—not a certainty, but only a moderately strong expectation, for something else, or in fact nothing, may have preceded the noun.

These expectations within the text constitute the structure within it; this structure within the text can be called its "grammar," or in another terminology it may be customary to say that the grammar of a text is only part of its structure, other parts being called its semology (which fits the text to mean something) and its phonolgy (which makes it fit the pronunciation-expectations of the community).

In any case, the structure of expectations within the text makes the text highly *redundant* within itself. One result is that when noise has obscured parts of a spoken text, the listener can reconstruct what he has failed to hear with more or less completeness according to how much noise there was and which parts of the text it covered.

Now "noise" is a very general term in technical discussion. For instance, the encountering of an unfamiliar word introduces semantic noise; an unexpected grammatical pattern (perhaps what is usually called a grammatical error or else an anacoluthon) introduces grammatical noise; an odd pronunciation introduces phonological noise.

Of course, what is noise for one listener may be clarity for another: it is a question of degree and kind of education. This is my general definition (and a very broad and general definition it is) of the term "education." It conflicts, naturally, with what is popularly meant by the same term; but I can find no better term for what I mean: the experiences which prepare a person to profit from a wider variety of texts, either in receiving them or emitting them. These experiences are what I mean by "education," no matter what they are.

When the text is not spoken but instead written (or printed), it contains a vastly greater amount of noise than a spoken text in an expected dialect. Its spelling, especially in English, covers half the phonology with noise; its grammar includes patterns that are seldom spoken and which are therefore noisy; its unexpected words introduce semantic noise. But experience in reading contributes rapidly to education, for the new words enrich the semology of the reader, and so does the wider range of grammar patterns, while he even gains enrichment of his phonology from print that has decent rhythms and from the rimes of verse. All this, of course, depends on good writing.

What is good writing? Since it is not heard as spoken outside the reader's skull, it is noisy: its blanks are to be rated as noise too. But there is a compensation that we get from even moderately skillful writing. The reason is that the reader has, compared to hearing, extra time for considering the text—time for reading it slowly, for rereading it, and (if he has looked at it thoughtfully) for reconsidering it after he has quit looking. The whole art of writing consists in providing rewards for the extra time, so that the reader gains in proportion to the time he spends; and when the total possible gain outweighs the loss from not hearing, the writing is called "good writing"; one important result is that good writing can and normally does employ words that are seldom or never spoken. That will be enough along this line; from now on, we can limit the discussion to speech and to texts that are only spoken.

There are still other kinds of background that are needed for a moderately full discussion of standards. One of them is the time dimension: the fact that standards change, even from decade to decade, and the various consequences of that; but that had better be postponed as long as possible. We have enough already for some quite substantial progress.

Normal text is highly redundant within itself. If every third word of this paragraph were blotted out, its message would come through still, and with very little loss. This fact has a number of interesting consequences. One is that the language provides a speaker (or writer) with a great deal of freedom in how to say what he wants to put across. The community profits from this freedom in a number of ways. Let us concentrate on those which affect the question of standards.

It is profitable for us to know as much as possible about what kind of person, or of mood, we are listening to. Persons and moods can differ in a number of important ways. The complete community's language provides devices for signalling each of them; the speaker has a social duty to mark his speech accordingly, and most speakers live up to this duty rather fully. Indeed, education (in the broadest sense) conditions us so thoroughly in this social discipline that we betray nearly everything about our personalities and moods even when we try to conceal some of it, and trains us to interpret the signals without conscious attention to them for the most part. That is to say, those signals have standards too.

For convenience in the discussion of standards, we can speak of several "scales" along which texts can differ and of the standard markers for points on the scale. Usually it is convenient to say that each scale has five marked points along its length. For simplicity's sake I begin with an extremely simple scale: the scale of sincerity. One of our standard markers for insincerity, oddly enough, means the opposite of what it seems to say. We say "as a matter of fact" to indicate that we are lying (or at least shading the truth somewhat) so that this is a sort of Freudian slip that is institutional in English. This does not mean that every utterance marked with that standard marker is a lie; and it does not mean that every lie is marked that way; but at least the probabilities are very strong in that direction.

The example is trivial, and not worth pursuing far enough for establishing five degrees of sincerity versus insincerity and listing the standard markers for each point. What I want it for is something much simpler. I want to show that the scales and their markers typically function automatically, without awareness, indeed subconsciously. The native speakers of English who *are aware* that "as a matter of fact" means insincerity are extremely few, but those who let it slip out with that real meaning are probably the majority, and those who profit from hearing it—who experience an unaccountable feeling of suspicion when they hear it—are numerous and include surely a majority of the socially sensitive and well-educated native speakers. See earlier for the definition of "education," and note that it is only decent to conceal the suspicious feeling even from oneself and to play along with the speaker who has given himself away in that fashion. It is usually considerably later, after parting from him, that we let the still-repressed suspicion prevail; and then we say, "I don't know why I didn't buy that car; I guess I just had a feeling that I could find a better one," or something like that.

In short, our standards are most effective when we are unaware of them; and, fortunately for us, we usually *are* unaware of them.

At this point let me insert a remark on what STANDARD means in this discussion and in others where it means something else. The difference between the two sorts of meaning is very much like the difference in two meanings of the word TEMPERATURE. I am going to continue to mark the two meanings by writing each word in one of its meanings with a small s or a small t, and for the other meaning I will write Standard and Temperature. Then we can say these things among others: Everybody always has a temperature; but a fever, an ominously elevated temperature, is called a Temperature. So far, I have been speaking of standards; but Miss Fidditch, who probably teaches English in your high school as she did in my daughter's high school, keeps talking about Standards and is sure that there is a Standard pronunciation and a Standard grammar and Standard meanings for words, poor dutiful soul. According to this popular theory, there are few speakers of Standard English; most people, louts that they are, flout Webster and flaunt their ignorance. Miss Fidditch is so clear about their lack of Standards that she probably never could be persuaded that they have standards. Enough of that for now: all I need to do for the present is define the two words "Standard" and "standard," so that I can use them both freely.

A community is not created by writing a constitution for it, the way the French try to create their political community over and over again. A community creates itself, informally and naturally, and its language is one of the institutions the community creates in creating itself. As in most civilized communities, so also in ours, there are schoolmen who don't understand this at all. Similarly, few people understand nature, so they assume a mythical Nature which serves to make them feel secure, as in ancient times the myths of the Sun God and the God of Storms served to provide security for a population ignorant of natural science. It is only human nature, then, to assume that there is a single Standard English.

The great merit of a myth is that it provides a First Cause, thereby relieving the Faithful of the burden of inquiring further; the corresponding disadvantage of any science is that as soon as it has found any causes it must look behind them for their cause in turn, and so on without limit. I am not going to promise you that linguistic science will provide us with any ultimate explanation of standards in the community language. All I can do is to enumerate (not completely, for that would be impossible) various kinds of standards. They are created by the community; they emerge in social living; life and human nature are that way, and no matter how much we understand about it we can never grasp all of it.

Meanwhile, Miss Fidditch will continue to protect her myth by a simple rule: "Among competing ways of saying things, only one is Correct." Corollary: "To teach Correct English, it is necessary to condemn what the pupils do already." Since Miss Fidditch typically comes from a family which does not speak Standard English, she feels insecure in her partial knowledge of Correct English; and since she knows she has little chance of learning it in a natural social way, she has adopted an auxiliary rule: "Whatever is less ordinary is more likely to be correct." For example, "I've got" (meaning "I possess") instead of "I have" is far more common in standard British than in standard American English; therefore, the British Miss Fidditches tell their London pupils that "I've got" is an ugly Americanism. (No, I really mean it! That is what they do, believe it or not.)

Now to finish swiftly. The age standards of English speech are: baby, child, teenage, mature, senile, and the last of these is used when one's old friends have nearly all died and one feels out of touch with the contemporary world. Some people age themselves prematurely, adopting senile usage by temperament and at an age when premature baldness is brought on by inheritance in others. Neither happens within the teenage years; either can happen soon thereafter; thus the teenage period is a teacher's last chance to help or hinder one of them. There is no effect on the pupil's usage from a school campaign; the effect comes, if at all, by example: the pupil adopts a personality model.

A superficially similar scale is the scale of breadth: popular, provincial, general, puristic, genteel. Here, as in all the five-step scales, it is the middle standard that serves best. The pupils know this as if by instinct, and the wise teacher's problem is to show them the way from the former end of the scale toward the latter end without encouraging them to go more than half-way. By stopping in the middle, the most useful result is attained: the speech is still identifiable according to its dialect origin, but the remaining dialect color does not interfere with general communication. The profit is that we know who we are listening to and are completely free to trust him as far as we choose. President Johnson is a convincing example. For the latter end of the scale, listen to Elizabeth II in her public utterances, for the British constitution requires the speech of the Royal Family to be genteel and thereby Non-U. This discussion makes it unnecessary to say any more about the extremely numerous dialects, each with its own standards.

Mature general usage (definitions just above) seem to have five "functional varieties," specialized to the various circumstances in which we speak: intimate, casual, consultative, formal, frozen. The last is reserved for print and declamation, and has therefore been called literary style. It is characterized by depth of ambiguity and of appeal to the reader's and listener's total life experience including reading, that is (by definition) to his education. Formal usage is for informative lectures and print; it is marked by impersonality and coherence, and requires many hours of preparation for one hour of presentation. Consultative usage, the middle of this scale, is the norm for coming to terms with strangers, as in finding the right ribbon for your portable typewriter. Casual usage is for spoken communion (not "communication") among close acquaintances; it is marked by devices which distinguish between insiders and outsiders, notably slang and ellipsis. Intimate usage is requisite between husband and wife, for example; it is marked by extreme simplifications (often leaving nothing but inarticulate murmurs) and by private jargon presumed to be different from the jargon of every other intimate group and invented within this one; the simplifications, on the other hand, are in principle shared by them all, and seem to derive naturally from the speech of babyhood.

This functional varieties scale is not the same as the next one; see later! Instinct, or something like it, carries each maturing person as far as the middle of this scale without any school help, provided he has normal social contacts, and the middle is the limit for most people. Beyond that, we try to teach formal composition; most teachers seem to believe that they are thereby preparing their pupils for literary writing too, but that is a professional illusion. Frozen styles are different for each writer, and simply can't be taught; they have to be invented, like intimate jargons. Another professional illusion is that progress along this scale is progress towards Correct English, Standard English. No other professional illusion seems to be quite as tenacious; and it is doubtful whether any other illusion is more pernicious.

No mature person can get along with a single one of these functional varieties; he has to be able to shift from each to its neighbors freely, and he does this within single social occasions too. He shifts from consultative to casual, for instance, when he becomes more friendly with the other party; or from consultative to formal when there is a temporary embarrassment or in proceeding from negotiation to contract-terms. (It is anti-social to shift more than one step at a time, for instance from casual to formal in a single jump, as teachers on a school picnic are likely to do in order to initiate a game or the like.)

Now the addressee has to be warned whenever there is a shift, and reassured from time to time when there is none. There are standard warning and confirmation signals for this. For instance "on" used as a vague or general purpose preposition is such a signal. In casual usage we say, "I wanted to see *about* that typewriter"; in consultative English we say, "I'd like to see you *on* that typewriter"; in formal English the preposition is again *about,* or else (and this is a warning or confirmation signal) it is *concerning* or *regarding* or one of the other formal substitutes. Here is the same message in three versions: Casual: "C'n I help you?" Consultative: "Can I help you?" Formal: "May I help you?" (Every small child knows that this *may* is Correct but not standard for this meaning; and the teacher who insists that it is standard is cheating the child by trying to make him a pupil instead of a citizen.) There is a long list of such signals, and they facilitate social life enormously. Their effect is that you always know where you are as long as they are being used. They are neglected or lied about in all traditional teaching.

The worst of these lies consists in pretending that the scale of functional varieties is identical with all the other scales and most particularly the scale of responsibility. Now *responsibility* is the genuine usage-scale which corresponds most closely to the mythical single scale which runs: bad, fair, good, better, best = Correct. We use this scale to tell the world how much responsibility we are willing to accept. The speaker who says "hisself" is not ignorant of the form "himself"; to be ignorant of it, he would have to be a hermit. He says it in order to convey the message "No responsibilities wanted!" And he conveys that message in obedience to his social duty to give fair warning, although he is not consciously aware that this is what he is doing. Some of us have never learned enough of these warning-words, such as "hisself" and "ain't," having been protected from such vulgarity; then we employ effeteness-formulas instead to convey the same warning, for vulgarity and effeteness are equivalent in this social function. Thus "either" pronounced "eyether" is usually effete in Wisconsin. Still, it must be admitted that the impulse to use it can often be called a

vulgar impulse. At the other end of the scale, the speaker who habitually uses only the best or better English is telling us that he would like
to be elected President of the United States; but the public prefers the
middle of the scale (good English) and makes him a teacher instead,
or causes him to be appointed Ambassador to the United Nations.

There are other scales and their standards, but these will do for now.
Logically, it would be every teacher's duty to be aware of them all,
and to offer as models those which are profitable in the mature business of the community, this model for one employment and that
model for another. Few teachers can both become sufficiently mature
for this and remain in teaching positions thereafter; hence my practical
advice for most teachers can only be a makeshift compensation for
their professional disabilities. They must trust their pupils to find their
own way around in the world, as the pupils did before they fell under
school discipline, and concentrate on the model— which is what literature is for. Literature is not to be taught for excellence in English, but
instead for diversity in English; and the teacher's discussion task is to
adequately locate the different voices in the total community, a task
for which the customary lies about Correctness do no good whatever
and often considerable harm. Following this program, the teacher can
also gain a useful awareness of what mature people know without
awareness.

The community (not teachers, and above all not the grammarians!)
creates all the standards for the community language. Now and then
some grammarian invents a "logical" substitute for some community
standard, as when "It is I" was invented to replace "It's me." Some
few of these are adopted (by the community!) as standard forms for
the *puristic* step on the *breadth scale*. From there, they can drift either
way; "It is I" has drifted into the *genteel* position, while "not all is"
(for Shakespeare's "All is not gold that glisters") has drifted into the
general position or even farther, a triumph for Miss Fidditch. The un-
splitting of the standard split infinitives may soon be another triumph
for her in America; it has recently taken place in Britain. The triumphs
are, however, not anything she can rightfully take credit for: it is
always the community's doing. We more traditional speakers are
naturally pained when we hear or read the unfortunate results, but our
grandchildren will no longer be pained by them when they have become usual in turn; they may even like the sound of this recently
printed silly sentence: "I am not in the least impressed by this circumstance, which seems so greatly to please our professors of linguistics." (Clifton Fadiman, *Any Number Can Play*, page 213 in the Avon
edition.)

For languages change, smoothly or in jumps, and nothing can be done about it. The smooth changes have been called "drifting" above. One kind of jump has been mentioned: the inventions of grammarians. The other principal kind of jump is the borrowing of items from other dialects or languages, as when "hopefully" for "we hope" was borrowed from German about twenty years ago: it has now become a standard item in technical and journalistic writing, and it may even become general English in time. For the present, it is still a marker for them; "hopefully" it will disappear before too late, for unity in the language is a contribution to solidarity. Drifting, on the other hand, does no harm at all; it may be regarded as a contribution to solidarity too. Yet we must not forget that the scales, as wholes, must survive: they are part of the social structure, the integrity of the community.

Is there a program for teachers in all this? A program of self- training is implied, but there isn't room here for a teachable program. Books by modern linguists (not the popularizers or the journalists) can be helpful. My book on some of the scales is *The Five Clocks* (Rayl House, Indiana University, 1962); and in an article in the *Harvard Educational Review* (XXXIV, 2, Spring 1964: pages 203-210) "Language and the School Child," I have detailed what happens when Correctness wreaks its traditional havoc. Otherwise, the best single book is *That* Dictionary, the one that raised such a storm among the journalists after its publication late in 1961. In place of a Program, all I can offer are the rewards of discovery and self-training; to gain them, simply set yourself free from the myth that traditional schooling, with its Standards, corresponds to something real. A teacher's natural interest in high standards will do the rest.

5

Dimensions
of English Usage

DAVID DECAMP

The Tragerian structural linguist, the Chomskian generative linguist, and Miss Fidditch, our dear old English teacher from P. S. 19, are all plagued with the same problem: that of reconciling two very different views of language. Most of the time the linguist looks on language as an abstract theoretical structure, which exists—if it can be said to exist anywhere—in the mind of its speaker, perhaps in the collective mind of all its speakers. He hopes that the grammar he is writing will be an accurate map of that structure, but the means of verifying his hypotheses are complicated and indirect. He will never with his own eyes actually see such a thing as "the English verb" naked and pure. Similarly when Miss Fidditch teaches her grammar class, she too deals in abstract structures and moves in a world of nouns, verbs, subjunctives, gerunds, and other "unreal" postulated entities. Her theories may differ slightly from the linguist's theories, but they are still theories rather than observed facts.

When the linguist heads for a Navajo village and a summer of fieldwork, however, or when he dabbles in dialectology or phonetics, he must see language not as an abstraction but as people talking and writing, a complicated profusion of people and circumstances and

David DeCamp, Professor of English and Linguistics at the University of Texas at Austin, has published widely in technical journals on dialectology, sociolinguistics, and creole languages. Among his books are *Jamaican Creole* and *A Collation of Checklists Used in the Study of Jamaican Creole*.

social mores and sounds and marks on paper. Similarly Miss Fidditch faces three or four classes, consisting of more than a hundred bewilderingly diverse youngsters, all of them constantly engaged in unique and unpredictable acts of language. That odd sentence in Johnny's last composition, the even odder one in the poem assigned for next week—how to reconcile these with the comfortable mathematical security of the grammar class? For there is indeed something comfortable and secure about grammar. It is like geometry with its ideal perfect circles, squares, and triangles, whereas most of English teaching is more like surveying, where none of the measurements ever come out exactly right, where even a straight line is only approximated, and where the surveyor must triangulate on the basis of imperfect triangles.

This double view of language was most articulately expressed at the turn of the century by the Swiss linguist de Saussure, who applied the term *la langue* to the underlying, abstract, constant structure, and applied the term *la parole* to the infinitely variable, empirically observable acts of language. The dictionary translations of these two terms (*language* for *la langue,* and *word* or *speech* for *la parole*) fail to convey the same idea, and many linguists continue to use the French words as technical terms. Linguists since de Saussure have developed various approaches to reconciling these two views of language. The Tragerians, for example, have tried to structure both an "overall pattern" to account for the composite of all English language acts and a "common core" restricted to those characteristics which all varieties of the language share in common. The generative linguists are working on sets of supplementary rules which, hopefully, may map out the relationships between the general grammatical principles which you find in your textbooks and the linguistic diversity which you daily face in your classrooms. Much progress has been made; much more such work needs to be done.

Here, however, I wish to discuss not linguistic theory but Miss Fidditch's own approaches to the paradox of *la langue* and *la parole.* The older Miss Fidditch operated on the principle that optional alternatives were intolerable. There was one and only one correct form for everything. Free choice was anarchy. Try to imagine how many arguments were settled, thanks to her influence, and how many bets paid off by looking up a word in the dictionary to see which form came first and which second—all this despite the fervent disclaimer by the editors in the prefaces to most dictionaries, insisting that the second entry is in no way substandard. After all, you can't print two alternatives and have them both come first! The half truth so widely mouthed by the semanticists in the 1930's, that there are no synonyms, only confirmed her conviction that there is no permissible variation in language. The parents of her pupils were bent on middle-class social climbing, a parlor game in which gaucheries like *it don't* automatically disqualify a player, and any teacher foolish enough to deviate from the unrelenting pursuit of the one and only correct form of English would be crucified at the next PTA meeting.

The older Miss Fidditch's intuitions on this matter were not entirely wrong. They seldom were. Like her rules of grammar, they were too vague and too limited and sometimes erred in detail, but they had some basis in fact. No sensible, well-informed person today wants to leave your language alone, not even the author of the book whose first edition bore that unfortunate title. Given enough context, not only the linguistic context of what is said before and after the form in question but also the social and cultural context in which it is used, it is almost always possible to choose and say that this word is better than that one *under these circumstances.* Value judgments can be— in fact, must be—made, but only in reference to larger contexts. We cannot evaluate elements in isolation. Hydrogen supports life when we drink it in water, but few of us choose concentrated hydrochloric acid as our cup of tea. Hydrogen is not in itself either a good element or a bad element. It is indeed better to use the letter *c* than the letter *k* in spelling the word *cat,* but we hardly insist that *c* is a better letter of the alphabet than *k.* Miss Fidditch stopped short of this absurdity of evaluating letters of the alphabet, but she did consider herself capable of isolated and absolute judgments on *shall, irregardless, might could,* and *you all.* For one thing, this simplified her problem of reconciling *la langue* and *la parole.* By outlawing all variation, she thought she could establish a simple one-to-one relationship between her grammatical principles and the written and spoken word. This she called logic. At this point my grammar has only triangular holes; square and oval pegs need not apply!

The 1920's were a decade of usage surveys. J. Leslie Hall's book *English Usage* had appeared in 1917, challenging the single standard. Hall's source was 75,000 pages of English and American literature, and his book bristled with incontrovertible statistics: e.g., found in 65 reputable authors 453 times. Yet teachers did not accept Hall's conclusion that "Custom is the most certain mistress of language." Even Matthew Arnold and Walter Pater may have exercised poetic license, the teachers argued, and little Johnny had darn well better learn correct English first; there will be plenty of time for him to experiment with the language after he has become an established great author. So do as I preach, not as Pater practices.

The presence of variable usage in literary masterpieces failed to move Miss Fidditch. In the 1920's, therefore, three major surveys were launched, attempting this time to examine the living usage. In 1927, Sterling Leonard and H. Y. Moffett published their article "Current Definition of Levels in English Usage."[106] Their research was expanded to a survey of the usage attitudes of 229 prominent members of our society, including well-known authors, editors of influential publications, and leading businessmen, and was published in full by Leonard in 1932 in his *Current English Usage*. In 1926, C. C. Fries began his survey of the English usage found in about three thousand letters written to a U. S. government agency. The socio-economic backgrounds of the people who wrote these letters were correlated with the usage in the letters, and Fries' report, *American English Grammar*, not published until 1940, divided English into three types: *standard* English, characteristic of writers with college education and professional standing in the community, *popular* or *common* English, normally used by high school graduates, and *vulgar* English, characteristic of uneducated laborers. Both the Leonard and the Fries surveys were published by the National Council of Teachers of English. In their time they were shockingly controversial, though they seem quite innocuous to us now. Fries was—and still occasionally is—subjected to many vitriolic attacks as the advocate of laissez-faire in linguistics and in morality in general, the arch-conspirator whose treason finally culminated in the great betrayal at Springfield in 1961. The third great survey begun in the 1920's was the *Linguistic Atlas of America*. Although field work for the atlas did not begin until 1931, the project began with the formal proposal in 1928, and plans involving the social levels to be surveyed were worked out before the end of the decade. Hans Kurath, director of the atlas, adopted Fries' three types, and the tradition became firmly established that American English exists in high, middle, and lowbrow varieties.

Miss Fidditch was not quick to change. Unless she was the type who attended NCTE meetings and regularly read such publications as the *English Journal*, she probably did not even know about these surveys until the 1940's when the publication of Fries created such a stir. R. C. Pooley's *Handbook of Current English Usage* appeared in 1930, but it had little immediate influence. Pooley did not become a common classroom word until 1946, when his *Teaching English Usage* was published. And of course the appearance in 1934 of the second edition of *Webster's New International Dictionary* set off a flurry of controversy as violent as that following the publication of the third edition in 1961. But few changes in the teaching of usage filtered down to the classroom until the postwar years.

The status of linguistics was considerably elevated by the success of the wartime accelerated language courses. Both the colleges and the high schools installed language labs and overhauled their creaky curricula in foreign languages. It is inconceivable that we would ever go back to the slow old translation methods by which languages were taught in the 1930's. The teaching of English as a foreign language became a recognized and respectable professional specialty, a branch of applied linguistics. It was inevitable that linguistics would invade Miss Fidditch's grammar class. Textbooks in the new English grammar began to appear. The NCTE, which always had been sympathetic toward linguistics, was thoroughly infiltrated by linguists and became the subversive organization it is today. A course in English structure became a requirement for the teacher's certificate in most states. The summer institutes pioneered by the College Board's Commission on English and now the entry of the U. S. Office of Education have hastened the capitulation, and Miss Fidditch has been so thoroughly brainwashed that she no longer opposes the linguists' theories of grammar, but too often expects the linguist to bring her the revealed word of truth from on high.

A revised attitude toward usage entered the classroom as a fellow-traveler with the new grammar. Miss Fidditch reluctantly gave up the fight for *I shall* as a lost cause. The three Fries-Kurath types (standard, common, and vulgar) became the new dogma. Miss Fidditch stopped thinking about correct and incorrect English and began to think in terms of good, not so good, and awful. With the dike breached by the acceptance of *I will* and *it's me* even in her textbooks, she believed that the good was no longer attainable, that she had no choice but to support the not-so-good and to shore up fragments against the influx of the awful. Quit trying so hard for perfection, she was told, or just quit trying altogether. Leave your language alone. Be descriptive, not prescriptive—whatever that means.

The results have been dismal. Miss Fidditch now vacillates between her old unenlightened despotism and a new unenlightened anarchy. She is trapped in a pincer maneuver between the NCTE and the PTA. The confusion in today's attitudes toward usage is well illustrated in an Ann Landers column which appeared recently:

> "DEAR ANN LANDERS: I'm a Chicagoan who is stationed at Fort Hood, Texas. Your answer will settle a small civil war in our barracks. We have guys in our outfit who hail from all parts of the country. The fellows from New York and Texas pronounce the letters 'u' and 'ew' as if there was a 'Y' in front. It comes out 'You.' For example, they say 'Nyoo York' and 'nyoospaper.' The midwesterners and the west coast guys say 'Noo York' and 'noozpaper.'

"The words 'produce,' 'consume,' and 'student' get the same treatment from the Texans and New Yorkers. They put a little 'y' sound in. We notice that Chet Huntley says, 'N.B.C. Nyoos, Nyoo York' and David Brinkley says, 'N.B.C. Nooz, Washington.'

"Can you tell us which is correct?—FORT HOOD GANG.

"DEAR GANG: I have checked four dictionaries. No two agree.

"The best answer to your question is in Fowler's Modern English Usage. It says 'We deserve not praise but censure, if we decline to accept the popular pronunciation of popular words.' This means there is no right or wrong, so imitate the natives.

"Good night, David. Good night, Chet. We enjoy your nooz in Chicago."

Of course Ann Landers' answer is half right, but oh that statement that there is no right or wrong in language—and imagine citing Fowler, of all people, to support it!

If Ann Landers is indeed echoing the new popular attitude toward usage, as I fear, then it is later than we think. It means that the authors of all those slick shiny new pretty textbooks and handbooks, each of which competes to be the most modern and up to date, have so distorted the real and eminently sensible conclusions of Fries and Kurath and the other surveyors of usage that it may take us a decade to get back to sanity. For when these textbook writers and a whole gaggle of new self-appointed experts on English language teaching who have never even read those surveys, though they invariably cite the titles in their footnotes and bibliographies—when these camp followers substituted the Fries-Kurath scale for the old invariable absolute, they loaded that scale with all kinds of extraneous junk. The "standard" end of the scale was equated with literary, formal, rhetorically effective, and other irrelevant adjectives. The "vulgar" end was equated with illiterate, slang, colloquial, jargon, and dialect.

Such a composite scale is, of course, illogical and unusable. Is *ain't* to be considered literary because it appears in *Huckleberry Finn*, or illiterate because it is used by the garbage man? And how about those little dialogues between Mercutio and his friends in *Romeo and Juliet?* Are they literary or vulgar? The Bostonian "Pahk youh cah beside the Hahvahd pahts depahtment" is a local dialect, but hardly restricted to the speech of illiterates. Faced with such an inconsistent scale, on which one end was obviously mother, home, and heaven, the other end the black pit, but along which Miss Fidditch was completely unable to navigate because these inconsistencies kept spinning the compass, she simply gave up and concluded that all virtue is relative and it doesn't really matter very much. Let's be descriptive, not prescriptive, anyway!

Even some of the highly competent and responsible authorities must share some of the blame for this absurd all-purpose usage scale and the consequent lapse into laisez-faire. Porter Perrin's *Writer's Guide and Index of Usage* replaced the conservative *Harbrace Handbook* as the most widely adopted freshman text, largely because of his elaborate scale of usage, ranging from literary at one end (the highest, naturally) to vulgate, slang, and dialect at the other. Pooley's *Teaching English Usage*, the most influential of the how-to-do-it books, used a five-tone scale: Literary, Standard Formal, Standard Informal, Homely, and Illiterate. Pooley was apparently following George Philip Krapp, one of the finest scholars on the English language, whose classification was Literary, Formal Colloquial, General Colloquial, Popular, and Vulgar.

In 1948 John S. Kenyon published a very important paper entitled "Cultural Levels and Functional Varieties of English" in which he attacked the single, multi-purpose scale and insisted that functional varieties (i.e., written vs. spoken) must be considered separately from cultural levels (i.e., upper vs. lower class usage). One dimension is not enough to fix a point of usage. The same warning had appeared in the first chapter of Fries, but no one had paid it much attention. Kenyon's article did indeed have some effect: Subsequent editions of Perrin, for example, adopted a two-dimensional scale of usage. But only a few of the textbook writers heeded the warning.

Even Kenyon combined many incompatibles. His examples of the lower cultural level included "illiterate speech, narrowly local dialect, ungrammatical speech and writing, excessive and unskilful slang, slovenly and careless vocabulary and construction, exceptional pronunciation." Kenyon was committing the very sin against which he preached so eloquently: loading one end of a value scale with a whole wastebasketful of miscellaneous evils. The "Hahvahd Yahd" pronunciation is "narrowly local" and perhaps even "exceptional" but certainly not of low cultural level. The slang of our teenagers may be inappropriate in an essay on *Silas Marner*, but it has little in common with the speech of illiterates. And I have been most offended by "solvenly and careless vocabulary" in graduate theses and dissertations written by pompous prudes who would sooner die than to ever split an infinitive.

Today we find three different and incompatible attitudes toward usage simultaneously current: The old invariable absolute of Miss Fidditch, moribund but not yet dead; the single sliding scale of the early Perrin, unfortunately now the most popular in the classroom; and Kenyon's two-dimensional scale distinguishing functional varieties from cultural levels. Now two dimensions are better than one, or none, but I suggest that they are not enough. To push the geometrical metaphor a bit further, two intersecting lines can indeed define a point, but it takes three dimensions to define a solid object, and a fourth to place it in time. For a concept so complex and elusive as usage, we need at least six dimensions.

One of these dimensions, as Kenyon quite rightly insisted, is functional variety or style. This is not a single binary contrast between written and spoken English, however, for there are many occasions on which we talk like a book, and we often write, or try to write, in a friendly conversational style. I am now speaking to you, but from a prepared written text. Does that make this lecture a sample of spoken English or of written English? No, style is a scale with more than two values, perhaps a continuous dimension. The most sensitive and sensible attempt I have yet seen to articulate this scale is Martin Joos's *The Five Clocks*—an absolute essential on your reading lists, for it is written both to and for the new enlightened Miss Fiddich. Joos calibrates this scale with five values, five styles, each of which may be either written or spoken: The *intimate* style, which communicates the person and the situation rather than information (after all, who could paraphrase the content of the "conversation" of nuzzling young lovers?); the *casual* style, that easy discourse which so comfortably keeps you a member of your in-group; the *consultative* style with which we earn and buy our daily bread, informative conversation normally punctuated at six-second intervals with cooperative interruptions from the listener (. . . yes . . . that's right . . . m-hm . . . yeah); the *formal* style, to be interrupted only by someone raising his hand or invoking some similar device of parliamentary procedure; and the *frozen* style, the language of those texts which we value enough to keep intact and periodically repeat verbatim, each time thawing the frozen text enough to savor the taste and aroma. It is no wonder that we prefer reading literature to hearing public lectures: any normal child prefers sucking a popsicle to drinking orange pop.

A second dimension of usage is geographical. Too many English teachers still think of a dialect as "what the other fellow speaks; I myself speak General American." The myth of a "general American" dialect was obsolete even before Kurath published his *Word Geography of the Eastern United States* in 1949, yet it lingers on in our classrooms. Yankee Miss Fidditches still condemn *you-all* as an illogical, illiterate vulgarism, just as they did when I was a child in their classes. And the Yankee is in turn reviled for his use of *dove* as the past tense of *dive*. Indeed some expressions are so narrowly localized, like the Bostonion *tonic*, for example, that they are better avoided when writing for nationwide publication, but they are certainly not sub-standard. Each of us speaks a dialect, and our regionalisms inevitably creep into our writing. If we try to avoid them, or warn our students to avoid them, it should be because they interfere with communication. If and when there is a case against *you-all*, it must rest on grounds very different from those relevant to *ain't* and *it don't*.

A third dimension is time. Historical change in language is both inevitable and continuous, not just something that happened at the time of the Norman Conquest. Nostalgia for the linguistic past is also nothing new. Remember that Spenser thought of Chaucer as a "well of English undefiled." The smart Miss Fidditch no longer cites Shakespeare to prove a point of usage, for she has learned that the Bard can be a two-edged sword in the hands of a bright and rebellious student. Yet she often uses *Silas Marner* and *A Tale of Two Cities* as prescriptive models for her students' prose. No one really wants or welcomes linguistic change, but the teacher is powerless to stop or even to retard it. She should be moderately conservative linguistically and there is no need for her to champion every emergent neologism just because it has appeared once in *Time* magazine. But continued tilting at the windmill of *disinterested/uninterested* only reduces her to an anachronism without any of the nobility of the gentle knight.

A fourth dimension is age. There is no reason why the child should talk like his grandfather, or vice versa. The language of Holden Caulfield's monologue would be singularly inappropriate for Hemingway's old man talking to his fish, but it is not in and of itself bad English. The speeches of John F. Kennedy were youthful and vigorous; we can only guess how he might have written as an elder statesman. A fifth dimension is sex. Can you imagine one of the football players in your senior English class describing the day of the big game as "utterly lovely"? We recognize that the masculine idiom differs from the feminine when we make critical judgements about Jane Austen, but do we sufficiently recognize the rights and needs of our students to speak and write in a manner appropriate to their sex and age group?

This leaves a sixth dimension, that of cultural level. Does Johnny speak and write in a social dialect which types him as coming from the wrong side of the tracks? If so, it is not because he is stupid or sloppy-thinking or even ignorant of English grammar. Explaining the principles of English verb agreement will not make him stop saying *it don't*. If you try to tell him that *I don't have no money* really means "I do have some money," he merely recognizes you for the fool you are. He knows very well—and so do you—that his sentence means nothing of the sort. He speaks this way because his parents and his friends speak this way. We acquire a social dialect the same way we acquire a geographical dialect, and no study of grammar (traditional, structural, or transformational) is going to change it. Dialects cannot be compared and evaluated in terms of logic, only in terms of appropriateness to the situation. After all, one can make a pretty strong logical case for *ain't: He's a student, isn't he? You're a student, aren't you? I'm a student, . . . ?* The research of my students in a seminar on social dialectology has clearly established that this linguistic social stratification in usage is firmly ingrained by kindergarten age. This is the logic in which these children think; to them, the teacher's dialect seems illogical.

If we tell Johnny that the use of *ain't* in certain social circles may prevent him from getting an invitation to join the country club (and from getting a good enough job to pay the club dues), then he starts to listen. But—and here is the controversial point on which so many critics have misinterpreted the linguists—we should not condemn *ain't* as a word, only its use in circumstances where it will evoke social disapproval. We hear a lot about aid to "disadvantaged youth" in these days of the War on Poverty, but no one holds that making a child ashamed of his family and friends is a legitimate goal of such programs. Ideally we should make Johnny bidialectal, able to travel in the country-club set without linguistic handicap, yet able to return to his home and friends without alienating them with pretentious manners and speech. We should help him to social-climb without becoming a snob, minimize rather than contribute to the cultural conflict which results from social mobility. People used to think that they could improve a bilingual child's English by stamping out his foreign language. Therefore Spanish-speaking children in Texas were punished for speaking Spanish, and both Spanish language and Spanish culture (except Castillian, of course) were treated with contempt. We now know that this unfortunate policy only rendered the child incapable of living comfortably in either culture. We found that when we encouraged pride in his bilingualism and in his Spanish heritage, he actually learned English faster, provided, of course, that he could see the important social and economic motives for doing so.

Bidialectism is like bilingualism, better approached positively than negatively. If your school has a dominant clique of students from "culturally advantaged" middle-class homes, your job is easy. You have only to assist Johnny in acquiring the linguistic social tools he needs to break into the circle of friends he admires. Teenagers are great conformists, with a classicist's respect for proper form, and they will learn more about usage on the ballfield and in the schoolyard than you can teach them in the classroom. But if the top dogs in your school are the gang of leather jacket and *it don't* boys, you have a problem, for the child will inevitably adopt whatever English usage gives him the most status among his peers. All you can do is try to supply the motivation which he does not get through natural channels. If your invocations of the country club and good job and your parade of heroes who don't say *it don't* all fail to move him, then you will almost certainly fail. In either case, you will get further with a positive approach. Johnny is a lot more likely to say *isn't* in the English class if you don't try to stop him from saying *ain't* in the schoolyard.

Even if the worst happens: the social organization of your student body does make your task hopeless and you do fail, and Johnny goes right on saying *ain't,* this is not a very important failure, certainly not worth making nagging old curmudgeons out of yourselves and breaking diplomatic relations with your students. There are so many things that you can do to help your students, even if you can't make a dent in their vulgate. You teach them composition, literature, grammar. And there are the other five dimensions of usage, in which you are not bucking the system and so can get through to the student. Johnny may be very interested in learning how language varies geographically, for example, and an understanding of regional variation may awaken an interest in how language can also vary socially, so that you eventually get through to him after all. Perhaps the society on the right side of the tracks is too remote and alien to motivate him at all; then let him wait a few years. When his life later does produce a need to associate with people outside his purloined-hubcap fraternity, he will make his own adjustments in social usage; that is, he will if you have given him some understanding of the usage problem rather than just loading him down with so many negative inhibitions that they only block his later attempts to find himself linguistically. Your proper goal is linguistic awareness of self and of society.

These six dimensions of usage must be carefully distinguished, both from one another and from a seventh but different scale, what we might call the scale of *responsibility*. On this scale, value judgements are indeed relevant: how responsible has Johnny been in selecting exactly those points on the other six dimensions which will make his language most appropriate for this specific occasion, and how responsibly has he combined these language forms into a logical, coherent, effective discourse? It is this which we should be evaluating when we put a grade on his composition. Another name for this scale is *rhetoric*. It is the legitimate subject matter of the course on composition. The six dimensions of usage must also be taught in the English class, however, for they are the factors which condition the long, almost continuous string of linguistic decisions which one must make in putting together a responsible composition.

But, Miss Fidditch will protest, how can we teach Johnny to make the hundreds of decisions on English usage which are so necessary in any responsible writing or speaking if every decision is itself such a complicated problem as you say, a function of six variable factors? Wouldn't he be paralyzed by having to stop at each word and work out the mathematics? Indeed he would, *if* the entire process had to operate at the deliberate, fully-conscious level. Fortunately our minds contain a wonderful mechanism which reduces a great deal of this decision-making to subconscious habit. Given enough experience—and good English teaching is mostly a matter of providing and directing that experience—a good writer or speaker learns to continuously evaluate the context and the situation and make the proper choices with little or no conscious awareness of the process.

Permit me another analogy: When you first learned to drive a car, you perhaps despaired of ever mastering the complicated coordination of your hands on the wheel and gearshift lever and your feet on the pedals. The worst part was that the proper thing to do with your hands and feet kept changing from moment to moment, depending on what you saw through the windshield and on the dashboard dials and what you heard and felt the car do. If your approach to this complex problem was to oversimplify it by reducing it to a set of invariable rules ("Always keep your eyes on the road." "Apply the brakes when you see danger ahead."), then you became a bad driver, the kind that slams on the brakes when skidding on an icy road, and who forgets to look in the rear-view mirror before changing lanes. If you are a good driver (as I am sure that all of you are), it is because you developed flexibility rather than rigidity in your reactions to new situations, and because you practiced driving under varying conditions until the appropriate reactions became second nature to you, so that now people compliment you by saying that you "instinctively" do the right thing in an emergency.

When I was a child in seventh grade, the local school system decided that we young barbarians needed social polish and so hired to lecture to us on etiquette an elderly widow, then living in modest circumstances but earlier, so she told us, the flower of Eastern Society. Her lectures were straight out of Emily Post, and the society she described might as well have been on Mars. I remember her telling us that when we went to call on our little friends, their butler would of course greet us at the door. If the young master were not at home, the butler would always present a silver tray, on which we were to lay our visiting cards. But, she warned us, before we placed the card on the tray, we had to bend down the proper corner of the card—I believe it was to be the lower right-hand corner, but I have forgotten that detail. Now in that little piney-woods community, a few of the more affluent families may have owned silver trays, but certainly no butlers. And visiting cards?! No, this instruction was absurd, not because there was anything wrong with butlers and visiting cards, nor because her rule of the proper corner was incorrect, but because she presented these as inflexible absolutes, ideals of social behavior for anyone anywhere. Even if we were too poor to buy visiting cards, she graciously assured us, we could write them out ourselves in a good Palmer hand and carry them along with us when we went to ask Butch or Spike to come out for an afternoon of stealing apples from the orchard behind the insane asylum.

Certainly we show much more sense today, both in driver training and in teaching our kids social manners. What excuse then is there for the English teacher's vacillating between the old invariable absolute and a game of laissez faire on a sliding scale. I don't propose a compromise, for I believe that both alternatives are equally dead wrong. To insist that square pegs go in square holes, triangular pegs in triangular holes, is not a proposal of a compromise between the idiocy of one fool who insists that square pegs are always nicer than triangular ones, and that of the other fool who claims that the shape of the pegs isn't really very important. What I propose is that we be uncompromisingly demanding of our students that they employ the *correct usage*, the *responsible* usage.

Of course you will be criticized for doing so, but then the good teacher has always found his cup of hemlock to be both inevitable and strangely rewarding. There are conservatives who will accuse you of "giving up all standards of right and wrong." There will be liberals who, with equal injustice, will accuse you of being "prescriptive old grammarians hostile to modern linguistic science." Hardest of all to bear will be those who will accuse you of being compromisers or, even worse, eclectics.

But you can defend yourselves. I was recently interviewed by a news reporter who was preparing a syndicated feature series on the "new grammar" and English teaching. I talked with him for two hours, but I am afraid that he went back to his newspaper not yet thoroughly converted, for a few days later I received the following letter from him:

> Dear Dr. DeCamp:
> Many, many thanks for the interesting interview last week. I came away from our talk much better informed than before.
> However (life is a whole series of "howevers"), there is something that bothers me. This is in what my limited knowledge of the modern movement sees as a too indulgent attitude toward the standard or prestige dialect.
> If the standard dialect were divested of its authority, if the level of language represented for example in the writing of Churchill is placed on the same value scale as the cottonfield jargon of Alabama—if we no longer have the goal of "correct" English, then what will we really have?
> As I see it the existence of precriptive norm creates an upward thrust to the language. That is, the existence of a The Correct Way tends to urge an upward striving which continuously works for the betterment of communication. Without an authority level would not the upward striving be brunted? Would not the course of the language's evolution become slightly degraded?
> As I see it there must be a prescribed goal to all human endeavor. As I see it a bad king given to arbitrary, inconsistent action is to be preferred, still, to anarchy. A semblance of order is better than confusion, I feel.

This is not a foolish letter. This newsman is not an idiot or a fanatic. He is an intelligent man of affairs, genuinely trying to find out what is going on in English classes today. That even he would write such a letter proves what a great task lies before us to inform the public as well as to teach their children. The newsman deserved an extended reply, and I wrote one. I will conclude today by reading that reply, not that I offer it as a model for replies to letters of this sort which you will certainly receive, but because it sums up most of the ideas of this lecture and arrays them in battle formation. For it is your battle too: a fight for your rights to be prescriptive, but correctly prescriptive, a fight for your freedom to get on with the job of helping Johnny learn, not to use better English, but to use English better. And that is really what usage is all about. Here is what I wrote:

> There is no danger of "the course of the language's evolution" becoming "degraded," as you fear. Language is only the medium of communication. Shakespeare was a great dramatist because he knew how to write well, not because Elizabethan English was superior. To assume otherwise is like saying that Rembrandt was a great painter because he had better paints and canvas than modern artists have. The English language is now, always has been, and probably always will be perfectly adequate—*equally*

adequate—as a medium of good writing. Unfortunately not all people are equally adept at using that medium. Therefore we need English teachers.

The attitude toward the standard or prestige dialect held by the linguist or the responsible English teacher is no more indulgent than it ever has been in any century. Of course we do not place the writing of Churchill on the same value scale as the cottonfield jargon of Alabama—your example—because there is no value scale including both these. There are at least three variables involved here. Remember my telling you about the several dimensions in which language may vary? Well, to begin with, Churchill is formal writing; the cottonfield is informal conversation. Second, Churchill was a well-to-do, upper-class English gentleman, whereas the cottonfield worker is economically and culturally lower class. Third, Churchill was a disciplined mind and an experienced and talented writer, whereas very few of the field workers would have the ability to write the history of the second world war even if someone gave them the opportunity. The first of these is a dimension (or scale, if you prefer) of functional varieties of language. After all, Churchill did not always speak as he wrote; he was a delightful informal conversationalist. Of course his informal conversation was not the same as that of the field worker, but we would have to compare the two men either by their formal writing or by their informal speech. Formal written prose is not in and of itself better than conversation. Each has its place in situations demanding the other—could you imagine your wife greeting you in Churchillian periods? —and there are both good and bad examples of each.

The second dimension by which your two examples vary is cultural level. The kid from the slums speaks differently, despite our efforts at democratic education. This is one way we can tell a judge from a janitor even if both are wearing bathing suits at the beach and we only hear them talking about the weather. The two simply speak different dialects, social dialects.

The third dimension relevant here is rhetorical. In this dimension, value judgments are indeed in order. A disciplined, logical mind, a clear sense of organization, a feel for the most effective and persuasive expression. We admire these characteristics in Churchill and deplore their absence in the field laborer, though they occasionally do appear in the speech and writing of an uneducated laborer. No one defends sloppy thinking. Now it is true that the clear-thinking, rhetorically-competent man is often upper class socially, simply because his competence advances him to a higher income bracket. It is also true that he is usually in a position where he will be producing more formal writing than will the laborer. But the three dimensions are not necessarily correlated. Disorganized, illogical trash is written in formal style by persons of upper class using impeccable "grammar"—witness the current government gobbledygook or the correspondence and memos written by most industrial executives. I won't even mention journalese. Churchill's table talk was colloquial yet superb. So was

Mark Twain, even when through the mouth of Huck Finn he used *ain't* and all the other shibboleths of lower class usage.

No, we are not "indulgent." We complain that the old-line English teachers were too indulgent. They gave (and some still do give) the student an A on a paper, no matter how inane and disorganized, just as long as the verbs all agreed in number, the commas were in the right places, and the student refrained from using *ain't*. Therefore, as you yourself admitted, their training had little to offer you in your career as a writer.

We believe that the teacher should be far more demanding rhetorically than ever before, that there should be no compromise with sloppiness in composition. On the cultural dimension, we believe that the teacher should deal with all the social variants, giving the student facility in shifting to different varieties, and being honest about the social implications of using each; after all, in some circumstances saying *it don't* is indeed socially equivalent to spitting on the carpet, but *I shall* and *Whom did you meet* are kisses of death to a politician—and possibly to a newspaper writer as well. Finally, on the functional or stylistic dimension, the teacher should give attention to all the stylistic levels which her students are likely to use. Instead of damning informal English or apologizing for it, she should help her students use it well.

In summary, I find it as illogical to attribute Churchill's greatness as a writer to his use of upper-class standard grammar as to attribute it to the fact that he always smoked big cigars.

Part III

Standard and Nonstandard English: Learning and Teaching Problems

Introduction

IRWIN FEIGENBAUM

The range of the English teacher's interests and abilities has to be very wide since his field extends from literacy training through productive control of standard English to literary appreciation. At the same time, every teacher's focus is necessarily on the individual students with him in class, and he is constantly searching for new ways of teaching them. Wherever and whenever two teachers meet, we find a universal phenomenon, "sharing"; teachers discuss what they have found useful in specific teacher-student situations. A large store of ways to teach typifies an experienced, innovative teacher. Acquiring new ways of teaching—new methods and new materials—will continue as the teacher expands his control of the subject matter as well as his ability to teach every student. However, it is also important that he periodically step back to reassess the larger teaching context.

Sometimes such a reassessment is forced on the individual teacher or on the entire teaching profession. This is the case at present. As integration proceeds on its slow, forward route, and as the mobility of our population forces contact among many languages and dialects, our schools are faced with large numbers of linguistically different students. Ruth Strickland has described the situation:

Irwin Feigenbaum is a Research Linguist in the Sociolinguistics Program at the Center for Applied Linguistics. His main concern has been the development of methods and materials for the teaching of standard English to nonstandard speakers. He is the author of several articles and a book, *English Now*.

219

It is well known that a high percentage of failure or of low achievement exists among children whose oral language differs from the language of the textbooks . . . Research is needed to determine whether there are problems here, the nature of them, and what should be done about them to permit children with the handicap of deviant language to reach maximum achievement.[107]

LINGUISTIC DIFFERENCE

In the past, recognized linguistic difference was of two types: different words for the same use (traditionally we have handled this by teaching alternate forms—not *He brang it* but *He brought it*) and different languages (for which we instituted classes in English-as-a second-language). Now we realize that there is—and has been—a third type of linguistic difference that falls somewhere between the two types mentioned above. This is the case, for example, of black nonstandard English.

In investigating linguistic variation in English, sociolinguists have contributed much information about the forms and structure of nonstandard English dialects. They see that such a dialect is as logical and structured as any other variety of English (or, to describe the situation more carefully, that it is impossible to prove that any variety of English is more logical or structured than any other).

STANDARD AND NONSTANDARD ENGLISH

How to define "standard English" and "nonstandard English"? This question is difficult to answer because of the variety of views on determining standard and nonstandard usage, but it is a concern that cannot be ignored since precise information is necessary for prescribing effective pedagogical strategies. Should we recognize several standard dialects that have some common features but that differ from region to region? Or is it a matter of recognizing what is sometimes called "network English"; that is, the English used by broadcasters throughout the country? Central to the problem of definition is the extent of the difference between standard and nonstandard dialects. It is central because the degree of difference will affect educational decisions.

One viewpoint is that the differences between standard and black nonstandard English are superficial; the differences, though apparent, are not deep. Some linguists describe standard/nonstandard speech differences in terms of the frequency of occurrence of forms. They say that the forms found in the standard-English speaker's repertoire are also found in the repertoire of the speaker of nonstandard English, but the differences, as William Labov states, reflect different selection from this common repertoire or a different order of selection. Labov argues very strongly that the differences are superficial:

> Despite the obvious differences between standard and nonstandard, they are both based upon the same deep structure and are used to convey the same underlying logical propositions.[108]

The other side of the argument is upheld with vigor and conviction. Beryl Bailey sees the differences as being so great that she proposes an underlying creole grammar for black nonstandard English.[109] And even Labov has to temper the strength of his argument. He admits that black nonstandard English differs in deep structure from standard English (he cites the absence of a future perfect tense and the presence of the verb *be*, separate from the copula), "but the main body of dialect differences do not affect the semantic or 'deep structure' level."[110]

The "main body"—however large it is—may be identical, but what about these exceptions? And, although standard and nonstandard dialects may have essentially the same deep structure, the extent to which they differ in surface structure must be considered. Dialect difference should be examined in terms of depth as well as length and breadth. There are many apparent differences between standard English and black nonstandard English. How widespread are these surface differences? For example, do the dialects differ in marking the third person singular present tense verb form (standard English *he works;* black nonstandard English *he work*)? Or must we say that the entire present tense paradigms differ?

On a slightly different tack, Labov suggests that conflicts exist between standard English and the structure of the black speech community. The conflicts can be structural or functional. Structural conflicts are due to grammatical differences between dialects; they have different rules and categories in their linguistic structures. Functional conflicts arise from differences in values assigned to language usage; what is linguistically valuable in one community may not be in the other.[111]

ISSUE: EFFECTS OF DIALECT DIFFERENCE

In describing nonstandard dialects, a linguist focuses on dialect difference and similarity. An educator, on the other hand, asks another type of question: how important is the difference? what are the effects of the difference? The linguist is not required to make the value judgments that the educator must. The educator must decide what is important to teach and how to teach it. Bailey, in raising the issue of a possible creole grammar underlying the structure of black nonstandard English, says that the effect of this type of difference would be that linguistic features of the nonstandard dialect are "more deeply rooted, more systematic" than we had previously thought. Our approach to teaching additional language skills might have to be different because the depth of the problem would be greater than we are used to seeing in our public school native-language English classes.

One effect of dialect difference could be social. Incomplete control of oral standard English could prevent job advancement, independent of a person's ability to read, write, or do other tasks necessary to the job in question. Carrying this reasoning even further, we can see that language could be used to enforce a segregation that is no longer practicable on other bases. What can be done if the student's language (and perhaps other behaviors) are not "standard"? One approach would be to try educating the child in the ways of the mainstream culture, the ways of the middle-class school. Another approach would be to try to change thinking so that these types of differences would be accepted.

Another effect of dialect difference might be lack of inter-dialect comprehension. What happens when the speaker of black nonstandard English encounters a standard English sentence like *He wants to know whether we* can go? (The speaker would probably use a sentence like *He want to know can we go.*) What happens when the dialect speaker says, "It ain't no desses"? (In standard English, that sentence would be *There aren't any* desks.) Does communication break down? and, if so, to what degree?

Does dialect difference affect the acquisition of other skills, such as reading? In his article, Goodman says, "The more divergence there is between the dialect of the learner and the dialect of learning, the more difficult will be the task of learning to read." Knowing the type(s) and degree of divergence would help us in pinpointing the difficulties children are having in learning to read, write, and speak standard English and perhaps in acquiring other academic skills. This knowledge would permit us to make rational judgments about what steps to take, if any. It may also keep us from taking unnecessary or unwise steps.

ISSUE: PEDAGOGICAL DECISIONS

Should standard English be taught in school? Why? Is employ-
ability a good reason for teaching it? Much of what is taught to students is not done with the view that they will be able to use this skill
or knowledge to get and hold a job. In his paper, Shuy suggests that
there are other reasons for teaching standard English. Bloomfield, Hill,
and Sledd say that the public makes judgments about a person's
language. How are we to react to these judgments in our educational
decisions? Since every decision involves a value judgment, people's
attitudes are important and, although linguists say that every dialect
seems to be as sophisticated as any other, the public's placement of
value on the standard dialect will affect the decisions we make.

If we are to teach standard English, what features do we present?
This will depend on how we see standard English. Dillard and Allen
see a type of "network English" as the goal. Goodman would consider
regional standards as the goal. In considering Labov's two categories
of conflicts (structural and functional), one might raise the question
of what we should teach. Are we to teach linguistic forms? different
value systems? What about the effective use of language?

At what age is instruction to be undertaken? Do some skills require
the prior mastery of standard English? Will we then have to sequence
our instruction to account for this order in skill acquisition? And what
age is best for instruction? Feigenbaum raises the last question in his
article on teaching oral standard English. The same question has to be
raised for instruction in all language arts.

How to teach standard English to the student who has always
spoken English? If the dialect differences are superficial, new approaches may not be needed. If, on the other hand, we are teaching
students whose language is so different from standard English that we
have a "quasi-foreign language situation",[112] we may need to look to
foreign-language instruction for suggestions of how to teach standard-
English language skills. Allen, Feigenbaum, and Troike suggest using
foreign-language methodology, but they differ somewhat in how they
would use them.

The linguist's contribution is in shedding light on a complex situation. He describes standard English and the nonstandard English
encountered by teachers in class, and he may suggest strategies for
achieving a specific educational objective. He can add to the teacher's
understanding and ability to cope with the situation, for, as Hill says,"
. . . all that a linguist can discover about his subject should not merely

limit what the English teacher can say but is of positive though potential value to him in all his work." In making use of these discoveries, the teacher can gain new insights into the teaching context and new ways of teaching. The following articles discuss teaching from many points of view. They can serve as a beginning for a reassessment of the larger teaching context and as sources of new ways of teaching the linguistically different student.

1

The Problem of Fact and Value in the Teaching of English

MORTON W. BLOOMFIELD

The increase of accurate knowledge about the history of the English language and of linguistic processes in general during the last hundred years has begun only recently to have its impact upon the teaching of English, and especially of grammar, in the schools. Greater and more accurate knowledge is bound to affect the attitudes toward and the aims of any academic subject as well as its content. It is therefore proper to consider just what changes are called for in the teaching of English on the basis of our enlarged knowledge.

Some linguists in America during the last two decades have become exercised over the traditional prescriptionist attitude toward grammar which has long been one of the chief factors contributing to the conviction held by a vast majority of Americans that the "rules" of grammar are laws, in the same sense as the regularities of nature were laws in nineteenth-century eyes, or moral imperatives on a level with the Ten Commandments. Some, in disgust, have been led to the extreme of suggesting that "anything goes," that one should leave one's language alone, and that all teaching of English should be confined to a description of the state of the language or to its history. Very recently, in American cultural and literary journals, there have been disputes between these ardent linguists and those who favor some kind of prescriptionist approach. At the same time, one hears over and over again, in the teaching and other professions, the wail that young people do not know how to read and write their own language.

225

Embedded in these disputes and complaints is a philosophic problem of the first magnitude of which many participants do not seem to be aware—the relation of fact to value. In the background are tacit assumptions about this relationship which, if they cannot be simply solved, should at least be thrust into the light. The purpose of this article is to point up some of these basic issues in their bearing on the teaching of English in the schools.

The problem of what to teach to youngsters in English is first of all a question of value not of fact. As Professor Northrop has written: "The characteristic of a problem of value . . . is that, in part at least, it raises a question concerning what ought to be, rather than what is, the case."[113] The question of the relation of fact to value is an exceedingly complex one. That facts have some bearing on value is clear. What man ought to do is at least limited by what he is; the values set up or discovered cannot violate his nature. On the other hand, the mere presence of certain facts does not make them valuable. Possibly more than 50 per cent of humanity desire to steal, at least on occasion, but this "fact" does not mean that stealing is a value. When Hegel wrote that whatever is is right, what he meant was that everything has a reason, that is, capable of rational explanation. He did not necessarily approve of whatever is. Some social scientists and linguists, however, follow Hegel's dictum to the letter.

The problem of value impinges on the science of linguistics on various levels, but it is not my intention here to discuss the general philosophical issues involved but to limit myself to their bearing on the subject of teaching English. There is, for example, the problem of value involved in the very subject matter of the science. The question of what language is must be answered, implicitly or explicitly, before the subject matter of linguistics can be properly delimited and understood. This involves general values, but they shall not be my concern here. I shall start with the assumption—not completely agreed upon— that we know what language is and what its facts are.

In relation to the teaching of English the question of what ought to be taught about the language to students cannot be completely answered by a knowledge of the facts of the language (or by linguists as linguists), because, first, value questions are never completely answered by the facts and, second, facts and values from areas other than language must be taken into consideration. Furthermore, the aim of education is not a linguistic question.

In order to decide what ought to be taught in elementary English classes, we not only have to find out what are the facts of language but what are the facts of society and man, problems which are difficult and which involve from the very beginning value questions. We are concerned with what we want to do for a child; with the desirability of advocating norms in the speaking and writing of English and with educational aims generally. Everyone who argues what ought to be taught in English classes—even those who believe that nothing should be recommended—has made certain value judgments as to the nature of man, society, and education and as to what a command of language means. Ultimately, the question which we must basically consider in dealing with the teaching of English is what kind of men we want to make of our students. This cannot be solved by a knowledge of the history of the English language.

The general picture of man behind the pure descriptionist's recommendation is a completely passive one. Having discovered that language is always changing and that past attempts to fix it have failed he concludes that language should be left alone. It will change anyway; usage determines correctness; all will work out well. This argument is on the level of another: All men must die eventually; therefore, when you are sick, do not go to the doctor.

But man is not a purely passive creature of circumstance. Circumstances help to make him, but he also makes circumstances. He is limited by historical, biological, and psychological forces, but within these limits he can do a great deal—with language as with other instruments and structures. The picture of the purely passive man acted upon by forces over which he has no control is not only untrue but dangerous—and an out-of-date picture of the human personality to boot.

The key to the whole problem as regards English is the doctrine of usage. We must recognize today that usage is sovereign in the long run; but man determines usage, whether consciously or unconsciously, and the long run can make a lot of difference. In the long run we will all be dead, but this need not lead us to commit suicide.

Is there any value in the relative stability which grammatical norms can give a language? The question cannot be answered from the history of language alone. Other factors must be considered. The eighteenth century had a genuine point when it foolishly tried to "ascertain" the language. It did not realize how impossible it was because of its lack of knowledge, but it did know how useful a relative stability could be in making for clarity, exactitude, and an understanding of the past. To slow down the rate of language change—putting the eighteenth-century desire into modern terms—is a desirable goal.

What are the reasons for teaching some kind of prescriptionist grammar on a formal and informal level in the schools? Why must we decide that this is a value? I do not necessarily approve of the present methods of teaching grammar, nor do I think that old-fashioned drill and rules are the most satisfactory method, but I do think some choice on the side of prescription must be made. Why?

1. *Social utility.* It is a fact that society as a whole, however mistaken, believes that there is a correct grammar and will judge our students by it. Ultimately this attitude may be changed but certainly not in the foreseeable future. The honest teacher is as responsible for teaching the static in language as he is for teaching the dynamic. His task is neither to hinder nor to hurry change—but to teach realities. A certain amount of standardization in practice is also useful and valuable.

2. *Aid in understanding the past.* The quicker language changes the sooner the literature and documents of the past become unreadable to the majority of the American people. With the precarious situation of the humanities in America, those who believe in the spiritual value of the humanities must not labor to make them even more difficult and strange to our students.

3. *Aesthetics.* The beauty and value of the literature of the past and present are lost to those who speak only vulgate English (the language of the majority). Vulgate English has an advantage over the other levels only in vigor, when vigor is appropriate, as in the obscene, but in almost every other sense—in subtlety, sonorousness, ambiguity, cleverness, breadth—it is deficient. A person who cannot recognize the superior beauty of "Forever wilt thou love and she be fair" to "I ain't got no dough" is not fit to be teaching English.

4. *Intellectual breadth.* Speakers limited to vulgate cannot discuss a variety of ideas because they do not have the vocabulary and grasp of linguistic structure for ideas beyond those of a most primitive type. It is most improbable that one who speaks and has command only of vulgate English could write a book on leaving one's language alone. A whole range of ideas is inaccessible to him. He cannot even talk about his talking vulgate in vulgate.

For these reasons, most of which are independent of the facts of linguistics, we can defend some form of study of formal and informal English (the language of the educated) on some kind of prescriptionist level.

The problem facing the teacher and supervisors of English is similar to that facing the teacher of civics. To the political scientist qua scientist, all political constitutions are of equal importance, all come down to the level of facts and per se no fact is more important than any other fact. To him as scientist the political constitution of Tibet—

if there is one—is as important as that of the U.S.A. But in the schools and universities we emphasize the constitution of the U.S.A. and ignore, for all practical purposes, the constitution of Tibet. For teaching purposes a value judgment is made on grounds other than those provided by the facts of political science. On utilitarian grounds we recognize that the student is an American who will presumably become an adult citizen of America and will exercise his democratic rights here. A knowledge of his government is most desirable. Also, on philosophical grounds, we assume that intrinsically the American Constitution is a more profound and more satisfactory constitution than that of Tibet. But, as a science, political science says nothing of this at all. Similarly, as a science, linguistics cannot favor formal and informal English (or for that matter Bantu) to vulgate English. All linguistic facts are per se of equal importance or of equal unimportance. But on other grounds we can and must choose our values and say that we can justifiedly teach a type of prescriptive grammar and emphasize formal and informal English in the schools. Majorities in language matters are not necessarily decisive. For five hundred years at least the contraction "ain't" has been used by, I'm sure, a majority of English-speaking people, but it still is not used in formal and higher informal discourse. The fact that a majority of the people may be dishonest does not mean that we should teach dishonesty in the schools, though we may, of course, be concerned to understand the ways in which dishonesty originates or to describe dishonesty so that it can be recognized.

But, the question arises, what good then is a knowledge of linguistics and an awareness of the doctrine of usage? Is the great increase in linguistic knowledge of no value or use in teaching English? I think it is of great value, though in a different way from that in which many regard it.

The facts of language set a limit to our application of values. In a negative sense they make us aware of where prescription dare not tread. They make us more openminded, more willing to accept divided usage, more willing to give up unimportant battles (as, e.g., over "contact" as a noun). They contribute to the peace of mind of the teacher and thereby to that of the pupil. If the teacher recognizes that the "rules" of grammar are not heaven-sent, he can with equanimity discuss with his students the problems involved. He will be more apt to avoid mechanical drill and avoid the *odium grammaticum*. He can make grammar and language study more pleasant and exciting by giving a sense of the past to his drive toward the present and future. He can create a sense of the excitement of linguistic awareness and language study. And, above all, he can keep the prescriptions down to a minimum, stress usage as the final arbiter, and concentrate on style, which is certainly even more important than grammar.

Some of the new work in structural linguistics may be of practical value in actually teaching the structure of present day English. We are not necessarily tied to the traditional grammatical analysis of English which is largely based on that of Latin and Greek. In fact, the categories laid down in a recent work by Charles Fries may prove to be more useful in teaching English.[114] We are not necessarily committed to the traditional approach. But the problem of value is still with us, no matter what system we may adopt. It is never solved merely by reference to the internal facts of a subject. More is needed, and the teacher or supervisor must face the problem if he is to be successful in his task.

2

❦ Prescriptivism and Linguistics in English Teaching

ARCHIBALD A. HILL

In a recent article in *College English* Morton W. Bloomfield presents a cogent, informed, and admirably good-natured account of the problem involved in teaching English to native speakers of the language, now that linguistic scientists (a notably prickly group of men) have begun to question many traditional attitudes and even to deny vehemently, not always wisely but sometimes certainly with good evidence, some of the things we all learned in the classroom as gospel truth. Professor Bloomfield comes to the conclusion that what is taught in an English class must be some form of wise and moderate prescriptivism, checked by the limits of fact as established by linguistics. The reason for his position is that the teaching of English involves questions of value, which characteristically are not settled merely by the accumulation of facts.

It is probably natural that Bloomfield, as a man primarily interested in the discipline of English, though aware of linguistics, should lean in the direction of value, just as it is natural that a linguist, even though he be a practicing teacher of English, should lean in the direction of fact. I do not wish to question Bloomfield's central thesis or to add fuel to an already unfortunate blaze. Rather it seems to me pos-

Archibald A. Hill, Professor of English and Linguistics at the University of Texas at Austin and former president of the Linguistic Society of America, has published extensively in linguistics. Among his books are *Linguistics Today* (ed.), *The Oral Approach to English,* and *Introduction to Linguistic Structures.*

sible, if a linguist states some modifications of what Bloomfield seems to believe the linguists' position to be, that the area of mutual understanding may be increased, with benefit to all.

Bloomfield defends prescriptivism first because it has social utility. That is, the public judges, and will continue to judge, our students by the language they use. Therefore, he says, the honest teacher must neither hinder nor hurry change but teach realities; and unwise liberalism will expose students to censure. With this position the majority of responsible linguists would agree. We are to blame for not having made ourselves clear on the point, though my own experience in the failure of serious attempts at explanation leads me to believe that perhaps not all the blame lies with the linguists. No intelligent linguist would think of denying that the use of a given linguistic form will have inevitable social consequences for the user—the position that language patterns are a part of larger patterns of social behavior and that each reacts on the other is central to linguistics. In my own classes, as an example of social consequences from language use, I often tell a story told me by an old Charlestonian. She had brought a beau home for family inspection, and her father was proudly displaying his collection of art. "Now this," he said, "is called 'The Broken Pitcher.' "

"Yes," said the young man, "I see the corner's damaged." The suitor was never invited to the house again. The form "pitcher" cannot be ugly in itself—we use it as a perfectly good word. Nor can the confusion of two words, as the result of natural tendencies of change, be a very heinous sin. Millions probably confuse them, just as even more millions confuse *affect* and *effect*. The point, however, is not that it would be easy to defend the young man's misunderstanding. It is rather that the consequences of it were very real for him and presumably unpleasant. The nonlinguist often argues violently that there is something inherently wrong, ugly, or illogical in such a form as "pitcher" and equates any denial of the inherent "wrongness" of the form with a denial of the social consequences of using it.

The linguist maintains merely that in itself a form, say *golpet*, is as good as another form, say *thaltep;* the difference between them is merely one of attitudes, not of inherent qualities. I have chosen nonsense illustrations deliberately, in an effort to find forms to which the reader has not already learned to respond with conditioned attitudes of value. It seems to me that a linguist is performing a service in attempting to separate such conditioned value reactions from the inherent qualities of the stimulus and that we have a right to complain when our attempts to do so are received as further illustrations of the blindness of men who are supposed to believe that "anything goes."

Bloomfield's second reason for teaching a prescriptive grammar and usage is that it is an aid in understanding the past. Again a linguist cannot quarrel, at least with the aim. Yet it is to be doubted whether prescriptive grammar is always conservative. For instance, one of Bloomfield's examples of vulgate (the language of the majority) which he would rightly resist in classroom use is "I ain't got no dough." Two of the three objectionable forms in this sentence, *ain't* and the double negative, are older than the prescriptivist objection to them and are therefore more in line with past usage than are the modern condemnations. A linguist would hope to accomplish Bloomfield's aim of understanding past language structures not by reliance on prescriptivism but by knowing the structures of the present, with adequate recognition of the fact that different forms and structures are in use in the English-speaking community, in different places, on different social levels, and for different purposes. With such a background a student would, we hope, be ready to deal with the language of the past not as a primitive jargon less perfect than his own speech but as structure to be respected and understood—a structure different from others, as all language structures are, and by virtue of difference, capable of artistic effects as good as any open to Hemingway or Housman.

Bloomfield's third and fourth reasons for rejecting vulgate in favor of a prescriptive norm are that vulgate is deficient in all artistic qualities except vigor and is likewise deficient in intellectual breadth and depth. The two statements are closely related and should be discussed together. In a measure, a linguist can agree. If we listen to talk heard on street corners or in grocery stores, it is true that we hear little that is memorable for beauty or intellectual penetration. Language use is an art, and all can agree that great practitioners of any art are few in number. Similarly it is a truism that intellectual leaders are anything but numerous—otherwise they would not be leaders. Yet many linguists would feel that, when Bloomfield says that vulgate is deficient in beauty and intellectual qualities, he is confusing the language with its use. We can agree with him heartily that good models of language use should be given to our students, but we would maintain that the nature of an instrument is different from its employment.

Language structure, with which linguists are primarily concerned, remains relatively constant, and in all important ways is shared by all members of the community, both those who use the language well and those who use it ill. For instance, though it is not universally agreed to by all linguists, many would now say that English has four degrees of stress. If so, this is an example of an important structural feature shared by normal English contemporary speech on all levels and in all localities. Even if we grant that such structural characteristics can only be created by the habitual usage of the community and are further changed only as these habits change, the striking fact about such structural features is how slowly and how little they change. If English has four stresses, it has acquired the fourth at some time since the Norman Conquest; otherwise the stress system has apparently remained unchanged for approximately two thousand years. If there should be only three significant stresses in Modern English, there has been no change at all. If such structural features can remain so little changed in the face of all the social upheavals and linguistic rivalries of two millenniums, it would seem that we should not worry too much over such details as where a student stresses a word like *justifiable*. At most the choice can affect the student and this particular word; the system of stress distinctions will remain the same. It should be emphasized that structure in language is something more, and more important, than a collection of items. A change in the number or type of stress distinctions would be vastly more important (for good or ill) than the introduction or the loss of vocabulary items. I am aware, for instance, that confusion of *disinterested* and *uninterested* destroys a useful vocabulary item and one which I would have been glad to see preserved, even though nowadays I cannot talk of "disinterested judges" for fear of being misunderstood. But, though vocabulary items can be lost, others can be gained, and somehow we manage to carry on our necessary business with the vocabulary we have at any one time. Therefore, it seems to me that we need not fear that the whole of our language will be damaged by those who would say "bored, disinterested judges." For the individual and the community, structure is a broad, pervasive pattern, already determined, and capable of very little change. As such it is relatively neutral and colorless. Indeed, in large measure, it is something which escapes the user's conscious attention. The use he makes of his structure and the items within it is something different. Language use is important to the individual; he is highly conscious of it and rightly seeks advice and help in improving it.

For the reasons which I have tried to outline, when Bloomfield goes on to say that to accept the use made of our language by the majority would be to destroy the beauties of the language itself, I think it is necessary to disagree. He is here assuming that poor use is essentially the same thing as poor structure. I should rather say that the use of language is an area in which value judgments must indeed be made, and is an area in which English teachers should increase both their vigilance and their research, but that structure is different and is not subject to the same kind of criticism we would bring to bear in order to evaluate a paragraph by Winston Churchill or a sonnet by Shelley. Bloomfield goes so far as to say that one who does not recognize the beauty of "Forever wilt thou love and she be fair" is unfit to teach English. But the example belongs to art and is beautiful because it is a part of a literary work the totality of whose beauty we all admire. It is difficult to argue that the forms contained in the line—considered either as separate items or as a special dialect—are in themselves any better or more beautiful than the forms of vulgate. For instance, if *wilt* is more beautiful than *will*, does that lead us to the conclusion that the sequence *-lt* is beautiful, so that *kilt* is better than *killed?* Or if a dialect employing a distinction between singular and plural in second-person pronouns is better and more logical than one which does not, are we to defend the metropolitan low-class distinction between *you* singular, and *youse* plural? I wish, however, to be as clear as possible and therefore to say as emphatically as I can that I agree that anyone who cannot appreciate the beauty of the Keats poem is unfit to teach English. And I should add further that, if there is any student who has drawn from linguistics the idea that the poem is in a strange and inferior dialect because its vocabulary and forms differ from contemporary everyday usage, he holds a horrifying and absurd conclusion. If linguistics leads to such beliefs, it earns nothing but opposition. May I hope, however, should any student of literature be led into the equally horrifying and absurd idea that the dialect employed by Keats is better than vulgate in all social and even in all artistic situations, that Bloomfield would join me in giving such a fallacious conclusion as vigorous opposition as I am sure he would give the other?

Much the same sort of objection applies to Bloomfield's fear that too much liberalism would destroy intellectual activity. It is usual in our culture to write about intellectual matters in a very formal kind of English, which is is all too easy to identify with the intellectual activity itself. The same thing is true of other cultures, yet elsewhere in the world the disappearance or replacement of a special intellectual language or dialect has not meant the disappearance of intellectual activity. Such replacements have almost always been by the form of language originally regarded as an unintellectual vulgate. Yet, when the replacement takes place, the old vulgate quickly becomes the new intellectual language. For instance, no one would maintain that the body of intellectual writing in the vernacular tongues is inferior to that in Latin or that intellectual vigor has been circumscribed by the disuse of the scholar's language. For once, therefore, I think I am safe in denying one of Bloomfield's theses. If, by vulgate, Bloomfield means the language structure used by the majority, then I should oppose him with this statement: Good style, whether artistic or intellectual, is possible in any language structure. Mark Twain, in *Huckleberry Finn,* employed the vulgate structure of rural America in his day, yet Huck's descriptions of a village funeral and of a backwoods front parlor are among the classics of our literature. It seems to me that as teachers of English, whether with or without linguistic training, we should strive for clarity. If we assume that style and structure need no differentiation, we are in danger of obscuring both.

I have tried to equal Bloomfield's urbanity and his grasp of first things first. I may have failed, but I hope I may permit myself to believe that he as English teacher, I as linguist, might agree that all who teach the native language have a solemn duty in understanding language, its structure, its social implications, and the use, beautiful or otherwise, which men have put it to. Further, since literature is necessarily a part of language, all that a linguist can discover about his subject should not merely limit what the English teacher can say but is of positive though potential value to him in all his work.

3

❀ Teaching Standard English as a Second Dialect

VIRGINIA F. ALLEN

Few people today need to be told that standard English is virtually a "second language" for millions. Almost every teacher knows students who cannot speak, read or write the sort of English that educated persons consider standard, even though some variety of English may be the student's mother tongue. Not only is the problem prevalent, of course, it is also old. It dates back past the days of Huck Finn and Topsy to the eighteenth century, and beyond.

Yet two facts do appear to come as news—good news.[115] One is that some teachers are developing a fresh and clearer view of what is involved in learning a standard dialect of English in school when some other dialect is spoken in the home. A second newsworthy fact, and an even more cheering one, is that these fresh insights have suggested some practical classroom procedures which are being tried with encouraging results. Some of those promising procedures will be described in this paper.

Virginia F. Allen is Professor of English Education in the College of Education at Temple University. Professor Allen, the author of several articles on the teaching of standard English as a second dialect, is currently writing a book on the learning of standard English.

STANDARD ENGLISH

First, however, it would be wise to show what the term "standard English" will mean in the context of this discussion. For our present purposes, standard American English is the kind of English *habitually* used by most of the *educated* English-speaking persons in the United States.

Thus "He doesn't want any" would qualify as a sample of standard English—not because some "authority" has certified it as being "correct," but because evidence suggests that educated speakers habitually *say* "He doesn't want any" in situations where less educated speakers might say "He don't want none."

It is important to note the emphasis on *habitually* and *educated* in this definition of standard English. A teacher who undertakes to familiarize her students with the standard dialect of English as here defined is careful to focus attention upon grammatical forms which educated speakers are in the *habit* of using. For instance, even though some grammar books decree that the "comparative" form *more* "should" be used in place of the "superlative" form *most* when only two are being compared, an enlightened teacher today would be undismayed if a student said, "Both Pete and Bill get good grades in school, but I think Pete really has the most sense." Habitual usage among educated speakers is what counts—whether or not that usage obeys some grammarian's rule.

On the other hand, the stress on the word *educated* in this definition is significant, too. What is being advocated here is emphatically *not* an "anything goes" approach to English usage. Standard English, as defined here, is the variety of English generally used by the *educated* members of the American speech community. Statistically speaking, one has reason to suspect that the number of Americans who say "you was" exceeds the number who say "you were." This fact does not establish "you was" as standard usage, however. Standard English is what the majority of *educated* speakers habitually use.

Teachers who start with this definition then go on to link it up with their student's experience and observation. They point out that the kind of English they have in mind is the sort used on radio and television by announcers, sportscasters, civil rights leaders, and news commentators, as well as by practically all TV heroes, including Batman, Superman and Flash Gordon. It is the English heard in the public statements of astronauts, bankers, congressmen, and movie stars. It has been called "the language of educated ease," because it is used by people who *know* they sound "educated" and so do not have to think about their use of language.

When the target language is defined in these terms, even young children know what the teacher means by "standard English." Martin Joos, who has made a special study of people's attitudes toward language, says:

> Long before any teacher began to correct his English, the child has learned all he needs to know, at his age, about people and their places; he has developed considerable skill in judging adults by their speech . . .[116]

MORALITY AND COMPREHENSIBILITY

Class time invested in discussing standard English along such lines is time well spent. For one thing, such discussions remind both teachers and students that the presence or absence of standard forms in a person's speech is not a moral or ethical issue; among announcers, congressmen and movie stars there are some who are moral, honest and upright and some who are not; yet both kinds are speakers of standard English.

Then, too, such discussions give the teacher an opportunity to grant that people who speak standard English do not always and invariably communicate any more clearly or forcefully than speakers of non-standard dialects do. Since the students themselves will doubtless have observed this fact, they will appreciate the candor of teachers who acknowledge that a person's grammatical usage has little effect—for better or for worse—upon the clarity and vigor of his message. Too often, teachers try to convey the opposite impression by feigning incomprehension when a student says something like "I don't have no pencil"—a statement whose import is perfectly clear, as the student well knows. The reason for learning to say "I don't have any pencil" has little to do with comprehensibility; when teachers imply that the standard English way is better because it is clearer, students can hardly be blamed for regarding English teachers as "phoneys" or, more charitably, as living in an unreal world.

There is a further advantage to be gained from discussing standard English in terms of professional groups who characteristically use it. Such discussions help to dispel the impression that what the class is being urged to learn is a language spoken chiefly by teachers, by *English* teachers, at that. As a motivating force, such an impression has very low potential.

A SCALE OF IMPORTANCE

Moreover, a definition which identifies the target of instruction as "the kind of English habitually used by educated speakers" gives teachers a useful scale for weighing the relative importance of various items found on English tests and in English textbooks. Textbook "rules" which would teach the class usages no longer habitual among most educated Americans can be passed over lightly or omitted altogether, and time thus saved can be more profitably spent in a study of usages that actually do distinguish the standard dialect from other varieties.

Thus far we have been concerned with identifying the kind of English that teachers should be helping their students learn to use. We have stressed the need for frankness and realism. It is good strategy to acknowledge that this standard dialect, this variety of language habitually spoken by educated Americans, has no inherent virtue of its own, unpossessed by other dialects. It was not divinely bequeathed to some Moses on tablets of stone. Furthermore, language problems are very different from arithmetic problems, though for centuries this difference has traditionally been ignored. Standard English is not a set of "right" answers, like the answers found at the back of an arithmetic textbook. (The right answer to "two plus two" is "four"; any other is, has always been, and doubtless always will be, wrong. Yet one cannot in the same sense assert that it would be "wrong" for a slum child in a rat-ridden flat to say to his mother, "That landlord, he *mean*. Ain't nobody no meaner'n him.") Hence, in good programs for students of standard English as a second dialect, the terms "right" and "wrong" are not often used. When they are, "right" means "appropriate to the situation," and "wrong" means "likely to put the speaker at a disadvantage," much as one might say it is "wrong" to chew gum while being interviewed for a job.

STANDARD VS NON-STANDARD

There is another truth that teachers in modern programs publicly acknowledge. Students whose families speak some variety of English other than the standard dialect appreciate being told that several features of their home language were once characteristic of standard speech. In seventeenth century England there would have been nothing non-standard about a sentence like "My brother and his family, they live in Atlanta." After all, the authors of the King James version of the Bible wrote: "Thy rod and Thy staff, they comfort me." Double negatives, too, were features of standard English for hundreds of years: Chaucer and Shakespeare often used them. For that matter, double negatives are regularly used in Spanish even to this day.

Teachers who share this sort of information with their students earn a reputation for honesty and reasonableness that stands them in good stead when the hard work of learning the standard dialect begins. For of course the standard dialect must be taught, and it should be learned. Even though there is nothing inherently "wrong" or "bad" about using a non-standard dialect, there are times when it can harm the person who uses it. No matter how tastefully he may dress, no matter how impeccable his grooming may be, the applicant for white collar employment does not enhance his chances by saying, "I come because I seen your ad."

"FRONT DOOR ENGLISH"

Undemocratic and unfair as it may seem, the fact is that standard English is "front door" English. And American schools are committed to the task of making it possible for every citizen to enter by the front door if he wishes to do so.

Just as candor and a clear view of the facts are essential in defining what standard English is, so also one needs to be factual and frank in saying why the standard dialect ought to be learned. The student needs to understand that a command of standard English is vital to any American (particularly any "minority-group" American) who aims to associate with speakers of the standard dialect on anything like an equal footing.

Note the phrase: "A *command* of standard English." To command something is not merely to have a vague notion of it, but rather to be able to *summon it up at will.* The student must be given the ability to summon up the standard dialect whenever he himself wants to use it, in any situation where fluency in that dialect would be to his advantage.

Often, in the development of such fluency, the school can count on little help from the environment outside. In urban "gray areas," for example, and in the rural South, a non-standard dialect is generally the medium of communication for most members of the student's immediate community, standard English being used only by members of the school staff. It is then entirely up to the school to teach young people how to use the standard dialect with ease and self-confidence when occasions demand.

Teachers are well aware of this responsibility, and they have worked at the task, year in and year out, but often with little success. Why? Partly because many a teacher antagonizes the very people she is trying to help. She makes her students feel that their natural way of talking is a shameful thing, marred by "errors" that need to be rooted out. She seems determined to wrest the students' familiar dialect from them, leaving in its place a language that may well estrange them from homefolks and lifelong friends. Small wonder that many students resist!

TOWARDS LINGUISTIC VERSATILITY

Nowadays, luckily, there *are* teachers who recognize that other varieties of English have validity for many communication situations profoundly important to their students. Such teachers offer standard English as a second—or additional—dialect without demanding that it *supplant* the students' home language.

In Europe, such a view of the standard dialect would be taken as a matter of course. In France, for example, it is taken for granted that a citizen will learn to use a standard dialect of the national language for communication in relatively formal situations involving educated speakers, and in conversations with persons from regions other than his own. It is not expected, however, that the standard dialect will replace for all time and for all occasions the dialect the individual learned at home. He retains his local dialect and uses it when he goes back to his home community, switching from one language-track to the other as he moves from scene to scene. This two-track versatility in language usage seems to be characteristic of most societies, especially the older ones. It is unfortunate that the possibility of achieving such versatility has been given so little systematic attention in the United States. To the traditional teacher in America, any and all non-standard utterances have seemed like evil tendencies, to be stamped out with Calvinistic zeal.

In earlier times, this may have been because so many teachers in American public schools were themselves members of immigrant families, to whom the learning of English had meant an unremitting struggle. Frequently, by dint of prodigious effort and some pain, these teachers had cut their ties with families whose "broken English" posed a threat to the teachers' own hard-won status as new members of an American middle class. One can understand how the experience could have accounted for a teacher's inability to tolerate the thought that a non-standard dialect might have a right to live on in some of the relationships her students held dear.

One of the new things to be said about the teaching of standard English is that some teachers now feel secure enough in their own middle class status to view the school's language-teaching responsibility in a somewhat different light. Such teachers try not to treat non-standard forms with abhorrence and disdain. At the same time, they press vigorously toward the goal of developing in every student the ability to use the standard dialect in any situation that *requires* its use. When this is the teacher's policy, many students eventually do stop using non-standard varieties of English altogether. They find themselves moving over to the standard dialect in a widening range of situations as they develop fluency and confidence in handling the standard modes. In time, many are willing to risk speaking standard English with family and friends. But even if a student continues to use the home dialect with his family and peer-group associates, the teacher need not feel that the language program has failed. The test of success is the student's readiness to "turn on" the standard dialect in situations where his standing as a person will be judged in part by his speech.

INSTRUCTIONAL STRATEGY

Sometimes, however, even when the teacher has managed to avoid arousing hostility through her attitude toward the home dialect, results have fallen short of success. A realistic, understanding attitude is not enough: one must also take stock of tactics and techniques.

Just what must be done by anyone who tries to become fluent in standard English when his home dialect is something else? His problem is much like that of someone learning a foreign language in school. Of course there are differences, too. On the debit side, the learning of a second dialect is harder to motivate than the learning of a language entirely foreign and new. And on the other hand, the non-standard dialect speaker has at least the advantage of knowing far more of the *meanings* of the target language than the foreign learner knows.

Still, despite these differences, the needs of second-dialect students and second-language students are alike in one important respect: in both cases the learner needs to develop a new set of language *habits*. He needs new habits that will enable him to utter appropriate responses instantaneously, whenever the need arises, without having to stop and think.

A student who has to stop and think whether to say "I done it" or "I did it" in a standard English speech situation has not *mastered* the target dialect. A person who has mastered a language or a dialect is no more conscious of making such decisions than he is conscious of deciding how to tie his shoes. The problem for teachers, then, is how to lead students to develop a repertoire of routine habits in connection with the forms and arrangements that make up the grammar of the standard dialect.

CLUES FROM FOREIGN LANGUAGE TEACHING

Teachers of foreign languages give much thought to this matter of "automatic control over the patterns of the language" as it is often called. Hence some of the foreign language teacher's procedures will suggest useful strategy to teachers of standard English as a second dialect.

The first element in the foreign language teacher's strategy is *selection*. Even the most skillful teacher cannot give a student a thorough mastery of every individual linguistic feature. The teacher (or the textbook writer) tries to select the smallest possible number of really essential items to be learned. The students concentrate on these, item by item, until they are able to "produce" each essential type of utterance without hestitation. After that, if time remains, attention is turned to finer points, minor patterns, alternate forms of expression. And once the student has been given a substantial start through the development of control over the major patterns of the language, he is able to fill in the remaining gaps on his own, through observation and analogy.

What does this mean for teaching English as a second dialect? It suggests that teachers and students need to concentrate their energies on features that truly do distinguish standard English from nonstandard usage. These need to be taught before items that do not conspicuously characterize one dialect or the other—items which are prescribed or proscribed by some grammar books, but which are used in much the same way by speakers of both standard and non-standard dialects.

Some concrete illustrations may be needed in order to clarify this point. In the list below, certain sentences contain obvious examples of non-standard usage. Any novelist who put those sentences into the mouths of his bankers, stock brokers, optometrists, head nurses or airline hostesses would be accused of having a poor ear for talk.

Other sentences in the list would seem quite at home in the discourse of educated Americans. Let us sort out the fifteen sentences, noting which ones would sound out of place in the "language of educated ease"—and which ones would not.

1. Cartwright don't want nobody to help him.
2. They give the burglar five dollar, which was all they had.
3. The man die after he had drank the poison.
4. This author explain why everything cost more now.
5. They always trying to find a way to get rich, no matter how it hurt other people.
6. Their children has went to Washington to spend six week with Mrs. Green sister.
7. I hope William and his family, they going to be more happier now.
8. In my opinion, neither Adams nor Reeves are really qualified for the job.
9. In each of these novels, the hero has to choose between riches, fame and happiness.
10. Somehow this hotel looks different than it did the last time we stayed here.
11. Both Detroit and Denver have possibilities, but I believe Denver would be the best for our conference.
12. But who could Patty stay with if we went abroad without her?
13. Even though I try not to be over-protective, I can't help but worry every time the children are away from home.
14. Carson is efficient, but Peters is certainly easier to work with.
15. Don't look so startled, Janice; it's only me!

Every one of the fifteen sentences contains something that violates some "rule" in grammar books still extant in American schools, but that fact is beside the point here. What has significance to the teacher of standard English as a second dialect is that only seven of the fifteen sentences would sound out of place in conversations among educated Americans. Those are sentences one through seven. The patterns represented by those sentences are the ones that need to be given intensive study by students who are trying to master the standard dialect. If the class has not yet learned to use these high-priority features of standard English, it will be pointless to spend valuable time on grammar-book rules which are "violated" by sentences like the last eight above —rules which condemn usages like "different than" and neither are." It will be futile and foolish to dwell upon rules governing *between* and *among* and *who* and *whom*. It is sad to think how much precious energy is being squandered on such esoteric distinctions in courses for students who need all the help they can get in mastering the basic hallmarks of standard speech.

In essence, then, the strategy of teaching a second dialect (as in teaching a foreign language) amounts to teaching the smallest possible number of vitally significant items—and *teaching each of them hard.*

TEACHING VS SCOLDING

What does a teacher do about a language pattern when she really wants students to learn it? Above all, she gets the students to *use* the pattern, to say sentences illustrating the pattern, again and again, until that mode of speech begins to sound natural to the students themselves. The skillful teacher of a second dialect does not simply remark in class, "Stanley should have said 'I saw it,' not 'I seen it.' You remember that, Stanley, don't you? All right then, let's go on."

Yet this is the sort of "teaching" that often takes place, and it has not been of much help to children from non-standard dialect homes. Year after year they have brushed briefly up against the same features of standard English; they have been "corrected" for the same "mistakes" from grade to grade in the same reproachful but off-hand way.

Now to get back to Stanley, a hypothetical child in perhaps the third or fourth grade. Supposing he has just said, "I seen it on my way to school this morning." Supposing the teacher has murmured, "You *saw* it. Stanley. You know that don't you?" and Stanley has mumbled, "Yeah."

As a matter of fact, Stanley probably does "know it"—in a way. That is, he has heard something about *I seen* as opposed to *I saw* a number of times before. The trouble is, no one has ever made him settle down on this bit of the standard dialect long enough to learn to use it. He has never been given a chance to *command* the form "I saw." Naturally, then, even in situations where he would be willing to use standard English—if only to mollify the teacher—the standard form is just not *in* him to be summoned up. If the teacher wants Stanley to *focus* on this bit of language, the very least she can do is ask him to repeat the sentence after her: "I saw it on my way to school this morning." (And she waits while Stanley repeats the sentence.) If several of the students share Stanley's problems, and she wants the class to master this use of *saw*, something like the following has to take place:

TEACHER: Let's practice using saw in some standard English sentences. Let's start by saying Stanley's sentence: I saw it on my way to school this morning. Class!

CLASS: (in unison): I saw it on my way to school this morning.

TEACHER: (to Thomas): Thomas, when did Stanley see it? Use *saw* in your answer.

THOMAS: He saw it on his way to school this morning.

TEACHER: Right! Gloria, who saw it on his way to school? Use *saw* in your answer.

GLORIA: Stanley saw it.

TEACHER: Yes! Now let's all mention things we saw on our way to school this morning. I saw a fire engine. What about you, Paul?

PAUL: I saw a garbage truck on my way to school.

TEACHER: Good! Laura, tell us what Paul saw, and then tell us something you saw.

LAURA: Paul saw a garbage truck on his way to school. I saw a . . . a . . . I saw a black kitten in front of the supermarket.

TEACHER: Fine! Anthony, what did Laura see?

ANTHONY: She seen . . .

TEACHER: She saw. Please say, "She saw . . ."

ANTHONY: She saw a kitten.

TEACHER: Yes. And what did you see?

ANTHONY: I seen . . . I saw a . . . a motorcycle.

TEACHER: Good. Class, what did Anthony say he saw? Use *saw* in your answer.

CLASS: He saw a motorcycle.

TEACHER: Right! Now, then, let's play the game in a different way. Did anyone see a taxi or a jeep on the way to school today? Gregory, did you see a taxi or a jeep?

GREGORY: I didn't see a jeep, but I saw a taxi.

TEACHER: Good. Daphne, did you see any dogs or horses on your way to school?

DAPHNE: I seen—saw some dogs, but I didn't see no horse.

TEACHER: I didn't see any horses. That's the standard English way to say it. Say: "I didn't see any horses."

DAPHNE: I didn't see any horses.

TEACHER: Fine! George, what did Daphne see and what didn't she see?

GEORGE: She . . . she . . . (silence)

TEACHER: Daphne, tell George what you saw and what you didn't see.

DAPHNE: I saw some dogs, but I didn't see no . . . I didn't see any horses.

TEACHER: Good for you, Daphne! You did it the standard English
    way without any help. Say it again.
DAPHNE: I saw some dogs, but I didn't see any horses.
TEACHER: Fine! George, what did she tell us?
GEORGE: She saw some dogs, but she didn't see any horses.

*(And so on, with contributions from all who need to gain command
over this feature of the standard dialect. The last to speak is Stanley,
who is asked to say what various classmates saw on their way to
school.)*

This is the kind of drill—disguised as a conversation—that has become important in foreign language teaching. Its aim is to make a
language pattern begin to sound natural, feel right, through repeated
uses in sentences that have some interest and meaning for the speaker
and his listeners. It belongs, in fact, to the species of drill that is often
called "pattern practice" or "substitution practice." For several years
it has been widely used in courses for students of English as a Foreign
Language (or Second Language); and it is used when people teach
foreign languages along "audio lingual" lines today.

True, it takes time to teach patterns of speech in this way. The
easier way is merely to mention the student's "error"—or to give him a
workbook exercise that he can do at home—though he probably won't.
But to deal thus with a language habit is not to deal with it at all. Next
year Stanley and the rest will still be using the same non-standard
forms on occasions that call for the standard dialect, and next year's
teacher will still deplore and nag, rather than teach. True, too, the
list of items to be learned is long (particularly if the student's home
dialect differs greatly from the standard) but the number of really
crucial items is finite: these *could* be mastered during the many years
English teachers are given for the task. In no other subject do teachers
in all grades try to work on everything at once. Why can't English
teachers divide up the list of linguistic habits to be learned? If the
fourth grade teacher could make her students fluent with regard to a
specified few of the items on the list, the fifth grade teacher could go
on from there, and so on up through the grades.

SOME SOURCES OF HELP

As yet little has been written about the possibilities of this kind of
"fluency practice" for students of standard English as a second dialect,
but three helpful studies will be mentioned here. One is Marjorie

Barrows' *Good English Through Practice,* which shows how to use a set of cleverly devised games for getting junior high school students to use many troublesome standard English forms over and over again while taking part in entertaining, creative language activities.[117]

A second helpful text is Ruth Golden's *Improving Patterns of Language Usage,* in which the problems and attitudes of students learning the standard dialect are analyzed, and many language-learning activities are suggested, including games, stories and role-playing skits.[118]

There is irony in the fact that both *Good English Through Practice* and *Improving Patterns of Language Usage* perpetuate in their titles the older, unhelpful policy of condemning non-standard dialects as intrinsically "worse" than the standard dialect and needing to be "improved." Fortunately, however, the attitudes reflected in the texts themselves are more harmonious with the spirit of modern courses in this field.

A third, and particularly fruitful, source of help for teachers is Sansu C. Lin's report on a three-year research project financed by the U. S. Office of Education, in which Dr. Lin and her associates experimented with pattern-practice techniques as a means of helping students in South Carolina master standard English.[119]

The setting for the Lin program was Claflin College, a small church-supported school serving mainly Southern Negroes from rural communities. The speech of many freshmen at Claflin included patterns like these: *three apple; nine childrens; I arrive here last week; Claflin have a new dormitory; They looks after theirselves; He don't want nothing; She's more prettier; She sang beautiful; I had wrote it; My uncle, he work in Richmond.* It was evident that the efforts of students and staff would need to be concentrated upon the mastery of basic grammar patterns distinguishing the standard dialect (in writing and in speech) from non-standard varieties. Consequently, problems of pronunciation were not permitted to occupy the center of attention in the Claflin project. However a few pronunciation problems (such as difficulties in adding the -s and -ed endings) did come within the scope of the project because these interfered with the mastery of grammatical forms.

Early in 1961, when the Claflin Project was conceived, there were few guidelines for teachers of a second dialect. Dr. Lin's 1965 report tells an absorbing story of trials, false starts, frustrations, accomplishments, and—above all—cumulative learnings on the part of both students and staff. The report tells of questions to which answers were found. First there was the need to understand why the problem existed:

What makes a college freshman from a culturally deprived Negro community persist in the use of nonstandard dialect in spite of many years of
English instruction through high school and elementary school? The dialect, no matter how other people may judge it, has evidently proved
socially and psychologically satisfactory to the individual who uses it. It
is the language of his family—a symbol of security and love. It is the language of his initiation into life—from the dawn of awareness through suc-
cessive steps in which he learned to adjust to different groups and to
establish rapport with the world around him.[120]

Next came the questions of approach, growing out of the staff's
analysis of the human aspects of the problem. Certain fundamentals
had to be established:

First of all, the teacher must become aware, and help the student become
aware, of the infinite variations that exist in the many dialects of American English, both regional and social. Both teacher and student must also
understand the social implications of these variations. If any change is
desirable, the decision to change must come from the individual himself.
The teacher, with sympathetic understanding, can help speed the process
of change by supplying the necessary methods and materials.[121]

In their search for procedures that could help these students achieve
proficiency in the use of standard English, the Claflin staff turned to
the field of foreign language teaching, particularly to the teaching of
English as a foreign language, in which Dr. Lin had had training and
experience. As the report points out:

. . . there has been little recognition among English teachers of the need
for a program basically different from the English program catering to
those who speak standard English at home. Not only are these linguistically different young people more sensitive to intolerance and tactless
criticism, they also differ from standard speakers in being faced with the
task of establishing a new set of language habits. In other words, if they
are learning a second language to be added to their indigenous dialect,
they must be taught with methods and procedures that are used in learning a second language.[122]

However, after a few weeks' experience with the "repeat-after-me"
type of practice material found in most language-learning laboratories,
the Claflin staff realized that major adaptations had to be made, since
English was, after all, not a foreign language to American students.
Quite apart from the psychological resistance to having one's national
language treated like a foreign tongue, there were difficulties arising
from the fact that standard English and a non-standard dialect of

English are so closely related that, as San-su Lin puts it, "the socially significant differences may be over-shadowed by the similarities and fail to present a real challenge to the students." Moreover, much as the students themselves wished to acquire skill in using standard English, they naturally resented having their entire Freshman English course devoted to drill on grammar patterns: they wanted to learn about literature, composition, stylistics, and other matters that they considered appropriate to a college course.

Thus the Claflin staff was faced with the task of devising procedures and materials that would give the students the kind and amount of drill they needed for mastery of the standard patterns, while at the same time satisfying the students' natural desire for "college level" instruction. Since much this same task is faced everywhere by teachers whose students are already fluent in some variety of English, Dr. Lin's report on solutions to the problem offers much practical advice. The Claflin staff learned to avoid the use of example sentences and drill sentences that merely illustrated a grammar pattern without offering information or ideas. They learned to construct practice exercises that gave these students information about science, etiquette and job-hunting techniques. They learned to design drills that increased a student's vocabulary, or improved his spelling and punctuation, while simultaneously strengthening his control over standard grammar forms.

For example, noting that the students needed to acquire the habit of using the *-s* ending for the third person singular form of verbs, the staff prepared an exercise which required each student to use third-person singular forms again and again while discussing "college level" vocabulary words that he knew he needed to learn to pronounce and spell.

The exercise was conducted about as follows: The teacher mentioned a polysyllabic word, such as *curriculum*. A student was then directed to analyze the word, using this sequence of sentences:

The word *curriculum* begins with the letter *c*.
It ends with the letter *m*.
It contains two *r*'s.
It has four syllables.
The accent falls on the second syllable.

A second student would then analyze another word (e.g. *accommodation*) using the same set of sentences:

The word *accommodation* begins with the letter *a*.
It ends with the letter *n*.

It contains two *c*'s and two *m*'s.
It has five syllables.
The accent falls on the fourth syllable.

The exercise would continue in the same way, until most members of the class had had an opportunity to construct sentences in this mold, each sentence containing at least one word with an -*s* ending. If any student said, "It *end* with . . .," or "The accent *fall* . . ." he was asked to repeat the sentence, using the -*s* ending appropriately. In this way, for the first time, the -*s* ending began to "sound natural" and "feel right" to these students, because they had said and heard it over and over again. Moreover, they had accepted the drill as being appropriate to their level of educational maturity because it sounded like "college English."

CONDUCTING MEANINGFUL DRILLS

Exercises of this sort are not nearly as easy to construct as they may seem. First the teacher must know precisely what grammatical point it is that the students need to have illustrated and repeated again and again; and then the teacher must elicite many repetitions of the pattern from the students in the course of a discussion that is more than a mere mechanical drill.

In the Claflin project, the staff realized that just one drill on the -*s* ending would not be enough to ensure the ready use of this feature of standard English when next the student found himself in a situation calling for fluent, effortless use of the standard dialect. There were many other exercises leading to the same goal by different routes. For example, on one occasion the class discussed reading techniques, within the framework of "Five Things a Good Reader Does." Each student offered his own five sentences, based on a discussion of reading in the essay anthology. Sentences constructed by the class included the following:

A good reader keeps his mind on his work.
A good reader looks for answers to certain questions in his mind.
A good reader distinguishes between main ideas and details.
A good reader summarizes the writer's ideas from time to time.

(Note that this exercise would have lost its effectiveness so far as practice on the third-person -*s* ending was concerned if the students had been permitted to alternate between "a good reader" and good readers." What they needed was to say and to hear a singular subject plus the -*s* form of the verb again and again, in order to forge a link between the form of the subject and the form of the verb.)

In similar fashion, the Claflin project students practiced the -*ed* ending for verbs within the context of a discussion of a chapel program, in which, they said, "The president introduc*ed* the guest speaker. The speaker talk*ed* for twenty minutes. He describ*ed* . . . and explain*ed* that . . . , etc." Once again the strategy called for an oral account, with contributions from all members of the class, carefully elicited by the teacher so as to ensure many repetitions of the standard English form (in this case, the -*ed* ending) over which the students needed to develop control.

ROLE PLAYING

In addition to those "structured discussions" or "fluency drills," the Claflin staff experimented with skits and other role-playing activities. The most successful skits were those that simulated life situations in which standard English would obviously be the appropriate dialect to use. Some dialogs illustrated forms of etiquette relevant to job interviews, employer-secretary conferences, and the like. After the students had taken part in skits written by the project staff, the students themselves—working in small groups—wrote a number of role-playing exercises. Each student practiced his part with the aid of a taped standard English recording of it in the language laboratory. The best skit in each class was chosen for performance in a chapel program. The students found the experience interesting and helpful: among a few students, the speech patterns changed dramatically as a result.

Although the Claflin project extended from 1961 to 1964, a different Freshman class participated during each of the three years. Thus no student was enrolled in the program for more than one academic year. As the final report pointed out, it would be wrong to claim (in San-su Lin's words) that "any method can, in nine months, give the student a full command of the standard dialect when it is psychologically and socially difficult for him to use anything but the non-standard dialect in his daily life, even on a college campus."

Even so, some very encouraging results emerged. From the taped interviews which formed part of the evaluation data, it was evident that the students had become more self-confident and more determined to develop dialectal versatility. Their enunciation had become clear, they found it easier to communicate, and they appeared more ready to correct themselves after using non-standard forms. On the locally prepared grammar test, the project students proved to be more successful than the control group in identifying non-standard patterns and "translating" them into standard modes. In addition to items that were indisputably non-standard, the test also included items like "Everyone was supposed to bring their lunch," and "This color is different than that"—usages decried by grammar books but often heard in the speech of educated persons. Since such items had been given little attention in the experimental program, most of them were "missed" by project students on the final test. However, in terms of the conspicuous hallmarks of standard English (as contrasted with the nonstandard dialect) the experimental students demonstrated significant improvement.

READING AND WRITING

Nor were the gains at Claflin limited to matters of speech and social dialect. Somewhat to the surprise of the staff, scores on the Cooperative English Test revealed that the experimental group made greater gain in *reading* after a year of grammar pattern practice than did the members of the control group (which had engaged in free conversation in place of the structured grammar drills). What made this result the more striking was that the control group (the group not employing the experimental techniques) had given more attention to reading, as such, and to discussions of the material read. The Lin report points out that apparently "the use of pattern practice techniques can sharpen students' awareness of structural matters in such a way as to improve their comprehension of material that they read. After a year of working systematically and intensively with various patterns of English, the experimental students were apparently better equipped to read passages which required an alert attention to structural signals."

Another skill which benefited from the application of second-language teaching techniques in the Claflin project was *writing*. At the end of the second year of the program, the director reported that the compositions written by students in the project were "not only more free of errors, but more purposeful and more interesting" than any she had previously read during seven years' experience at the same institution.[123]

Above all, what has been proved by the Claflin project (and by similar programs) is that speakers of non-standard dialects can make significant progress toward the mastery of standard English, even in a program of very short duration. (It should be remembered that no Claflin student was involved in the project for more than nine months.) How much could be accomplished if teachers at all levels of the instructional ladder were to apply the lessons learned from such experiments!

TARGET LANGUAGE

Fortunately, more and more teachers are coming to realize that attitudes, approaches and procedures germane to the teaching of foreign languages have relevance to the teaching of standard English as a second dialect. More and more teachers are defining the target language as "the kind of English habitually spoken by most of the educated members of the American speech community." Guided by this definition, classes for non-standard speakers are concentrating upon language usages which indisputably characterize "the language of educated ease." Teachers are thus freeing class time for practice upon these crucial features of the target dialect by passing lightly over esoteric distinctions that carry little or no weight outside some grammar textbooks.

In their classrooms, these teachers guard against treating the students' home dialect as something faulty, flawed and inferior. They are willing to grant that the home dialect may even be the "right" one for a student to use in some interpersonal relationships deeply important to him. At the same time, they help their students achieve fluency in standard English by patiently guiding the class through practice exercises based on second-language teaching techniques, but adapted to second-dialect purposes with artistry and tact.

In programs conducted along these lines, there is much hope for students striving to command the dialect that is required for advancement in our national life—for entering fully into American affairs, through the front door.

4

Using Foreign Language Methodology to Teach Standard English: Evaluation and Adaptation

IRWIN FEIGENBAUM

With the current interest in urban education and the language of the "culturally-different" Negro student, educators have been looking for new methods that might prove useful in teaching standard English. One such approach that has received quite a bit of attention is that of teaching standard English in the same way that English is taught as a foreign language (abbreviated in this paper as "EFL"). There are several labels for this methodology, among which are "the aural-oral approach", "the linguistic method", "the audio-lingual method", and "pattern practice". Heretofore, teaching standard English has been concerned with the correction of word forms and usages that differ from the standard. In EFL teaching, new patterns of grammar and pronunciation are taught as additional language skills for the student to use when English is required.

For several years now, there has been much discussion and some work in implementing EFL-like programs to teach standard English. Some of the programs have done valuable work toward assessing the applicability of foreign language techniques to teaching standard English. They have contributed to determining which features of the aural-oral approach could be profitably utilized and which ones could not.

This paper discusses some of the early contributions, the roles of the classroom teacher and the student in bringing innovation to the classroom, the adaptation of EFL methodology to the native language English class, and new features that are required to replace the features

256

that have been discarded or to meet needs that have not been adequately met.

EARLY WORK

One of the earliest and better-known programs was directed by San-su C. Lin. From September, 1961 to June, 1964, various drills and taped activities were tried with college students at Claflin University in South Carolina. As Dr. Lin stated in her report:

> The purpose of the project . . . was to find out to what extent pattern practice techniques might help Negro students who needed to master standard English as a second language, and to work out materials and procedures to implement such techniques.[124]

She states her immediate objective as "how to organize and integrate content so that pattern practice could be used in more meaningful context and more palatable form."[125] She concludes that many of the students succeeded in establishing greater control of standard patterns. Her restrained tone is noteworthy; wisely, Dr. Lin does not claim to have found a panacea. Later, she says:

> Native speakers of English who wish to master the standard dialect do need pattern practice, and they do benefit from pattern practice. However, pattern practice for native speakers of English must take a form quite different from that customarily used in teaching English to speakers of other languages.[126]

Her principal concern is subject matter. Although subject matter is important, one wishes for more specific discussion about the changes and adaptations that must be made in the pattern practice approach to make it more effective and palatable to the students.

In 1964, William A. Stewart recommended using an aural-oral approach for teaching standard English. He says, ". . . it would appear that the most satisfactory approach to the teaching of standard verb usage would be of a type similar to one now being used in many of the new foreign language teaching materials."[127] In this article, he mentions general similarities between teaching standard English and teaching foreign languages and the difference between standard English and traditional native language instruction. He lists many differences between standard and nonstandard English, information which he rightly maintains must be known in order to construct effective teaching materials. Unfortunately, he does not mention any specific drill-types or teaching techniques when he describes the specific learning problems.

In an article in the *English Journal*, William R. Slager advocates the use of EFL techniques and drill-types in teaching standard English. He says that "one of the most effective means of achieving automatic control of pronunciation and grammar is through the techniques of oral drill that have been so widely used in the teaching of foreign languages".[128] He then goes on to describe in useful and usable detail several types of oral drill that have been used with success in teaching EFL. Also mentioned are practical suggestions about the construction of drills and about using the drills in the classroom.

In the *TESOL Quarterly*, William S. Carroll describes an experiment undertaken by the Urban Language Study at the Center for Applied Linguistics, with the cooperation of the District of Columbia public schools.[129] In the first year of work in the schools, Mr. Carroll and the author of the present article tried conventional EFL materials and teaching techniques in order to determine which ones worked well and to discover the particular problems of training teachers in this new methodology.

In the beginning we went into the classroom with the notion that EFL techniques and materials could be profitably employed there, but since we were not teaching a foreign language, we expected that some of the foreign language methods introduced would prove to be unsuitable. The following discussion deals with some areas of methodology that must be reevaluated in the context of teaching standard English in the native-language class.

THE TEACHER'S ROLE IN INNOVATION

In attending conventions, one is struck by the frequency with which papers are begun with a disclaimer like the following: "This paper is addressed to teachers. It is not meant for the specialist in linguistics or second language pedagogy." The person giving the paper has dismissed the specialists in two fields while failing to see that although the teacher is not a specialist in theoretical matters she has her own area of specialization, the classroom. It is, of course, true that one must be concerned with the fundamentals on which a theory or methodology is based, but teachers have different considerations from the materials writer and the researcher. The teacher's focus is very specific since her concern is necessarily with the moments in the classroom, face to face with the students. Because of this focus, the teacher is eager to acquire many different techniques and materials to use when the need arises. Basic attitudes are important, and theoretically sophisticated teachers are valuable. But in becoming concerned with attitudes, concepts, and "the whole child" to the exclusion of methodology and specific skills, one fails to take advantage of the essential contribution that the teacher can make in classroom innovation.

Does a teacher's role in innovation mean that she should be called on to develop materials? Materials development is a time-consuming undertaking, and because of the specialized nature of the content teachers may not be trained to develop course materials, at least not in the customary sense of writing textbook lessons. There is ample opportunity for a teacher to be creative in using materials in the classroom and getting them to work. A teacher is essential to the materials developer precisely because of the specific viewpoint that is required in the classroom. The teacher can tell 1) what is easy to use and what is not, 2) what goes over well with the students and what does not, and 3) what is effective and what is not. These three questions are answered in the context of specific considerations: the classroom and the students in it.

Teacher trainers should be aware that the teachers want specifics in methodology more than general attitudes and concepts; the fact that teachers request materials and techniques more often than they request attitudes and concepts bears this out. It is easy to talk in generalities about "basic attitudes and concepts"—teacher trainers have been doing this in EFL for a long time. It is time to shift the focus to the teacher and the students in the classroom.

THE STUDENT'S ROLE IN INNOVATION

In teacher training and in professional meetings, valuable time is spent reaffirming that one should appreciate and understand the student. The time is wasted because 1) what a classroom teacher needs is a collection of techniques and materials to draw upon during the teaching process and 2) no one would seriously oppose the idea. More attention should be paid to the student, especially to his reactions to what happens in the class, and more time should be spent in discussing effective, interesting ways of teaching the material to be mastered. We must make certain that the class activities are maximally beneficial. To do this, we should look at the activities not only in terms of what it is the students are called on to do and what, in fact, they are doing.

It is easy for a teacher of EFL or one using EFL methodology for standard English to master a series of techniques or for a materials writer to develop lesson after lesson of well-written drills; this orientation to the technology of drilling is one of the bases of EFL teacher training. What must also be done is to evaluate these techniques and materials in use in the classroom. This is what good teachers do and always have done. If something seems to work, it is retained; if not, it is changed or discarded. Such considerations as economy of effort and time, student interest, and relative effectiveness are always present in the teacher's thinking. A professional EFL teacher trainer may recommend something without knowing that within the specific context of a native language class it is not workable. Too often, teachers assume that because the EFL specialist has some background in linguistics (currently the magic word in the field of English) the recommendations must be taken literally and that if they do not work it is the fault of the teacher or of the students.

One often hears that although a given activity may not be interesting to the students or immediately effective the activity should be performed nevertheless: "I tell them that I know it will be boring, but they should put up with it for a few minutes." This "medicine" approach (it may taste bad, but it is good for you!) dooms the teaching from the outset. It will be difficult to instill the feeling of possible success if we begin by admitting that there has already been a lack of success and that his failure is to be accepted as inevitable.

The most obvious feed-back that can be gained from the students during a drill is their willingness to continue the drill. If they are involved in the activity, this is a strong indication that the activity is worth retaining or modifying in order to make it more effective. If an activity is not accepted by the students, we should welcome the additional information. A temporary set-back should not be considered an irreversible failure but an indication of an area needing further creative work.

IMITATION AND REPETITION

One of the foundations of the EFL approach is the cycle that consists of imitation, repetition, and manipulation. It is a basic tenet that, to master a new pattern, the students must spend time imitating a model of correctness presented by the teacher or on a tape. This imitation must be followed by many repetitions of the material so that saying it can become automatic and easy. The third step is using this pattern with other vocabulary items and relating it to other patterns (see below: Grammatical Manipulation Drills). The first two parts of the imitation—repetition—manipulation cycle are especially necessary when there are difficult sounds or when the sequence of sounds is troublesome.

But we have a situation that is not identical to the foreign language situation. Do the students need the amount of work in imitation and repetition that a foreign language student needs? Dr. Lin seems to think so:

> . . . it is believed that only repetitious practice imitating model sentences can bring about firm neuro-muscular control and the habit of using the new language patterns at the appropriate moment.[130]

Ruth W. I. Golden would also answer the question affirmatively:

> . . . we should take (the child) back to the period of lallation, sharpen his ear-voice reflex, and take him again through a stage of echolalia, giving him effective patterns to imitate. . . . We need to re-educate him to the more exact production of these sounds, giving him practice in repeating them in the combinations which he needs for effective language use.[131]

On the other hand, those students with whom the author has worked, especially those in junior high and senior high schools, do not like to imitate and repeat. They do not feel that these two activities are interesting or that they are making very much progress in learning new skills. The students are justified in this feeling. Consider the sentence *He begins to read.* It is not difficult for the students to say; there are no problem sounds; and the sequence of sounds does not present any problems. What, then, is gained by having the students repeat the sentence? Provided that the sentence is observed as different from *He begin to read,* it does not seem that much will be gained from imitation and repetition. And Dr. Lin points out that repetition will not assure that the student can hear the difference between the two sentences.[132]

The author observed this same phenomenon during a repetition drill conducted in a 10th-grade class. Three of the words in the drill were *desks, masks,* and *tasks.* The students were earnestly trying to imitate the teacher's pronunciation, but some of them were perplexed when the teacher said that they were not repeating the words accurately. (The inaccurate imitations were of two types: 'desses', 'masses', 'tasses'; and 'deskes', 'maskes', 'taskes'.) They could not hear the difference between the teacher's model and their imitation.

In teaching standard English, the usefulness of repetition and imitation drilling is limited to such a degree that the need for some other kind of activity is evident.

CONTRAST AND MINIMAL PAIR DRILLS

Fortunately, another type of drill from EFL methodology offers promise of compensation for the lack of interest and effectiveness found in imitation and repetition activities. This is the minimal pair drill. In this drill-type the students are presented with pairs of words or sentences, to which they respond "same" or "different". Drill Number 1 is an example of the minimal pair drill.

Drill Number 1

Teacher stimulus
1. masks
   'masses'
2. masks
   masks
3. 'masses'
   'masses'
4. 'tasses'
   tasks
5. desks
   desks

       Student response
       1. different
       2. same
       3. same
       4. different
       5. same

This drill is easy to present. It takes little time, and it focuses on the feature in question. If the students can respond correctly to the pairs, we know that they can hear the difference before they are called on to produce the standard.[133] We can adapt this EFL drill to the standard English context in another way, by using it for grammar work. Drill Number 2 illustrates this use.

Drill Number 2

Teacher stimulus
1. He work hard.
   He works hard.
2. He work hard.
   He work hard.
3. Paula likes leather coats.
   Paula likes leather coats.
4. She prefers movies.
   She prefer movies.
5. Robert play guard.
   Robert play guard.

     Student response
     1. different
     2. same
     3. same
     4. different
     5. same

It is not necessary to spend lots of time in imitation and repetition in order to be sure that the students are aware of the point in question. A minimal pair drill does this directly and effectively. We have also found that the above type of drill is interesting to students. It presents a challenge that rote work does not, and, if the teaching pace is brisk, the class does not bog down.

The following statement by Dr. Lin raises an important issue that must be considered:

> The interference between two closely related dialects—such as a non-standard dialect and standard English—is far greater than between two completely different languages, and the socially significant differences between the standard and nonstandard forms may be overshadowed by the similarities and fail to present a real challenge to the students.[134]

It is clear that students often do not see the difference between the standard they are to practice and the nonstandard they use. To counteract this interference, we must sort out the two dialects. This can be readily done by using both the nonstandard and the standard in minimal-pair-type drills.

THE CONCEPT OF APPROPRIATENESS

One of the differences between EFL and standard English pedagogy lies in making the point that standard English is appropriate in certain social situations and nonstandard in others. This is not necessary in EFL classes because it is relatively clear when one is to use English or one's native language. In standard English instruction, the language teaching must be preceded by a discussion of the concept of appropriateness. When the students are aware of other areas of behavior in which the concept holds true, adding this new area is not difficult. Secondary school students are aware of social appropriateness, and we have been able to take advantage of their awareness of appropriate modes of dress to establish the idea of appropriate modes of speaking.

But what is to be done with students who are not mature enough to understand this concept? The author would suggest that if a student is too young to understand appropriateness, teaching standard English and when to use it will be very difficult and perhaps fruitless. Some language teachers wish to begin foreign language instruction as early as possible. The NCTE Task Force seems to feel that teaching standard English at the earliest time is not a primary concern:

> The NCTE Task Force recommends that nonstandard English dialect be a concern at the preschool level only to the extent that it interferes with the acquisition of fundamental language learnings.[135]

In the case of standard English it might be advisable to wait until the idea of social suitability can be drawn upon, for the students *are* learning and using English, even though it is a nonstandard variety.

In presenting the concept of appropriateness, we go through a process that is not necessary in teaching English as a foreign language. Another aspect of this difference between the two situations is that in the foreign language class it is clear when the foreign language is being used and when the native language is being used. In the standard English classroom this may not always be so clear to the students. Our teaching task involves the sorting out of standard from nonstandard. The students must be taught to identify the standard and the nonstandard dialects on the basis of the grammar and pronunciation features that are taught. This can be readily handled in drills of the type described above in conjunction with drills in which the students identify English words or sentences as standard (appropriate for use in class) or nonstandard (appropriate for use on the street). Drills Number 3 and Number 4 work on this identification.

Drill Number 3

Teacher stimulus
1. masks
2. 'desses'
3. 'tasses'
4. tasks
5. desks

> *Student response*
> 1. class
> 2. street
> 3. street
> 4. class
> 5. class

Drill Number 4

Teacher stimulus
1. He work hard.
2. She prefer movies.
3. Robert plays guard.
4. He works hard.
5. Robert plays guard.

> *Student response*
> 1. street
> 2. street
> 3. class
> 4. class
> 5. class

GRAMMATICAL MANIPULATION DRILLS

In teaching EFL, one makes extensive use of two drill-types that are often called "manipulative". These are "substitution drills" and "transformation drills". In these drills, the students are given practice in extending the use of the pattern they have learned through imitation and repetition to other situations. In substitution drills, the students are given new words or phrases that they are to substitute in the pattern learned. For example, one might use the following substitution drill:

Drill Number 5

Teacher stimulus
1. We waited around after class.
2. They
3. John and Henry
4. after lunch
5. John

> *Student response*
> 1. We waited around after class.
> 2. They waited around after class.
> 3. John and Henry waited around after class.
> 4. John and Henry waited around after lunch.
> 5. John waited around after lunch.

In the following transformation drill, the students change the sentence from the past tense to the present or from the present to the past, according to the stimulus presented:

Drill Number 6

Teacher stimulus
1. We waited around after class.
2. Henry stood near the gym.
3. We often have tests.
4. Sometimes they came to class late.
5. He drove to work.

> *Student response*
> 1. We wait around after class.
> 2. Henry stands near the gym.
> 3. We often had tests.
> 4. Sometimes they come to class late.
> 5. He drives to work.

In teaching standard English, one might wish to use the two drills shown above, but there is an additional complication that must be handled. In the nonstandard, the students have two possibilities for a sentence in the past, where the standard permits only one. There are contexts in which the sentence *Yesterday we wait around* is permissible and other contexts in which the sentence *Yesterday we waited around* is permissible.[136]

Both of the sentences are found in the nonstandard, and there is no reason to believe that one is easier or more natural for the students to say. As in the case of the sentence *He begin to read* cited above, we have an example of the students' producing a form not from laziness or lack of care but because of the grammatical structure of their own dialect. It is crucial to realize that with some nonstandard dialects we are not dealing with only surface differences of pronunciation but also with deeper grammatical differences.

Repetition obviously will not be an effective way of dealing with the problem. If we tell the students that in a certain drill they are to produce only *waited, stood,* and *drive,* they may do so. But what will happen when they are required to use standard English in free-conversation situations, when the verb form to be used has not been specified? What about the students who are confused when they produce *Yesterday we wait around,* and are told they are wrong? Here again, we see that the instruction must do some sorting out—separating what is acceptable in standard English from what is acceptable in nonstandard English—before work with material in the standard dialect can be effective.

Sorting out can be accomplished by using minimal pair drills and "identification drills". In this way, we can be sure that the students are focusing on the feature that we are dealing with. It is a vain hope that by asking the students to be more careful they will automatically put the past tense marker where standard English requires it.

Students find grammatical manipulation drills interesting and challenging. We can take advantage of the students' interest by having them practice putting together standard English sentences under controlled circumstances. They would be using the feature or features that we are teaching, without interference from other potentially confusing factors.

One way to assure maximum student interest and involvement is to have the drill led by one of the students in the class. If the drill leader has a copy of the drill which includes the expected students responses, and if he is instructed to have the students repeat a response when there are mistakes, the drill will go over with a degree of success that will surprise those who observe this for the first time.

In the substitution and transformation drills above, the students were called on to make one or a small number of changes in the sentence. The drills are short because they are used for illustration. It would be more efficient to have ten to fifteen items per drill because it takes one or two items for the students to understand how they are to respond and to establish a pace that will carry the drill.

There are many possibilities for varying the difficulty in manipulation drills. A few of these are illustrated in the following drills. In Drill Number 7, the students substitute the verb given; they are not required to make any other changes.

Drill Number 7

Teacher stimulus
1. He relaxes in English class.
2. plays
3. sleeps
4. works
5. talks

> *Student response*
> 1. He relaxes in English class.
> 2. He plays in English class.
> 3. He sleeps in English class.
> 4. He works in English class.
> 5. He talks in English class.

In Drill Number 8, the students must decide where to substitute the new item in the sentence. The sentences are cumulative; the students must pay attention to every response.

Drill Number 8

Teacher stimulus
1. He relaxes in English class.
2. in history class
3. in assemblies
4. sleeps
5. Robert
6. after school

7. works
8. Rhonda
9. before school
10. practices

Student response
1. He relaxes in English class.
2. He relaxes in history class.
3. He relaxes in assemblies.
4. He sleeps in assemblies.
5. Robert sleeps in assemblies.
6. Robert sleeps after school.
7. Robert works after school.
8. Rhonda works after school.
9. Rhonda works before school.
10. Rhonda practices before school.

In Drill Number 9, the students do not have to decide where to substitute the new items, but they must decide whether to change anything else in the sentence.

Drill Number 9

Teacher stimulus
1. He relaxes in English class.
2. Paul
3. Rhonda
4. Paul and Rhonda
5. She

Student response
1. He relaxes in English class.
2. Paul relaxes in English class.
3. Rhonda relaxes in English class.
4. Paul and Rhonda relax in English class.
5. She relaxes in English class.

In Drill Number 10, the students have to decide where to substitute the new item as well as whether to make any other changes. Again, the sentences in the drill are cumulative.

Drill Number 10

Teacher stimulus
1. He relaxes in English class.
2. Paul
3. in history class
4. plays
5. Rhonda
6. Paul and Rhonda
7. sleep
8. She
9. in assemblies
10. They

    Student response
    1. He relaxes in English class.
    2. Paul relaxes in English class.
    3. Paul relaxes in history class.
    4. Paul plays in history class.
    5. Rhonda plays in history class.
    6. Paul and Rhonda play in history class.
    7. Paul and Rhonda sleep in history class.
    8. She sleeps in history class.
    9. She sleeps in assemblies.
    10. They sleep in assemblies.

In Drill Number 11, the students transform the model sentence to the question form.

Drill Number 11

Teacher stimulus
1. He relaxes in English class.
2. He works on Saturdays.
3. He practices after school.
4. He sleeps in assemblies.
5. He talks in history class.

    Student response
    1. Does he relax in English class?
    2. Does he work on Saturdays?

3. Does he practice after school?
4. Does he sleep in assemblies?
5. Does he talk in history class?

In Drill Number 12, the students transform the model sentence to the question form; they must also select the form of the auxiliary verb.

Drill Number 12

Teacher stimulus
1. He relaxes in English class.
2. Paul works on Saturdays
3. They practice after school.
4. Rhonda sleeps in assemblies.
5. Rhonda and Paul talk in history class.

 Student response
 1. Does he relax in English class?
 2. Does Paul work on Saturdays?
 3. Do they practice after school?
 4. Does Rhonda sleep in assemblies?
 5. Do Rhonda and Paul talk in history class?

Drill Number 13 is a combination of the substitution and transformation types. It is relatively difficult to teach the first time because of the large number of factors at play. The pace in such a drill must also be slower than in any of those previously shown. We have used the combination type as a game with two sides. The sides are called on alternatively, and a point is scored for each correct answer.

Drill Number 13

Teacher stimulus
1. He relaxes in English class.
2. sleeps
3. NEGATIVE
4. Her boyfriend
5. in history class

6. The students
7. AFFIRMATIVE

   8. work
   9. Paul
  10. on Saturdays
  11. QUESTION
  12. Rhonda
  13. after school
  14. Paul and Rhonda
  15. STATEMENT

> *Student response*
> 1. He relaxes in English class.
> 2. He sleeps in English class.
> 3. He doesn't sleep in English class.
> 4. Her boyfriend doesn't sleep in English class.
> 5. Her boyfriend doesn't sleep in history class.
> 6. The students don't sleep in history class.
> 7. The students sleep in history class.
> 8. The students work in history class.
> 9. Paul works in history class.
> 10. Paul works on Saturdays.
> 11. Does Paul work on Saturdays?
> 12. Does Rhonda work on Saturdays?
> 13. Does Rhonda work after school?
> 14. Do Paul and Rhonda work after school?
> 15. Paul and Rhonda work after school.

These are only a small number of the possibilities for drilling with grammatical manipulation. The challenge and interest that this type of activity generates recommends it for further work. A creative materials writer will come up with a number of variations that maintain student attention while giving practice with the particular standard English feature or features being worked on.

RESPONSE ACTIVITIES

The conventional EFL drill-types such as imitation and repetition have a greatly reduced utility in teaching standard English. Substitution and transformation drills have shown some promise, but we must not stop here, for manipulation does not provide instruction or practice in *creating* new sentences. Imitation drills are too confining and free conversation is too loose for effective control in teaching new forms and giving students practice with these forms. The problem is to develop ways of restricting the students in the grammar and pronunciation features of standard English that they can use while providing them the freedom to create new utterances.

One area of EFL methodology that does hold promise is that of the question-and-answer drill. In practice, this is often limited to several drills in which questions are asked and the students answer either with a preset sentence pattern or in any suitable way. This area should be expanded to include not only question-and-answer drills but many kinds of "response activities" that call for sentence generation.

Drill Number 14 is one type of response activity. It combines a transformation format with somewhat greater freedom; a student changes the model sentence and adds any other statement.

Drill Number 14

Teacher stimulus
1. It's my camel.
2. It's his elephant.
3. It's your baboon.
4. It's their giraffe.
5. It's our eagle.

> *Student response*
> 1. You have a camel, and . . . (he eats a lot. (or) we don't like it, etc.)
> 2. He has an elephant, and . . .
> 3. I have a baboon, and . . .
> 4. They have a giraffe, and . . .
> 5. We have an eagle, and . . .

We assure that the students practice different verb forms in the present tense while they feel the freedom to include any additional statement after the *and*. In teaching this drill, we have found that the students use a variety of other verbs in the second clause, although it sometimes takes a little prompting for them to become original in making the additions.

Another type of activity is one in which the students are called on to create a sentence using one item from the left-hand list and another one from the right-hand list.

Drill Number 15

My monkey	fins
This elephant	four feet
The fish	gills
That teacher	two feet

This drill must, of course, be done in the right spirit, but, once that spirit is present, the students will create affirmative and negative sentences like the following:

1. This elephant has four feet.
2. My monkey doesn't have gills.
3. That teacher doesn't have gills, either.

The creative teacher can involve other students by calling on them to affirm or deny the statements. For example, if one student says, *That teacher has fins,* another student can be called on for agreement or denial such as *No, she doesn't* or *Yes, he does, and they're red.*

One other activity is mentioned here as a further illustration of the types of drilling activities that serve the teaching purpose without sacrificing interest.

Drill Number 16

The class is divided into several teams. The teacher selects a number from one to one thousand. The students on the first team ask questions that can be answered with "yes" or "no", until they have narrowed down the field and guessed the number. This is repeated for each team. The team with the lowest score is the winner. The teacher will only answer questions that have been asked in standard English, but any question, standard or nonstandard, scores a point. This game can be varied by having a student lead the game in the teacher's place.

In some respects, this resembles a repetition practice because the students will settle down to a small number of question patterns; *Is it . . .?* is usually the predominating pattern. But the students become caught up in the game and do not feel that they are doing rote drill work.

If we are concerned with teaching the concept of appropriateness, the pedagogy must include instruction and practice in responding appropriately. The area of response drilling offers a place for activities in which the students respond with standard or nonstandard English according to the linguistic features presented: if the teacher stimulus is standard, the correct response is standard; if the teacher stimulus is nonstandard, the correct student response is nonstandard. In Drill Number 17, the students are to contradict the statements with an *appropriate* response.

Drill Number 17

Teacher stimulus
1. He gets good grades.
2. His girlfriend chews gum all the time.
3. Her boyfriend don't drive fast.
4. The teacher doesn't give too much homework.
5. Your math teacher give easy tests.

> *Student response*
> 1. No, he doesn't.
> 2. No, she doesn't.
> 3. Yes, he do.
> 4. Yes, she does.
> 5. No, she don't.

In Drill Number 18, the students are free to answer the questions in any *appropriate* way.

Drill Number 18

1. Do his sister go to this school?
2. Does your brother get good grades?
3. Does your English teacher give lots of tests?
4. Do your worst enemy go to this school?
5. Does he have a brother?

There are many activities of this type, in which we can restrict the scope of the student responses to the points we are working on while the students do not feel the restrictions of the drill. Here is the area that offers most promise for the future of teaching standard English (and in teaching English as a foreign language as well).

Too often teacher training becomes bogged down in the techniques of the imitation-repetition-manipulation cycle. One reason for the great attractions of this cycle may be that these three drill-types are easy to present in training programs. With such considerations as "constant intonation" and "backward build-up"—the EFL "stocks-in-trade"—they are easy to discuss. It is in the less controlled areas of the instruction that more emphasis must be placed. More time should be spent on "response activities", an area in which the students are freer to approximate natural speech but with some constraints so that they are practicing the grammar and pronunciation features that distinguish standard from nonstandard English.

THE USE OF WRITING

In more conservative EFL teaching, it has been common practice to present the oral forms of the language before the written ones. The idea is that, since the written word is a reflection of the oral language, it is better to teach students to read what they have already learned orally. In addition, it has been felt that the written word might cause problems in the acquisition of accurate pronunciation because the students would be concentrating on reading and not on oral imitation. Within these two areas—the oral and the written—it has been felt that the passive skills (hearing and reading) should be presented before the active skills (speaking and writing). Therefore, the sequence of the language skills has been: Hearing, speaking, reading, and writing.

It appears useful to continue the general practice of "passive before active" in teaching standard English. The students must be able to discriminate between the two dialects and between two similar items in the standard before we can call on them to produce. However, the principle of "oral before written" should be reexamined. If the students are literate in either dialect of English, we can take advantage of this skill in teaching the oral standard. It is easy to show the difference between the standard and the nonstandard with two written sentences. Before going on to the oral production steps, we can be sure that the students are focusing on the area of the sentence that is crucial. For example, writing the following two sentences on the board is a simple and efficient way to begin work on the present tense verb forms:

He begin to read.
He begins to read.

The two sentences can be left on the board during the following drill work as a reminder of the point being worked on.

To delay the use of writing because it seems to be a useful working principle in EFL is not sufficient reason for refusing to make effective use of it in teaching the oral form of standard English. The students feel more comfortable when they can see what is being discussed, and we can avoid wasting time on student guessing.

The recent interest in EFL methodology can be seen in the various summer workshops and in-service teaching programs during the school year. Many of the people starting out will probably trace some of the steps others have trod several years earlier. In order to avoid this waste of time and effort and in order to direct our efforts to those areas of the pedagogy which require further development, we should exchange the ideas and experiences we have had.

Although there seems to be a lot that can be borrowed from EFL and used advantageously, there must be some adaptation. The foreign language context is different from the standard dialect context. Accepting EFL methodology without critical examination would be a mistake. We must search for ways to innovate for increased interest, efficiency, and effectiveness.

5

🌺 Bonnie and Clyde Tactics in English Teaching

ROGER W. SHUY

The decade of the 1930's will long be remembered for the depression, the rise of The New Deal and a mood which produced some of the more exciting gangsters of all time, including Bonnie and Clyde. Few need to be told that Bonnie and Clyde were noted for their fast eradication of those who stood between them and their various coveted goals. Although it may strain the analogy to refer to the Bonnie and Clyde syndrome in relationship to English teaching past or present, such a metaphor seems appropriate. One may argue, for example, that English teachers wipe out evil while Bonnie and Clyde eradicated without discrimination. Those who so argue either point bear the burden of proof. It is the eradication *per se* that concerns us here.

English teachers have long borne the secret guilt of overly negative evaluation. Most of the marks and comments on any given composition will support the assertion that English teachers are overly concerned about what is wrong with the universe, the student and the student's ability to write and think. We set about to note the negative aspects of a written composition, we correct oral language lapses and we search for weaknesses in the formal properties of the debates and interpretations of our speech courses. The paucity of positive criticism is carried on even through graduate seminars in Shakespeare where term papers have been known to return with a lone grade and a number of corrections concerning style, mechanics, and punctuation.

278

Although it is customary for such long nourished pedagogical traditions to be given frozen immortality, recently the English teachers' accent on the negative has been reexamined in connection with the description, analysis and application of data about non-standard English. In this paper I will describe several current approaches to the problem, suggest the motivations for and effects of changing the current system, and note some of the materials currently available.

CURRENT APPROACHES TO THE PROBLEM OF NONSTANDARD ENGLISH

1. Eradication

In an editorial in the San Diego Union (September 10, 1967), Dr. Max Rafferty, State Superintendent of Public Instruction for the State of California, strongly urged the return to a pedagogical strategy of teaching that right is right and wrong is wrong with regard to the social varieties of American English:

> It is precisely education's job to deal in rights and wrongs. Because a child may count on his fingers and toes at home is no reason for his arithmetic teachers to let him keep doing it at school. And because a bigoted neighborhood may revel in racism doesn't make it okay for the civics instructor to neglect teaching the Bill of Rights to youngsters who call that neighborhood home.
>
> Neither does the fact that mom and pop say "De cat ha just split" when they mean "The man has just gone" make it right, any more than my Irish great-grandfather was permitted by his American teachers to go around voicing such Old Sod barbarisms as "Shure and begorra, 'tis a foine spaleen ye are, bad cess to ye."
>
> After his teachers had finished with him, great-granddad spoke good English, and he was thankful for it all his life. His parents went to their graves speaking brogue.

Although justifiable criticism may be made for selecting this particular representation of the position of those who possess what might be called the Bonnie and Clyde syndrome, it nonetheless establishes the position with pristine clarity.

A more scholarly position statement in support of eradication was made by Robert Green in reference to the more generally held sympathy toward biloquialism noted at the 1964 Conference on Social Dialects and Language Learning:

It was further indicated that if a person has a dialect that is peculiar to a given area and moves to another area, we should not attempt to change the dialect since it is acceptable in other parts of the United States. I would say that this point of view is not necessarily a defensible one, and I would again present the argument stressed previously—that area dialects which allow one to be identified and discriminated against perhaps should be restructured . . . The very inadequate speech that is used in the home is also used in the neighborhood, in the play group, and in the classroom. Since these poor English language patterns are reconstructed constantly by the associations that these young people have, the school has to play a strong role in bringing about a change in order that these young people can communicate more adequately in our society.[137]

It is not surprising that two leading educators such as these men would adopt the Bonnie and Clyde syndrome with respect to the teaching of standard English to nonstandard speakers. The English teaching profession has long nourished such a position. Children are corrected in speech and writing from their earliest days in the classroom to the last rites of graduation. The anomaly of the situation is perhaps best seen in the report of Murray Wax in his observations of how English was being taught to the Pine Ridge Sioux Indians:

> Teachers are trained to criticize (the local dialect) as 'bad English,' and so, no sooner does the Indian child open his mouth to speak English, than he is branded publicly as speaking incorrectly.[138]

If it seems undesirable to produce predictable regional features such as those found among the Pine Ridge Sioux Indians, how much more undesirable it must be to produce socially identifiable features such as those found in ghetto communities. The great American assumption, it then follows, is to rid oneself of the stigma of those features by simply eradicating the features, a time honored tradition in the English Departments of our country.

2. Biloquialism

A second position is easier to describe than to name. The term, *functional bidialectalism* was suggested at the Conference on Social Dialects and Language Learning as a way of identifying a person's right to continue speaking the dialect of his home (which may be nonstandard) even after he has learned a school dialect (which may be standard). Since the term *dialect* seems to carry such a heavy pejorative connotation these days, other terms have been suggested in place of bidialectalism, including the recently coined terms, *biloquialism,* and the term borrowed from the field of bilingual studies, *diglossia.* It is relatively safe to assume that both of the latter terms are more neutral than any term which involves the word *dialect.* Whatever it is called, most linguists will agree that a speaker of any language will make linguistic adjustments to specific social situations. These adjustments in phonology, grammar and lexicon will range anywhere from the obvious adjustments between adults and small children to the more complicated sociolinguistic switching between school, home and playground talk. Those who encourage the adoption of biloquialism feel that the teacher's job is not to eradicate playground English—or any other kind. Instead, teachers should help children to make the switch comfortably from one setting to another.

3. Non-Standard for Standard Speakers

Recently a third position has received considerable attention. Although the topic has been discussed for several years now, I know few linguists who have publicly advocated that instead of offering standard English to non-standard speakers, we should do exactly the opposite— present non-standard to standard speakers. However, in his review of the *Roberts English Series,* Wayne A. O'Neil observes:

> Instead of "enriching" the lives of urban children by plugging them into a "second" dialect (if that enterprise is too "enriching" (sic): why don't we let everyone in for the fun and games; "enrich" the suburban kid with an urban dialect), we should be working to eradicate the language prejudice, the language mythology, that people grew into holding and believing. For there is clear evidence that the privileged use their false beliefs about language to the disadvantage of the deprived. One way to stop this is to change nonstandard dialect speakers at least for some of the time, i.e. when the nonstandards are in the presence of the standards, currying favor of them, jobs of them, etc. This seems to me intolerable if not impossible. Another response to language differences would be to educate (especially the people in power) for tolerance of differences, for an understanding of differences. This could be naturally done, easily done in elementary schools, but only by teachers who are themselves free of language prejudice. In many ways this is the more important kind of language study that needs to be accomplished in the schools.[139]

Those who share O'Neil's position will argue that a brutal frontal attack on the problem, such as the one advocated by those who encourage the development of biloquialism, will be fruitless. They argue that this is not simply another case of bonehead English, that a frontal attack will alienate nonstandard speakers from us and from education, and that indirection is likely to work better than a head-on attack since their language will change of itself as they are introduced to a wider and wider world. Furthermore, advocates of this position feel that it is as morally defensible to change the rest of the world as it is to change the linguistic behavior of the nonstandard speaker.

These three positions, then, characterize current thought on the question of what to do about nonstandard English. A further position might be added in order to account for an even larger portion of the teachers of America—that of historic lethargy. One might opt for continuing to ignore the problem.

MOTIVATIONS FOR CHANGING THE CURRENT SITUATION

Before delving too deeply into the techniques of the approaches of eradication, biloquialism, or nonstandard for standard speakers, it may be wise to examine briefly the reasons most frequently listed for engaging in such behavior.

The eradicators, of course, carry the flag of unquestionable morality. Standard is better because it's nicer, but why it is nicer is never really explained. To accuse the people who hold this notion of ethnocentrism would be to involve the fierce wrath of the Mortimer Smiths of America on one's head. Smith, in fact, has recently observed:

> We can only hope that teachers of English, especially of the deprived, can resist the notion of linguistic equality. We hope, as we have said before in these pages, that teachers will continue to operate on the theory that education must seek to enlarge the horizon of the student, to improve and change and refine him, and to move him on to something better than he now knows.[140]

The eradicating Bonnies and Clydes of Smith's persuasion apparently feel that "enlarging the horizon of the student" means that he should forsake his old ways, his old culture for something vaguely represented as "refinement" and "something better than he now knows." That this runs counter to the natural flow of education and life experience in general seems not to have occurred to the editor of the *Bulletin* of the Council for Basic Education. At least it seems reasonable to assume that learning one thing does not necessarily require the eradication of another thing, even if they are diametrically opposed to each other.

One can only hypothesize how eradication can be conceived as enlarging one's horizon, particularly in a free society.

The motivations of the advocates of the biloquial position are considerably more complicated and deserving of attention. I will mention two motivations relating to social goals and two relating to intellectual goals.

SOCIAL GOALS

1. Upward Mobility

By far the most commonly stated reason for teaching children to be biloquial is to enable them to ascend the social ladder. Whether this is viewed crassly or altruistically, it must be listed as the goal most frequently cited.[141] Those who are critical of upward mobility as a goal of American education feel that our concern should be not with economic achievement but, instead, with expanding one's intellectual potential. It is difficult, of course, to disagree with this reasoning and there may be, in fact, no real reason to disagree with it. At least some of those who favor biloquialism do not consider upward mobility as mere social climbing. Instead, they mean to provide the learner with the linguistic tools with which he can operate synchronically on a number of social levels at one time. He can identify with and communicate comfortably to a wide spectrum of people. He can refrain from both talking down to and talking over the heads of his audiences. If such teaching is accompanied by condescension toward the lower socio-economic groups and fawning toward the uppers, it is the practice which errs, not necessarily the philosophy. And this, of course, can be a serious problem. If the practitioners of biloquialism hold only a hollow regard for nonstandard and do not view it as a legitimate form of language which, like other legitimate forms, has boundaries of propriety and ludicrousness, they are not really advocates of biloquialism anyway. They are only masquerading Bonnies and Clydes.

2. Manipulation

With the healthy advent of black self-awareness and ethnocentrism comes a different possible goal for learning standard English—that of increasing one's ability to manipulate whitey. The overtones of such a development range from the most extreme form of hatred of whites to the less excitable need for establishing an economic base within the black population. In some ways this goal is subject to the same criticism which we noted for those whose goal is upward social mobility. One can reasonably wonder whether the aim of English teaching is to help people become powerful every bit as much as we can wonder if it is to help people become financially secure. Yet certainly many teachers would agree that the black community needs to develop this power and ability to manipulate its environment. If biloquialism helps contribute to this goal, well and good. If it is used to foster hatred, however justifiable this may seem, again it is the practice, not necessarily the philosophy which needs to be repaired.

INTELLECTUAL GOALS

1. Understanding Language System

A relatively untapped but perfectly legitimate reason for encouraging biloquialism is that it can provide a convenient and interesting way to observe the systematic nature of language. Those who feel that learning can take place effectively by the use of contrast will want to seriously consider aspects of the contrast of systems between standard and nonstandard language. We can make no claim, in this case, for the use of such contrast merely to teach standard English, however much this might be true. A more likely outcome could be that students will learn something important about the systematicity of language, a fact which may be very helpful in building important understandings across social classes in both directions. And they just might learn something about how languages operate too. It seems reasonable to assume that studying the system of nonstandard English can lead to an appreciation of its speakers.

2. Observing Language Dynamics

If English teachers seriously believe that their subject matter is one of the most dynamic in the curriculum, they can be strengthened in their belief by observing language variation in process. It seems to be totally relevant to study the varieties of our contemporary language in relation to the current social scene. This can be done poorly—and probably will be by some. But if linguistic variety is approached as a means of developing self-awareness—what it is like, linguistically, to be thirteen years old rather than thirty-five or what it is like linguistically to be black rather than white, we may be on the verge of presenting the English language in its most meaningful and dynamic dimension.

The motivation for changing current pedagogy, then, differs considerably for the eradicators and the biloquial advocates. The former lean heavily on time honored notions of rightness, giving little concern to cultural relativism or social pluralism. The advocates of biloquial education feel that it is their duty as educators to provide the learner with the alternatives to make his life what he wants it to be. If he chooses to cut cleanly with his past, he can do so by learning standard and eradicating nonstandard forever and ever. If he chooses to become fluent in both standard and nonstandard, he is given this option also. If the student's motives are selfish, the educator may be sorry about this, but he can do more about it than my former college literature teacher who worried herself sick over what might happen to us if our reading D. H. Lawrence would lead us to sexual promiscuity. Her worries were real and well motivated. But the decision of whether or not to offer D. H. Lawrence was really never hers. The course demanded it. Our education required it. Her duty as an educator was to offer the material and let us decide what to do with that knowledge. She had to provide us with that option. Our application of it, whether altruistic or selfish, whether we remembered it or forgot it immediately, was, in one sense, none of her business.

The motives of those who advocate presenting nonstandard to standard speakers are undoubtedly good. The reasons for the low esteem in which nonstandard English is held derive from mankind's lowest points. Snobbery, hatred, inequality, racism and jealousy are all likely candidates. There can be no question about the need for removing these aspects from human life and there can be no doubt that we will continue to fail to do this. But there is no reason why we shouldn't try and I hold very great sympathy with the advocates of non-standard for standard speakers in this respect. To be sure, we need to engage in a massive attack on the legitimacy of nonstandard English for and by itself. This might be done through the study of Black English grammar (once one is written) in the high schools, through the study of language variety and change (noted earlier) and, more likely for now, through an enlightened social studies program.

In order to do any of these things, however, linguists need to tell us a great deal more than we now know about nonstandard English—particularly that variety used by Negroes. If we are going to use English as a Second Language technique for teaching standard to non-standard speakers, educators need to tell us why we should use this method and exactly how to delineate the differences between learning a second language and learning a second dialect. From psychology we need to learn at what age a child can best learn adult norms of standard English along with other aspects of the problem of motivation. From many disciplines (or perhaps from none) we need to learn how to direct men's hearts away from hatred, jealousy and greed.

CURRENT MATERIALS

A majority of the materials currently available for teaching standard English to nonstandard speakers rest on the uneasy assumption that TESOL techniques are valid for learning a second dialect. They do this without any solid proof. We do not have a viable evaluation tool at this time nor are we likely to get one until the linguists complete their analysis of the language system of nonstandard speakers. Most current materials deal with pronunciations although it has long been accepted that grammatical differences count more heavily toward social judgments than phonological or lexical differences.

It stands to reason that there is a hierarchy of importance in matters of teaching standard to nonstandard speakers, whether from the stance of biloquialism or Bonnie-and-Clydery. If grammatical matters count more heavily in social judgments, it seems reasonable to assume that grammatical matters should receive high priority in materials development. I know of only one set of oral language materials which has done this so far.[142] Most focus on pronunciations and few specify the nature of the problem beyond the usual list of aberrant features. Until a clear hierarchy of importance with respect to nonstandard features is established, however, it will be difficult to decide when a learner has reached the point at which no negative social judgment is made of his oral language (or to decide the point at which pursuit of standard forms buys him so little that it is not worth the effort.)

An even more perplexing problem has to do with distinguishing those features which black speakers wish to retain in order to be identified as black from the features which give them low social status. Contributing to our difficulty here is the unsettled state of things in general at this time. Ron Karenga, for example, has argued that black people need to become socially distinct as a basis on which to function politically and economically with unity. In order to do this he advocates a cultural revolution which involves developing a mythology, a historical tradition (with new heroes and new holidays), the restoration of emasculated black males, the development of new political and economic organizations, and an education, art, literature, and music which will create and support a black ethos. At his center for instruction in Los Angeles, Karenga also encourages black people to learn an African language, Swahili, to tie language to the cultural revolution. Although it is quite perceptive to recognize that language is an extremely important part of developing black ethnocentrism, three things might be said of Karenga's choice of Swahili. First, it is quite unlikely that Swahili was an ancestral language of very many of the black people of America. It is an East African language and most slaves were uprooted from West Africa where other languages, such as Hausa and Yoruba, were spoken. Second, one may legitimately wonder whether Karenga is not making his job harder than it need be by going back to Africa to resolve the language question. Third, it is unlikely that blacks will be any more successful in teaching Afro-Americans to speak Swahili than are our high schools in teaching Euro-Americans to speak French, German or Spanish.

Certain distinctive characteristics of contemporary Negro speech may well suffice to serve the same purpose. At this point, this is only a hypothesis, of course, but could it be that two or three phonological features such as the final consonant cluster reduction and the devoicing of the final voiced stop consonants /b/, /d/, and /g/, will suffice to provide this black identity? A major difficulty with such a suggestion is that phonological features are not very high in the threshold of speaker awareness. These features, for example, are often the last remnants of nonstandard Negro speech primarily because the speaker is not aware that they so identify him. Indeed, it might be easier to select grammatical features which Negroes can use to satisfy their black consciousness since it would be easier to restructure conscious indices than to make unconscious ones conscious. At this point, one can most sensibly observe that the topic bears further investigation.

It would appear that the three positions described in this paper (The Bonnies and Clydes, The biloquialists and The advocates of non-standard for standard speakers) are not necessarily in mutual opposition. As in politics, it is frequently difficult to tell the Republicans from the Democrats. There are eradicators who claim to be biloquialists and biloquialists who sympathize with the idea of presenting nonstandard to standard speakers. The latter two positions have more in common, however, than either of them with the eradicators.

It is difficult to tell exactly what the most efficient procedure will be from here on but it seems clear that all English teachers should concern themselves with the following questions:

1. Is what I am teaching about the English language the most important thing that my students can study at this time?

2. Is my English language teaching completely unbigoted?

3. Am I honoring my obligation as an English language teacher to provide the most useful alternatives or options for my students' self-fulfillment (not just job opportunities)?

4. Is my English language teaching utilizing the most dynamic and timely principles and data for undertaking the system of language?

5. Am I taking every advantage of the opportunities in my English language class to develop healthy attitudes toward social justice, brotherhood and human rights?

If the answers to any one of these questions is no, we had better re-examine our motives for being where we are and for doing what we are doing.

6

🌼 How to Tell the Bandits from the Good Guys: or, What Dialect to Teach?

J. L. DILLARD

As one of those who lived along Highway 80 in Texas during the days when Raymond Hamilton and his now better known associates were more or less terrorizing the area, I have too much sympathy for the victims of the gunmen and for those who feared that they would become victims to aspire to be a kind of Texas gunman who would do murder on our cute little regional dialects. Quaintness has its charms, as will be attested by those who have been attracted to the archaic concept of *ye olde dialecte* as practiced by the *Linguistic Atlas of the United States and Canada* for the past forty years. Yet quaintness is not all innocence, as those of us can testify who have tried to flavor the dialect picture with our own Creole blend of *de dahleck* only to meet with the fury of the back-to-East Anglia Establishment. Live and let live—even if it doesn't make for Award-winning movies. But another dialect is asserting its claims; and surely not even Murder, Incorporated, would have mowed it down simply because it cannot lay claim to a geographic locale.

This dialect, which is the preferred brand of English on the part of

J. L. Dillard is Visiting Lecturer in Linguistics in the Ferkauf Graduate School of Humanities and Social Sciences, Yeshiva University. His writings reflect a concern with the inadequacy of the *Linguistic Atlas* methods, the nature and creole origin of Negro dialects, and relevant educational problems.

those who speak the equally non-territorial variety called Negro Non-Standard or Black English, is the consensus dialect—or Network Standard in the terminology used by Wallace Lambert and William A. Stewart.[143] It is widely acknowledged among sociolinguists although harshly proclaimed to be non-existent by the dialect geographers in some faulty-appearing analogies with Parisian French and Florentine Italian.[144] It is no new linguistic sin invented by the wicked twentieth century—no taking off of the clothes of linguistic respectability in public as in *Hair*—for its congeners have been around since the days of *koiné* Greek. Whatever the status of Paris or Florence, we know that it takes no dominance by Berlin to make possible the German Bühnenausspra-che, and we suspect that it takes no permission from Chicago to provide a consensus dialect for the United States.[145] For the Holy Land itself, we have Haim Blanc's excellent testimony that a *koiné* dialect of Hebrew is developing; we cannot, therefore, be trafficking with a sacrilegious development.[146]

Not only does the consensus dialect have its present diglossic relationship with regional and other dialects as described by Fishman, but some such dialect has stood in that relationship in the United States since at least the early years of the nineteenth century. This was especially true in the South, where the Plantation Creole-influenced home dialect was the language of the slave-owning women and one of the varieties used by the men.[147] The latter shifted into the consensus dialect when they talked to Lyell, Dickens, or some other distinguished visitor.[148] The women had only a dialect which reminded everyone of the speech of their Negro slaves.[149] In like manner, New York researchers today have found that Puerto Rican men may speak a very American-like brand of English at the office but that Puerto Rican women, who stay at home, speak the home language—Puerto Rican Spanish—and very little else.[150] Although a home language or dialect is as good as any other kind of dialect, it has been an almost worldwide tradition for centuries that the school should concern itself with teaching the language to be used outside the home. Even most "primitive" cultures have long known what super-modern American linguistics keeps telling itself—that the physiologically normal human being learns the language of his home circle and peer group *without* assistance from the school. This does not, of course, mean that the school is not to be concerned with such *uses* of language—whether it is the home and peer group language or not—as reading and writing, nor do such considerations have any bearing on whether the home language or some language of wider communication or *koiné* dialect should be the medium for learning such language-related skills.

It therefore seems reasonable that a part of the English teaching in the United States should be concerned with imparting another dialect to the students. Because the principle of dialect extermination has long been deprecated by linguists and by their camp followers, many linguists and educators have advocated the second language/dialect teaching approach rather than the remedial approach.[151] The change from remedial-destructive to SESD (Standard English as a second dialect) seems like a very promising future development in English teaching methodology.

In the elementary school, some students may have little or no need for such a second dialect. Many a speaker of a Northeastern middle-class variety of English has little trouble in adjusting to the fact that the printed marks which we must learn to decode have *r* where he has none in *war* and lack *r* where he has one in *idea of it*. Basilect speakers of Negro Non-Standard English,[152] on the other hand, frequently find so much difference between their own language and that of the classroom that their acquisition of the skills of reading and writing is seriously impeded.[153] The new Stewart-Baratz project is based upon the theory that Negro children will learn to read better in their own dialect, and I am totally in sympathy with that view. It also assumes that they will eventually move toward the reading of Standard English. Teachers who have such experiences as teaching Haitian Creole speakers the reading process first in Creole before beginning them on Standard French are unanimously sympathetic with such procedures. Those whose experience is bounded by mainstream American culture tend to be somewhat more difficult to convince.

All of these approaches plan for the teaching of Standard English to the students at some time. If it could be effectively taught to Negro Non-Standard speaking children in the pre-school, there would, of course, be no reason why they could not begin learning to read in Standard English. The brand of Standard English taught might as well be the most useful one. Insofar as speakers of Negro Non-Standard dialects are concerned, there is a solid preference for that dialect indicated by the Lambert-Tucker experiment. Others may have practical use for it, as Fishman has indicated:

> . . . Many of them [commuters to New York City jobs] also [in addition to their local dialects] can and do employ a more regionally neutral variety, which is their approximation to "Standard American."[154]

No one seriously advocates gunning down Boston dialect, Texas cotton country dialect, or Negro Non-Standard. But those of us who will not be content all our lives to be home folks twenty-four hours a day—and which of us will be?—will find some need to use the relatively un-marked dialect. I can mystify and amuse my Yeshiva students with a sentence like *This milk is blinky;* but I have not had a serious need for the area dialect word in thirty years. It has been even longer since I had occasion to talk about what we used to call *snake doctors;* but, on the very unlikely chance that I ever need to have the janitors chase one out of my office, I might as well learn to call it a *dragon fly.* (As a matter of fact, the janitors are Puerto Ricans and would not under-stand that term either.)

To the teacher, the important information is not that *shrunk* is used as a preterite by 86.5% of all informants in the Upper Midwest but that such usage is not characteristic of the supra-regional consensus standard.[155] The teacher should not, of course, denounce the usage in terms so violent as to risk scaring the child out of six years or more of language development; the teacher might as well accept the preachings of a generation of linguistic reformers and give up talk of localisms and social dialect forms as "errors." But this surely does not mean that the teacher should give up teaching anything else. With a great deal of SESD methodology available as an alternative to puristic condem-nation, the teacher need be impaled on neither horn of the dilemma—condemn or teach localisms. Those who continue to give the teacher only that choice are surely suffering from, and trying to infect others with, culture lag.

What is this consensus dialect like? With the absolute revulsion which some dialectologists have felt toward the mere mention of the phenomenon, there has been a not surprising lack of progress toward a description. But we can be fairly sure that it has /r/ in *barn, war, Har-vard* (twice) but not in *idea of it* or *Cuba.* Verbs like *drink* and *sink* tend to have three forms, rather than two; there is, on the other hand, no tendency toward the archaic seeking out of the four forms of Old English or Germanic strong verbs. *Ain't* is for its casual style if it's there at all; casual style is more nearly the domain of other dialects, anyway. A double negative doesn't make a positive; but, then, it isn't a likely structure in this dialect so we're spared that worry. We don't need to determine its terms for farm implements, since we aren't likely to talk about *singletrees* or *whiffletrees* in the consensus dialect. We don't have to worry about breaking students of the bad habit of using *olicook;* college students in the area where it's supposed to be one of the characteristic words are vastly amused at being told that there's such a word in the English language. And we won't have to worry too much about which term the students, in urban schools anyway, use for fishing worms. (That will be one minor use for the forthcoming *Dictionary of American Regional English:* City residents who are going fishing in rural areas can look up the specific area's word for fishing worm—provided they want to fish with worms). *Nice white rice* has three dipththongs; *bird and Boyd* can never be confused; *ten* and *tin* (alas!) contrast.

The cute little regional dialects aren't in danger so much of being gunned down as of being turned out to pasture—or, more precisely, to fish. Those few who feel nostalgic for them can meet on special nights to speak them as Leopold says certain East German refugees in West Germany have been doing.[156] It would be good if a lot of people read Leopold's article, for one reason or another. It might even start some people to thinking about whether the migration of area dialects with their speakers is a normal and regular part of human language history.

We can tell the good guys in the movies because they wear white hats and only turn bloodthirsty when there are bad guys around to be slaughtered; they do their killing in defense of peace and of human life. It's harder to tell the good guys where dialects are concerned, because what seems to be a noble urge to protect one kind of dialect may in fact be an evil scheme to do in another. Perhaps we would be better advised to forget about good guys and bandits, and about metaphors from the movies, and concentrate on determining which dialects are most useful for educational and other purposes.

7

❀ Dialect Barriers to
Reading Comprehension

KENNETH S. GOODMAN

The task of learning to read is not an easy one. But it's a lot easier to learn to read one's mother tongue than to learn to read a foreign language, one which the learner does not speak. Actually each of us speaks a particular dialect of a language. Each dialect is distinguished from all other dialects by certain features as: some of its sounds, some of its grammar, some of its vocabulary. The dialect which the child learns in the intimacy of his own home is his mother tongue. All physically normal children learn to speak a dialect. Whatever happens to his language during his life, however fluent and multilingual he may become, this native dialect is his most deeply and permanently rooted means of communication.

Since it is true that learning to read a foreign language is a more difficult task than learning to read a native language, it must follow that it is harder for a child to learn to read a dialect which is not his own than to learn to read his own dialect.

This leads to an important hypothesis: *The more divergence there is between the dialect of the learner and the dialect of learning, the more difficult will be the task of learning to read.*

This is a general hypothesis. It applies to all learners. If the language

Kenneth S. Goodman is Professor of Elementary Education and Director of Reading Miscue Research at Wayne State University. Professor Goodman is the author of several articles and the co-author of *Choosing Materials to teach Reading* and *The Psycholinguistic Nature of the Reading Process*.

of the reading materials or the language of the teacher differs to any degree from the native speech of the learners some reading difficulty will result. To some extent also there is divergence between the immature speech of the young learner and adult language norms in the speech community. Children have mastered most but not all of the sounds and syntax of adult speech. A further divergence reflects the fact that older members of any language community are less influenced by language change than are the youth. Thus the teacher may cling to language which is obsolescent in form or meaning. Books particularly lag behind language change since they freeze language at the date of composition. Though this paper is mainly concerned with gross dialect differences it must be remembered, then, that the reading problems discussed apply to some extent to all learners because minor dialect differences are features of even homogeneous speech communities.

The Divergent Speaker

For purposes of discussion we'll call the child who speaks a dialect different from that which the school, text, or teacher treats as standard, *the divergent speaker*. Divergence, of course, is relative and there is by no means agreement on what standard American English is. Divergent is a good term however, because it is neutral as a value term and it is important, perhaps critical, in considering the problems of the divergent speaker to avoid labeling his language as bad, sloppy, or sub-standard. We need to keep clear that, though some dialects may carry more social prestige than others, they are not necessarily more effective in communication. Gleason has said, "It is a safe generalization to say that all languages are approximately equally adequate for the needs of the culture of which they are a part." Dialects represent subcultures. Therefore it can similarly be said that all dialects are equally adequate for the needs of the subculture of which they are a part.

Every child brings to school, when he comes, five or six years of language and of experience. His language is closely intertwined with the culture of his community; it embodies the cultural values and structures the way in which he may perceive his world and communicate his reactions to others.

His language is so well learned and so deeply embossed on his subconscious that little conscious effort is involved for him in its use. It is as much a part of him as his skin. Ironically, well-meaning adults, including teachers who would never intentionally reject a child or any important characteristic of a child, such as the clothes he wears or the color of his skin, will immediately and emphatically reject his language. This hurts him far more than other kinds of rejection because it endangers the means which he depends on for communication and self-expression.

Things that other people say sound right or funny to a child depending on whether they fit within the language norms of his dialect. He has become exceedingly proficient in detecting slight, subtle differences in speech sounds which are significant in his dialect and he's learned to ignore other differences in speech sounds that are not significant. He uses rhythm and pitch patterns of his language with great subtlety. He enjoys puns on language which employ very slight variations in relative pitch and stress. By the time divergent speakers are in the middle grades they have learned to get pleasure from the fact that an in-group pun based on their common divergent dialect is unfunny to an outsider like their teacher who doesn't share the dialect.

All children develop vocabulary which falls generally within the vocabulary pool of their speech community. Through repeated experience common for their culture they have begun to develop complex concepts and express them in their mother tongue.

In every respect the process of language development of the divergent speaker is exactly the same as that of the standard speaker. His language when he enters school is just as systematic, just as grammatical within the norms of his dialect, just as much a part of him as any other child's is. Most important, it is a vital link with those important to him and to the world of men.

There are some differences between the problems of the divergent speaker in an isolated rural community where a single dialect is the common speech and has been for several generations and the problems of the divergent speaker in the center of one of our great cities. This latter child may live in a virtual ghetto, but his friends and neighbors represent a variety of language backgrounds. Transplanted regional dialects become social class dialects. As the city-dweller grows older he comes into increasing contact with the general culture and its language. In the home community the idiolects, the personal languages of individuals, will cluster closely around a dialect prototype. But the dialects of urban divergent speakers are much more varied and shade off from distinct divergent dialects to standard speech. Variables such as family origin, recency of migration, degree of isolation from influences outside the subculture, attitudes toward self, personal and parental goals are some of the factors which may determine idiolect.

Divergent Language or Dialects

Language diversity among divergent speakers complicates the task of understanding the literacy problems which they have. The basic problems will be the same but the specific form and degree will vary among individuals.

Teachers need to give careful consideration to the separate characteristics of several kinds of language divergence. They need to first differentiate immature language from dialect-based divergence. Language which is immature is always in transition toward adult norms. Teachers need not worry too much about immaturity in language since desired change is virtually inevitable. On the other hand, whatever the teacher does to speed this change is in the direction the child is moving. He can confirm the teacher's advice in the speech of his parents. But if the teacher "corrects" the dialect-based divergent language, this is at cross purposes with the direction of growth of the child. All his past and present language experience contradicts what the teacher tells him. School becomes a place where people talk funny and teachers tell you things about your language that aren't true.

Another point that needs to be clarified is the difference between standard regional speech and some imaginary national standard which is correct everywhere and always. No dialect of American English ever has achieved this status; instead we have a series of standard regional dialects, the speech of the cultured people in each area.

It's obvious that a teacher in Atlanta, Georgia, is foolish to try to get her children to speak like cultured people in Detroit or Chicago, just as it's foolish for any teacher to impose universal standard pronunciations which are not even present in the teacher's own speech. I'm referring to such hypocrisies as insisting that *u* before *e* must always say its own name and therefore *Tuesday* is /tyuzdey/. Cultured speech, socially preferred, is not the same in Boston, New York, Philadelphia, Miami, Baltimore, Atlanta, or Chicago. The problem, if any, comes when the Bostonian moves to Chicago, the New Yorker to Los Angeles, the Atlantan to Detroit. Americans are ethnocentric in regard to most cultural traits but they are doubly so with regard to language. Anybody who doesn't speak the way I do is wrong. A *green onion* is not a *scallion*. I live in Detróit not Détroit. I can carry my books to work but not my friends. *Fear* ends with *r* and *Cuba* does not. Such ethnocentrisms are unfortunate among the general public. They may be tragic among educators. Too often we send children off to speech correction classes not because their speech needs correction but be-

cause it isn't like ours. Pity the poor child who finds himself transplanted to a new and strange environment and then must handle the
additional complication of learning to talk all over again. And, of
course, if the child is a migrant from the rural South to the urban
North, his speech marks him not only as different but socially inferior.
He is told not just that he is wrong but sloppy, careless, vulgar, crude.
His best defense is to be silent.

In his classroom the divergent speaker finds several kinds of lan-
gauge being used. First is the language or bundle of idiolects within
dialects which he and his classmates bring with them as individuals.
Represented in their language or dialect is the language or dialect of
their parents and their speech community. Next there is the language
of the teacher which will exist in at least two forms. There will be the
teacher's informal, unguarded idiolect and his version of correct standard speech; the way he says things off guard; the way he strives to
speak as a cultivated person. Another version of the standard language will be the literary form or forms the child encounters in books.
To this we must add the artificial language of the basal reader. Artificial language is not used by anyone in any communicative situation.
Some primerese is artificial to the point of being non-language, not
even a divergent one.

The Consensus of Language and the Uniformity of Print

Two things are in the divergent child's favor. First, all speakers have
a range of comprehension which extends beyond the limits of their
own dialect. All of us can understand speech which differs from our
own, particularly if we are in frequent contact with such speech. As
they grow older, urban children are in increasing contact with a number of dialects other than their own. Secondly, the English orthography
has one great virtue in its uniformity across dialects. No matter how
words are pronounced, printers across the country usually spell them
the same. Though we get some mavericks like *guilty* and *judgment,*
we spell *pumpkin* the same whether we say *pəŋkin or pəmp-
kən* and *something* the same whether we say *səmpthin* or
səmpm. This standardization of print for a multidialectal speech suggests that part of the problem of learning to read for divergent speakers
could be eliminated if teachers let children read in their own dialects
and if teachers got rid of the misconception that spelling determines
pronunciation. One child asked his teacher how to spell /ræt/. "R-a-t,"

she said. "No, ma'am," he responded, "I don't mean rat mouse, I mean right now."

Points of Divergence Among Dialects

Now if we examine the areas in which dialects differ we can perhaps shed some light on the barriers divergent readers face. Let us start with sound.

SOUND DIVERGENCE

Intonation

Dialects differ in intonation. Perhaps what makes an unfamiliar dialect most difficult to understand is its unexpected pitch, stress, and rhythm. Teachers often complain when they first begin to work with divergent speakers that they can't understand a word. But after a short time they seem to tune in on the right frequency. They catch on to the melody of the dialect. Since intonation is essential in understanding oral language, it is logical to assume that it must be supplied mentally by readers as they read in order for comprehension to take place. How much comprehension is interfered with if the teacher insists on intonation patterns in oral reading which are unnatural to the divergent reader can only be conjectured at this time. But there is no doubt that this is a source of difficulty to some extent.

Phonemes

Phonemes are the significant units of speech sounds which are the symbols of oral language. All American dialects share more or less a common pool of phonemes. But not all dialects use all these phonemes in all the same ways. They pattern differently in different dialects. Since phonemes are really bundles of related sounds rather than single sounds, it is likely that the range of sounds that compose a particular phoneme will vary among dialects. Vowel phonemes are particularly likely to vary. Even within dialects there are some variations. Good examples are words ending in -og, such as /dog/, /fog/, /frog/, /log/; or are they /dɔg/, /fɔg/, /frɔg/, /lɔg/? In my own idiolect I find I say /frɔg/, /fɔg/, /dɔg/, /lɔg/, but I also say /cag/, /bag/, /smag/.

Obviously, phonics programs which attempt to teach a relationship between letters and sounds cannot be universally applicable to all dialects. The basic premise of phonics instruction is that by teaching a child to associate the sounds which he hears in oral language with the letters in written language he will be able to sound out words. But a divergent speaker can't hear the sounds of standard speech in his nonstandard dialect because he does not have them or because they occur in different places in his dialect than other dialects. The instruction may be not only inappropriate but confusing. When he reads the lesson he may then be forced to sound out words which are not words in his dialect. To illustrate: Take a child who normally says /də/ rather than /ðə/ and /nəfin/ rather than /nəθin/. Teaching him that the digraph <th> represents the first sound in *the* and the medial consonant in *nothing* makes him pronounce words not in his dialect and throws a barrier across his progress in associating sound and print.

New Reading Materials and Sound Divergence Among Dialects

Recent attempts at producing beginning reading materials which have regular one-to-one correspondence between letters and phonemes will not solve this problem and may actually compound it since there will be a tendency for teachers to assume that the matched correspondence of sound and letter is to be uniform throughout the reading materials. For example, they might assume *frog* and *log* to have the same vowel sound and so teach the sounds to be the same when a student might well use /a/ as in *father* in one and /ɔ/ as in *caught* in the other. The matched phonemic-graphemic books assume that there is a uniform spoken set of sounds that can by ingenuity and counting of data be inscribed with a uniform written alphabet. This is not true, when the spoken language is viewed as a national-international phenomenon or when it is viewed as a local phenomenon in a heterogeneous cultural country as one of our urban centers.

Transcription of the sound language in ITA faces the same problems. It has a wider alphabet and can therefore transcribe more literary and sensible English than the limited lexicon of the American linguistic readers. The British ITA materials, however, cannot be read literally except with the "received pronunciation" of the BBC. When as an

American I read about "levers" in an ITA book I must say /liyvərz/.
The principle that spelling is the same across dialects is sacrificed and
ITA spelling requires pronunciation narrowed to one special class
dialect. Teachers using these materials need to make some adjustments
for the dialects used by themselves and their students. There may be,
no doubt is, a spoken language in common but it is not so uniform as
is the common spelling system.

Another place where sound divergence among dialects affects the
handling of reading materials is the traditional sets of homophones.
Homophones, words that sound alike, will vary from dialect to dialect.
Been and *bin* are homophones in my speech. In another dialect *been*
would sound the same as *bean* and in still another *Ben* and *been* would
be sounded alike. Bidialectal students may bring up new sets of homophones. One teacher asked her class to use *so* in a sentence. "I don't
mean sew a dress", she said. "I mean the other so." "I got a *so* on my
leg", responded one of her pupils.

GRAMMAR DIVERGENCE

The Suffix

Inflectional changes in words involve using suffixes or internal
changes in words to change case or tense. In certain dialects of American English speakers say *He see me* rather than *He sees me*. They are
not leaving off an *s*. There isn't any in their dialect. Similarly, plurals
may not use an *s* form. *I got three brother*, is common in Appalachian
speech. One teacher reported to me that her pupils could differentiate
between *crayon* and *crayons* as written words and respond to the difference by selecting plural and singular illustrations, but they read the
words the same, one crayon, two /kræyən/. The problem is not an
inability to see or say the *s*. It doesn't seem to belong to the pronunciation of *crayons*. The inflectional ending *s* to indicate plural is not in the
grammar of this dialect.

Most Americans will add /əz/ to form plurals of words ending in /s/
/z/ /š/ /ĵ/ /č/ as in *busses, mazes, washes, colleges, churches,* but in
the Blue Ridge Mountains this ending also goes with words ending in
/sp/, /st/, /sk/ as in /waspəz/ /pohstəz/ /tæskəz/ (H. A. Gleason,
An Introduction to Descriptive Linguistics, New York: Holt, Rinehart
and Winston, p. 62). This kind of difference will be reflected in the
child's reading. The differences are systematic within the child's dia-

lect. In terms of the school and teacher they may be divergent, or as
we say, incorrect, but in terms of the reader and his speech community
they are convergent, that is, correct.

Not only suffixes vary, but also verb forms and verb auxiliaries. When
a child says, "I here, teacher", as the teacher calls the roll, he is not
being incomplete. No linking verb is needed in this type of utterance
in his dialect. There is a difference in the syntax of his dialect and
other American English dialects. Fortunately such differences are minor
in American English. One area of difference seems to be the use of
verb forms and verb markers. *We was going, They done it, We come
home,* all are examples of this phenomenon.

Vocabulary Divergence

An area of dialect divergence that people are most aware of is vocabulary. Most people are aware that *gym shoes* in Detroit are *sneakers* in
New York, that in Chicago you may *throw* but in Little Rock you
chunk, that a Minnesota *lake* would be a *pond* in New Hampshire. Perhaps there is less awareness of words which have similar but not identical meanings in different dialects. All words have a range of meaning
rather than a single meaning. This range may shift from place to place.
The meaning of *carry* may be basically the same in two dialects but
some uses will be correct in one dialect but not in the other.

Vocabulary differences among dialects may cause reading difficulty
and must be compensated for by the teacher who uses texts printed for
a national market.

I've dealt primarily here with the barriers to learning how to read
that result when the readers have divergent languages. There are of
course other important problems which grow out of the differences in
experience, values, and general subculture of the divergent learners.
Readers can't comprehend materials which are based on experience
and concepts outside their background and beyond their present
development.

The Reading Program for Divergent Speakers

Let's address ourselves to a final question. What is currently happen-
ing as the divergent speaker learns to read? I've found that divergent
speakers have a surprising tendency to read in book dialect. In their
oral reading they tend to use phonemes that are not the ones they use

in oral language. Their reading often sounds even more wooden and unnatural than most beginners. There is some tendency to read their own dialect as they gain proficiency, but in general it appears that teachers are more successful in teaching preferred pronunciations than reading. What is lacking is the vital link between written and oral language that will make it possible for children to bring their power over the oral language to bear on comprehending written language.

There seem to be three basic alternatives that schools may take in literacy programs for divergent speakers. First is to write materials for them that are based on their own dialect, or rewrite standard materials in their dialect. A second alternative is to teach the children to speak the standard dialect before teaching them to read in the standard dialect. The third alternative is to let the children read the standard materials in their own dialect, that is, to accept the language of the learners and make it their medium of learning. The first alternative seems to be impractical on several counts. Primarily the opposition of the parents and the leaders in the speech community must be reckoned with. They would reject the use of special materials which are based on a non-prestigious dialect. They usually share the view of the general culture that their speech is not the speech of cultivation and literature. They want their children to move into the general culture though they are not sure how this can be brought about.

The second alternative is impractical on pedagogical grounds in that the time required to teach children who are not academically oriented to another dialect of the language, which they feel no need to learn, would postpone the teaching of reading too long. Many would never be ready to learn to read if readiness depended on losing their speech divergence in the classroom. The problem is not simply one of teaching children a new dialect. Children, the divergent among them, certainly have facility in language learning. The problem involves the extinction of their existing dialect, one which receives continuous reinforcement in basic communications outside of the classroom. Labov's research in New York indicates that divergent speakers do not seem to make a conscious effort to use language forms which they recognize as socially preferred until adolescence. Younger children may hear differences but lack the insight to realize which forms are socially preferred. Of course, teenagers may deliberately avoid preferred forms, too, as they reject adult ways and adult values.

In essence the child who is made to accept another dialect for learning must accept the view that his own language is inferior. In a very real sense, since this is the language of his parents, his family, his community, he must reject his own culture and himself, as he is, in order to become something else. This is perhaps too much to ask of any child. Even those who succeed may carry permanent scars. The school may force many to make the choice between self-respect and school acceptance. And all this must be accomplished on the faith of the learner that by changing his language he will do himself some good. As one teen-ager remarked to me, "Ya man, alls I gotta do is walk right and talk right and they gonna make me president of the United States."

The only practical alternative I feel is the third one. It depends on acceptance by the school and particularly by the teacher of the language which the learner brings to school. Here are some key aspects of this approach:

1. Literacy is built on the base of the child's existing language.
2. This base must be a solid one. Children must be helped to develop a pride in their language and confidence in their ability to use their language to communicate their ideas and express themselves.
3. In reading instruction, the focus must be on learning to read. No attempt to change the child's language must be permitted to enter into this process or interfere with it.
4. No special materials need to be constructed but children must be permitted, actually encouraged, to read the way they speak. Experience stories must basically be in their language.
5. Any skill instruction must be based on a careful analysis of their language.
6. Reading materials and reading instruction should draw as much as possible on experience and settings appropriate to the children. While special dialect-based materials are impractical, we may nonetheless need to abandon our notion of universally usable reading texts and use a variety of materials selected for suitability for the particular group of learners.
7. The teacher will speak in his own natural manner and present by example the general language community, but the teacher must learn to understand and accept the children's language. He must study it carefully and become aware of the key elements of divergence that are likely to cause difficulty. Langston Hughes has suggested an apt motto for the teacher of divergent speakers: "My motto as I live and learn, is dig, and be dug in return."

My own conviction is that even after literacy has been achieved future language change cannot come about through the extinction of the native dialect and the substitution of another. I believe that language growth must be a growth outward from the native dialect, an expansion which eventually will encompass the socially preferred forms but retain its roots. The child can expand his language as he expands his outlook, not rejecting his own sub-culture but coming to see it in its broader setting. Eventually he can achieve the flexibility of language which makes it possible for him to communicate easily in many diverse settings and on many levels.

I'd like to close with a plea. You don't have to accept what I've said. I don't ask that you believe or that you agree with my point of view. My plea is that you listen to the language of the divergent. Listen carefully and objectively. Push your preconceptions and your own ethnocentrisms aside and listen. I think that you'll find beauty and form and a solid base for understanding and communication. And as you dig you'll find that you are indeed dug in return.

8

❦ English and the Bilingual Child

RUDOLPH C. TROIKE

Bilingualism can be defined simply as the use by a single speaker of two or more languages. The phenomenon of "interference," which Weinreich has defined, concerns the occurrence in an individual's speech of features or elements of one language while he is speaking a second language. From a knowledge of the structure of two languages, it is often possible to predict problems of interference which will come up in the speech of an individual speaker. Armed with such foreknowledge, the teacher in the classroom can readily identify these problems when they occur and, understanding what causes them, carry out appropriate remedial treatment.

Problems of interference may be phonological, grammatical, or lexical in nature. Typical phonological problems for the Spanish speaker learning English involve the distinction of the vowels of *sheep* /šiyp/ and *ship* /šɪp/, and of the final consonants of *wash* /waš/ and *watch* /wač/. One day a student in my class of English for foreign students asked "What is the difference between /čiyp/ and /čiyp/?" As he had pronounced both items identically, I asked him to repeat the question, to which he replied, "What is the difference between /čiyp/ and /čiyp/?" When I continued to show my puzzlement, he added, "You

Rudolph C. Troike, Professor of English and Linguistics at the University of Texas at Austin, has been closely associated with the East Texas Dialect Project and is the author of articles dealing with anthropological linguistics and child language learning and of *Introduction to English Linguistics for the Teachers of English.*

know, /čiyp/ *cheap* and /čiyp/ *chip*," spelling each word out. This boy, who was a native Spanish speaker but who used English quite fluently, had never *heard* the difference in the vowels of /čiyp/ and /čɪp/, so that for him they were homophones. The trouble lay not in his intelligence or in his hearing, but in the fact that he was a speaker of Spanish, which does not make a phonemic distinction between these two vowels.

The burden which such a problem of interference places on the learner can readily be imagined. English contains enough differently-spelled homonyms now to form a considerable learning problem, but we can see how a failure to differentiate /iy/ and /ɪ/ in English greatly increases the number of homophones for an individual with this problem. In the case of *cheap* and *chip*, he simply has to memorize the fact that the adjective is spelled one way and the noun another. He would also regard such words as *peat* and *pit*, or *list* and *least*, as having purely arbitrary spellings. This is an added imposition on the student's visual memory, for as far as he is concerned the words are pronounced exactly alike. The *wash/watch* difficulty involves similar problems, and the list can be extended for hundreds of words.

Spanish speakers learning English will often say such things as "Is a book?" or refer to a table as *she*. What they are doing, of course, is carrying over Spanish syntactic patterns into English. They have probably got the idea that English is really just another way of speaking Spanish, and all that is necessary is to translate word for word in order to have perfectly good English. But it does not come out that way, and it is a little hard on them psychologically to learn that they cannot just use English words in Spanish word order and come out with perfectly good English sentences.

Another vexing grammatical problem facing the Spanish speaker is the use of *in*, *on*, and *at* in English. The problem exists because Spanish has only one preposition, *en*, corresponding to all three English prepositions in different contexts. This may be shown as follows:

	in
en	on
	at

The situation illustrates a basic language learning problem: one habit pattern or one unit in the native language must be broken into two or more habits or units in the target language. The student has to learn how to restructure his native perception and habits, and at the same time how to structure space, time, events, and entities in the other language. Wherever the structures of the two languages differ, there will always be a learning problem.

The extent of lexical problems for the student of English will vary with his own language background. Speakers of other Germanic languages, or of one of the Romance languages, will find more familiar words in English than will a speaker of Japanese or Turkish. Even so, the natural tendency on the part of students to translate words "literally" (*i. e.*, in terms of the limited equivalents they know) often causes difficulties. I recall the experience of a Turkish friend of mine who was in this country, and was taken to visit a country fair in South Texas. His host wanted him to try some typical American food and offered to buy him a hot dog. Now the idea of eating dog meat was extremely repugnant to this good Moslem, but his host kept insisting, and finally wanted to buy him a "super dog;" this was too much for my friend, who became quite angry with his host at this point. Less extreme examples occur frequently as a result of students' failure to recognize (and of teachers' failure to point out) that words do not have fixed unitary meanings, but that the meaning is often relative to the context.

The problem of dividing one unit in the native language into two or more elements in the second language is relevant to such items as Spanish *esperar* vs. English *hope, expect,* and *wait for.* Another type of problem which is mildly troublesome is that of "false cognates;" an example is the Spanish speaker's use of *assist* in talking about "assisting to a class," where English uses *attend a class;* the error arises from an attempt to anglicize the Spanish expression in a context where it does not fit.

PHONOLOGY

One of the most important things in helping us to understand language behavior and bilingual problems, particularly problems of second language learning, is the concept of the phoneme. This has been one of the great scientific discoveries of this century, and one of the things linguists have been very much interested in. The concept of the phoneme should be as important to the language teacher as the notion of an atom is to a chemistry teacher. It is difficult to imagine a chemistry course being taught without a mention of atoms, yet we go ahead teaching language, and have gone on teaching it, without ever talking about phonemes. But the concept does shed so much light on the process of communication that we need to consider it here.

We may define a phoneme as one of the *psychologically significant sound units in a language, i. e.*, a class of sounds which the speakers of a language react to as being identical. Operationally, we may identify the phonemes of a given language as the mutually contrastive classes of sounds which serve to signal differences in meaning. We know that the native speakers of a language do not hear raw sounds as such, but rather they hear only those classes of sounds which function in their own language to signal a difference in meaning, and they do *not* perceive sound differences which do not function in this way in their language. As an illustration, you might say the following words to yourself to see if you notice any difference in the sounds represented by the italicized letters in each pair of words:

*p*in	:	s*p*in
*r*ain	:	t*r*ain
he*l*p	:	hea*l*th
*k*eep	:	*c*aught

Physically (phonetically) all of these sounds are quite distinct, yet most English speakers will perceive little or no difference between the pairs of sounds represented by the italicized letters. This reaction simply reflects the fact that, for example, the initial sound of *pin* and the second sound of *spin* belong to the same phoneme in English. Physically, phonetically, objectively they are different, but functionally, phonemically, psychologically they are the same. We ignore—in fact we learn to ignore in the process of learning the language—the actual physical differences which do exist. We have to ignore these if we are going to learn to communicate in English. So we are unaware of *phonetic* differences which are not *phonemic;* in other words, we are not aware of differences of sound in our own language which do not serve to signal a difference in meaning. This realization is extremely important, then, when it comes to the matter of sound language learning.

CONTRASTIVE PHONOLOGY

Linguists have known for a long time that the most efficient way to predict pronunciation problems for speakers of one language learning another is to compare the phonemic systems of the two languages. Such comparison of two linguistic systems is known as *contrastive linguistics.* We may illustrate some of the procedures involved in predicting problems of phonological interference by comparing the phonemic systems of English and Mexican Spanish.

Phonemes of English					*Phonemes of Spanish (Mexican)*			

p		t	č	k		p		t	č	k
b		d	ǰ	g		b		d		g
	f	θ	s	š		h		f	s		x
	v	ð	z	ž					
m		n		ŋ		m		n	ñ
w		l	y	r		w		l	y
									r
									r
iy		uw				i		u
ɪ		ʊ						
ey		ow				e		o
	ə							
ɛ		ɔ						
æ		a					a

In comparing two such phonemic systems, the first step is to draw a circle around the symbols for phonemes in the target language—which in this case is English—which are absent in the native language. If we compare the English and Spanish systems, we find that both of them have /p t č k b d g/, but the /ǰ/ is absent in Spanish; we can predict, then, that English /ǰ/ will be a problem for Spanish speakers, because it is a new unit in the sound system, one that does not exist in their native system as a separate phoneme.

Continuing our comparison, we find /f/ in both languages, but /θ/ (the initial sound of *theta*) is not present in Mexican Spanish. Nevertheless, many Spanish speakers know how Castilians sound, for the /θ/ does exist in the Castilian dialect of Spanish, and they may know how to imitate the sound. However, they will still have perceptual difficulties discriminating /θ/ as a separate phoneme. We note that Spanish has no phonemic contrast, as English does, between /s/ and /c/; it is predictable, then, that Spanish speakers will have trouble hearing and producing the contrast between *share* and *chair*, or *wash* and *watch*.

Spanish has a /x/ (voiceless velar fricative), which English lacks, while English has a /h/ not found in Spanish (it must be remembered at this point that we are talking about speech, not writing). It is normal for the speakers of either language to use their native phoneme in speaking the other language; in this situation, where one phoneme is simply substituted for another, the result contributes to a foreign

"accent" but does not really impede communication. Thus the Eng-
list speaker who pronounces *mujer* as /muwher/ and Spanish speaker
who pronounces *hot* as /xat/ are still intelligible, though their accent
is unmistakable.

An entire series of English phonemes, the voiced fricatives /v ð z
ž/, are absent from Spanish, so that all of them will pose a learning
problem for the Spanish speaker. The problem is complicated by the
fact that some of these sounds occur in Spanish phonetically, but not
phonemically, hence Spanish speakers will find it difficult to perceive
them as distinct sounds. Going on down our chart to the nasals, we
find /m/ and /n/ in both languages; Spanish has an /ñ/, which
English lacks, so this will pose no problem for the Spanish speaker
learning English, to whom this phoneme will merely be "extra baggage," so to speak. English, on the other hand, has the phoneme /ŋ/
which does not occur in Spanish as a phoneme. Although both [n]
and [ŋ] occur phonetically in Spanish, they never contrast to signal a
difference in meaning as they do in English. For Spanish speakers, then,
both sounds are members of the same phoneme, whereas in English
they belong to different phonemes.

Finally, we find /w y l/ in both languages, but Spanish has /r/ and
/r̄/, while English has only /r/. In this instance it is the English
speaker studying Spanish who must learn to subdivide his /r/-habits
into two. We know from considerable experience that the *r*-problem
is one which English speakers have in learning Spanish, and not
vice-versa.

Comparing the vowels, we see that the vowel system of English is
extremely complex. English has one of the most complex vowel
systems in the world, which is certainly unfortunate considering its
status as a world language. English speakers make phonemic distinctions between /iy, ɪ, ey, ɛ, æ/ among the front vowels, in such words
as *beet, bit, bait, bet, bat;* in the central vowel column we have the
distinction between /ə, a/ as in *cut* and *cot;* and in the back the
differences between /uw, ʊ, ow, ɔ/ are phonemic, as in *pool, pull,
pole,* and *pall.* While we have all these different vowel distinctions
to make in English, the Spanish speaker has only five to worry about.
The English speaker learning Spanish finds a much simpler system
and so has no real problem aside from the differences in articulatory
norms which contribute to an accent. On the other hand, the Spanish
speaker learning English has to divide his system of five vowels into the
eleven vowels of English, which is to say that he must more than
double the number of distinctions he makes in his native vowels in
order to understand and be understood in English. The size of this
learning problem can readily be appreciated.

PHONOLOGICAL PROBLEMS

The phonemic system of a language acts as a kind of filter through which the native speaker hears the sounds of other languages. This "phonemic filter" assigns the sounds of foreign languages to the nearest equivalent phoneme in the native language, and often prevents the learner from recognizing any phonemic differences between his own and the target language. If the native language lacks /θ/, the student learning English will often fail to hear it as a new sound, but will perceive it as the phonetically most similar sound in his language; *e.g.*, as /t/, /s/, or occasionally as /f/. If the native language has no phonemic distinction between /ə/ and /a/, for example, they will be heard as identical sounds. The perceptual system of the brain automatically pigeon-holes all language sounds (unless they are too novel) into the phonemic categories to which the speaker has been conditioned by his previous language experience.

Some of the problems of phonemic differentiation which the Spanish speaker faces in learning English are listed below. We have previously identified most of these in our initial contrastive analysis of the two phonemic systems, but the mode of presentation adopted here may help to bring these into sharper focus.

Spanish	English	Spanish	English
/č/	/č/ chair, watch /š/ share, wash	/d/	/d/ den, ladder /ð/ then, lather
/s/	/s/ sip, racer /z/ zip, razor	/i/	/iy/ cheap /ɪ/ chip
/n/	/n/ sin /ŋ/ sing	/e/	/ey/ bait /ɛ/ bet /æ/ bat
/b/	/b/ bat, rabble /v/ vat, ravel	/a/	/ə/ cut /a/ cot
/t/ /s/	/t/ tin /θ/ thin /s/ sin	/u/	/uw/ pool, Luke /ʊ/ pull, look
		/o/	/ow/ coat /ɔ/ caught

Certain sounds which are phonemically distinct in English are found to occur in Spanish as members of the same phoneme. For example, both of the sounds [d] and [ð] occur in Spanish, where they never contrast and are both members of the phoneme /d/. Their distribution may be illustrated by the following examples:

/d/

[d]	[ð]
*d*ormir, cuan*d*o	la*d*o, Uste*d*

As shown, the stop [d] occurs initially and after nasals while the fricative [ð] occurs between vowels and in final position. Their occurrence is predictable and automatic, and the two sounds never contrast to signal a difference in meaning between two words, as they do in English. The Spanish speaker is therefore unaware that the two sounds exist, and hears them as phonemically equivalent. As a result, he fails to hear or produce any distinction between such pairs of English words as *dare-there, ladder-lather,* and *read-wreathe.*

A similar situation involves the sounds [n] and [ŋ], which in English belong to different phonemes but in Spanish are members of the same phoneme. Their distribution is as follows:

/n/

[n]	[ŋ]
*n*orte, cua*n*do, so*n*	ba*n*co, so*n*

Words which end in /n/ may be pronounced indifferently either with [n] or [ŋ], though in some dialects there is a greater tendency to use [n] in this position. Before velar stops or fricatives, only [ŋ] is found; [n] occurs in all other positions. Spanish speakers, therefore, have great difficulty detecting any perceptible difference between such English pairs as *sin* and *sing,* and even greater difficulty producing such a distinction. Occasionally they are misled by the orthography and actually attempt to pronounce the *g* in *sing,* often saying something closer to *sink.*

THE AUDITORY MONITOR

When a person wishes to express his thoughts, he puts them into linguistic form, *i.e.,* he encodes them. The brain then sends instructions to the vocal organs to carry out their respective and coordinated functions for the formation of speech, by which the linguistically-encoded information is transmitted. As speech is produced, the vocal output reaches the speaker's own ear and is fed into the linguistic decoding component of his brain, where it is monitored and matched against the intended output (at least as long as he listens to what he is saying). The brain, then, depends upon feedback through the ear as a check on whether its instructions have been fulfilled. This monitoring process has been compared to the way in which a thermostat controls a central heating system, with the auditory monitor acting much as a type of servo-mechanism.

The analogy is a useful one, for it sheds considerable light on the problems of phonemic perception. A heating control, for example, may be set to operate over varying ranges of temperature difference: it may come on at 65° and go off at 80°, or the critical temperatures may be set closer together, at 70° and 75°. Similarly, as a child learns the limits of phonemic variation is his language, his "phonostat" becomes "set" to react to certain *ranges of sound variation* as functionally equivalent, and to ignore fluctuations within each of these limits.

A comparison of the permitted latitude for the variation in the high front vowels of Spanish and English would give this result:

Spanish	English
	iy
i	
	I

For the Spanish speaker, any sound within this range qualifies as the same phoneme; the English speaker, however, is conditioned to hear two significantly different vowels within this range.

The speaker's internal "phonostat", therefore, affects not only his perception, but even more critically for production, it governs his oral output. Note, for example, the very slight muscular adjustments which suffice to change *eat* to *it;* unless the "phonostat" has been properly set beforehand, the motor centers of the brain will not be able to control the critical muscular movements necessary to produce a consistent distinction between these sounds.

Pedagogically, then, it is important to give learners adequate ear-training in the phonemic distinctions of a new language even before they are asked to produce these distinctions themselves. They must internalize a clear acoustic image of the new phonemic contrasts in order to have a reference target to guide the performance of their own vocal organs. Otherwise they will be able to do no more than carry over the phonemic distinctions of their native language into the new one.

PHONOLOGICAL TRAINING

We now have a better theoretical basis for viewing the phonological problems of second-language learning. We are thus in a better position for understanding why phonological interference arises in the speech of a bilingual (or incipient bilingual), and how we might devise a teaching approach for dealing with these problems. The first important focus must be on training the student's ear to hear the phonemic distinctions of the second language. The aim, then, is to condition the individual to respond to a different set of signals from that which he has learned previously. He must learn a whole new system and must overcome the constant interference from the native system. The older the learner, the more ingrained will be the perceptual habits of the native language, and the more difficult will be the task of establishing a new set of contrasts.

Drills to teach phonemic discrimination are best set up on the basis of minimal pairs—words that differ by only one phoneme, and are otherwise identical, *e.g., leave-live, berry-very*. In the initial stages, students should not be called upon to pronounce the sounds, or the words, but merely identify which one of a pair the teacher may say. They should have ample opportunity to hear the words, and the contrast between the pairs, before they are asked to differentiate them.

Suitable drill material might be presented in some such way as the following:

"Which one do you hear?"

A	B
sheep	ship
heel	hill
beet	bit
bean	bin
cheek	chick

After hearing the teacher pronounce all the words in each list, then hearing her contrast each pair of words, the students may be called upon to identify single words pronounced by the teacher as *A* or *B*.

This procedure provides a convenient way for the teacher and the student himself to check on the progress of his perception. With young children, flash cards containing pictures could be used in the same way. The important thing is to teach the student to realize the great difference in meaning signaled by the slight difference in sound, so that he will learn to respond to these differences. For this reason it is necessary for students to know the meaning of the words in the drills.

Once students are able to recognize the contrasts correctly about ninety percent of the time, then they will be ready to start pronouncing the words themselves. It is important to get students to practice the words in short contexts as soon as possible; spending too much time on isolated word pairs is not desirable in production practice. Many students can memorize entire drill lists and recite them with phonetic perfection, but when asked to use a word in a sentence, they will slip back into their native phonology. Such behavior clearly shows that they have learned the pronunciation not as a part of language, *i.e.,* as part of a system of phonemic contrasts, but merely as an isolated task unrelated to language.

Suitable contexts for initial drill in minimal-pair contrasts could consist of such simple frames as these:

> I see a . . . .
> It is a . . . .
> A . . . . is not a . . . .

As more phonemic contrasts are introduced and drilled, and students' vocabulary is enlarged, more complex sentence frames can be employed. The mastery of a new phonemic system does not come easily or quickly, however, and contrastive drill and constant correction must be maintained long enough to insure that new pronunciation habits become fixed and automatic.

THE PROSPECT

It is abundantly clear that linguistics has a major contribution to make toward an understanding of the phenomenon of bilingual interference. Equally, because of the light it sheds on the nature of language, language acquisition, and bilingualism, linguistics offers valuable insights and suggestions for second-language teaching. We have touched on only a few of these in our discussion of phonological training, but enough has been said about the prediction of problems in grammar and vocabulary to indicate that teachers of bilingual students should be informed about linguistics and the techniques of language comparison.

In considering the social implications of bilingualism, we need to keep uppermost in our minds the realization that language is a system of communication. The bilingual who has mastered two such systems, has thereby effectively doubled the range of social contexts in which he is able to function successfully. The monolingual or partial bilingual, on the other hand, is the prisoner of his linguistic environment. Especially if his native language is not the dominant one in the community, if it is not the medium of education and commerce, then he will be severely handicapped in his attempts to achieve economic and social advancement.

The linguistically sophisticated teacher can do a great deal to guide her students to an adequate command of the official or prestige language, while at the same time preserving intact their respect for their native language. The teacher needs to recognize that English is truly a foreign language for many children entering first grade. Such a child faces the task of acquiring a completely new code system for communicating about his experiences. If he is particularly apt, he may be able to learn the language and get ahead educationally. In this the home environment can be a crucial factor, depending on whether it supplies reinforcement for his motivation to learn English. Unfortunately, the classroom situation rarely provides adequate opportunity for that *sine qua non* of language learning, oral practice. Ordinarily the child is relegated to the role of a purely passive learner, while his active oral communication, both at home and within his peer group, continues to be in his native language.

If we accept the proposition that English is truly a foreign language for these children, we can begin to see immediately the applicability of techniques worked out for teaching the modern foreign languages to English speakers by the oral-aural or audio-lingual method. Children need a great deal of opportunity to practice repeating simple sentence patterns after the teacher and to make their own sentences using vocabulary they have learned. The teacher must serve as the oral model and the corrective monitor of their linguistic output, until they have internalized enough of the language to freely generate English utterances without going through a translation process. As we know, children are capable of acquiring a new language very rapidly at this age if the proper environment for learning is provided, and full advantage should be taken of this capacity.

We should work to foster the achievement of successful bilingualism in our students, conscious of the advantages it bestows upon the individual. The non-English-speaking child who comes to us possesses a potential handicap or an advantage; he may become either a social cripple or one who can enjoy the best of two worlds. The alternatives are clear; our teaching can make the difference.

9

🎴 Bi-Dialectalism: the Linguistics of White Supremacy

JAMES SLEDD

Because people who rarely talk together will talk differently, differences in speech tell what groups a man belongs to. He uses them to claim and proclaim his identity, and society uses them to keep him under control. The person who talks right, as we do, is one of us. The person who talks wrong is an outsider, strange and suspicious, and we must make him feel inferior if we can. That is one purpose of education. In a school system run like ours by white businessmen, instruction in the mother tongue includes formal initiation into the linguistic prejudices of the middle class.

Making children who talk wrong get right with the world has traditionally been the work of English teachers, and more recently of teachers of that strange conglomerate subject which we call speech. The English teacher in the role of linguistic censor was once a kind of folk heroine (or anti-heroine), the Miss Fidditch of the linguists' diatribes. Miss Fidditch believed in taking a strong stand. It never occurred to her that her main job was making the lower classes feel so low that they would try to climb higher. Instead, Miss Fidditch taught generations of schoolchildren, including future linguists, to avoid *ain't* and double negatives and *used to could* and *hadn't ought,* not because

James Sledd, Professor of English and Linguistics at the University of Texas at Austin, has published widely in linguistics and is the co-author of *Dr. Johnson's Dictionary, Dictionaries and That Dictionary,* and the author of *A Short Introduction to English Grammar.*

ain't would keep them from getting ahead in the world, but because *ain't* was wrong, no matter who used it, and deserved no encouragement from decent people who valued the English language. She did her job all the better for thinking that she was doing something else.

Miss Fidditch is not popular any longer among educators. Though the world at large is still inclined to agree with her, the vulgarizers of linguistics drove her out of the academic fashion years ago, when they replaced her misguided idealism with open-eyed hypocrisy. To the popular linguists, one kind of English is as good as another, and judgments to the contrary are only folklore; but since the object of life in the U.S.A. is for everybody to get ahead of everybody else, and since linguistic prejudice can keep a man from moving up to Schlitz, the linguists still teach that people who want to be decision-makers had better talk and write like the people who make decisions. The schools must therefore continue to cultivate the linguistic insecurity which is already a national characteristic but must teach the youngsters to manipulate that as they manipulate everything else; for neither Miss Fidditch's dream of a language intrinsically good, nor a humbler ideal of realizing the various potentialities of the existing language in its responsible use, can get in the way of the citizenry in its upward anguish through the pecking order. The linguists think that people who do knowingly what Miss Fidditch did in her innocence, will do it more efficiently, as if eating the apple made a skilled worker out of Eve.

As long as most people agreed that up is toward Schlitz and another TV set, and as long as they could pretend that every American eaglet can soar to those great heights, Fidditch McFidditch the dialectologist could enforce the speech-taboos of the great white middle class without complaint: either the child learned the taboos and observed them, or he was systematically penalized. But the damage done to the Wasps' nest by World War II made difficulties. People who talked all wrong, and especially black people, began to ask for their share of the loot in a world that had given them an argument by calling itself free, while a minority of the people who talked right began to bad-mouth respectability and joined the blacks in arguing that it was time for a real change. Some black people burned up the black parts of town, and some students made study impossible at the universities, and in general there was a Crisis. Optimists even talked of a revolution.

The predictable response of the frightened white businessman's society was to go right on doing what it had done before—which had caused the crisis—but to do it harder and to spend more money at it. Education was no exception. Government and the foundations began to spray money over the academic landscape like liquid fertilizer, and the professional societies began to bray and paw at the rich new grass. In that proud hour, any teacher who could dream up an expensive scheme for keeping things as they were while pretending to make a change was sure of becoming the director of a project or a center and of flying first-class to Washington twice a month. The white business-man strengthened his control of the educational system while giving the impression of vast humanitarian activity.

Black English provided the most lucrative new industry for white linguists, who found the mother lode when they discovered the inter-esting locutions which the less protected employ to the detriment of their chances for upward mobility. In the annals of free enterprise, the early sixties will be memorable for the invention of functional bi-dialectalism, a scheme best described by an elderly and unregenerate Southern dame as "turning black trash into white trash." Despite some signs of wear, this cloak for white supremacy has kept its shape for almost a decade now, and it is best described in the inimitable words of those who made it. Otherwise the description might be dismissed as a malicious caricature.

The basic assumption of bi-dialectalism is that the prejudices of middle-class whites cannot be changed but must be accepted and in-deed enforced on lesser breeds. Upward mobility, it is assumed, is the end of education, but white power will deny upward mobility to speakers of black English, who must therefore be made to talk white English in their contacts with the white world.

An adequate florilegium may be assembled from a volume entitled *Social Dialects and Language Learning* (NCTE, 1964), the proceed-ings of a conference of bi-dialectalists which was held in 1964. William A. Stewart of the Center for Applied Linguistics begins the chorus (p. 13) by observing among our educators "a commendable desire to emphasize the potential of the Negro to be identical to white Ameri-cans"—a desire which is apparently not overwhelming, however, among the Black Muslims or among the young men who have enjoyed pot-shooting policemen for the past few summers. Editor Roger W. Shuy next speaks up (p. 53) for social climbing by our American Indians, who have been notably reluctant, throughout their unfortunate asso-ciation with their conquerors, to adopt our conquering ways. Our lin-guistic studies, Shuy remarks in the purest accents of fidditchery, "should reveal those elements, both in speech and writing, which pre-vent Indians from attaining the social status which, with socially ac-ceptable language, they might otherwise attain." A similar desire to be at peace with status-holders is suggested (p. 66) by Ruth I. Golden, who opines that "a human being wants most of all to be recognized as an individual, to be accepted, and to be approved." Since Southern speech brings "negative reactions when heard by employers in Detroit," where Dr. Golden labors in the schools, she devotes herself to stamping out /i/ for /e/ in *penny* and to restoring /l/ in *help* (pp. 63 f.).

An admirable scholar from New York, William Labov, then agrees (p. 88) that "recognition of an external standard of correctness is an inevitable accompaniment of upward social aspirations and upward social mobility," and advises that people who (like Jesus) prefer not to take excessive thought for the morrow can probably be made to. In Labov's own words, "since the homes of many lower class and working people do not provide the pressures toward upward social mobility that middle-class homes provide," and since adults in those lower reaches are sometimes resistant to middle-class values, we must "build into the community a tolerance for style shifting which is helpful in educational and occupational advancement," and we must build into the children, "starting from a level not much above the nursery school and going on through high school, a tolerance for practice in second role playing" (pp. 94-97, 104).

Presumably Labov sees nothing wrong in thus initiating children into the world of hypercorrection, insecurity, and "linguistic self-hatred" which marks, as he has said elsewhere, "the average New Yorker" (*The Social Stratification of English in New York City*, Center for Applied Linguistics, 1966, Chapter XIII); and Charles Ferguson, the eminent ex-director of the Center for Applied Linguistics, is equally confident of *his* right and duty to remake his fellow men in his directorial image. Talking about the Negroes in our Northern cities, Ferguson says that "we have to face a rather difficult decision as to whether we want to make these people bi-dialectal . . . [please to remark Ferguson's choice of verbs] or whether we want . . . to impose some kind of standard English on these people and to eradicate the kind of substandard English they speak" (p. 116). To cite another NCTE volume (*Language Programs for the Disadvantaged* [NCTE, 1965], p. 222), if the black children of the ghetto "do not learn a second kind of dialect, they will be forever prevented from access to economic opportunity and social acceptance." Middle-class white prejudice will rule eternally.

The bi-dialectalists, of course, would not be so popular with government and the foundations if they spoke openly of the supremacy of white prejudice; but they make it perfectly clear that what they are dealing with deserves no better name. No dialect, they keep repeating, is better than any other—yet poor and ignorant children must change theirs unless they want to stay poor and ignorant. When an NCTE "Task Force" set out to devise *Language Programs for the Disadvantaged* (NCTE, 1965), it laid down a perfect smoke screen of such hypocrisy, as one would expect from persons who felt called upon to inform the world that "without the experience of literature, the individual is denied the very dignity that makes him human" (p. v) but that not "all disadvantaged children are apathetic or dull" (pp. 24 f.).

"In this report" (p. 117), "teachers are asked to begin by accepting the dialect of their students for what it is, one form of oral communication. . . ." Teachers are warned particularly that they "need to accept the language which Negro children bring to school, to recognize that it is a perfectly appropriate vehicle for communicating ideas in the Negro home and subculture" (p. 215), that it is "essentially respectable and good" (p. 227). But though teachers must not attack "the dialect which children associate with their homes and their identity as Negroes" (p. 215), they must still use all the adult authority of the school to "teach standard informal English as a second dialect" (p. 137), because the youngster who cannot speak standard informal English "will not be able to get certain kinds of jobs" (p. 228).

The most common result of such teaching will be that white middle-class Midwestern speech will be imposed as mandatory for all those situations which middle-class white businessmen think it worth their while to regulate. In the words of Chicago's Professors Austin and McDavid (p. 245), "future educational programs should be developed in terms of substituting for the grammatical system of lower-class Southern speech [read: black Chicago speech] that of middle-class Chicago white speech—at least for those economic and social situations where grammatical norms are important." Labov goes so far as to ask (*Social Dialects and Language Learning*, p. 102) whether Northern schools should tolerate Southern speech at all—whether they should not also correct the "cultivated Southern speech" of privileged children who move North.

The description of compulsory bi-dialectalism may be completed by examining the methods which its proponents advocate for perpetuating the supremacy of white prejudice. Essentially, those methods are derived by analogy from structuralist methods of teaching foreign languages—methods whose superiority has been claimed but never demonstrated and whose intellectual foundations vanished with the demise of structuralist ideas. As an eminent grammarian privately observed after a recent conference, "The achievements of the operators will continue to lie in the field of getting and spending government money. . . . They seem to have an unerring instinct for finding ways of spending it unprofitably—on conferences at which they listen to each other, for example. Now they're out to teach standard English as a second dialect through techniques that have served very poorly in teaching second languages."

High on the list of those techniques is incessant drill on inessentials. In theory, the drills are the end-product of a long process of systematic comparison of the children's nonstandard dialects with the standard dialect which they are to be taught; but since the systematic comparisons have never been made, the bi-dialectalists fall back on a simple enumeration of a few dozen "features of pronunciation, grammar, and vocabulary which can be considered indices of social stratification" (Roger Shuy, "Detroit Speech," in A. L. Davis, ed., *On the Dialects of Children,* p. 13). Professor Rudolph Troike of the University of Texas was thus simply platitudinizing piously when he told the TESOL convention in 1968 that "any instructional program . . . must begin with as full an *objective* knowledge as possible" of both or all the dialects involved. The escape hatch in Troike's statement is the phrase *as full as possible.* What is usually possible is an unsystematic list of shibboleths —the simplification of consonant clusters, the Southern pronunciations of *walk* and *right, ax* for *ask,* the dropping of post-vocalic /r/, *ain't* and *fixin' to, bofe* and *mouf* for *both* and *mouth,* and the like. These innocent usages, which are as familiar as the sun in the late Confederacy, are apparently the terror of Northern employers, who the bi-dialectalists assume are almost suicidally unconcerned with such details as character, intelligence, and training for the job. The fact is, of course, that Northern employers and labor leaders dislike black faces but use black English as an excuse.

Having established, however, that a child of darkness under her tutelage says *mouf,* the pretty white lady sets out to rescue his soul. First she plays tapes of Southern speech to convince her victims, who understand Southern speech far better than they understand hers, that Southern speech often makes "complete understanding of content . . . difficult," "not readily comprehensible"—as is demonstrated by the fact that the pretty white lady would never have detected her victim's four-letter word just by listening and without watching his lips (New York Board of Education, *Nonstandard Dialect,* pp. 1, 14, 17). The difficulty of detecting him is all the more reason for fearing the iniquitous *mouf*-sayer: it proves he is a cunning devil who probably says *dentissoffice* too and who perpetrates such subversive "malapropisms" as "The food in the lunch room is not fitting to eat" (*On the Dialects of Children,* p. 23). How else *would* he spell *fitten?* But for such a hardened rogue, a good many "motivational activities" are likely to be necessary before the pretty white lady can really start twisting the thumbscrew with her drills.

Yet the drills are available, and the pretty white lady will use them when she sees her time. She has drills of all kinds—repetition drills, substitution drills, replacement drills, conversion drills, cued answer

drills, the reading in unison of long lists of words like *teeth / reef,
toothbrush / waffle, bathtub / alphabet, weather / weaver.* To get rid
of *dentissoffice,* she may have students debate such propositions as
"Ghosts do exist" or "Formal school tests should be eliminated"; and
before a really "culminating activity" like playing "Pack the Trunk"
she may "divide the class into consonant-cluster committees to seek out
words containing" clusters like *sks, sps,* or *kt* (*Nonstandard Dialect,
passim*). At this point the class might be invited to suggest a context
for a replacement drill—maybe something like "Teacher! teacher! Billy
Joe say that Tommy ———— Bessy!" This last suggestion, it must be
confessed, has not yet been made in the literature, but it seems considerably more stimulating than choral recitation of Poe's "Bells" (*ibid.,*
p. 35).

Perhaps it need not be added that existing tests and evaluations of
such "instructional materials" are something of a farce. If bi-dialectalism is really harder to acquire than bilingualism (Einar Haugen in
Social Dialects and Language Learning, p. 125), teachers and texts
ought surely to be superb, and judgments on them ought to be severe;
but New York City's curriculum developers can give "highest priority"
to making the children change *a* to *an* before nouns beginning with a
vowel (*Nonstandard Dialect,* p. 14), and Texas' Professor Troike can
argue the success of his methods by showing that after six months of
drills a little black girl could repeat *his hat* after her teacher, instead
of translating automatically to *he hat.* Unfortunately, tapes do not record psychological damage, or compare the effectiveness of other ways
of teaching, or show what might better have been learned in the same
time instead of learning to repeat *his hat.*

So much for a description of mandatory bi-dialectalism, a bit en-
livened (since the subject is dreary) by irreverent comment, but not
distorted in any essential way. In the U. S. A., we are being told, everybody wants approval—not approval for doing anything worth approv-
ing, but approval for doing whatever happens to be approved. Because
approval goes to upward mobility, everybody should be upwardly
mobile; and because upward mobility is impossible for underdogs who
have not learned middle-dog barking, we must teach it to them for use
in their excursions into the middle-dog world. There is no possibility
either that the present middle class can be brought to tolerate lower-
class English or that upward mobility, as a national aspiration, will be
questioned. Those are the pillars on which the state is built, and the
compassionate teacher, knowing the ways of his society, will change
the color of his students' vowels although he cannot change the color
of their skins.

It is not at all certain that the bi-dialectalists, for all their absurdities, can be dislodged from their well-carpeted offices. They are supported by the National Council of Teachers of English, the Modern Language Association of America, the Center for Applied Linguists, the federal government, the foundations, the governments of a number of major cities, and by black people who have made it into the middle class and so despise their origins and their less efficient fellows. In the best of times our top dogs are pleased by docility, if not mobility, among the beasts below; and in 1969 a new ice age is beginning. Newspaper headlines tell us that the Department of Health, Education, and Welfare has been urged to relax its requirements for desegregation of schools immediately but quietly, and President Nixon loses his Miami tan at the thought that militant students will "politicize" our universities—as if government grants to upwardly mobile faculty had not politicized them long ago. In Lyndon Johnson's Texas the citizens of Austin vote down an open housing law, their board of education then justifies segregated schooling by the established pattern of segregated housing, and the governor of the state praises the state university as the source of brain-power to assist the businessman in the lucrative exploitation of what the governor proudly calls the "insatiable appetite" of Texans. The only revolution we are likely to see is the continued subversion, by the dominant white businessman, of the political and religious principles on which the nation was founded.

Yet though the times are bad, they are not hopeless, at least not in the small, undramatic world of English education; and the bi-dialectalists are so gorgeously absurd that the breath of laughter may collapse their card-house if only enough people can be brought to see it as it is. It is not simply quixotic, then, to add to a laughing description of imposed bi-dialectalism a more serious statement of reasons why it cannot succeed and should not be tolerated even if it could—a statement which can lead, in conclusion, to the proposing of an alternative policy.

The argument that bi-dialectalism cannot be forced is easy to make out, even, in part, from the reluctant admissions of some of its proponents. Two principal reasons have already been suggested, the ignorance and unproved methods of the bi-dialectalists. The term *ignorance* is used literally, and in all fairness. Whatever one thinks of teaching standard English by methods like those for teaching foreign languages, constrastive analyses of our different dialects are a prerequisite—but a prerequisite which has not yet been supplied. Until very recently, the principal sources of information were the collections for the *Linguistic Atlas;* but they are unsystematic, partially out-of-date, and in some respects inaccurate and superficial. Where, for example, should one go for descriptions of intonation and its dialectal variants, for accurate accounts of the system or systems of verbal auxiliaries, for analyses of the speech of ghetto children instead of rustic ancients? Such minimal essentials are simply lacking. In fact, it might be said that for all the talk about revolutionary advances in linguistics, neither the structural nor the generative grammarians have yet produced a satisfactory basic description of even standard English.

The best descriptions of all our kinds of English would still not be enough to make coercive bi-dialectalism a success. The English teacher's forty-five minutes a day for five days in the week will never counteract the influence, and sometimes the hostility, of playmates and friends and family during much the larger part of the student's time. Formal education could produce real bi-dialectals only in a vast system of state nurseries and boarding schools to which the children of the poor and ignorant would be consigned at an early age; but such establishments would be prohibitively expensive, intolerable to the people, and still not absolutely certain of success, because the most essential of all conditions might not be met—namely, the desire of the children to talk like the white middle class.

When one thinks about it in these realistic terms, the whole argument about bi-dialectalism begins to look schizophrenic, as out-of-this-world as an argument whether Lee should surrender at Appomattox or fight back. There is no evidence that the bi-dialectalists, if they actually had good textbooks, better teachers, and as much money as the country is spending to devastate Vietnam, would really know what to do with those fictional resources. Instead of clear ideas, they offer clichés, like the familiar attacks on "traditional methods and approaches" or the protected pedagogue's arrogant assurance that illiterates can have no human dignity. They fly off quickly into high-sounding vaguenesses, talking (for example) about "differences in social dialect and associated versions of reality" *(Social Dialects and Language Learnng, p. 68)*, as if metaphysics rested on a preconsonantal /r/. At their most precise, they suggest the prudential avoidance of Southern pronunciations of *walk* and *cough* in Washington because Negroes there look down on new arrivals from Georgia and the Carolinas. They happily assume what they should prove—that intensive training in "standard informal English as a second dialect" has produced or can produce large numbers of psychologically undamaged bi-dialectals, whose new accomplishment has won them or will win them jobs that otherwise would have been impossible for them to get. When their guard is down, the bi-dialectalists actually confess that they *have* no concrete program, since "no one program at any level yet seems applicable to a significant number of other classes at the respective level" *(Language Programs for the Disadvantaged,* pp. 30 ff.).

Some awareness of their difficulties, and some uncertainty about priorities, seem indeed to be spreading among the bi-dialectalists (though it would be too much to hope that if their present band wagon falls apart they will consider themselves discredited and resign their membership in the Society of Mandarin.) For one thing, they have become aware of the significance of reading, which William A. Stewart, as late as 1964, could reduce to the level of "socially desirable embellishments" *(Social Dialects and Language Learning,* p. 10). In his latest book, however, *Teaching Black Children To Read,* Editor Shuy announces "the simple truth that speaking standard English, however desirable it may be, is not as important as learning to read" (p. 118). His colleagues Walter A. Wolfram and Ralph W. Fasold are even closer to enlightenment. In the same new volume (p. 143), they hesitantly admit that "there is some question about the degree to which Standard English can be taught to the ghetto child in the classroom at all"; and Fasold meant what he said, for he had said it before at the Milwaukee convention of the NCTE. Though that august body was still congratulating itself on its concern with "a language component for the so-called culturally divergent," it had to bear with Fasold's embarrassing confession: "Because of the operation of social forces in the use of language," he said, "forces which are only poorly understood, it may not be possible to teach Standard English as a second language to Black English speaking children unless they are interacting with Standard English speakers in a meaningful way outside the classroom" *(Convention Concerns—1968,* p. 10). The Center's linguistician came as close as standard English would allow to saying that it is segregation which makes black people talk different and that there would be no slum children if there were no slums.

No doubt the most important of Fasold's poorly understood social forces is one which everybody but white linguists has understood for a long time: black people may just not want to talk white English. Several years ago, Labov observed that some of his more rebellious New York subjects were deliberately turning away from social-climbing New York speech toward a black Southern model *(Social Dialects and Language Learning,* pp. 96 f.), and today comment on "the new feeling of racial pride among black Americans" *(Teaching Black Children To Read,* p. 142) is a platitude. Wolfram and Fasold go on to the quite unsurprising speculation that pride may even extend to the Negro's speech. "If a realization develops that this dialect, an important part of black culture, is as distinctively Afro-American as anything in the culture, the result may well be a new respect for Black English within the community' (p. 143). More plainly, condescending middle-class white charity is not wanted any more, if it ever was, in language-teaching or anywhere else. We should learn from the example of the British: the social cataclysm of the Second World War, and the achievement of political power by labor, did more to give the "disadvantaged" English youngster an equal chance than charitable bi-dialectalism ever did. We are past the stage when white teachers, whether Africans or Caucasians, can think well of themselves for trying to turn black people into uneasy imitations of the whites.

The immorality of that effort is the chief reason why enforced bi-dialectalism should not be tolerated even if it were possible. Predators can and do use dialect differences to exploit and oppress, because ordinary people can be made to doubt their own value and to accept subservience if they can be made to despise the speech of their fathers. Obligatory bi-dialectalism for minorities is only another mode of exploitation, another way of making blacks behave as whites would like them to. It is unnecessary for communication, since the ability to understand other dialects is easily attained, as the black child shows when she translates her teacher's prissy white model *"his hat"* into *"he hat."* Its psychological consequences are likely to be nervous affectation, self-distrust, dislike for everyone not equally afflicted with the itch to get ahead, and eventual frustration by the discovery that the reward for so much suffering is intolerably small. At best the altered student will get a somewhat better job and will move up a few places in the rat-race of the underlings. At worst he will be cut off from other blacks, still not accepted among whites, and economically no better off than he was before.

White teachers should hope, then, that their black students will be recalcitrant, so that bi-dialectalism as a unilateral condition for employment can be forgotten. It would make better sense, if pedagogues insist on living in a fantasy world, to require whites to speak black English in their dealings with blacks, since the whites have more advantages than the blacks and consider themselves more intelligent, or perhaps we should be hard-headedly consistent in our brutalities and try to eradicate the vices which really do enrage employers—like intellectual questioning, or the suspicion that ours is not the best of possible worlds.

Indeed, the educationists' faith in education would be touching if it were not their way of keeping up their wages. Nothing the schools can do about black English or white English either will do much for racial peace and social justice as long as the black and white worlds are separate and hostile. The measure of our educational absurdity is the necessity of saying once again that regimented bi-dialectalism is no substitute for sweeping social change—*necessity* being defined by the alternative of dropping out and waiting quietly for destruction if the white businessman continues to have his way.

The reply that the educational system should not be politicized is impossible for bi-dialectalists, since bi-dialectalism is itself a political instrument. They may purge themselves of inconsistency, and do what little good is possible for English teachers as political reformers, if instead of teaching standard English as a second dialect they teach getting out of Vietnam, getting out of the missile race, and stopping the deadly pollution of the one world we have, as horribly exemplified by the current vandalism in Alaska.

One use for a small fraction of the resources that would thus be saved would be to improve the teaching of the English language. Bi-dialectalism would never have been invented if our society were not divided into the dominant white majority and the exploited minorities. Children should be taught that. They should be taught the relations between group differences and speech differences, and the good and bad uses of speech differences by groups and by individuals. The teaching would require a more serious study of grammar, lexicography, dialectology, and linguistic history than our educational system now provides—require it at least of prospective English teachers.

In the immediate present, the time and money now wasted on bi-dialectalism should be spent on teaching the children of the minorities to read. Already some of the universal experts among the linguists have boarded this new bandwagon, and the next round of government grants may very well be for programs in reading and writing in black English. That might be a good thing, particularly if we could some- how get rid of the tired little clique of operators who have run the professional societies of English teachers for so long. Anyway, the direct attack on minority language, the attempt to compel bi-dialect- alism, should be abandoned for an attempt to open the minds and enhance the lives of the poor and ignorant. At the same time, every attempt should be made to teach the majority to understand the life and language of the oppressed. Linguistic change is the effect and not the cause of social change. If the majority can rid itself of its prejudices, and if the minorities can get or be given an education, differences between dialects are unlikely to hurt anybody much.

(The phoniest objections to this proposal will be those that talk about social realism, about the necessity for doing something even— or should one say particularly?—if it's wrong. That kind of talk makes real change impossible, but makes money for bi-dialectalists.)

10

Speech Differences and Teaching Strategies: How Different is Enough?

ROGER W. SHUY

In past years linguists have been working diligently in different parts of the country to define the exact linguistic features which characterize people of different social status. The work of the Linguistic Atlas of the United States and Canada, begun in the thirties, made some attempt at obtaining socially interesting information along with invaluable data which revealed important historical and geographical insights. The rise of interest in urban problems in the sixties, however, has called for an entirely new strategy. As the interest of linguists shifted from historical and geographical concerns to synchronic social matters, it became increasingly difficult for them to hang on to older ways of operating. They learned more about sampling design, about data gathering techniques, about analytical procedures, about social stratification. Major linguistic research in urban areas has been conducted recently in New York, Detroit, Chicago and Washington, D.C. These research projects are just beginning to bear fruit to the educators.

These projects are not involved in the study of phonetic or grammatical "deficiencies." And they are not saying that the child cannot learn to read because he does not know Standard English. They are saying, instead, that the linguistic system of the ghetto Negro is different in a number of identifiable features from that of Standard English.

331

THE NEED FOR LINGUISTIC DESCRIPTION

The theoretical assumption made by the linguist in his study of these linguistic differences is that whatever pedagogical strategy is devised for black children, whether in reading, oral language or composition, one of the first stages in the process is a careful delineation of the exact differences.

IN THE DEVELOPMENT OF ORAL LANGUAGE MATERIALS

The earliest applied work which related to the systematic differences between the speech of lower socio-economic black people and other middle class Americans focussed heavily on oral language materials. The battles over whether it was better to eradicate entirely non-standard English (as it was then called) or to teach children to be biloquial (to control two or more dialects) generated considerable heat in the mid-sixties. Toward the end of the decade, some well-meaning white liberals overstated their dismay over the long-recognized but uncontrollable intimidation processes involved in language standardization by presenting strong, if not self-righteous, arguments that it is the standard English speaker who should become biloquial by learning Black English (as it is called) (Sledd, 1969).[157]

Whatever lack of clarity may exist with regard to pedagogical strategies, political alignment, the will of the community, teacher attitudes and the inner motivations of researchers, one fact remains clear. It was good to have isolated, as much as possible, the linguistic features which set off the speech of ghetto children from middle class norms. It was good because *any* of the pedagogical strategies, political positions and community pressures require us, ultimately, to specify exactly what it is we are talking about when we say that the speech of ghetto children is different from that of their middle class peers.

That is, if your position is that black children should acquire standard English speech, for any reason you might suggest, it is necessary for teachers and materials writers to know exactly where the speech of black children differs from that of other people. If, on the other hand, you believe that white people should learn Black English, you first have to know essentially the same sort of information.

IN THE DEVELOPMENT OF READING MATERIALS

Likewise, in the field of reading, such specifications are critical, regardless of whether it is finally decided that the best approach to beginning reading in the black ghetto is to:

1. first teach them standard English (McDavid, 1964),[158]
2. accept their dialect reading of traditional material written in standard English (Goodman, 1965),[159]
3. develop materials in standard English which minimize dialect and cultural differences (Venezky, 1970),[160]
4. develop materials which incorporate the grammar of black children (Stewart, 1969).[161]

If it is decided that children must be taught standard English before they learn to read, the teachers and the materials must surely begin with an exact account of the differences between Black English and Standard English. If the schools decide to accept the oral renderings of the standard English *she goes* as *she go*, the teacher will have to be alerted to the precise conditions in which such renderings are to be expected. If an avoidance strategy is set up to neutralize the mismatch between the written text and the child's oral language, the materials developers will have to rely on this same delineation of the contrast between standard English and the speech of black children. And if it should be decided that special reading material should be developed utilizing Black English grammar, it will be necessary to know precisely what that grammar is.

What should be perfectly clear, at this point, is that regardless of the pedagogical task or the proposed teaching strategy, we will not get very far without a rather thorough description of the language of the black child. Although it may seem to the anxious public that more time should have been spent on developing materials during the past five years or so in which American education developed its belated interest in the language problems of black children, the simple truth is that it was first necessary to try to isolate the characteristics of the problem. And this was considerably harder to do than anyone would have imagined. The growing literature in the field clearly documents the sorts of problems we faced as we moved slowly toward the goal of developing classroom materials.

BACKGROUND OF THE LINGUISTIC DESCRIPTIONS

The early materials developed for teaching standard English to non-standard speakers clearly suffered from lack of accompanying linguistic analysis. It was fashionable, for example, to be concerned for the future welfare of children who said /pɪn/ for both the instrument you write with and the thing that holds two pieces of cloth together. Nor was there much perceptiveness about whether a given feature was grammatical or phonological. That is, the child's use of *jump* as the past tense form was generally thought of as carelessness with the ends of words. The obvious solutions to both problems were to give the students practice in producing a distinction between the two sets of words in question, *pen-pin* and *jump-jumped,* and to develop care in articulating the ends of words rather than, say, "swallowing them."

The next phase through which material-development seemed to pass was that of the audio-lingual stage. In the mid-sixties, TESOL was still held in high regard in most circles and it suddenly became fashionable to talk about the speech of black children as a foreign language. And if it was a foreign language, one might well consider the use of foreign language teaching techniques for ghetto kids (Lin, 1965; Stewart, 1964).[162] Some researchers rushed immediately to the task, building lessons filled with repetition drills, pattern practice and long assignments in the language laboratory, despite the early warnings by Lin that such activities seemed to have little effect on the children other than boredom. A recent intensive survey of such materials by C.A.L. staff managed to identify 28 such sets of materials, only four of which are currently available commercially. Most of the laborious efforts of hundreds of hours of various curriculum revision and materials development committees which produced many of these programs ended in anonymity. Like so many such innovative projects, the materials were used only as long as the funding for the program lasted. In some cases, it is now even impossible to discover where the materials have been stored.

During the development of the foreign-language teaching phase, it became apparent to many people that a careful description of black speech was necessary in order to determine what features to build lessons upon. It was at this point that the importance of careful linguistic descriptions became obvious. Linguistic descriptions of the speech of black people began to be made in the second half of the decade of the sixties, especially in New York (Labov and Cohen), Chicago (McDavid and Pederson), Detroit (Shuy, Wolfram and Riley), Washington (Stewart, Fasold), Florida (Houston) and Los Angeles (Legum).[163] These descriptions vary in scope and philosophy, but they constitute a considerable step in meeting the goal of a large scale description.

THE CURRENT STATUS OF LINGUISTIC DESCRIPTIONS OF BLACK ENGISH

Several types of information about the nature of Black English are now available. The earlier reports were largely lists of various features, frequently oversimplified and occasionally inaccurate, as far as Black English is concerned (Wolfram, 1970).[164] As more and more linguistic research was done, a second type of information source developed: that of the technical report which, though accurate, made for difficult reading by non-linguists and generally dealt with only a few aspects at a time (Labov, 1966; Wolfram, 1969).[165] Now a third source of information has been made available: that of the rather complete, linguistically accurate but relatively non-technical description of the most crucial features of Black English (Fasold and Wolfram, 1970).[166] This article is of great importance in that it provides the first thorough analysis of Black English while, at the same time, being accessible for the lay audience. Since this information about Black English is now readily available, there is no point in merely summarizing it here. Instead, let us review some of the kinds of problems which such a description is helping to solve. Some educators have been critical of the depth and extent of the linguistic description and analysis which sociolinguists have insisted upon. To some, it has seemed like an unnecessary luxury and it is now time to assess what it is that these descriptions have bought us.

In brief, five years or so of description and analysis have revealed some answers to the following questions:

1. What role does linguistic environment play in the contrast between Black English and standard?
2. How does one determine a pronunciation characteristic from a grammatical one?
3. How does one tell how much of a given feature a child knows and how much he doesn't?
4. How does one determine which features are most crucial or most stigmatizing?

1. The Role of Linguistic Environment

Much of the recent research of Labov, Wolfram and Fasold and others has pointed out, consistently, the importance of being able to determine the exact linguistic environments of the features which are said to contrast between standard and Black English. This particular type of knowledge enables the teacher or materials developer to build lessons with desirable precision. For example, it is important to note that the frequently observed lack of -ed past tense marker in the speech of black children is not an indication that such children have no past tense sensitivity. Indeed, their use of irregular verb past tense forms is substantially similar to that of white people of similar socio-economic status. What must be seen, here, is the working of the word final consonant cluster. Since most regular past tense formations are merely the addition of /t/ to verb bases ending in certain voiceless sounds (i.e. *jumped, picked*) and /d/ added to verb bases ending in voiced sounds (i.e., *pinned, hanged, zoomed, rubbed, begged*), and since these *t* and *d* sounds tend to be lost in certain kinds of word final consonant clusters whether they are part of a past tense formation or not, this past tense reduction must be interpreted as directly related to phonological environment.

Fasold and Wolfram clearly point out how consonant cluster reduction operates both in Black English and in the colloquial speech of standard English speakers. Both groups reduce the second member of the cluster when the following word or suffix begins with a consonant. Thus we all normally say, *bes' kind* or *wes' side* in casual speech. The major difference between Black English and standard English, however, occurs when the following sound is a vowel, as in *bes' one* and *wes' end*. Another aspect of consonant cluster reduction, noted earlier by Wolfram, is that it operates only when both members of the cluster are either voiced or voiceless. Where the consonants are of mixed voicing, as in *jump, cold* or *belt*, this reduction does not take place. These two clarifications of the general nature of consonant cluster reduction in black speech should prevent future material writers from producing lessons on the non-existent problems involving clusters of mixed voicing (as in *jump, colt* and *belt*) as well as wasting the time of black children by trying to get them to produce consonants in positions where even colloquial standard English does not require them (as in *best kind* and *west side*).

Whether the user of this information wants to eradicate nonstandard, teach biloquialism, or teach standard English speakers to use or appreciate Black English, the data provided by an exact description of the linguistic environment involved will enable him to accomplish his task with a high degree of efficiency.

2. Distinguishing Between Phonological and Grammatical Features

To indicate how important it is to examine the phonology of Black English in its entirety rather than in bits and pieces, we may observe the often noted pluralization rules of certain black children. Fasold and Wolfram point out that in Negro dialect, words ending in *s* plus *p, t* or *k* take the *-es* plural form (*-es* is also regularly used in words ending in *s, sh, z* or *zh* sounds). Thus, black children often say *wasses* for *wasps*, *ghosses* for *ghosts* and *desses* for *desks*. Because the *p, t,* and *k* sounds are so often removed by the word final consonant cluster reduction noted earlier, the plurals of *wasp, ghost,* and *desk* are formed as though these words ended in *s* rather than the consonant cluster.

It would be pedagogically wrong to assume that black children who produce words like *wasses, ghosses* and *desses* have problems with the rules of Standard English pluralization. This, indeed, is only a superficial view of the situation. At the heart of the issue is the consonant cluster reduction rule which induces these children to treat these words, quite regularly, as though they were spelled with word final *s*. It is reasonable to assume that a classroom lesson which addresses itself to consonant cluster production will be of considerably more relevance than a lesson which attempts to teach children to produce the past tense.

3. Discovering How Much of a Given Feature a Child Knows

If black children are completely unfamiliar with a given phonological or grammatical feature, the pedagogical strategy is considerably different from when they are familiar with part of the system or when they have two systems operating at the same time. For example, Fasold and Wolfram show that word final consonant clusters are not foreign to the speech of black children (Fasold and Wolfram, 1970).[167] Their clusters are simply different from standard English because they can undergo reduction in certain contexts where reduction is not possible in standard English (e.g. when the following word begins with a vowel). Unless one determines whether or not consonant cluster reduction operates consistently in Black English, one cannot build teaching materials efficiently. If the students have no morpheme final consonant clusters at all, they will produce utterances like *tes pattern, tes in math* and *tesser.* If they are like most blacks in the North, they will not produce utterances like *tesser* for *tester* or *tessing* for *testing.* These speakers evidence familiarity with the cluster before suffixes beginning with a vowel and, like standard speakers, they reduce the cluster to *s* before words beginning with a consonant. The specific contrastive environment is before words beginning with a vowel.

Any materials developed to help such speakers to produce full consonant clusters before vowels should most certainly take into account that the speakers are perfectly capable of producing the full cluster in certain environments. We should not fool ourselves into thinking that we are teaching such children something that they cannot already produce. On the contrary, what we are doing is extending the territory in which they are to produce a sound that they are, in other environments, quite capable of producing.

Another dimension of the question concerning how much a child really knows of a given linguistic feature is found in linguistic variability. Labov has observed that some of the variation between forms of a given grammatical or phonological feature are an inherent part of the child's dialect (Labov, 1969).[168] That is, a child may produce the *s* form of the plural part of the time and delete it part of the time. The sociolinguist tries desperately to focus on the exact non-linguistic environments accompanying this variation and to describe this variation accordingly. He looks for clues in terms of switching based on stylistic requirements, relative excitement, audience inter-action, etc. But even after exhausting all such clues, he frequently discovers that a certain amount of variability may exist within the same style, context and setting.

With respect to the current discussion of potential dialect inter-ference to beginning reading, linguistic variability plays a vital role. Those who are testing the hypothesis that beginning reading material should be prepared in the child's own dialect must decide how to handle this linguistic variability. Should dialect readers use the pure, invariable dialect or should they incorporate this documented varia-bility? Wolfram goes so far as to observe: "Some of the beginning dialect materials which start with pure dialect may, in effect, be creating a new type of mismatch between written and spoken language. That is, they have made the dialect to be more divergent from standard English in written form than it actually is in spoken form (Wolfram, 1970)."[169]

This whole issue of variability, in fact, helps solve the question concerning teaching strategies for nonstandard speakers. As was noted earlier, for several years it was thought that foreign language teaching techniques would be useful to teach standard English to non-standard English speakers. But a careful assessment of their speech indicated that such speakers actually produce the standard form in some con-texts or even variably within a single context. We seldom find a paral-lel to this situation in foreign language teaching, where it is reasonably clear which language is which and few, if any, English words or grammatical forms creep into a French sentence. If such an intrusion were to take place, meaning signals would start flashing a warning. Between dialects, however, such switching seldom carries with it a switch in meaning, so that *She goes to the store* means exactly the same thing as *She go to the store.*

Thus it is clear that we cannot call on the traditional foreign language teaching techniques in teaching about contrastive forms when there are no contrastive semantic functions accompanying the transfer. What is at stake is the social status of the speaker, and only minimally is there a problem of communication loss.[170] This recognition of a speaker's variability has caused materials developers to realize what we probably should have known all along: that we are seldom teaching the child something new; we are only helping him to realize how and when to switch from one system to another. This task is of tremendous importance and is by no means simplified by this discovery.

4. Discovering Which Features are Most Crucial

As linguistic geographers have long observed, it is not enough to point out where the speech of one group differs from that of another. We must also try to discover how crucial that difference is, particularly if we intend to use such information as a basis for shaping classroom activities. It has long been known, for example, that some people use relatively little aspiration at the beginnings of words with an initial *wh* spellings. Consequently, *witch* and *which* are homophonous in their dialects. This minor pronunciation difference carries relatively little social consequence even for those who produce a contrast between these two words. Those who pronounce them the same are often not even aware that some speakers produce a contrast. There are several reasons for the lack of social stigmatization attached to either side of the issue, not the least of which involves the relatively light functional load which the sounds carry. In isolation, there is potential ambiguity between *which* and *witch* but in real-life speech there are obvious syntactic clues which prevent confusion. That is, one seldom utters sentences like, *"Look, there goes a relative pronoun* (witch) *on a broom!* or *"This is the story old hag* (which) *I heard last night."*

Of late, considerable attention has been given this matter of relative cruciality, by sociolinguists who are concerned about which linguistic features are most stigmatized. The most comprehensive treatment of this issue to date is Wolfram's set of criteria for ranking such features (Wolfram, 1970):[171]

1. *sharp versus gradient stratification.* Since all linguistic features do not correlate with social status in the same manner, it is obvious that those features which show sharp breaks between social classes are more crucial that those which show only slight differences across so-

cial status groups. Wolfram's research clearly shows that verb third person singular *-s* absence *(My sister go to school every day)* stratifies sharply whereas pronominal apposition *(My brother he came home late)* has only gradient (gradual) stratification across social class.

2. *the generality of the rule.* "Some nonstandard forms affect only a small subset of words or a single item whereas others involve general rules that operate on the form of every sentence of a particular structural type (Wolfram, 1970)."[172] The Black English rule of multiple negation, *(He didn't do nothing)* for example, is a general rule that affects all negative sentences with an indefinite pronoun, determiner or adverb. On the other hand, the Black English equivalent of the *there is-there are* construction, *it is,* concerns only one item.

3. *grammatical versus phonological.* It has already been pointed out how important this difference can be to the development of materials. Nonstandard grammatical features, which tend to show sharp stratification between socioeconomic groups, are generally considered more stigmatizing than most phonological features by sociolinguists working in this area.

4. *social versus regional significance.* Although some features which are perfectly acceptable in one part of the country become stigmatized in another, other features have negative social values everywhere. It has been discovered that the latter, the generally stigmatized features, tend to be the most crucial for they always display sharper stratification than the regionally distributed items and they do not run the risk of developing regional snobbery.

5. *the relative frequency of the items.* Since some Black English patterns occur infrequently, they take less precedence than those which occur often. It is obvious that features which occur frequently are more crucial than those with low frequency.

To be sure, considerably more research needs to be done to refine our current knowledge in this area, but considerably more is now known than ever before about the relative values placed on socially stigmatized differences.

THE IMPLICATIONS OF THESE DIFFERENCES

It is clear from the emerging picture of the contrast between Standard and Black English that we have a situation which is unique in the study of language variation in this country so far. Until the mid-sixties most dialect research in America focussed on historical and geographical concerns. It used the data of pronunciation and vocabulary in particular, since these categories revealed reasonably sharp contrasts when plotted on dialect maps. The study of grammar usually pinpointed regional contrasts between different groups of lower class speakers, most frequently in the verb forms. But very little research before Labov addressed itself on the most crucial problems involved in socio-linguistic variation or degrees of stigmatization (Labov, 1966).[173] Indepth studies which determined whether a feature was a phonological or grammatical component in a person's language are extremely recent and comparatively little information is extant, even yet, about the general distribution of Negro speech in this country.

Research has progressed far enough, however, to enable us to say that the speech of most American Negroes is certainly not as different from standard English as a foreign language and it is certainly more different than the concept of dialect which we most commonly hold. In their treatment of the linguistic features of Negro dialect, Fasold and Wolfram have written the clearest statement yet about the nature of Negro speech:

> First, it should be understood that not all Negroes speak Negro dialect. There are many Negroes whose speech is indistinguishable from others of the same region and social class, and there are many whose speech can be identified as Negro only by a few slight differences in pronunciation and vocal quality. Second, Negro dialect shares many features with other kinds of English. Its distinctiveness, however, lies in the fact that it has a number of pronunciation and grammatical features which are not shared by other dialects. It is important to realize that Negro dialect is a fully formed linguistic system in its own right, with its own grammar and pronunciation rules; it cannot simply be dismissed as an unworthy approximation of standard English. In fact, there are some grammatical distinctions which can be made more easily in Negro dialect than in standard English. Negro dialect, then, as the term is used here, is a cohesive linguistic system which is substantially different from standard American English dialects. It is spoken by some, though not all Negroes, particularly those of the lower socio-economic classes. Furthermore . . . almost all the features associated with Negro dialect alternate with standard English forms in actual speech (1970).

Within the confines of the preceding qualifications, then, Black English may be said to be different enough from the schoolroom norms to merit special attention. It is different enough from these norms to require specially developed teaching strategies and materials which address themselves specifically to the beginning points of these speakers.

Research has revealed some things about Negro speech that come as a surprise to certain teachers. For example, black children have neither more nor less difficulty with irregular past tense forms than do Standard English speakers (black and white). But Black English is different enough from Standard English (and still more different from the prose of beginning reading materials) to merit serious research into the use of this indigenous system in the teaching of early reading skills. Venezky dismisses this possibility on the following grounds: (1) there is no proof that it will work, (2) it is too complicated and expensive, (3) the problems of attention span, motor coordination and cognitive skills usually accompany non-standard speech and these may be the real root of the problem, and (4) it has been shown that lower socio-economic status Negro children do not find educated speech any less intelligible than Negro speech (Venezky, 1970).[174] Not one of these objections is adequate for stopping the ongoing research and testing in this area. To the objection that there is no proof that it will work we must respond that there is also no adequate proof that it will not work. Likewise, there is less than adequate proof that any approach to reading works, at least as it is conceived of by its author.

The objection based on complexity is irrelevant. It is argued, for example, that if native literacy materials were constructed for Hawaiians, this would have to be done for Hawaiian pidgin, Japanese, Chinese, the various Philippine languages, Korean, etc. This may or may not prove to be true. Whether it is true or not, the issue involves making children literate, not how hard it is to do so. The creative American spirit has not yet been stifled by arguments of expense or complexity, and there is no reason to expect it to be stifled here.

The argument that non-standard speech accompanies cognitive deficit has been rejected by almost all linguists since educational psychologists first presented it publically and there is evidence even from psychology that data which appear to show such conclusions are measuring test-taking ability, cultural difference or something else rather than cognitive ability (Labov, 1969).[175] Furth, in fact, has clearly demonstrated that children who are deaf from birth have no cognitive deficits whatsoever despite their total lack of language environment. (Furth, 1970).[176]

That lower socioeconomic black children find educated white speech intelligible should not be surprising in light of what has been said about the two linguistic systems. Even ghettoized Black children come in contact with Standard English on the television set but it appears that they develop an editing process quite similar to the apparently universal contrast between two kinds of vocabulary. We all have a "use" vocabularly and a "recognition" vocabulary. We can input through either set but we usually output only through the former. Baratz's sentence repetition tests seem to verify this phenomenon (Baratz, 1969).[177] Given a stimulus sentence in Standard English, black children converted the sentence into their own linguistic system when they "repeated" it. That black children can do this says little or nothing, however, about what interference a different language system might have on them as they acquire beginning reading skills, especially at the time when heavy emphasis is traditionally placed on developing skills in decoding and when the flow of predictability from what children already know (their oral language) to what they are learning (the written manifestation of that oral language) is of such great significance (Shuy, 1969).[178]

To dismiss any promising hypothesis on such grounds as those stated above is dangerous business, especially in a field of study which historically and, perhaps, necessarily may be characterized as hypothesis-oriented. The entire tradition of educational research suffers from much the same problem. We are engaged in research which is quite different from that of the hard sciences. That is, we have precious little that can be thought of as a scientific base. Any serious researcher in reading will verify that in this area, the variables tend to multiply so fast that experimental control becomes extremely difficult, if not impossible. Since we know relatively little about how humans acquire learning, how they process language input or control its output, and how their knowledge and use of language relates to all this, we are probably doing well to operate even at the level of hypotheses. What we are finally beginning to know something about is the broad outline of the linguistic system of the target population. It would seem reasonable to try to utilize this small segment of what may be called a scientific base in connection with reasonable hypotheses about the acquisition of reading skills.

To those who claim that nonstandard English speakers should be taught standard English before they are taught reading we can only say that there is also relatively little upon which this hypothesis is based. But it probably should be thoroughly investigated with as much rigor as we can marshal for the occasion, despite the apparent contradictory positions of researchers concerning the ability of children to acquire language skills at this age.

Likewise those who argue for beginning reading materials written in standard English but which avoid the grammatical and cultural mismatch of Black English speaking children with the printed page also work from a reasonable but unproved hypothesis, but one which should certainly not be ignored.

It seems likely, then, that the combined effects of our current frustration concerning what to do about teaching black children to read and our developing knowledge about the linguistic system of such children should work together in a new phase of our research in which these various hypotheses should be given a fair and thorough try, and not necessarily always by those who have been grinding axes for their own hypotheses.

A far more potent reason for discouraging any of the hypotheses noted in this paper may come from the black community itself. In a time such as this, when it is commonplace to be suspicious of the motives of researchers, it is particularly difficult to address ourselves to the problems of minority groups, whether in reading, economics, family planning or almost anything else. There is little reason for us to agonize over this situation or to feel sorry for ourselves as a result of it. The fact remains that no matter what route we take toward addressing these problems, we stand a pretty good chance of being called racist, Uncle Toms, communists or empire builders. Perhaps this matters; perhaps not. It should be clear by this time, however, that any experimentation in the various teaching strategies which grows out of our descriptions of language differences must have the approval and support of the community in which the experimentation takes place. It is not likely that teaching strategies which grow out of 1) teaching standard English before reading, 2) teaching reading by using dialect materials, 3) developing teaching materials which neutralize dialect differences and 4) teaching teachers to accept oral dialect renderings of written standard English will seriously harm the students in the experiments. But if the community *thinks* these will be harmful, it has the right to say no. Personally, these approaches seem to me to be no more harmful than the other strategies currently in vogue, including phonics, the whole-word method and ITA. But since a specific minority population is identified, the public relations problem is intensified.

CONCLUSION

In this paper I have attempted to demonstrate the importance of a careful and thorough sociolinguistic description of the speech differences which characterize different groups of people. It has been observed that such a description is at the heart of any pedagogical strategies, whether for teaching standard oral English or reading ability and that until such descriptions were made, the teaching materials were frequently based on less crucial aspects of the problem or on features which were not problems at all. Such descriptions enable us 1) to develop materials which relate more specifically to the exact linguistic environment in which the features are found, 2) to devise strategies determined by whether the feature is grammatical or phonological in nature, 3) to help us assess what the child already knows about given features of language which otherwise we might have overlooked, and 4) to help us determine which features are most stigmatized by the society as a whole.

During the past five years, while most of the sociolinguistic research concerning Black English was undertaken, various teaching strategies have taken shape. We are currently at that stage of the research in which we can best take advantage of our knowledge of the specific differences between black and standard English. Since there is no known way to determine exactly what it is that keeps children from learning to read, it will pay us to take that next logical approach to the problem—hypothesis testing. This should come as no shock to reading researchers, since hypothesis testing has certainly characterized the work of the profession to date. To be sure, certain aspects have already begun to be tested, particularly with respect to the development of materials written in the black child's dialect. Now it is time to urge researchers to coordinate their work in such a way that the four models involving potential dialect interference to reading (noted above) are thoroughly examined.

Sociolinguistic research to date has clearly shown that the systematic difference between black and standard English is great enough to cause people to be clearly marked socially with great consistency (Shuy, Baratz, and Wolfram, 1968).[179] This difference is great enough to be a clear handicap to employers (Shuy, 1970)[180] and, whether desirable or not, it is great enough to enable listeners to achieve 80 percent accuracy in racial identification tasks (Shuy, 1969).[181] Research to date has not clearly established whether or not this difference is great enough to affect the acquisition of reading skills. But the evidence suggests that every effort should be made to discover which of the four strategies noted in this paper will be most helpful, in what settings and under what circumstances. The stakes are too great for us not to try.

Notes

Part I: Standard and Nonstandard English: Temporal, Regional, and Social Variations

1. "Language and Environment" in *Selected Writings of Edward Sapir in Language, Culture, and Personality,* David G. Mandelbaum, ed. (Berkeley and Los Angeles: University of California Press, 1949), pp. 102-103.

2. Raven I. McDavid, Jr., abrid., *The American Language* (New York: Alfred A. Knopf, 1963), p. 450.

3. "American Linguistic Geography: A Sociological Appraisal," *Word* 12 (1956): 225.

4. Allan F. Hubbell, *The Pronunciation of English in New York City* (New York: King's Crown Press, 1950), p. 11; Mary M. Galvan and Rudolph C. Troika, "The East Texas Dialect Project: A Pattern for Education," *The Florida FL Reporter* 7, 1 (Spring/Summer 1969): 31.

5. "Urban Negro Speech: Sociolinguistic Factors Affecting English Teaching" in *Social Dialects and Language Learning,* Roger W. Shuy, ed. (Champaign, Ill.: National Council of Teachers of English, 1964), pp. 15-16.

6. William Labov, "A Proposed Study of Negro and Puerto Rican Speech" in *Project Literacy Reports* (Ithaca, N. Y.: Cornell University, 1964), p. 15. For a complete report of Labov's work see his Columbia University dissertation, "The Social Stratification of English in New York City (Washington, D.C.: Center for Applied Linguistics, 1964).

7. Quoted in Walter A. Wolfram, *A Sociolinguistic Description of Detroit Negro Speech* (Washington, D. C.: Center for Applied Linguistics, 1969), p. 123.

8. Marvin D. Loflin, "A Note on the Deep Structure of Nonstandard English in Washington, D.C.," *Glossa* 1 (1967): 26, footnote 3; J. L. Dillard, "Non-Standard Negro Dialects—Convergence or Divergence," *The Florida FL Reporter* 6, 2 (Spring 1968): 9-10, 12.

9. In this volume see pp. 96-106.

10. In this volume see pp. 107-122.

11. William A. Stewart, *Non-Standard Speech and the Teaching of English*

(Washington, D.C.: Center for Applied Linguistics, 1964); "Urban Negro Speech;" "Sociolinguistic Factors in the History of American Negro Dialects," *The Florida FL Reporter* 5, 2 (Spring 1967): 11, 22, 24, 26; "Continuity and Change in American Negro Dialects." J. L. Dillard, "Negro Children's Dialects in the Inner City," *The Florida FL Reporter* 5, 3 (Fall 1967): 7-8. Beryl Loftman Bailey, "Toward a New Perspective in Negro English Dialectology, "*American Speech* 40 (October 1965): 171-177; "Some Aspects of the Impact of Linguistics on Language Teaching in Disadvantaged Communities," *Elementary English* 45 (May 1968): 570-577.

12. In this volume see pp. 96-106.

A detailed study of Gullah is presented in Lorenzo Trumen's *Africanism in the Gullah Dialect* (Chicago: University of Chicago Press, 1949).

13. William A. Stewart, "Creole Languages in the Caribbean" in *Study of the Role of Second Languages in Asia, Africa, and Latin America,* Frank A. Rice, ed. (Washington, D.C.: Center for Applied Linguistics, 1962), pp. 34-52; Bailey, *op. cit.,* p. 172; Dillard, "Non-Standard Negro Dialects," p. 9.

14. Dillard, *Ibid.*

15. Dillard, "Negro Children's Dialect in the Inner City," p. 8; Stewart, in this volume see pp. 96-106.

16. Since eastern Pennsylvania and the Hudson Valley share many phonological features—such as the homonymy of *morning* and *mourning,* /w-/ in *whip,* etc., /eh/ in *had* and /oh/ in *law*—it is possible, on phonological grounds alone, to class them together in a Middle Atlantic area, extending from Albany to the Baltimore-Washington area. Certainly, with the growth of population and the heavy industrialization of this area, the more peculiarly local speech characteristics are disappearing.

17. *Linguistic Atlas* data supplemented by W. S. Avis, "Speech Differences along the Ontario–U.S. Border," *Journal of the Canadian Linguistic Association,* preliminary issue (1954): 13-17; I (1955): 14-19; II (1956): 41-59.

18. E. B. Atwood, *The Verb Forms of the Eastern United States* (Ann Arbor, Mich.: University of Michigan Press, 1953).

19. The regional designations are those found in H. Kurath, *A Word Geography of the Eastern United States* (Ann Arbor, Mich.: University of Michigan Press, 1949), and in articles by Kurath, E. B. Atwood, Raven McDavid, and A. L. Davis. Linguistically the North includes New England, the Hudson Valley (including New York City) and derivative settlements in upstate New York, Pennsylvania, and further west. The Inland North is the northern area exclusive of the Hudson Valley and eastern New England. The Midland includes most of New Jersey and Pennsylvania, with derivative settlements to the west and south. The North Midland includes most of New Jersey and Pennsylvania, plus northern West Virginia. The South Midland includes the Shenandoah Valley, southern West Virginia, southwest Virginia, and the mountain and upper Piedmont areas of the Carolinas and Georgia. The South includes the older plantation areas of eastern Virginia and the coastal plain and lower Piedmont of the Carolinas and Georgia. The boundaries between these sections are much less sharp west of the Appalachians than along the Atlantic Seaboard.

20. The particular type of analysis one favors will often determine the category to which he assigns these differences. The analysis here used is basically that of *The Pronunciation of the Eastern United States* as adapted to the system of transcription generally used in *Language Learning.* Phonetic symbols are enclosed in brackets; phonemic symbols in slated lines. Phonemic equivalents are as follows:

Vowels:

/i/	as in *beet*
/ɪ/	as in *bit*
/e/	as in *bait*
/ɛ/	as in *bet*
/æ/	as in *bat*
/a/	as in *hot, father*
/ɔ/	as in *bought*
/o/	as in *boat*

/ŏ/ the New England "short *o*" as in *coat, road, home*
/u/ as in *put*
/u/ as in *boot*

Diphthongs:

/ai/ as in *write*
/au/ as in *rout*
/ɔi/ as in *oil*
/æi/ as in the common Southern and South Midland *bag, half*
/ɔu/ as in the common Southern and South Midland *law, hog.* This diphthong also occurs in New Hampshire.
/iu/ as in the common New England *beautiful, music.* This diphthong also occurs along the south Atlantic coast.
/'/ primary stress
/ı/ secondary stress

21. We will assume throughout this article that the question of whether or not there is such a thing as "Negro dialect" distinct from white nonstandard dialects has been answered in the affirmative. Discussion of this issue is to be found in any of the articles by William A. Stewart. The use here of the term "Negro dialect" is equivalent to our use of "Black English" elsewhere and approximately equivalent to the use of "Negro Non-Standard English" by others. Unfortunately, there is no consensus about an adequate label for this variety of English, so that we have adopted the more traditional term.

22. "Consonant blends" is sometimes used by educators where we have used consonant clusters, but the meaning is the same.

23. "Base words" refers to the part of the word to which inflections may be added. For example, in the words *drowned* and *drowns, drown* is considered the base part of the word.

The rules which govern standard English as it is actually spoken are often quite different from the prescriptive norms that are set up in school grammar textbooks.

24. In standard English, these sequences are often pronounced by lengthening the *s* instead of pronouncing the full sequence (e.g. *tess* for *tests* or *dess* for *desks*).

25 In some parts of the South *t* or *d* occurs at the end of the word in Negro dialect, regardless of what precedes *th.* Thus we may get *toot* or *Rut'* for *tooth* and *Ruth.*

26. There are, however, two exceptions. Some verbs, like *berate*, end in *t* or *d* followed by "silent *e.*" When *-ed* (actually only *d*) is added to these verbs, the pronunciation is still *id.* In the second case, English has a set of verbs ("strong verbs") like *hit* and *cost*, which never take the *-ed* suffix. All "strong verbs" end in *t* or *d.*

27. This seems to be a different rule from the *d*-elimination rule discussed in the pronunciation section of this article.

28. Teachers are sometimes doubly surprised when they hear sentences like *He don't suppose to bring his books to class.* Not only is the *-s* suffix absent from auxiliary *don't*, but the presence of *don't* instead of a form of *to be* is strikingly different from standard English. In Negro dialect, the word is not the participle *supposed,* but *is* a verb *suppose* which functions grammatically like the verb *intend.* Thus we get *He don't suppose to bring . . .* parallel with *He don't intend to bring . . . .*

29. It is difficult to indicate the pronunciations intended by the spellings *mon* and *gon.* The *on* in each case is to be taken as a nasalized *o*- like vowel (giving $m\tilde{o}$ and $g\tilde{o}$).

30. In Negro dialect, of course, the third person singular *-s* suffix would ordinarily not be present and this sentence would be *Nobody don't know it.* For simplicity in comparing standard and nonstandard sentences, we will ignore this fact.

31. This was true of studies in New York, Detroit and Washington, D. C.

32. This statement is not to be taken as implying that Negro dialect at this or any other stage is a cognitively deficient system. Many languages in which there is an abundance of philosophical and literary works, like Chinese, also lack plural as a grammatical category.

33. There seems to be some evidence that this regularization is coming into

standard English, since sentences like the last two are sometimes heard in the standard dialects.

34. See Stewart, *Non-Standard Speech and the Teaching of English.*

35. The American Dream notwithstanding, it is well known to social scientists that American society is stratified into a number of social classes and ethnic groups, and that each of these exhibits a "characteristic" configuration of customs, attitudes, roles, life-ways and, as it turns out, speech patterns. The literature on social and ethnic stratification is extensive, but good introductions are Egon Ernest Bergel, *Social Stratification* (New York: McGraw-Hill Book Co., 1962), and Tamotsu Shibutani and Kian M. Kwan, *Ethnic Stratification* (New York: The Macmillan Co., 1965). For an exhaustively documented study of the correlation between language variation and the social class, ethnicity, and age in an American metropolis, see William Labov, *The Social Stratification of English in New York City* (Washington, D.C.: The Center for Applied Linguistics, 1966).

36. These two facts may not be entirely unrelated. For a graphic indication of the relatively more non-standard grammatical norms of Negro children over white children in a single city, see Figure 18 (page 53) in Walter Loban, *Problems in Oral English: Kindergarten Through Grade Nine* (Champaign, Ill.: National Council of Teachers of English, 1966).

37. For a discussion of Negro dialect in one urban community see Stewart, "Urban Negro Speech." The non-standard dialect patterns cited earlier in the present article are also Negro dialect.

38. In referring to types of languages, linguists use the term *pidgin* and *creole* in a technical sense which has none of the derogatory or racial connotations of popular uses of these terms. When a linguist says that a variety of language is pidginized, he merely means that it has a markedly simplified grammatical structure compared with the "normal" (i.e., unpidginized) source-language. This simplification may be one way in which speakers of different languages can make

a new language easier to learn and use —particularly if they have neither the opportunity nor the motivation to learn to speak it the way its primary users do. In addition, some of the unique characteristics of a pidgin language may be due, not to simplification, but to influences on it from the native languages of its users. What is important to realize, however, is that pidginized languages do have grammatical structure and regularity, even though their specific patterns may be different from those of the related unpidginized source-language of higher prestige. Thus, the fact that the sentence *Dem no get-am* in present-day West African Pidgin English is obviously different from its standard English equivalent "They don't have it" does not necessarily indicate that the Pidgin English speaker "talks without grammar." In producing such a sentence, he is unconsciously obeying the grammatical rules of West African Pidgin English, and these determine that *Dem no get-am* is the "right" construction, as opposed to such ungrammatical or "wrong" combinations as *No dem get-am, No get dem-am, Get-am dem no,* etc. If a pidgin finally becomes the native language of a speech community (and thereby becomes by definition a creole language), it may expand in grammatical complexity to the level of "normal" or unpidginized languages. Of course, the resulting creole language may still exhibit structural differences from the original source-language, because the creole has gone through a pidginized stage. For more details, see Robert A. Hall, Jr., *Pidgin and Creole Languages,* (Ithaca, N. Y.: Cornell University Press, 1966).

The same citation is given in a fuller form, along with a number of other attestations of early New World Negro speech, in George Philip Krapp, *The English Language in America* (New York: The Century Co., 1925), Vol. 1, pp. 255-265. Other attestations are cited in Tremaine McDowell, "Notes on Negro Dialect in the American Novel to 1821," *American Speech* 5 (1930): 291-296.

39. J. D. Herlein, *Beschryvinge van de volksptantinge Zuriname* (Leeuwar-

den, 1718), pp. 121-123. Herlein gives the Negro English dialogues in Dutch orthography. I have retranscribed these sentences in the kind of spelling which his English contemporaries would have used in order to show better the relationship between the Surinam dialect and the other examples. In the Dutch spelling, these sentences appear as *My belle wel, Jou wantje sie don pinkinne?*, and *Jo wantje gaeu wakke lange mie?*

40. See, for example, Basil Davidson, *Black Mother: The Years of the African Slave Trade* (Boston: Little, Brown and Co., 1961), particularly p. 218.

41. In the West Indies, creole English is usually called *patois*, while in Surinam it is called *Taki-Taki*. In the United States, the only fairly "pure" creole English left today is Gullah, spoken along the coast of South Carolina.

42. These were Pieter van Dijk, *Nieuwe en nooit bevoorens geziende onderwijzinge in het Bastert Engels, of Neeger Engels* (Amsterdam, undated, but probably 1780), and G. C. Weygandt, *Gemeenzame leerwijze om het Basterd of Neger-Engelsch op een gemakkelijke wijze te leeren verstaan en spreeken* (Paramaribo, 1798).

43. Martin R. Delany, *Blake: or the Huts of America* in *The Anglo-African Magazine* 1, 6 (1859): 163.

44. Raven I. McDavid, Jr. and Virginia Glenn McDavid, "The Relationship of the Speech of American Negroes to the Speech of Whites," *American Speech* 26 (1951): 3-17.

45. See for example, *The Florida FL Reporter* 4, 2 (Winter 1965-66): 25. Frances Anne Kemble, *Journal of a Residence on a Georgian Plantation in 1838-1839* (New York, 1862) pp. 52, 118.

46. E.g., "The Negroes born in this country invariably used, according to these records, good English," Allen Walker Read, "The Speech of Negroes in Colonial America," *The Journal of Negro History* 24, 3:258. The records which Read refers to are for the most part runaway slave advertisements published before the American Revolution. Of course, the evidence which they supply on slave speech is indirect (i.e., they give impressions of the particular slave's competence in English, but no examples of that English), since the information was merely intended to help identify the runaway. If these indirect records say what Read interprets them as saying, then they are certainly at variance with what direct evidence (quotations in slave dialect) is available from the same period. Furthermore, the far larger number of attestations of slave speech during the nineteenth century which show widespread use of non-standard dialect, together with a similar situation observable today, would mean that American Negro speech generally became less standard after the first generation of American-born slaves. Needless to say, such a process would be difficult to explain either structurally or historically. The trouble with Read's conclusion seems to be that, in interpreting such advertisements, he did not consider the possibility that in the parlance of slave owners a term like "good English" might have meant something very different when applied to Negroes than it would have if applied to whites. Indications that this was probably the case seem to exist in the advertisement quoted on pages 252-253.

47. The Gullah (or Geechee) dialect, spoken by many Negroes along the South Atlantic coast, appears to be a fairly direct descendant of the older kind of plantation creole.

48. The term "zero copula" refers to the absence of an explicit predicating verb in certain dialect constructions, where standard English has such a verb (usually in the present tense). Compare non-standard Negro dialect **He old, Dey runnin'**, and **She ateacher** with standard English "He is old," "They are running" and "She is a teacher." The term "zero possessive" refers to the absence of an explicit suffix in noun-noun constructions, where standard English has such a suffix. Compare non-standard Negro dialect **my fahver frien'** with standard English "my father's friend." The term "undifferentiated pronoun" refers to the use of the same pronoun form for both subject and object, and sometimes for possession as well. The pronominal form

used may be derived from either the standard English object form, or the subject form. Compare such non-standard forms as **Him know we, Him know us,** (beside **He know us**) with the standard English "He knows us" to which they are equivalent. Or compare **He fahver** (beside **His fahver**) and **We house** (beside **Our house**) with standard English "His father" and "Our house."

49. If the term "Negro dialect" is understood to refer to non-standard varieties of American English whose more unique (i.e., non-white and non-British) structural features are simply due to the historical influence of an earlier plantation creole, then it should be clear that such a term does not imply any direct genetic determination of speech patterns, in spite of its ethnic reference. The "Negro," in "Negro dialect" is merely a recognition of that fact that the creole predecessor for such structural features was itself the result of African migration to and acculturation in Anglo-Saxon America, and that those present-day dialects which show the greatest influence from such a creole are precisely those which are used by the descendants of the Negro field hands who originally spoke it. In addition, the speech of American Negroes is often characterized by special kinds of syllable and breath dynamics, as well as unique uses of pitch, stress and volume. But even these language habits are always socially learned and transmitted ones, although it is difficult to tell whether they represent survivals of African speech habits, creole speech habits, or are more recent innovations. That they are not the product of any special Negro vocal physiology should be obvious from the fact that some whites can mimic such features quite well, while there are some Negroes in whose speech the same features are not normally present.

50. Judging from the literary treatment of Negro dialect, these features were characteristic of the non-standard speech of even New England Negroes up to the close of the eighteenth century. Within the first decades of the nineteenth century, however, the northern limit

of their common occurrence in adult speech appears to have receded to the Delaware region, and to somewhere in the Carolinas by the middle of the same century. Of course, most of these creolisms still occur in Gullah—at least sporadically. And it is likely that the *for to* infinitives of some Deep South Negro dialects are the result of incomplete decreolization (the adding of non-creole *to,* without giving up the creole *for*), rather than the borrowing of a white non-standard dialect pattern, as some might suppose. In the first place, such white dialects (Appalachia, Georgia, etc.) usually have a contrast between *to* and *for to,* e.g. *I come to see it*" (i.e., "It dawned on me") vs. *I come for to see it* ("I came in order to see it"), while many Negro dialects in which *for to* occurs do not make such a distinction. In the second place, there is piecemeal evidence of the addition of *to* after *for* along the South Atlantic coast, where the change has been relatively recent. For example, in *Drums and Shadows: Survival Studies Among the Georgia Coastal Negroes* (Athens, Ga., 1940), p. 144 a team of the Georgia Writers' Project interviewed an old lady (then approximately one hundred years old) who, speaking of an African-born slave whom she knew in her youth, recalled "I membuh he say 'Lemme cook sumpm fuh nyam.' He mean sumpm fuh to eat." Notice also the de-creolization of the Gullah and Caribbean Creole English verb *nyam* "to eat." In some areas, the changeover was not so complete, if a literary reflection of a Gullah Negro's alternation between the same two verbs in Ambrose E. Gonzales, *The Captain: Stories of the Black Border* (Columbia, S. C.: The State Co., 1924), p. 149, "You hab mout' fuh nyam da' haa'd hoecake you juntlemun gi' you fuh eat."

51. The impression that the rustic and creole features of the older plantation dialects died out entirely during this period is easy to get, considering that the speech of children hardly appears at all in the records of folklorists or dialectologists, or even in the fictional use of dialect, since the main concern of the social scientist and the novelist alike has

been the adult. Evidence that the older dialects have in fact survived in the speech of children is only now coming to light through recent studies of present-day Negro speech communities. See Stewart "Urban Negro Speech" pp. 16-18, and Dillard, "Negro Children's Dialect in the Inner-City." It would seem that the preservation of a more conservative dialect by young children in communities where the older language forms are being encroached upon by imported ones is not limited to Negro communities. During a recent sociolinguistic survey of the Appalachian region, I found full-fledged mountain dialect still being used by pre-school-age white children in communities where it had been abandoned by all but the oldest adults.

52. Like Dillard, I feel that this constitutes the most plausible explanation of the sporadic but not infrequent occurrence in the speech of lower-class Negro children of such "mistakes" as *been* as a general past-time market (e.g. **He been hit me**), pronominal forms which are undifferentiated for case or gender, **Me gonna try** and **He out payin'**—the latter said in reference to a girl), etc., since these same features were quite normal in older forms of Negro dialect (and still are in Gullah) and since there is, after all, an uninterrupted chain of language transmission from those earlier speakers to Negro children of the present day. Because some of the features are similar (at least superficially) to ones which are characteristic of certain stages of language development in virtually all English-speaking children, most specialists have attributed the Negro child patterns to developmental causes. However, since the Negro patterns are sometimes used by children who are well beyond the developmental stage (which normally ends at age 3.6 or 4 for whites), this would imply that Negroes develop linguistically more slowly than do whites. And, since there are even Negro octogenarians who use these forms, one would be forced to the absurd conclusion that some Negroes must not have completed the developmental process at all.

53. In Washington, D.C., I know of an adolescent Negro who for some reason had retained many child-dialect features in his speech. His peers characterized his speech by saying that "He talk just like a small boy." And in her *Folk-Lore of the Sea Islands, South Carolina* (Cambridge, Mass.: American Folklore Society, 1923), Elsie Clews Parson gives a Negro folk-tale (No. 148, "The Girl Who Learned to Talk Proper") in which the speech of a young lady who was said to "talk very bad" is marked by the use of creole pronominal forms (e.g., "Me ain' col' suh!"). It is interesting that the conclusion of this tale also shows popular recognition of the effect of out-migration on speech habits, since the same girl did finally "learn to talk proper" when an outsider married her and "kyarried her to his country."

54. John Bennett, "Gullah: A Negro Patois," *The South Atlantic Quarterly* 7 (Oct. 1903) and 8 (Jan. 1909). Quote from Vol 7, p. 339. This same process had evidently been going on for at least a century and a half before Bennett's time. It was noted during the first half of the eighteenth century by G. L. Campbell, a British traveler to the American colonies. "One Thing they are very faulty in, with regard to their Children," he wrote of the white planters, "which is, that when young, they suffer them too much to prowl amongst the young Negros, which insensibly causes them to imbibe their Manners and broken Speech." (*The London Magazine,* July 1746). Quoted in Allen Walker Read, "British Recognition of American Speech in the Eighteenth Century," *Dialect Notes* 6, 6 (July 1933): 329. Since even the most aristocratic British children undoubtedly picked up non-standard English or Scottish dialects from children of the servant class, it must have been the "broken" (i.e., creolized) character of colonial Negro speech which Campbell found so disagreeable in the North American situation.

55. Elsewhere ("Urban Negro Speech," p. 13, footnote 7,), I have taken Ambrose E. Gonzales to task for his racistic explanation of some of the structural characteristics of the Gullah dialect. At the same time, one can see how he would come to such a point of view, since he was obviously unaware of pidginization as a linguistic phenomenon, and therefore unable to account scientifically for its operation in the speech of the Gullah Negroes. In addition, a genetic explanation of language differences fitted quite comfortably into the rhetoric of the caste-cloven society of which Gonzales was so much a product. This theoretical weakness notwithstanding, Gonzales' literary rendition of Gullah was superb. Considering the accuracy of his dialect phonology and syntax, and the ease with which he handled subtle dialect differences and even individual switching behavior, he can certainly qualify as America's greatest dialect writer. For a similar opinion of Gonzales, see Ann Sullivan Haskell *The Representation of Gullah-Influenced Dialect in Twentieth Century South Carolina Prose: 1922-30* (University of Pennsylvania Ph.D. Dissertation, 1964), pp. 238-241.

56. Because the structural relationships which hold between the two "dialects" in such a case are in part like those between completely foreign languages and in part like those between two style levels of a single language, I have coined the term "quasi-foreign language situation" to describe it. See my "Foreign Language Teaching Methods in Quasi-Foreign Language Situations" in *Non-Standard Speech and the Teaching of English.*

57. Linguistic and cultural relativists will be pleased to learn that the dialect tables have been turned on the normativists at least once. In his essay, John Bennett (*op. cit.,* 7, p. 340) reports that Gullah-speaking Negroes passed judgment on visiting Yankees with "Dey use dem mout' so funny!"

58. William Francis Allen, Charles Pickard Ware, and Lucy McKim Garrison, *Slave Songs of the United States* (New York: 1867), p. xxvii. What the father of the boy knew was that in Gullah, observable characteristics are usually indicated by means of the verb *stan'* (or *'tan*) which can be translated

roughly as "look," "seem" or "appear."

59. As one dialect geographer expressed his view of the matter, "the range of variants is the same in Negro and in white speech, though the statistical distribution of variants has been skewed by the American caste system." Raven I. McDavid, Jr., "American Social Dialects" *College English* 26, 4 (January 1965): 258, fn. 7. In an even more recent article, McDavid rejects the idea of a pidgin or creole background for American Negro dialects, saying "To a naive social scientist, what is generally known about the operations of the domestic slave trade should be sufficient to refute such an argument." Raven I. McDavid, Jr., "Needed Research in Southern Dialects" in *Perspectives on the South: Agenda for Research,* Edgar T. Thompson, ed. (Durham, N.C.: Duke University Press, 1967), p. 122. In view of the numerous attestations of the actual use of pidgin and creole forms of English by American Negro slaves in the contemporary literature (see pages 86-95 for references, ed.), it is difficult to imagine any historical basis for McDavid's statements. Since he must have seen at least the reprintings of some of these in scholarly books and articles, it can only be that he has not considered the linguistic implications of their non-European grammatical structure. Furthermore, if there is anything in what is known about the slave trade, slave life, or plantation social stratification in America which would call into question these early attestations of pidgin and creole English, it is strange that it has never been articulated in such standard works on American Negro slavery as Philip Alexander Bruce, *Economic History of Virginia in the Seventeenth Century* (New York: The Macmillan Co., 1895); Ulrich B. Phillips, *American Negro Slavery* (New York: D. Appleton and Co., 1918) and his *Life and Labor in the Old South* (Boston: Little, Brown and Co., 1929); Marcus William Jernegan, *Laboring and Dependent Classes in Colonial America: 1607-1783* (Chicago: University of Chicago Press, 1931); Frederick Bancroft, *Slave-Trading in the Old South* (Baltimore: J. H. Furst Co.,

1931); Kenneth M. Stampp, *The Peculiar Institution: Slavery in the Ante-Bellum South* (New York: Alfred A. Knopf, Inc., 1956); Herbert S. Klein, *Slavery in the Americas: A Comparative Study of Virginia and Cuba* (Chicago: University of Chicago Press, 1967). None of the four recent publications on American dialects which have been written for the use of English teachers contain any substantive reference to Negro dialect—not even a simple statement of the historical and definitional issues involved in the concept. This omission is probably due to the tacit acceptance on the part of the various authors of the theory that most Negro speech is identical to southern varieties of white speech, and therefore that the description of the latter in their manuals takes care of Negro speech as well. These four publications are: Jean Malmstrom and Annabel Ashley, *Dialects—USA* (Champaign, Ill.: National Council of Teachers of English, 1963); Jean Malmstrom, *Language in Society* (New York: The Hayden Book Co., 1965); Carroll E. Reed, *Dialects of American English* (Cleveland: World Publishing Co., 1967); Roger W. Shuy, *Discovering American Dialects* (Champaign, Ill.: National Council of Teachers of English, 1967).

60. The term *basilect* refers to that variety of a particular dialect which is structurally the most deviant from standard English. See Stewart, "Urban Negro Speech," pp. 15-17.

61. The literary dialect spellings which I have used in these examples may well make the individual words in WNS and NNS seem more alike than they actually are when pronounced. But, for the sake of argument, I would just as soon allow for the possibility that some words might have identical phonological forms in the different dialects.

62. This concession as to the creole nature of Gullah was largely forced upon an intensely Anglo-centric American dialect-studies tradition by Lorenzo Dow Turner's *Africanisms in the Gullah Dialect* (Chicago: University of Chicago Press, 1949) which, though it concentrated more on African survivals than on creole influences and dealt more with

naming practices than with linguistic structure, did at least make the point rather strongly that Gullah is a creolized form of English.

63. Those who have had enough contact with Negro non-standard dialects to know that constructions like *We tryin'* usually indicate the present tense (i.e., STE "We are trying") might assume that the superficially similar construction, we drinkin' in the NNS sentence *We was eatin'-an' we drinkin', too* also indicates the present tense—the whole thereby meaning "We were eating—and we are drinking too" with an erroneous lack of tense agreement between the two clauses. Although it is true that *we drinkin'* does mean *"we are drinking"* in most circumstances (cf. NNS *We drinkin' right now*), in the sentence cited the phrase really represents *we was drinkin'* with the past tense marker *was* omitted. By the same token, GUL *we duh drink,* can mean "we are drinking" as well, but represents *we bin duh drink,* with the past tense marker *bin* omitted, in the sentence cited.

64. For comparative purposes, I have written these languages in a spelling which is as close to that of standard English as the literary dialect spellings used in the preceding set of equivalent sentences. Scientific (phonemic) orthographies have been devised for these languages, however, and in them the same sentences would appear as: JMC *We ben a nyam—an we a dringk, tu;* SRA *we ben njan—en we de dringi, toe;* WAP *Wi bin de it—an we de dring, tu.* See Frederic G. Cassidy, *Jamaica Talk* (London: Macmillan Co., Ltd., 1961); Beryl L. Bailey, *Jamaican Creole Syntax* (Cambridge University Press, 1966); A. Donicie, *De Creolentaal van Suriname* (Paramaribo: Radhakishun and Co., 1959); Gouvernement van Suriname, Bureau Volkslectuur, *Woordenlijst van het Sranan-Tongo* (Paramaribo: N. V. Varekamp & Co., 1961); Gilbert D. Schneider, *West African Pidgin English* (Ph.D. Thesis, Hartford Seminary Foundation, 1966); David Dwyer, *An Introduction to West African Pidgin English* (African Studies Center, Michigan State University, 1967).

65. The past tense markers in this series are *ben* (JMC, SRA) and *bin* (WAP), the latter having a common variant—*be*. The preverbal *a* in JMC is a modern reduction of an older *da*, obviously related historically to GUL *duh*, as well as to SRA and WAP *de*. In fact, the preverbal *a-* in some southern Negro dialects (e.g., *he a-workin'*) may well derive from just such a source, rather than from the verbal prefix *a-* of many white dialects. This seems likely in view of the fact that, in those white dialects in which such a prefix is used functionally, there is usually a contrast between its presence and its absence (e.g., **he's workin'** "he is working within view" *vs.* **he's a-workin** "he is off working somewhere"), while Negro dialects with preverbal **a-** use it like Gullah uses preverbal **duh**—for the simple durative. Finally, Gullah actually has **a** (or **uh**) as a variant of **duh**, especially after **bin**.

66. Even persons who are quite familiar with American Negro dialects may be led, by dissimilarities in word-forms, to overestimate the difference between them. For example, as keen an observer of dialect as E. C. L. Adams stated in *Nigger to Nigger* (New York: Charles Scribner's Sons, 1928), p. viii, that the speech of the Congaree Negroes of inland South Carolina was "absolutely distinct" from the coastal Gullah. Actually, the many striking syntactic similarities between the two dialects would suggest that the former is only a slightly de-creolized form of the latter. Observers of Gullah, from John Bennett on, have all remarked on how the older "pure" form of the language has been undergoing modification (i.e., de-creolization), particularly in the cities and towns. Seeing this "modified Gullah" always as a new phenomenon, they never expressed any awareness of the possibility that they might have been watching a continuation of the same process which earlier gave rise to the contemporary forms of other American Negro dialects.

67. See Thomas R. Ford, *The Southern Appalachian Region: A Survey* (Lexington: University of Kentucky Press, 1962).

68. See Jack E. Weller, *Yesterday's People: Life in Contemporary Appalachia* (Lexington: University of Kentucky Press, 1966).

69. The history of one important part of Appalachia is chronicled in Harriette Arnow, *Seedtime on the Cumberland* (New York: Macmillan, 1963).

70. For an objective discussion of archaisms in the Ozark Mountain dialect see Randolph Vance and Patti Sankee, "Dialectal Survivals in the Ozarks—Armchair Pronunciation," "Dialectal Survivals in the Ozarks—Grammatical Particularities," "Dialectal Survivals in the Ozarks—Archaic Vocabulary" *American Speech* 5 (1930): 198-208; 246-269; 424-430.

71. Dialect differences analogous to those of spoken language may also occur in written language. Such is the case with variant spellings, e.g., British *centre* and *colour,* compared with the American *center* and *color.* These are purely written dialect differences, since the different spellings have nothing to do with differences in pronunciation.

72. See Harriette Arnow, *Flowering of the Cumberland* (New York: Macmillan, 1963).

73. The network of differences and similarities between Mountain Speech and Negro Dialect, and between each of these and standard English is a complicated one. For example, Mountain Speech is usually "r-ful" (meaning that final or preconsonantal *r* is pronounced in words like *war, dark,* etc.), while Negro Dialect is generally "r-less" (meaning that no actual *r* is pronounced in such words, although the vowel may be lengthened). Both usages are acceptable in standard English, except that r-less pronunciations of words like *door, more,* must end more like *Noah* than like *no.* A somewhat different relationship holds for the possessive suffix *-s,* however. While both Mountain Speech and standard English always use the suffix in constructions of the type *John's hat,* Negro Dialect can form its equivalent, *John hat,* without the suffix. While Mountain Speech and Negro Dialect both deviate from the standard English use of the verb *to be,* they do so in different ways. For standard English *we're friends,* for example, Mountain Speech is likely to yield *we's friends,* which does have the linking verb, although in a different form from standard English in that case. But in Negro Dialect one finds an additional equivalent, *we friends,* with no linking verb at all. Of course, the foregoing are only isolated examples of the structural characteristics of the three principal varieties of Appalachian English. An understanding of the total relationship of each of these forms of English to the others can only be gained by a rather complete description and comparison of their linguistic structures. Just the same, there seems to be enough evidence to justify the conclusion that, for historical reasons, Mountain Speech is structurally somewhat closer to standard English than Negro Dialect is. Even so, there are still instances in which Negro Dialect agrees with standard English, while Mountain Speech does not.

74. See in this volume pp. 86-95. Also see McDavid and McDavid, "The Relationship of the Speech of American Negroes to the Speech of Whites."

75. The "youth reference group" mentioned by Weller *(Yesterday's People,* pp. 68-72) might appear to be an example of white mountain age-grading, but it is really a young-adult group—quite different in structure and function from the age-grades so common among younger Negro children (particularly boys). Correlated with the apparent differences in age-grading between whites and Negroes in Appalachia seems to be a difference in the importance of the family unit itself.

76. To my knowledge, this phenomenon has not yet been dealt with in any serious way, or even remarked upon by Appalachian educators. I noticed it during a recent survey of language usage in Southern Appalachia. Although my sample for that survey was small, the distribution of this phenomenon was so striking within it that I would be quite surprised should further investigation show that either its distribution or its courses were other than I suggest here.

77. The same assumptions, clothed in technological guise, underlie proposals for exposing the disadvantaged child to increasing amounts of raw output from the media (radio and television). I will merely point out that in many parts of South America, where (because of the extensive use of videotaped programs from the United States) a substantial amount of local television broadcasting is in English, there seems to be no evidence that local Spanish or Portuguese speaking viewers are learning much English from the experience. As an adjunct to carefully planned and controlled teaching techniques, the media are of immense value. Used alone, they will probably remain ineffective.

78. The meaning of the verbal prefix *a-* in Mountain Speech as stated here is only approximate. It is based entirely on my own observations, since I have not seen any previous study of this phenomenon by other linguists or dialectologists. Admittedly, the use of *a-* seems elusive when one attempts to elicit the reactions of Mountain Dialect speakers, but this elusiveness probably lies, not in any marginal function, but rather in the fact that it expresses a distinction not easily translatable into standard English.

79. Unlike the *a-* of Mountain Speech, Negro Dialect *be* does not necessarily indicate that the action is remote in space. On the other hand, Negro Dialect *be* is also used with predicated adjectives (e.g., *he be busy,* "he is habitually busy" as distinct from *he busy,* "he is busy at this moment"), while *a-* cannot be used with adjectives in Mountain Speech. Furthermore, some Appalachian Negroes seem to have both *be* and *a-,* with the latter indicating only remoteness in space. For such speakers, *he be workin'* would mean "he is habitually working close by", while *he be a-workin'* would mean "he is habitually working way off somewhere". This kind of dialect usage was not included in the sample teaching problem, since it would have complicated it unnecessarily.

80. Once, while teaching a course on the language and culture of the disadvantaged at The Johns Hopkins University, I decided to show the class how different from standard English the

speech of some Americans is by reading a story in Gullah. A particularly observant teacher who was taking the course pointed out that, when I read the Gullah story, I exhibited many of the "pocr reader" phenomena which she had seen so often when her non-standard speaking pupils tried to read a standard English text, e.g., tenseness, false starts, corrections long pauses, etc. She was absolutely right; although I am a fluent reader of standard English, I was still learning Gullah at the time, and my reading of the Gullah story was adversely affected by my lack of familiarity with the linguistic system I was trying to decode.

81. The idea, often expressed by educators who should know better, that mountaineer children do poorly in science and technology because their way of life does not prepare them for such topics, seems to be particularly absurd in view of the extent to which technological skills are evident in and disseminated by many of the traditional mountaineer crafts. See Allen H. Eaton, *Handicrafts of the Southern Highlands* (New York: Russell Sage Foundation, 1937).

82. For a more complete account see Robert P. Stockwell and J. Donald Bowen, *The Sounds of English and Spanish,* (Chicago: 1965), Daniel N. Cárdenas, *Introducseón a una comparación fonológica del español y del inglés* (Washington: 1960); also Harold V. King "Outline of Mexican Spanish Phonology" *Studies in Linguistics* 10 (1951): 51-62; Robert Lado "A Comparison of the Sound Systems of English and Spanish," *Hispania* 39 (1956): 26-29; George L. Trager "The Phonemes of Castilian Spanish," *Travaux du Cercle linguistique de Praque* 8 (1939): 217-222; Hans Wolff "Partial Comparison of the Sound Systems of English and Puerto Rican Spanish," *Language Learning* 3 (1950): 38-40 and "Phonemic Structure and the Teaching of Pronunciation," *Language Learning* 6 (1956): 17-23.

83. Morphology means the structure of words and in English this is applied to inflectional endings: (cat-cat's-cats)

(walk-walks-walked-walking) (tall-taller-tallest), derivational affixes which may be before or after the base: *able unable, quick quick-ly;* in some languages infixes are used but they are very rare in English, such as the Australian *indebloody-pendent.* An English variation is vowel change as in *gold-gild,* or vowel change with suffix *strong-strength.* Inflections like *man-men, run-ran, child-children* are special forms of affixation. The order of affixation is usually determined: *nature-natural unnatural-unnaturally (or naturally-unnaturally).* Inflections are nearly always last, "they close the construction": *accelerate-accelerator-accelerators,* but *son-in-law-sons-in-law* (at least in books!). The word components are called morphemes, which are minimum meaning units: *un-child-like, cat-s.*

Compounds are made of two independent units (morphemes or combinations) which in English have stress features setting them off from mere sequences: *sandal, wood:* sándal + wòod, *ice, cream:* ice + creàm, ice +creám. A new commercial product is called Lémon + wàx. In some dialects the secondary accent is used: bárn + yàrd or bárn + yârd.

84. *American English Grammar* (New York: 1940). See also his *The Structure of English* (New York: 1952).

For more extensive treatments of English see W. Nelson Francis, *The Structure of American English* (New York: 1958); Archibald A. Hill, *Introduction to Linguistic Structures: From Sound to Sentence in English* (New York: 1958); George L. Trager and Henry Lee Smith, Jr., *An Outline of English Structure* (Washington: 1951); H. A. Gleason, Jr., *An Introduction to Descriptive Linguistics;* Robert B. Lees, *The Grammar of English Nominalizations* (Bloomington, 1960). Of great value for the comparison of English and Spanish is Robert P. Stockwell, J. Donald Bowen, and John W. Martin, *The Grammatical Structures of English and Spanish,* as is also Robert L. Politzer and Charles N. Staubach, *Teaching Spanish* (New York: 1965).

Part II: Standard English: The Problem of Definition

85. A widely accepted definition is Professor Pooley's: "Good English is that form of speech which is appropriate to the purpose of the speaker, true to the language as it is, and comfortable to speaker and listener. It is the product of custom, neither cramped by rule nor freed from all restraint; it is never fixed, but changes with the organic life of the language." Robert C. Pooley, "Grammar and Usage in Textbooks on English," *Bulletin No. 14,* (Madison, Wisconsin: University of Wisconsin, Bureau of Educational Research, 1922).

86. Leonard Bloomfield, "Secondary and Tertiary Responses to Language," *Language* 20 (1944): 49.

87. C. S. Forester, *Plain Murder* (London: Dufour, 1951), p. 102.

88. Sheridan Baker, "The Error of *Ain't,*" *College English* 26 (1964): 91-104.

89. From a commencement address entitled "This Is Worth Fighting For," delivered at Marlboro College, Vermont, 1966, and reprinted in the Chicago *Daily News,* "Panorama," August 6, 1966.

90. J. Donald Adams, "Does Anyone Know What Creative Writing Is?" *Saturday Review,* September 18, 1965, p. 23.

91. Quoted by Mario Pei in *Saturday Review,* July 21, 1962, p. 44.

92. All these linguistic animadversions occur in a review of George F. Kennan's *The West Under Lenin and Stalin* in the *New Yorker,* September 9, 1961, p. 141.

93. Quoted from the San Francisco *Chronicle* in the *New Yorker,* April 12, 1962, p. 90.

94. "But What's a Dictionary For?" *The Atlantic Monthly,* May, 1962, p. 62.

95. October 21, 1961, p. 196. I have used this citation and the following ones from Dorothy Parker and Clifton Fadiman in "The New Fowler," *Sewanee Review* 74 (Spring, 1966): 540-44.

96. *Esquire,* September 1961, p. 34.

97. F. G. Fowler, *Dictionary of Modern English Usage,* 1st ed. (Oxford: Oxford University Press, 1940), p. 381.

98. Henry Sweet, *The Sounds of English* (Oxford: Oxford University Press, 1910), p. 78.

99. S. A. Leonard and H. Y. Moffett, *English Journal* 26, 5 (May 1967): 345-359.

100. George Philip Krapp, *The Knowledge of English* (New York: Charles Scribners, 1927), pp. 55-76.

101. Arthur G. Kennedy, *Current English* (Boston: Little Brown Company, 1935) pp. 15-17.

102. Porter G. Perrin, *An Index to English* (Chicago: University of Chicago Press, 1930), pp. 364-365.

103. George Philip Krapp, *A Comprehensive Guide to Good English* (New York: Charles Scribner, 1927), p. 641.

104. H. L. Mencken, *The American Language* 4th ed. (New York: Alfred A. Knopf, 1938), p. 203.

105. Kennedy, *Current English,* p. 26.

106. *English Journal* 16 (May, 1927): 345-59.

Part III: Standard and Nonstandard English: Learning and Teaching Problems

107. Ruth G. Strickland, "Needed Research in Oral Language: Part I," *Elementary English,* 44 (March, 1967): 259.

108. William Labov, *The Study of Nonstandard English* (Champaign, Ill.: National Council of Teachers of English, 1970), pp. 46-47.

109. Beryl Loftman Bailey, "A Proposal for the Study of the Grammar of Negro English in New York City," in *Project Literacy Reports* (Ithaca, New York: Cornell University, 1964), p. 20.

110. Labov, *Nonstandard English,* p. 41.

111. Labov, "Negro and Puerto Rican Speech in New York City," p. 16.

112. Stewart, *Non-Standard Speech,* pp. 1-15.

113. *The Logic of the Sciences and the Humanities* (New York, 1947), p. 20.

For my views on this subject see "Some Problems of Method in Linguistics," *Studium Generale* 5 (August 1952): 437-443.

114. *The Structure of English: An Introduction to the Construction of English Sentences* (N.Y.: Harcourt, Brace & World, 1952).

I myself am not convinced that this work, which considers English almost completely in oral terms, which is based on behavioristic psychology, which plays down the basic characteristic of language—meaning—and which introduces categories as complicated and probably as inconsistent as the present system is really what we need. The book, however, has opened new perspectives in the practical analysis of our language and is an important contribution to its understanding. However, some kind of prescriptionist commitment such as I am advocating here is not tied to any particular type of language analysis—even the traditional one.

115. For front page news in the literary sense, see for example *The Wall Street Journal*, January 19, 1966, which featured an account of several current programs and approaches in standard English as a second dialect.

116. Martin Joos, "Language and the School Child," *Word Study* 11, 2 (December 1964).

117. Marjorie Wescott Barrows, *Good English Through Practice* (New York: Henry Holt, 1956).

118. Ruth I. Golden, *Improving Patterns of Language Usage* (Detroit: Wayne University Press, 1960).

119. San-su C. Lin, *Pattern Practice in the Teaching of Standard English to Students With a Non-Standard Dialect* (New York: Teachers College Press, 1965).

120. *Ibid.*

121. *Ibid.*

122. *Ibid.*

123. San-su C. Lin, "An Experiment in Changing Dialect Patterns: The Chaflin Project," *College English* (May 1963): 644-647.

124. Lin, *Pattern Practice in Teaching Standard English*, p. 8.

125. *Ibid.*, p. 47.

126. *Ibid.*, p. 145.

127. Stewart, *Non-Standard Speech*, p. 11.

128. William R. Slager, "Effecting Change Through Oral Drill," *English Journal* 56, 8 (November 1967): 1167.

129. William S. Carroll, "A Teaching Experiment," *TESOL Quarterly* 1, 3 (September 1967): 31-36.

130. Lin, *Pattern Practice in Teaching Standard English*, p. 41

131. Ruth I. Golden, *Effectiveness of Instructional Tapes for Changing Regional Speech Patterns*, doctoral dissertation, Wayne State University 1963, pp. 10-11.

132. Lin, *op. cit.*, p. 43.

133. For a discussion of the pedagogical use of nonstandard English, see Irwin Feigenbaum, "The Use of Nonstandard English in Teaching Standard: Contrast and Comparison" in Ralph W. Fasold and Roger W. Shuy, eds., *Teaching Standard English in the Inner-City* (Washington, D.C.: Center for Applied Linguistics, 1970).

134. Lin, *op. cit.*, p. 8.

135. Richard Corbin and Muriel Crosby, co-chairmen, *Language Programs for the Disadvantaged* (Champaign, Ill.: NCTE, 1965), p. 70.

136. In the midst of a narrative of events in the past, when the "past time" has been clearly established, we may find *Yesterday we wait around*. This is only one situation in which we may not find an overt marking of the past tense in the nonstandard. Others may exist, but they are still being investigated by linguistics.

137. From Shuy, ed., *Social Dialects and Language Learning*, pp. 122-123.

138. Murray Wax, Rosalie Wax, and Robert Dumont, "Formal Education in an American Indian Community," *Social Problems* (Spring 1969): 82.

139. Wayne A. O'Neil, "Paul Roberts' Rules of Order: The Misuses of Linguistics in the Classroom," in *The Urban Review* II, 7.

140. Mortimer Smith, "The New English," *Bulletin of the Council for Basic Education* 13, 1 (September, 1968): 4.

141. Lin, *Pattern Practice in Teaching Standard English*, p. 1.

142. These materials were developed

as part of the Sociolinguistics Program at The Center For Applied Linguistics under funding from the Carnegie Corporation of New York. The author, Irwin Feigenbaum, developed these materials in the Washington, D.C. schools over a period of two years. They have been published by Appleton-Century-Crofts under the title *English Now*.

143. Wallace A. Lambert, "A Social Psychology of Bilingualism," *The Journal of Social Issues* 23, 2 (April 1967) refers to the results of his Tougaloo University study which gave these results. Stewart's treatments of the subject have been given in public lectures. For study of relatively low prestige for older regional dialects, see e.g., William Labov, "The Reflection of Social Processes in Social Structures," in Joshua A. Fishman, ed., *Readings in the Sociology of Language*.

144. A statement of this type is made by Raven I. McDavid, Jr., in "Dialectology and the Teaching of Reading," in *Teaching Black Children to Read*, Baratz and Shuy, eds. (Washington, D.C., 1969). The statement "there is no regional variety of speech that has established itself as prestigious" (p. 4) seems almost like a deliberate attempt to confuse the issue. More likely, however, it simply reflects the fact that American linguistic geography is the only surviving branch of American Structuralism—a thoroughly outmoded approach to linguistics. See also, for example, Joshua A. Fishman, "Sociolinguistics," in *Social Psychology*, Kurt Black, ed.

145. The traditional view, reflected in many general works like W. P. Lehmann, *Historical Linguistics* (1962), is "Lacking the speech of a long-established political center like Paris or Florence, the accepted standard (for German) was fixed only at the end of the nineteenth century. The pronunciation was based on that of the stage." (p. 36). There are several ways in which such a statement may be misleading. The first is that the geography function ("center") of Paris or of Florence may be taken as more important than other factors ("political"). The second is that it might be assumed that German, unable to fulfill a kind of

"natural" function of language, is forced to a makeshift—deprived of its geographic locus for a standard dialect, it is forced to less desirable expedients. There is, of course, no evidence for this interpretation. In fact, a wide array of evidence from various languages of the world leads one to believe that it is the geographic locus itself which is accidental and relatively unimportant in the formation of a *koine* or standard dialect; that the social factors leading to a consensus dialect are the substantial considerations.

146. Haim Blanc, "The Israeli Koine as an Emergent National Standard." See also Blanc's *Communal Dialects in Baghdad Arabic* for an exposition of non-geographically (and non-spatially) influenced dialect variation, quite apart from the question of a *koine* or a consensus standard.

147. My chapter "The Negro Dialect and Southern Dialect" in *Black English in the United States* gives many examples in terms of citations from journals and other writings of the period.

148. Sir Charles Lyell, *A Second Visit to the United States of North America* (1849), 11, 20. A letter to Forster (April 15, 1842) specifies that ". . . all the women who have been bred in slave-states speak more or less like Negroes, from having been constantly in their childhood with black nurses . . ."

149. Fanny Kemble, *Journal of a Residence on a Southern Plantation*, pp. 210-211, is one of many who attest to this relationship.

150. See Gerard Hoffman, "Puerto Ricans in New York: A Language-Related Ethnographic Summary," in Joshua A. Fishman, ed., *Bilingualism in the Barrio*, U. S. Office of Education, Contract No. OEC-1-7-062817-0297, p. 34.

151. Especially Stewart, "Non-Standard Speech," pp. 1-15. Kenneth Johnson's University of Southern California dissertation (1968) reports positive results from a test of such a method against a control group taught by conventional methods.

152. Stewart, "Urban Negro Speech."

153. Joan C. Baratz, "Teaching Reading in an Urban School System," in

Teaching Black Children to Read (Washington, D.C.: Center for Applied Linguistics, 1969).

154. Joshua A. Fishman, "Sociolinguistics," in *Social Psychology,* Kurt W. Black, ed.

155. Harold B. Allen, "On Accepting Participial Drank," *College English* 18 (February 1957): 283.

156. Werner F. Leopold, "The Decline of German Dialects," *Word* 15 (1959): 134-153.

157. James Sledd, "Bi-Dialectalism: The Linguistics of White Supremacy." (In this volume see pp. 319-330.)

158. Raven I. McDavid, Jr. "Dialectology and the Teaching of Reading," *The Reading Teacher* 18 (December 1964): 206-213.

159. Kenneth Goodman, "Dialect Barriers to Reading Comprehension," *Elementary English* 42 (December 1965): 853-860. In this volume, pp. 294-305.

160. Richard Venezky, "Nonstandard Language and Reading," *Elementary English* 47 (March 1970): 334-345.

161. William A. Stewart, "On the Use of Negro Dialect in the Teaching of Reading," in *Teaching Black Children to Read.*

162. William A. Stewart, *Nonstandard Speech,* pp. 1-15; Lin, *Op Cit.*

163. Susan Huston, "A Sociolinguistic Consideration of the Black English of Children in Northern Florida," *Language* 45 (1969): 599-607; Stanley E. Legum, *et. al.,* "Social Dialects and Their Implications for Beginning Reading Instruction," Southwest Regional Laboratories for Educational Research and Development, Los Angeles, June, 1969.

164. Walter A. Wolfram, "Sociolinguistic Implications for Educational Sequencing," in *Teaching Standard English in the Inner City,* Ralph Fasold and Roger W. Shuy, eds. (Washington, D.C.: Center for Applied Linguistics, 1970).

165. William Labov, *The Social Stratification of English in New York City* (Washington, D.C.: Center for Applied Linguistics, 1966); Wolfram, *A Sociolinguistic Description of Detroit Negro Speech* (Washington, D.C.: Center for Applied Linguistics, 1969).

166. Ralph Fasold and Walter A. Wolfram, "Some Linguistic Features of Negro Dialect," in *Teaching Standard English in the Inner City,* Ralph Fasold and Roger W. Shuy, eds. (Washington, D.C.: Center for Applied Linguistics, 1970).

167. *Ibid.*

168. William Labov, "Contraction, Deletion and Inherent Variability of the English Copula," *Language* 45 (1969): 715-762.

169. Walter A. Wolfram, "Reading Alternatives for Nonstandard Speakers: A Sociolinguistic Perspective," mimeographed report (Washington, D.C.: Center for Applied Linguistics, 1970).

170. This is often denied by people who claim that they can't understand a thing their students are saying. This hyperbole can be easily remedied, as I have indicated elsewhere (see Roger W. Shuy, "Teaching Training and Urban Language Problems," in *Teaching Standard English in the Inner City.*

171. Wolfram, *op. cit.*

172. *Ibid.*

173. Labov, *Social Stratification of English in New York City.*

174. Venezky, "Nonstandard Language and Reading."

175. See Labov, "Contraction, Deletion and Inherent Variability for the English Copula."

176. Hans Furth, "On Language and Knowing in Paiget's Development Theory," paper presented at the 1970 Lincolnland Dialect Conference, Charleston, Illinois, March 18, 1970.

177. Joan Baratz, "Teaching Reading in an Urban Negro School System," in *Teaching Black Children to Read.*

178. Roger W. Shuy, "Subjective Judgments in Sociolinguistic Analysis," Georgetown Monograph *Series on Languages and Linguistics* 22 (1969): 175-188.

179. Roger W. Shuy, Joan C. Baratz and Walter A. Wolfram, *Sociolinguistic Factors in Speech Identification,* National Institute of Mental Health, Research Project No. MH-15048-01 (Washington, D.C.: Center for Applied Linguistics, 1968).

180. Roger W. Shuy, "Speech and Employee Selection, Training and Pro-

motion Pitfalls of Good Intentions," paper presented at the C.A.L.–N.C.T.E. Conference, Education and Training in the National Interest: The Role of Language Variety, Washington, D.C., February 14, 1970.

181. Roger W. Shuy, "A Linguistic Background for Developing Beginning Reading Materials for Black Children," in *Teaching Black Children to Read*.

Acknowledgments

"A Brief History of the English Language" by Morton W. Bloomfield is reprinted with permission from *The American Heritage Dictionary of the English Language* ©Copyright 1969, 1970 by the American Heritage Publishing Company, Inc.

"Dialects" by Jean Malmstrom is reprinted with the permission of the *Florida FL Reporter* and Jean Malmstrom from the special anthology issue entitled, *Linguistic-Cultural Differences and American Education* 7, 1 (Spring/Summer 1969): 47-49, 168, Alfred C. Aarons, Barbara Y. Gordon, and William A. Stewart editors. This article is an updated version of "Dialects" which first appeared in the Winter 66-67 issue of the *Florida FL Reporter*.

"The Principal Dialect Areas of the United States" by Raven I. McDavid, Jr., is reprinted with permission from *The Structure of American English* by W. Nelson Francis. Copyright © 1958 by The Ronald Press Company, New York.

"Some Social Differences in Pronunciation" by Raven I. McDavid, Jr., is reprinted with permission of *Language Learning* and Raven I. McDavid, Jr., from *Language Learning* 4 (1952-53): 102-116.

"Some Linguistic Features of Negro Dialect" by Ralph W. Fasold and Walter Wolfram is reprinted with the permission of authors and publisher from *Teaching Standard English in the Inner City*, edited by Ralph W. Fasold and Roger W. Shuy (Washington, D.C.: Center for Applied Linguistics, 1970), pp. 41-86.

"Sociolinguistic Factors in the History of American Negro Dialects" by William A. Stewart is reprinted with the permission of the *Florida FL Reporter* and William A. Stewart from Vol. 5, No. 2 (Spring 1967): 11, 22, 24, 26, 30, Alfred C. Aarons, editor.

"Continuity and Change in American Negro Dialects" by William A. Stewart is reprinted with the permission of the *Florida FL Reporter* and William A. Stewart from Vol. 6., No. 1 (Spring 1968): 3-4, 14-16, 18, Alfred C. Aarons, editor.

"Language and Communication Problems in Southern Appalachia" by William A. Stewart is reprinted with the permission of the author. Stewart prepared this report while at the Center for Applied Linguistics for the Appalachian Educational Laboratory, Inc., Charleston, West Virginia.

"English Problems of Spanish Speakers" by A. L. Davis is reprinted with the permission of the Bureau of Research, U.S. Office of Education and A. L. Davis.

"Sense and Nonsense About American Dialects" by Raven I. McDavid, Jr., is reprinted by permission of the Modern Language Association and Raven I. McDavid, Jr. from *PMLA* 81 (May 1966): 7-17.

"Cultural Levels and Functional Varieties of English" by John S. Kenyon was published in *College English* 10 (October 1948): 31-36. Reprinted by permission of the National Council of Teachers of English and the George Wahr Publishing Company.

"English Usage: The Views of the Literati" by Thomas Pyles was published in *College English* 28 (March 1967): 449-454. Reprinted by permission of the National Council of Teachers of English and Thomas Pyles.

"The Gentlemen's Guide to Linguistic Etiquette" by Patrick E. Kilburn was first published in *Union College Symposium* 9 (Spring 1970): 2-6. Reprinted with the permission of Union College, Schenectady, New York, and Patrick E. Kilburn.

"Standards in the Community Language" by Martin Joos was first published in *The National Elementary Principal* 45 (September 1965): 26-33. Reprinted with permission of the National Association of Elementary School Principals, NEA, and Martin Joos.

"Dimensions of English Usage" by David DeCamp is from *Reflections on High School English,* Gary Tate, editor, copyright 1966 by the University of Tulsa. Reprinted with the permission of the University of Tulsa and David De-Camp.

"The Problem of Fact and Value in the Teaching of English" by Morton W. Bloomfield is from *College English* 5 (October 1953): 33-37. Reprinted with the permission of the National Council of Teachers of English and Morton W. Bloomfield.

"Prescriptivism and Linguistics in English Teaching" by Archibald A. Hill is from *College English* 15 (April 1954): 395-399. Reprinted with the permission of the National Council of Teachers of English and Archibald A. Hill.

"Teaching Standard English as a Second Dialect," by Virginia F. Allen was first published in *The Teachers College Record* 68 (February 1967): 355-370. Reprinted with the permission of Teachers College, Columbia University and Virginia F. Allen.

"Using Foreign Language Methodology to Teach Standard English: Evaluation and Adaptation" by Irwin Feigenbaum is reprinted with the permission of the *Florida FL Reporter* and Irwin Feigenbaum from the special anthology issue entitled, *Linguistic-Cultural Differences and American Education* 7, 1 (Spring/ Summer 1969): 116-122, 156-157, Alfred C. Aarons, Barbara Y. Gordon and William A. Stewart, editors.

"Bonnie and Clyde Tactics in English Teaching" by Roger W. Shuy is reprinted with the permission of the *Florida FL Reporter* and Roger Shuy from the special anthology issue entitled, *Linguistic-Cultural Differences and American Education* 7, 1 (Spring/Summer 1969): 81-83, 160-161, Alfred C. Aarons, Barbara Y. Gordon William A. Stewart, editors.

"How to Tell the Bandits from the Good Guys, or What Dialect to Teach?" by J. L. Dillard is reprinted with the permission of the *Florida FL Reporter* and J. L. Dillard from the special anthology issue entitled, *Linguistic-Cultural Differences and American Education* 7, 1 (Spring/Summer 1969): 84-85, 162, Alfred C. Aarons, Barbara Y. Gordon and William A. Stewart, editors.

"Dialect Barriers to Reading Comprehension" by Kenneth S. Goodman is from *Elementary English* 42 (December 1965): 853-860. Reprinted with the permission of the National Council of Teachers of English and Kenneth S. Goodman.

"English and the Bilingual Child" by Rudolph C. Troike is printed here for the first time with the permission of Rudolph C. Troike.

"Bi-Dialectalism: The Language of White Supremacy" by James Sledd is reprinted from *English Journal* 58 (December 1969): 1307-1315, with the permission of the National Council of Teachers of English and James Sledd.

"Speech Differences and Teaching Strategies: How Different is Enough?" by Roger W. Shuy is from *Language and Learning to Read: What Teachers Should Know About Language,* to be published by Houghton Mifflin Company early in 1972, © HMCo, Boston, Massachusetts. Reprinted with the permission of the publisher and Roger W. Shuy.

A Selected Bibliography

BIBLIOGRAPHIES

Aarons, Alfred C. "TESOL Bibliography." *The Florida FL Reporter* 3 (Spring 1965).

Allen, Harold B. *Linguistics and English Linguistics.* New York: Appleton-Century-Crofts, 1966.

ERIC Clearinghouse for Linguistics. *A Preliminary Bibliography of American English Dialects.* Washington, D.C.: Center for Applied Linguistics, 1969.

Hoffman, Melvin A. "English and the Culturally Deprived: A Bibliography." In *Communication Barriers to the Culturally Deprived,* edited by Raven I. McDavid, Jr., and William M. Austin. Cooperative Research Project 2107. Washington, D.C.: U.S. Office of Education, 1966.

Shuy, Roger W. "A Selective Bibliography on Social Dialects." *The Linguistic Reporter* 10 (June 1968) : 1-5.

Tarone, Elaine. *A Selected Annotated Bibliography on Social Dialects for Teachers of Speech and English.* Seattle: University of Washington, Speech Science Laboratories, 1970.

Williams, Frederick and Rita C. Naremore. "An Annotated Bibliography of Journal Articles." In *Language and Poverty,* edited by Frederick Williams. Chicago: Markham Publishing Company, 1970.

———. *Language and Poverty: An Annotated Bibliography.* Madison: The University of Wisconsin, Institute for Research on Poverty, 1968.

COLLECTIONS

Aarons, Alfred C.; Barbara Y. Gordon; and William A. Stewart, eds. *Linguistic-Cultural Differences and American Education.* A Special Anthology Issue. *The Florida FL Reporter* 7 (Spring/Summer 1969).

Alatis, James E., ed. "Linguistics and the Teaching of Standard English to Speakers of Other Languages and Dialects." 20th Annual Round Table. *Monograph Series on Languages and Linguistics*, No. 22. Washington, D.C.: Georgetown University Press, 1970.

Allen, Harold B., ed. *Readings in Applied English Linguistics.* Rev. ed. New York: Appleton-Century-Crofts, 1964.

Baratz, Joan C. and Roger W. Shuy, eds. *Teaching Black Children to Read.* Washington, D.C.: Center for Applied Linguistics, 1969.

Corbin, Richard and Muriel Crosby, eds. *Language Programs for the Disadvantaged.* Champaign, Ill.: National Council of Teachers of English, 1965.

Davis, A. L., ed. *On the Dialects of Children.* Champaign, Ill.: National Council of Teachers of English, 1968.

———, et al. *Language Resource Information for Teachers of the Culturally Disadvantaged.* USOE Project 6-1340. Final Report. Washington, D.C.: U.S. Office of Education, 1969. (To be published by the National Council of Teachers of English under the title of *Culture, Class and Language Variety: A Resource Book for Teachers.*)

Evertts, Eldonna L., ed. *Dimensions of Dialect.* Champaign, Ill.: National Council of Teachers of English, 1967.

Fagan, Edward R., ed. *English and the Disadvantaged.* Scranton, Pa.: International Textbook Company, 1969.

Fasold, Ralph W. and Roger W. Shuy, eds. *Teaching Standard English in the Inner City.* Washington, D.C.: Center for Applied Linguistics, 1970.

Frazier, Alexander, ed. *New Directions in Elementary English.* Champaign, Ill.: National Council of Teachers of English, 1967.

Gunderson, Doris V., ed. *Language and Reading: An Interdisciplinary Approach.* Washington, D.C.: Center for Applied Linguistics, 1970.

Hill, Archibald A., ed. *Linguistics Today.* New York: Basic Books, 1969.

Horn, Thomas D., ed. *Reading for the Disadvantaged: Problems of Linguistically Different Learners.* New York: Harcourt, Brace, Jovanovich, 1970.

Hungerford, Harold; Jay Robinson; and James Sledd. *English Linguistics.* Glenview, Ill.: Scott, Foresman and Company, 1970.

Marckwardt, Albert H., ed. *Language and Language Learning.* Champaign, Ill.: National Council of Teachers of English, 1968.

McDavid, Raven I., Jr. and William M. Austin., eds. *Communication Barriers to the Culturally Deprived.* Cooperative Research Project 2107. Washington, D.C.: U.S. Office of Education, 1966.

Shuy, Roger W., ed. *Social Dialects and Language Learning.* Champaign, Ill.: National Council of Teachers of English, 1964.

Sledd, James and Wilma R. Ebbitt, eds. *Dictionaries and That Dictionary.* Chicago: Scott, Foresman and Company, 1962.

Stewart, William A., ed. *Non-Standard Speech and the Teaching of English.* Washington, D.C.: Center for Applied Linguistics, 1964.

Walden, James, ed. *Oral Language and Reading.* Champaign, Ill.: National Council of Teachers of English, 1969.

Williams, Frederick, ed. *Language and Poverty: Perspectives on a Theme.* Chicago: Markham Publishing Company, 1970.

THE ENGLISH LANGUAGE AND LINGUISTICS

Bolinger, Dwight. *Aspects of Language.* New York: Harcourt, Brace and World, 1968.

Bronstein, Arthur J. *The Pronunciation of American English.* New York: Appleton-Century-Crofts, 1960.

Dinneen, Francis P. *An Introduction to General Linguistics.* New York: Holt, Rinehart and Winston, 1967.

Francis, W. Nelson. *The English Language: An Introduction.* New York: W. W. Norton and Company, 1965.

Gleason, H. A., Jr. *Linguistics and English Grammar.* New York: Holt, Rinehart and Winston, 1965.

Hall, Robert A., Jr. *Introductory Linguistics.* Philadelphia: Chilton Book Company, 1964.

———. *Linguistics and Your Language.* Garden City, N.Y.: Doubleday and Company, 1950.

Herndon, Jeanne. *A Survey of Modern Grammar.* New York: Holt, Rinehart and Winston, 1969.

Langacker, Ronald W. *Language and Its Structure.* New York: Harcourt, Brace and World, 1968.

Langendoen, D. Terence. *The Study of Syntax.* New York: Holt, Rinehart and Winston, 1969.

Lehmann, Winfred P. *Historical Linguistics: An Introduction.* New York: Holt, Rinehart and Winston, 1962.

Pyles, Thomas. *Words and Ways of American English.* New York: Random House, 1952.

———, and John Algeo. *English: An Introduction to Language.* New York: Harcourt, Brace, Jovanovich, 1970.

Sapir, Edward. *Language.* New York: Harcourt, Brace and World, 1921.

Stevick, Robert D. *English and Its History.* Boston: Allyn and Bacon, 1968.

USAGE AND STANDARDS

Bloomfield, Leonard. "Literate and Illiterate Speech." *American Speech* 2 (1927): 432-439.

————. "Secondary and Tertiary Responses to Language." *Language* 20 (1944): 45-55.

Bryant, Margaret. *Current American Usage.* New York: Funk and Wagnalls, 1962.

Fries, Charles C. *American English Grammar.* New York: Appleton-Century-Crofts, 1940.

Gove, Philip B. "Telling the Truth About Words." *Word Study* 43 (1968): 1-8.

————. Usage in the Dictionary." *College English* 27 (1966): 285-292.

Hall, J. Leslie. *English Usage.* Chicago: Scott, Foresman and Company, 1917.

Hartung, Charles. "Doctrines of English Usage." *English Journal* 45 (1956): 517-525.

————. "The Persistence of Tradition in Grammar." *Quarterly Journal of Speech* 48 (1962): 174-186.

Heller, Louis B. and James Macris. "English Usage and Modern Linguistic Theory." *American Speech* 42 (1967): 131-135.

Ives, Sumner. "Grammar and the Academic Conscience." *College English* 24 (1962): 98-101.

Joos, Martin. *The Five Clocks.* New York: Harcourt, Brace and World, 1967.

Kenyon, John S. and Thomas A. Knott. *A Pronouncing Dictionary of American English.* Springfield: G. & C. Merriam Company, 1944.

Kilburn, Patrick E. "Labeling the Language." *Word Study* 44 (1968): 1-7.

Knott, Thomas. "Standard English and Incorrect English." *American Speech* 9 (1934): 83-89.

Leonard, Sterling A. *The Doctrine of Correctness in English Usage, 1700-1800.* Madison: University of Wisconsin, 1929.

Marckwardt, Albert H. "Dictionaries and the English Language." *English Journal* 52 (1963): 336-345.

————, and Fred Walcott. *Facts About Current Usage.* Champaign, Ill.: National Council of Teachers of English, 1938.

Perrin, Porter G. *Writer's Guide and Index to English.* 4th ed. Glenview, Ill.: Scott, Foresman and Company, 1965.

Pooley, Robert C. *Teaching English Usage.* New York: Appleton-Century-Crofts, 1946.

Quirk, Randolph. *The Use of English.* 2nd ed. New York: St. Martin's Press, 1968.

Reed, Allen W. "American Projects for an Academy to Regulate Speech." *PMLA* 51 (1936): 1141-1179.

Strevens, P.D. "Varieties of English." *English Studies* 45 (1964): 20-30.

The American Heritage Dictionary of The English Language. New York: American Heritage Publishing Company and Houghton-Mifflin, 1969.

Webster's Third New International Dictionary of the English Language, Unabridged. Springfield, Mass.: G. & C. Merriam Company, 1961.

LANGUAGE VARIATION

Atwood, E. Bagby. *A Survey of Verb Forms of the Eastern United States.* Ann Arbor: University of Michigan Press, 1953.
———. "The Methods of American Dialectology." *Zeitzchrift für Mundartforschung* 30 (1963): 1-30.
———. *The Regional Vocabulary of Texas.* Austin: University of Texas, 1962.
Bailey, Beryl L. *Jamaican Creole Syntax.* New York: Cambridge University Press, 1966.
———. "Toward a New Perspective in Negro English Dialectology." *American Speech* 60 (1965): 171-177.
Barker, George C. "Social Functions of Language in a Mexican-American Community." *Acta Americana* 5 (1947): 185-202.
Berrey, Lester V. "Southern Mountain Dialect." *American Speech* 15 (1940): 45-54.
Davis, Lawrence M. "Dialect Research: Mythology vs. Reality." *Orbis* 18 (1969): 332-337.
———. "Social Dialectology in America: A Critical Survey." *Journal of English Linguistics* 4 (1970): 46-56.
Dillard, J. L. "Non-Standard Negro Dialects—Convergence or Divergence?" *The Florida FL Reporter* 6 (Fall 1968).
———. "Principles in the History of American English—Paradox, Virginity, and Cafeteria." *The Florida FL Reporter* 8 (Spring/Fall 1970): 32-33, 46.
———. "The DARE-ing Old Men on their Flying Isoglosses or, Dialectology and Dialect Geography." *The Florida FL Reporter* 7 (Fall 1969): 8-10, 22.
Erickson, F. "'F Get You Honky! A New Look at Black Dialect and the School." *Elementary English* 46 (1969): 495-517.
Ferguson, Charles A. "Diglossia." *Word* 15 (1959): 325-340.
Fisher, John L. "Social Influences on the Choice of a Linguistic Variant." *Word* 14 (1958): 47-56.
Fishman, Joshua. "Sociolinguistics." *The Florida FL Reporter* 8 (Spring/Fall 1970): 40-42, 52.
Gumperz, John T. "Dialect Differences and Social Stratification in a North Indian Village." *American Anthropologist* 60 (1958): 668-682.
Hall, Robert A., Jr. *Pidgin and Creole Languages.* New York: Cornell University Press, 1966.
Houston, Susan. "A Sociolinguistic Consideration of the Black English of Children in Northern Florida." *Language* 45 (1969): 599-607.
Ives, Sumner. "Pronounciation of *Can't* in the Eastern States." *American Speech* 28 (1953): 149-157.
Krapp, George P. *The English Language in America.* 2 Vols. New York: The Century Company, 1925.
Kurath, Hans. "Area Linguistics in the U.S.A." *Orbis* 11 (1962): 57-60.

——. *A Word Geography of the Eastern United States.* Ann Arbor: University of Michigan Press, 1949.

——. "The Origin of Dialectal Differences in Spoken American English." *Modern Philology* 25 (1928): 385-395.

——, and Raven I. McDavid, Jr. *The Pronunciation of English in the Atlantic States.* Ann Arbor: University of Michigan Press, 1961.

Labov, William. "The Logic of Nonstandard English." 20th Annual Round Table. *Monograph Series on Languages and Linguistics,* no. 22, edited by James E. Alatis. Washington, D.C.: Georgetown University Press, 1969.

——. "The Social Motivation of a Sound Change." *Word* 19 (1963): 273-309.

——. *The Social Stratification of English in New York City.* Washington, D.C.: Center for Applied Linguistics, 1966.

Levine, William L. and H. J. Crockett. "Speech Variation in a Piedmont Community: Postvocalic *r*." *Sociological Inquiry* 36 (1966): 204-226.

Marckwardt, Albert H. *American English.* New York: Oxford University Press, 1959.

Maurer, David W. "The Importance of Social Dialects." *Newsletter of the American Dialect Society* 1 (June 1969): 1-8.

McDavid, Raven I., Jr. "American English Dialects." In *The Structure of American English* by W. Nelson Francis. New York: Ronald Press Company, 1958.

——. "American Social Dialects." *College English* 26 (1965): 254-260.

——. "Dialect Differences and Inter-group Tensions." *Studies in Linguistics* 9 (1951): 27-33.

——. "Dialect Geography and Social Science Problems." *Social Forces* 25 (1946): 168-172.

——. "Historical, Regional, and Social Variations." *Journal of English Linguistics* 1 (1967): 25-40.

——. "Postvocalic -*r* in South Carolina: A Social Analysis." *American Speech* 23 (1948): 194-203.

——. "Variations in Standard American English." *Elementary English* 45 (1968): 561-564, 608.

——, and Virginia Glenn McDavid. "The Relationship of the Speech of American Negroes to the Speech of Whites." *American Speech* 26 (1951): 3-17.

Mencken, H. L. *The American Language.* Abridged by Raven I. McDavid, Jr., with the assistance of David W. Maurer. New York: Alfred A. Knopf, 1963.

Pederson, Lee A. "The Pronunciation of English in Metropolitan Chicago." *Publications of American Dialect Society,* no. 44 (1965).

Pickford, Glenna R. "American Linguistic Geography: A Sociological Appraisal." *Word* 12 (1956): 211-235.

Reed, Allen W. "The Speech of Negroes in Colonial America." *Journal of Negro History* 24 (1939): 247-258.

Reed, Carroll E. *Dialects of American English.* Cleveland: World Publishing Company, 1967.

Reed, David W. "Establishing and Evaluating Social Boundaries in English." In *Studies in Language and Linguistics in Honor of Charles C. Fries,* edited by Albert H. Marckwardt, pp. 241-248. Ann Arbor: University of Michigan, The English Language Institute, 1964.

Shuy, Roger W. *Discovering American Dialects.* Champaign, Ill.: National Council of Teachers of English, 1967.

————, Walter A. Wolfram and William K. Riley. *Field Techniques in an Urban Language Study.* Washington, D.C.: Center for Applied Linguistics, 1968.

Sledd, James. "Breaking, Umlaut and the Southern Drawl." *Language* 42 (1966): 18-41.

Spencer, John. "The Anglo-Indians and their Speech: A Socio-linguistic Essay." *Lingua* 16 (1966).

Turner, Lorenzo D. *Africanisms in the Gullah Dialect.* Chicago: University of Chicago Press, 1949.

Williamson, Juanita V. "A Phonological and Morphological Study of the Speech of the Negro of Memphis, Tennessee." *Publications of American Dialect Society,* no. 50 (1968).

Wolfram, Walter A. *A Sociolinguistic Description of Detroit Negro Speech.* Washington, D.C.: Center for Applied Linguistics, 1970.

Wood, Gordon R. "Dialect Contours in the Southern States." *American Speech* 38 (1963): 243-256.

APPLICATIONS

Abercrombie, David. "The Social Basis of Language." *English Language Teaching* 3 (1948): 1-11.

Abrahams, Roger D. "The Advantages of Black English." *The Florida FL Reporter* 8 (1970): 27-30, 51.

Allen, Robert L.; Virginia F. Allen; and Margaret Shute. *English Sounds and Their Spellings.* New York: Thomas Y. Crowell Company, 1966.

Allen, Virginia F. "Some Strategies for Teaching Standard English as a Second Dialect." Tallahassee, Fla.: Spring Institute on Teaching English as a Second Language and as a Second Dialect, February 16, 1970.

Anderson, Lorena A. "Reading in Appalachia." *The Reading Teacher* (1967): 303-06, 312.

Bailey, Beryl L. "Some Arguments Against the Use of Dialect Readers in the Teaching of Initial Reading." *The Florida FL Reporter* 8 (1970): 8, 47.

———. "Some Aspects of the Impact of Linguistics on Language Teaching in Disadvantaged Communities." *Elementary English* 45 (1968): 570-578.

Baratz, Joan C. "Linguistic and Cultural Factors in Teaching Reading to Ghetto Children." *Elementary English* 46 (1969): 199-203.

Bernstein, Basil. "Language and Social Class." *British Journal of Sociology* 11 (1960): 271-276.

Brooks, Charlotte K. "Some Approaches to Teaching Standard English as a Second Language." *Elementary English* 41 (1964): 728-733.

Burling, Robbins. "Standard Colloquial and Standard Written English: Some Implications for Teaching Literacy to Nonstandard Speakers." *The Florida FL Reporter* 8 (1970): 9-11.

Carroll, William and Irwin Feigenbaum. "Teaching a Second Dialect and Some Implications for TESOL." *TESOL Quarterly* 1 (1967): 31-39.

Ching, Doris C. "Methods for the Bilingual Child." *Elementary English* 42 (1965): 22-27.

Cook, Mary Jane and Margaret Sharp. "Problems of Navajo Speakers in Learning English." *Language Learning* 16 (1966): 21-30.

Davis, A. L. "Dialect Research and the Needs of the Schools." *Elementary English* 45 (1968): 558-559.

Dillard, J. L. "Negro Children's Dialect in the Inner City." *The Florida FL Reporter* 5 (1967): 7-10.

———. "The English Teacher and the Language of the Newly Integrated Student." *Teachers College Record* 69 (1967): 115-120.

Feigenbaum, Irwin. "Developing Fluency in Standard Oral English." *Elementary English* 47 (1970): 1053-1059.

———. *English Now.* New York: New Century, 1970.

Fishman, Joshua. "Bilingualism, Intelligence and Language Learning." *Modern Language Journal* 49 (1965): 227-236.

Ford, Nick Aaron. "Improving Reading and Writing Skills of Disadvantaged College Freshman." *College Composition and Communication* 28 (1967).

Golden, Ruth I. *Effectiveness of Instructional Tapes for Changing Regional Dialects.* Detroit: Board of Education, 1963.

———. *Improving Patterns of Language Usage.* Detroit: Wayne State University Press, 1960.

Graham, Richard T., and E. Hugh Rudorf. "Dialect and Spelling." *Elementary English* 47 (1970): 363-376.

Green, G. "Negro Dialect, The Last Barrier to Integration." *Journal of Negro Education* 31 (1962): 81-83.

Hernandez, L. F. "Teaching English to the Culturally Disadvantaged Mexican-American Student." *English Journal* 57 (1968): 87-92.

Johnson, Kenneth R. *Teaching Culturally Disadvantaged Pupils.* Chicago: Science Research Associates, 1968.

Kurath, Hans. "Area Linguistics and the Teacher of English." *Language Learning.* Special issue no. 2 (1961): 9-14.

Labov, William. "A Note on the Relation of Reading Failure to Peer Group Status." *Teachers College Record* 70 (1969): 395-405.

———. "Some Sources of Reading Problems for Negro Speakers of Non-standard English." In *New Directions in Elementary English,* edited by Alexander Frazier. Champaign, Ill.: National Council of Teachers of English, 1967.

———. "Stages in the Acquisition of Standard English." In *Social Dialects and Language Learning,* edited by Roger W. Shuy, pp. 77-103. Champaign, Ill.: National Council of Teachers of English, 1965.

———. *The Study of Non-standard English.* Champaign, Ill.: National Council of Teachers of English, 1970.

Lefevre, Carl A. *Linguistics and the Teaching of Reading.* New York: McGraw-Hill Book Company, 1964.

Lin, San-su C. *Pattern Practice in the Teaching of English to Students with a Nonstandard Dialect.* New York: Bureau of Publications, Teachers College, Columbia University, 1965.

———. "Experiment in Changing Dialect Patterns: The Claflin Project." *College English* 24 (1963): 644-47.

Loflin, Marvin D. "A Teaching Problem in Nonstandard Negro English." *English Journal* 46 (1967): 1312-1314.

McDavid, Raven I., Jr. "Dialectology and the Teaching of Reading." *The Reading Teacher* 18 (1964): 206-13.

———. "Social Dialects and Professional Responsibility." *College English* 30 (1969): 381-385.

———. "The Cultural Matrix of American English." *Elementary English* 42 (1965): 13-21.

McDowell, Neil A. *A Study of the Academic Capabilities and Achievements of Three Ethnic Groups: Anglo, Negro and Spanish Surnames, in San Antonio, Texas.* Austin: The University of Texas, 1966.

Mellan, Olivia. "Black English: Why Try to Eradicate it?" *New Republic,* November 28, 1970, pp. 15-17.

Nonstandard Dialect. Champaign, Ill.: National Council of Teachers of English, 1968.

Ohannessian, Sirapi. *A Study of the Problems of Teaching English to American Indians: Report and Recommendations.* Washington, D.C.: Center for Applied Linguistics, 1967.

Peisach, E. Cherry. "Children's Comprehension of Teacher and Peer Speech." *Child Development* 30 (1965): 467-80.

Ramsey, Wallace. "Reading in Appalachia." *The Reading Teacher* 21 (1967): 57-63.

Randolph, Vance and Anna A. Inglemann. "Pronunciation in the Ozark Dialect." *American Speech* 3 (1928): 401-407.

Raspberry, William. "Should Ghettoese Be Accepted?" *Today's Education* 59 (1970): 30-31, 61-62.

Reed, David W. "A Theory of Language, Speech, and Writing." *Elementary English* 42 (1965): 845-851.

Rosenthal, R. and Lenore Jacobson. *Pygmalion in the Classroom.* New York: Holt, Rinehart and Winston, Inc., 1968.

Shuy, Roger W. "Detroit Speech: Careless, Awkward, and Inconsistent, or Systematic, Graceful, and Regular?" *Elementary English* 45 (1968): 565-569.

———, Irwin Feigenbaum and Allene Grognet. *Sociolinguistic Theory, Materials and Training Programs: Three Related Studies.* Final Report. Washington, D.C.: U.S. Office of Education, 1970.

Slager, William R. "Effecting Dialect Change Through Oral Drill." *English Journal* 56 (1967): 1166-1176.

Sledd, James. "On Not Teaching English Usage." *English Journal* 54 (1965): 698-703.

Stewart, William A. "Current Issues in the Use of Negro Dialect in Beginning Reading Texts." *The Florida FL Reporter* 8 (Spring/Fall 1970): 3-7, 46.

———. "Nonstandard Speech Patterns." *Baltimore Bulletin of Education* 43 (1966-67): 52-65.

———. "On the Use of Dialect in the Teaching of Reading." In *Teaching Black Children to Read,* edited by Joan C. Baratz and Roger W. Shuy. Washington, D.C.: Center for Applied Linguistics, 1969.

———. "Urban Negro Speech: Sociolinguistic Factors Affecting English Teaching." In *Social Dialects and Language Learning,* edited by Roger W. Shuy. Champaign, Ill.: National Council of Teachers of English, 1964.

Stryker, Shirley L. *Teaching American English.* Rowley, Mass.: Newbury House, 1971.

Venezky, Richard L. "Nonstandard Language and Reading." *Elementary English* 47 (1970): 334-345.

Wardhaugh, Ronald. *Reading: A Linguistic Perspective.* New York: Harcourt, Brace and World, 1969.

———. "The Implications of Linguistics for Reading." *The Florida FL Reporter* 7 (Fall 1969): 1-2, 23.

Wheatly, Katherine. "Southern Standards." *American Speech* 9 (1934): 36-45.

Wise, C. M. "Southern American Dialect." *American Speech* 8 (1933): 37-43.

Wolfram, Walter A. "Sociolinguistic Alternatives in Teaching Reading to Nonstandard Speakers." *Reading Research Quarterly* 6 (1970). Reprinted in *The Florida FL Reporter* 8 (1970): 16-23, 48.

———. "The Nature of Nonstandard Dialect Divergence." *Elementary English* 47 (1970): 739-748.

Index

377